The Literary Market

MATERIAL TEXTS

Series Editors

Roger Chartier   Leah Price
Joseph Farrell   Peter Stallybrass
Anthony Grafton   Michael F. Suarez, S.J.

A complete list of books in the series is available from the publisher.

The Literary Market

Authorship and Modernity in the Old Regime

Geoffrey Turnovsky

PENN

University of Pennsylvania Press
Philadelphia

Copyright © 2010 University of Pennsylvania Press

All rights reserved. Except for brief quotations used for purposes of review or scholarly citation, none of this book may be reproduced in any form by any means without written permission from the publisher.

Published by
University of Pennsylvania Press
Philadelphia, Pennsylvania 19104-4112

Printed in the United States of America on acid-free paper
10 9 8 7 6 5 4 3 2 1

Library of Congress Cataloging-in-Publication Data
Turnovsky, Geoffrey.
The literary market : authorship and the making of a modern cultural field in old regime France / Geoffrey Turnovsky.
    p. cm. — (Material texts)
Includes bibliographical references and index.
ISBN 978-0-8122-4195-2 (alk. paper)
1. French literature—17th century—History and criticism. 2. French literature—18th century—History and criticism. 3. Authorship—Economic aspects—France—History. 4. Litertaure publishing—France—History—17th century. 5. Literature publishing—France—History—18th century. 6. Book industries and trade—France—History—17th century. 7. Book industries and trade—France—History—18th century. I. Title.
PQ245.T87 2009
840.9'004—dc22   2009018799

Contents

INTRODUCTION   1

PART I: WRITING, PUBLISHING, AND LITERARY IDENTITY IN THE "PREHISTORY OF *DROIT D'AUTEUR*"

INTRODUCTION: THE STORY OF A TRANSITION: WHEN AND HOW DID WRITERS BECOME "MODERN"?   15

1. LITERARY COMMERCE IN THE AGE OF *HONNÊTE* PUBLICATION   25

2. THE PARADOXES OF ENLIGHTENMENT PUBLISHING   63

PART II: THE LITERARY MARKET: THE MAKING OF A MODERN CULTURAL FIELD

INTRODUCTION: RECONSIDERING THE ALTERNATIVE   105

3. "LIVING BY THE PEN": MYTHOLOGIES OF MODERN AUTHORIAL AUTONOMY   113

4. ECONOMIC CLAIMS AND LEGAL BATTLES: WRITERS TURN TO THE MARKET   145

5. THE REALITY OF A NEW CULTURAL FIELD: THE CASE OF ROUSSEAU   184

CONCLUSION   204

NOTES   211

BIBLIOGRAPHY 265

INDEX 279

ACKNOWLEDGMENTS 285

Introduction

TWO BRIEF AND UNDERSTATED ANECDOTES can frame this study. They illustrate the ambiguities that will be at the core of my account of the "modernization" of intellectual identities in the seventeenth and eighteenth centuries, particularly to the degree that this book explores the historical process of the "birth of the modern author" in light of continuities with the values and behaviors of the early modern period rather than, as is more traditionally done, in terms of a sharp break with them.

The first is told by Paul Pellisson in the history of the Académie française, which he wrote in the late 1640s and early 1650s at a time when he was lobbying for a seat in the assembly. Remembering the strong interest in theater of the Académie's first patron, Cardinal Richelieu, Pellisson recounts how the cardinal brought together five of the leading dramatists of the day in the mid-1630s—among whom the best known was Pierre Corneille—and commissioned them to write a series of plays based on subjects and arrangements of his own inspiration, including a 1635 *Comédie des Tuileries*, celebrating the palace next to the Louvre that Catherine de Médicis had built after the assassination of her husband Henri II in 1560; a now lost *Grande pastorale* from 1637; and a tragicomedy called *L'aveugle de Smyrne*, which was performed a month later.[1] Each of the *cinq auteurs* was assigned to write one act of each play. For this, Pellisson observes, the writer received a pension from the minister, along with "considerable gestures of generosity [quelques libéralitez considérables], when they succeeded to his liking."[2] To explain what he means by "libéralitez," Pellisson reveals what one of the playwrights, Guillaume Colletet, had confided to him:

Thus M. Colletet assured me that, having brought to him [Richelieu] the Monologue from *Les Tuileries*, the latter was especially drawn to the following two lines [*sic*] from the description of the *Carré d'eau*:
    [At the same time, I saw on the banks of a stream]
  The female duck dampened by the muddy water,
  With a hoarse voice and a flap of her wings,
  Reinvigorate the male duck which languished at her side,

[Au même temps j'ai vu sur le bord d'un ruisseau,
La cane s'humecter de la bourbe de l'eau,
D'une voix enrouée, et d'un battement d'aile,
Animer le canard qui languit auprès d'elle,]
And after listening to the rest, he gave him from his own hands fifty *pistoles*, with the obliging words *that they were only for those two lines which he had found so beautiful, and that the King was not rich enough to pay for the rest*.[3]

The second story dates from almost two hundred years later. When Victor Hugo published his play *Cromwell* in 1827, he removed from the famous preface a historical excursus originally intended as part of it. Having recently founded the *Revue de Paris*, Louis-Désiré Véron approached Hugo about printing the excerpt in his new journal in return for a reasonable fee. In a letter from May 18, 1829, Hugo laid out the terms on which he might agree to this:

I am eager, Monsieur, to respond to the kind solicitation that you addressed to me yesterday.

I have never sold a manuscript, however thin it might be, for less than 500 francs.

But I have, on occasion, given them away, and I could do it again.

If you are interested in the fragment for which you do me the honor of asking, you could have it for 500 francs (or for nothing). Choose. Whatever your choice, I will agree with pleasure.[4]

At one level, both exchanges highlight attitudes and views that seem appropriate for their times. Colletet's desire to please his patron appears as fitting for the seventeenth century as Hugo's aggressive response to the commercial journal editor for the nineteenth. At another level, however, both convey these attitudes and views in an unexpected way, in the evocation of a transaction through which the writer gained a specified sum of money. We really anticipate the opposite; we expect instead that the core values in question for both the Classical and the Romantic writers would be communicated through a repudiation, sublimation, or "euphemization" of monetary payment, whether in the pseudo-aristocratic indifference to gain of the court playwright or in the Romantic poet's grandiose rejection of commerce in the name of Art, Beauty, and Humanity. In these two stories, though, money is not only unconcealed, it is highlighted.

It is emphasized both to the degree that it is quantified—which in itself calls attention to its prominence—and inasmuch as it is incorporated into the heart of a representation that intends to valorize the writer on the receiving end of the payment. What is more, the money indicates more or less precisely what we would assume a rejection of money to signal; not the crass and unseemly commercialization of art and literature, but the fundamental incommensurability of the writer and his works with an economy presumed to measure only the ordinary and the mediocre. The fifty *pistoles* Richelieu hands to Colletet do not assess the base economic value of the verse and, in establishing such an equivalency, demean its true artistic worth. They gauge instead the inestimable beauty of the monologue insofar as the fifty *pistoles* express the minister's inability to compensate the lines and establish any fair equivalency, even with the king's fortune at his disposal. Likewise, the choice that Hugo presents to Véron between zero and what is clearly offered by the poet, with his reference to a "thin" work and emphasis on "no less than," as an extravagant price intended to challenge the commercial sensibility of the editor aims to put the writer off the scale, and in the process articulate the transcendent quality of his writing by summoning an image of the impossibility of its valuation by a middling market price.[5]

It is important to add as well that both images of money have what can be characterized as a tenuous, nontransparent relation to the "real" economic contexts to which they allude. Richelieu's praise—"the King was not rich enough to pay for the rest"—did not represent with any accuracy at all either the king's finances or the economic relationship between the monarch and Colletet, who, we can safely assume, would have felt that the king did have the funds to compensate him. Hugo's case is more complex due to the fact that his rhetoric is less hyperbolic than that of Richelieu, and conveys in this respect a more "realistic" image of the writer/publisher transaction. Five hundred livres was a lofty figure for Véron, who proposed a lower sum in response. This surely felt like a normal business negotiation to the editor. But the counter-offer, which was soundly rejected by Hugo who opted to give his text to the editor for nothing, speaks to the degree to which the poet's "500 livres" did not fully correspond to the "500 livres" that had entered into the economic calculus of Véron. Five hundred livres did not, for Hugo, open the door to a back and forth over the price of the text, but affirmed the opposite: his refusal or inability to negotiate his literary insight or talent. In this respect, the same sum carried two substantially different significations.

We are accustomed, of course, to considering hard numbers as privileged points of access into an undisputed reality. In their "quantitativeness," they conjure up the rawness, materiality, and noneuphemized nature of this reality, and thus its "objectivity." Yet here the numbers take us in a completely different direction. They lead us not toward but away from the "objective lives" of writers, and into a highly stylized symbolic universe whose logic is not the need to "make a living" or the maximization of economic profit, but the complex and polemicized dynamics of intellectual, literary, and artistic legitimacy as these play out in shaping the strategies of self-presentation through which writers seek to establish their credibility and authority.

The symbolic appropriations and transformations of commercial and economic images in the efforts of defining and articulating intellectual value are the subject of this book. Influenced by work on "self-fashioning" and the "presentation of self," the chapters that follow set out, in highlighting such efforts, to shed light on the evolution of intellectual identities in the seventeenth and eighteenth centuries, and to enhance our understanding of their "modernization," particularly to the extent that the latter process has so often been figured in the economically coded terms of a passage from an archaic, constraining patronage system into the realm of the market.[6] Accounts of this transition tend to view it as a self-evident move from the perspective of the author, who is assumed "naturally" to want to be free from any dependence on noble patrons, and thus to pounce on the chance to do so once the opportunities present themselves. The only question, then, is the availability of these opportunities in an underdeveloped Old Regime publishing industry, and accordingly, much attention has been given to tracing the evolution of the objective circumstances that made the transition seem inescapable, with an emphasis on rising payments to writers and the legislation of intellectual property law. But in truth writers had a far more complex relationship with the commercial publishing system. The latter did exist "objectively," of course, and established real conditions that would positively and negatively affect the attitudes and choices of writers. These conditions evolved throughout the period in question, and this evolution—consisting broadly in an expansion of the book trade as well as in a moderation of censorship, if not in any radical changes to the official regulations or to the underlying technology of the publishing industry—is an essential factor for understanding, in turn, how authorial practices developed into the modern era.

However, it is a central contention of this book that accounting for these conditions is not sufficient for explaining the modernization of intellectual identities. More exactly, it is not sufficient for explaining the particular "modernization" that has become the standard narrative in the history of authorship, and which identifies modernity with the specific vision of an autonomy from traditional political and social elites articulated in commercialized images of the writer following two distinct and contrary patterns: the writer is viewed as either economically self-reliant and "earning an independent living" or subject to the exploitation of cruel publishers. We shall see that these contrasting figurations of the writer in the "literary market" are ultimately two sides of the same coin. For now, though, it is enough to point out that the modernization process signaled by the idea of a transition from patronage to market has its roots not just in the "objective" expansion of the print trade. For they lie as well in the successive battles that were waged, from the *Querelle du Cid* in 1637 to debates over philosophical identity in the eighteenth century, over what constitutes legitimacy in the intellectual field and over who can lay claim to the exalted and authoritative designation of being an *homme de lettres* or an author. "Modernity" was not in these battles a self-evident or unambiguous state. Construed as an essential dimension of the prestige to which writers aspired, it was an upshot of the polemical claims of writers to authority and influence. It was, in other words, an assertion of legitimacy. "Commerce," in turn, conceived not in terms of writers' actual transactions with, say, agents of the publishing industry, but as a series of topoi projecting stylized images of their experiences in the book trade as central to their claims to legitimacy—in other words, conceived as "commerce" existed in the language of the writers themselves—emerged as a powerful signifier of this modernity; indeed, perhaps as the most powerful signifier of it.

This book describes, in a way, how that came to pass. It argues that the integration and elevation of images of commercial literary activity within the self-presentational rhetoric of writers engaged in the decisive battles over legitimacy comprise an equally important development for the evolution of intellectual practices in seventeenth- and eighteenth-century France. Though influenced by changing conditions in the publishing sphere, this development was not a direct translation of them. Instead, it was defined by two related aspects: first, an investment of meaning in economically themed images that then clearly conveyed the writer's authority and preeminence—thus the writer's refusal to accept income from a publisher stood as an instantly recognized sign of his or her aristocratic quality, and second, the *inevitable* noncorrespondence of these images to the "objective" reality of the writer's commercial dealings with publishers and patrons, inasmuch as the images sought not a "realistic" account but a conceptual transformation of the cultural sphere as a space in which the writer's transcendent status would be readable and widely accepted.

The "literary market" is an illuminating concept by which this process can be accessed in all its nuances. It has of course played a familiar and prominent role in much scholarship on the evolution of authorship in the Old Regime as one of the principal institutions allowing writers to make a transition out of the patronage system and into modernity. Such accounts, though, have not always adequately described the complexity of the passage, and thus of the market's function. Nor have they appreciated the capacity of the market, as a model, to figure the constitutive ambiguity of writers' engagements with money and commerce in the period, a fact that is suggested by a consistent inability to reconcile the contradictory articulations of the market's role in this process as an institution of liberation and economic self-reliance for writers, on one hand, and as a newly oppressive system subjecting *gens de lettres* to its mercantile logic, on the other. This is due, I would argue, to a tendency associated with the overriding focus on "objective" circumstances to identify the market too directly with the publishing industry or the book trade, and thereby to consider it primarily as another facet of the "true lives" of writers. But the "literary market" is a qualitatively different type of configuration, which finds its conceptual coherence not in the economic reality of the book trade but in the convergence of the book trade's "objectivity" with the evolving expectations of those who aspire to a literary identity.

Thus we can envision a publishing sector without writers, or more exactly without living writers with something at stake—whether income or esteem—in a particular print job. Explaining why property rights for the earliest works were nonexistent, Diderot described the Renaissance book trade as an authorless industry: "the first privileges had for their object only ancient works."[7] By contrast, we can hardly envision the literary market without living writers bringing into their contacts with the book trade an urgent investment in its outcomes, and engaging publication through an array of ambitions, anxieties, and frustrations which, in turn, clearly characterize for us the figure of the "modern author." This is because the literary market is the product of their investments and anxieties. For while it is not the book trade per se, the market is the perception and representation of the book trade by writers who turn to it and conceptualize it, through their aspirations and fears, as a system whose fundamental purpose is not making and selling books, but transforming manuscripts into Great Works, and identifying individuals, on the basis of these works, as esteemed and independent Authors. Its currency is legitimacy, autonomy, and prestige. Money has value to the extent that, by its abundance or its dearth, it can be converted.

A reconsideration of the market can therefore probe much more than changes in the publishing sphere. It also offers an entry into the shifting mentalities of writers and into their evolving ideals of legitimacy as they struggle, in the framework of an established cultural order whose standards and conventions were nonetheless a target of incessant debate, to lay claim to valorized identities. To push matters farther, the market is not just a specific image of the publishing sphere but also the effort to impose this image as a faithful representation both of an artisanal sector—the print industry— that *really* was about intellectual identities and values, and of a cultural field whose outlines were precisely those of the book trade. It is, as such, necessarily a rhetorical or a polemical construct, the pertinence of which lies in the degree to which its claim to being a faithful depiction of things is accepted, believed, or more subtly and accurately perhaps, indulged—by readers who do not so much wholeheartedly "believe" in the authors' biased view of the publishing world, as grasp the importance, for the realization of literary value and hence for their own self-esteem as consumers of Literature, of sustaining the illusion. Thus, they go along, for instance, with received ideas about the poverty of a writer in order to uphold a collective belief in his ennobling struggle, which then grounds the value of his work and the symbolic payoff of reading it. In this fashion, the literary market takes form as an "instrument . . . of the struggle for the definition of reality," to adapt the terms of Pierre Bourdieu.[8]

To be sure, Bourdieu's work, particularly his model of the "field," is paramount for my study, which argues, in a sense, that the market's emergence is concomitant less with the development of the book trade per se than with its conceptualization as a field of authorship. Formulated as a "literary" or "cultural" field, or as a "field of cultural production," the concept seeks to define, beneath these variances, the logic of the literary and artistic world with reference to a specifically modern vision of intellectual autonomy, traced to the late nineteenth century and defined in light of at least two key variables.[9] The first is the colonization of the cultural world by the bourgeois industrial economy of the Second Empire, with its "exaltation of money" and utilitarian ethic.[10] The field in this scenario defines the autonomy of writers in terms of a free space that they carve out for themselves where "artistic," not "economic," values predominate, and in which they can then ignore the demands of the industry and the conventional tastes of a large readership in order to act as their own public and judges, according to the "pure aesthetic" values of *l'art pour l'art*.[11] The second is the decisive role played by "cultural intermediaries," such as art dealers, agents, publishers, critics, and others who mediate the relation between artists and publics, shaping the perception of the former by the latter. Here the theory of the field stands in opposition to a sublimated, Romantic notion of artistic value as the pure emanation of the genius and travails of a singular individual by emphasizing the extended network of actors who collectively contribute—either supportively or antagonistically—to what Bourdieu called "the production of belief" in the value of the work and in the brilliance of the artist. Ultimately, the model problematizes rather than defines autonomy.[12]

This second conceptualization of the field is crucial for my analysis, which assumes literary value to be an object of mediation or, to recall Greenblatt, of negotiation between a diverse array of agents bringing heterogeneous interests—intellectual, social, political, economic—into the process.[13] Indeed, the battle is not simply about the amount of value or whether it is negative or positive, but over its quality and meaning: what is "literary value"? What effects—pleasure, utility, beauty, truth—generate this value? Who is authorized to determine and measure it? And what exactly does "literary" denote in this framework? For the "literary field" does not simply demarcate a space in which one could practice "literature," but one in which the concept of "literature" itself, as a specific kind of intellectual activity, became knowable and as a result debatable. The term is very much a dependent variable in this study. It is not a given and will not be presumed self-evidently to account for the success of a work or a writer. Instead, the assumption will be that a critical part of any writer's success lies in his or her ability to impose a specific conceptualization of his or her activity as "literary," to have the activity seen and appreciated as such.[14]

My focus on literary or intellectual value as a site of mediation leads me to depart in salient ways from Bourdieu's first view of the field as starkly bifurcated into autonomous and nonautonomous zones. For Bourdieu, the two zones are, as it were, ontologically equivalent in that both are assumed to be actual spaces in which individuals actually behave according to the logic imputed to their respective fields. A purely venal culture industry takes shape and sparks the opposition of a group of writers and artists who really do retreat into rarefied circles where they experience a radical disconnect—in the form of failure, obscurity, and poverty—from the industry and its commercial public. One consequence of such a bipolar schema is that the values and practices characteristic of the autonomous subfield tend to come across as defensive responses to the overbearing influence and philistinism of the bourgeois culture industry. Indeed, for Bourdieu, literary and artistic autonomy ultimately seems to rest on accepting the power and crassness of the nonautonomous zone, even emphasizing its corruption in order then to do everything in the opposite way and to have the contrarian gestures valorized, in turn, as heroic and necessary. In this respect, Bourdieu's famous description of the field as an "economic world turned upside down" should be understood in light of the immense efforts and suffering that go into such a reversal. Likewise, as an articulation of the field's basic rationality, "disinterested interest" explains not the facile indifference of an aristocrat to an economic gain that he hardly needs, but an urgent and sublime effort of self-denial.

Bourdieu draws in large measure on literary sources for this view, most famously on Flaubert's 1869 novel *L'éducation sentimentale*. I am not suggesting that we reject such sources as fantasies—this study will itself be primarily concerned with them—but it seems obvious to point out that their agenda is not an "objective" or totalizing depiction of the cultural sphere. Literary sources have "literary" interests at heart; they highlight particular issues— related to, say, the integrity or the livelihood of writers—at the expense of a whole host of other concerns that are of equal possible relevance for the broad functioning of the cultural sphere. Furthermore, if they do address such issues as the profitability of publishers or the preferences of readers, it is to address them not as such but only insofar as they affect authorial concerns.[15] The upshot is that the "autonomous field" as conceived by Bourdieu is not "out there" in the world. It is instead the effect of a specialized, partial vantage point, which sees the field as autonomous to the extent that the cultural sphere is viewed, against its inherent complexity and heterogeneity, through the narrow lens of literary priorities, and assumed to exist solely for the purpose of consecrating writers and their works. The same logic dictates that anything not serving literary interests first and foremost be relegated to "nonautonomy" and caricatured as pointedly *anti*-literary. It is in this effort that the language of economics is polemically wielded, in order to devalorize such influences as venal and profiteering. In any case, the "nonautonomous" field is no more "real" or "objective," but takes shape as a by-product of the conceptual fantasy of the "autonomous field" and the "autonomous writer." The "exploitative publisher" and the "bourgeois reader" are indeed part and parcel with those whom they are presumed to torment.

My contention is that the relation between autonomous and nonautonomous, as well as between symbolic and economic, is far more permeable than Bourdieu allows. Not because one is merely the denial of the other, but because neither has a real existence. The dichotomies belong to a single vision of purity that, in rescuing "literature" from the forces of co-optation, had to play up the danger of those forces, and indeed had perhaps to invent them. Nor is the literary market an actual place. Like Bourdieu's subfields, it offers a postulation or an argument about how the cultural world should operate, how it should function in the interest of bolstering the formation and valorization of certain intellectual identities. With roots in early modern debates over the definitions of literary legitimacy, the "market" developed in a prolonged effort to transform the field of play for specific writers—namely, for those seeking to define themselves as outsiders with respect to an established cultural order whose authority was increasingly open to contestation—by changing how the intellectual field was perceived. The market imposed new meanings on familiar outcomes—for instance, the noble leisure that was traditionally considered to be the most proper condition for *lettres* became, in this view, indecent and demeaning—and it offered new outcomes as meaningful: those, above all, which ensued from the print publication process.

For in the framework of the literary market print publication was symbolically invested in ways that it had never been.[16] "As an exhibition makes a painter," remarks Bernard Lahire in his recent study of *La condition littéraire*, "so publication, in a large measure, makes a writer."[17] The fact is, though, that there was no such clear-cut connection between literary identity and publication in early modern literary culture, in which writers endeavored to be recognized for their respectability and elegance as *honnêtes gens* rather than for the brilliance of their books. We shall see that publication was an intensely fraught issue, and writers were far more prone to obfuscate or downplay their contacts with the world of print rather than to appropriate them as decisive factors of their credibility. The connection was not given but forged in the same debates that advanced the market as a conceptualization of the cultural sphere. Accordingly, publication processes were integrated in new ways into the self-presentations of writers, who no longer underscored their distance from the book trade—say, by expressing indifference to or ignorance of its outcomes—but highlighted their involvement.

Most often, they did so by playing up the bad treatment to which they were subjected, along with their inabilities, as "disinterested" writers prepared to suffer for their art, to negotiate with publishers concerned only to make a profit. But decent pay could figure, too. In any case, both experiences at bottom proved exactly the same thing: that through contacts with the commercial publishing world the writer was independent from the corrupt elites who for so long had ruled the cultural sphere. This was without a doubt the fundamental logic of the "market," which in all of its positive and negative permutations envisioned a field in which the links tying a specific vision of intellectual legitimacy—based on social autonomy from traditional elites—to a vision of authorial economic participation in publishing (whether this was successful or not) were self-evident, such that an evocation of the latter easily and persuasively conjured up a belief in the former, that is, in the writer's credibility. Whether depicted being robbed by a *libraire* or as the recipient of a handsome payment, the writer at the center of such a representation was in either case independent from a patron, and extricated from the rationale of the corrupt world that patronage evoked: pleasing, leisure, entertainment.[18] With its roots in Old Regime polemics rather than in the "natural" desires of writers, the association of legitimacy, social autonomy, and economic self-sufficiency is at the core of our contemporary understanding of the author and the intellectual. A lack of a sense of its historical contingency and development has clouded many analyses of the modern cultural sphere and the condition of the modern writer within it.

From a broad historical viewpoint, the problem of the field has often imposed itself as a problem of identifying the first one. This is, of course, what inspired Alain Viala to describe in such influential terms the literary field of the seventeenth century, which he so famously called "le premier champ littéraire" in a refinement of Bourdieu's effort to situate the first field in the late nineteenth century.[19] He would back off from this assertion to some degree, despite the compelling nature of the argument.[20] Nothing, though, could be farther from the spirit of how this study employs the concept of the field. My goal is to understand authorial modernity not in terms of a decisive break with an old culture of *honnête* intellectual activity, but as "modernity" took root and developed within early modern culture. Thus, one of my assumptions is that the key principles of *honnête* publication— and in particular, the construal of autonomy as a function of legitimacy rather than legitimacy as a function of a specific ideal of autonomy—remain at the heart of modern literary life and identity, even though the latter, oriented around ideals of sincerity and selfless dedication, are presumed to be in fierce opposition to the ritualized codes of *honnêteté* (the duplicity— another notion advanced by Viala—is critical to my account). Moreover, to the degree that literary *honnêteté*, as it evolved in the seventeenth century and into the Enlightenment, was predicated on assertions of its own innovativeness and progress with respect to previous intellectual traditions and strategies, depicted as more constrained and primitive, we might add that the literary field, to the extent that it is always in some measure a field of *honnête* publication, is by the same token always a "first literary field."

Finally, this book is both about Old Regime France and not about it. Seventeenth- and eighteenth-century France presents a rich historical context in which to explore how these issues play out. And inevitably they do so, as the term itself of *honnête* publication implies, in ways that are specific to the time and place. My study seeks, of course, to identify and elucidate these particularities. My hope, however, is that this study will also broach, and propose some answers to, broader questions regarding the engagement of writers with commerce, and the ways in which commerce in turn shapes and is shaped by writers' battles over legitimacy and its definitions, not just in France or under the Old Regime, but anywhere and anytime that money enters into the literary enterprise.

PART ONE

WRITING, PUBLISHING, AND LITERARY IDENTITY IN THE "PREHISTORY OF *DROIT D'AUTEUR*"

The Story of a Transition:
When and How Did Writers Become "Modern"?

The "literary market" has been a key concept in accounts of cultural and literary practices in Old Regime France, particularly for studies of the author as a "modern" principle of intellectual coherence and legitimacy. In these accounts, the birth of the author is predicated on the writer's growing independence from early modern political, social, and cultural institutions, which for their part are presumed to inhibit the sincere, personal expression that will be at the core of the claim to distinction and credibility conveyed by the emerging ideal. This independence has been interpreted in no small measure as a function of the new possibilities extended to *gens de lettres* by a book trade whose expansion becomes, in turn, a measure of the growing ability of writers, by selling their works to publishers, to extricate themselves from the networks of Old Regime literary life in order to address a broader public, and in so doing claim a new kind of authority.

In the effort to map out this process, scholars have been drawn to identify the first writer "to live by the pen." Both Alain-René Le Sage and the abbé Prévost have been presented as inaugurators of such an independence for *gens de lettres* in eighteenth-century France, not for anything that either said on the topic, it should be stressed, but due to the fact that direct earnings from publishing seem to have played a relatively more important role in their overall trajectories than in those of other writers of the time.[1] Still, as Wallace Kirsop points out, "it is not easy—even in the eighteenth century—to discover someone who lives exclusively by the pen."[2] Whatever place publishing income occupied in their lives, potential candidates invariably turn out, on closer examination, to have also been deeply implicated in the traditional patronage system, ultimately relying on noncommercial forms of support as much as or more than earnings from manuscript sales. Dubious of the received wisdom about Le Sage and Prévost, John Lough calls attention to their non-market income, including for the former a 600–livre pension from the son of Louis XIV's foreign minister and for the latter a remunerative priory.[3]

More fundamentally, though, the search itself is flawed, since it presupposes that writers had already discerned and internalized an essential, qualitative distinction between commercial and noncommercial pay, and that they therefore considered any move on their part toward market-based compensation as, in and of itself, a gesture of repudiation of noble protection in the name of "autonomy." In early eighteenth-century France, it is not clear that even money-making authors such as Le Sage or Prévost perceived what they earned in the book trade as representing such a choice. Payment from *libraires* was scarcely destined to replace traditional revenue sources, but to supplement them when the pensions and sinecures proved inadequate to support the livelihood of the writer. In this sense, Prévost wrote for the commercial press not in order to free himself from the protection of the prince de Conti, whose almoner he became in 1735, but because this position, while offering protection and credibility, did not furnish income. It would therefore be more accurate to say that Prévost wrote for the book trade not to escape Conti's household but to uphold his place within it, and to continue to reap the benefits that such a position brought him.

As a result, more persuasive contributions to the debate have instead focused not on the first economically self-sufficient writers, but on those who initially imagined such independence, even if they were not able to live it out. Rather than identify the "first writers to live by the pen," these studies seek out those who first postulated the idea, highlighting the conditions in which "living by the pen" initially became thinkable: "at least [a] possibility," writes Lough.[4] "In the course of the eighteenth century . . . we see progressively emerge, if not payment to authors as we understand it, at least the principle of a specific monetary remuneration for literary activity," observes Henri-Jean Martin.[5] Jules Bertaut's 1950s study of Enlightenment-era "literary life" similarly emphasizes an emerging psychological landscape—the rising hope of autonomy through publishing—which anticipates but is not identifiable with actual self-sufficiency: "around 1770, the situation slowly modifies: writers have learned to defend themselves. . . . On the eve of the Revolution, they foresee that one day—perhaps—they will be able to live by their pens."[6] Among those considered to have glimpsed this day early on, Diderot tends to count as a prescient advocate of "professionalism" for writers.[7] So does Rousseau, if in a different kind of mode, given that he mobilized not for writing as a "métier" but for the legal and commercial recognition of the inviolable connection between a writer and a work.[8]

Yet while they are surely more convincing as descriptions of the hybrid conditions under which writers of the Enlightenment operated, such studies are probably no less idealistic in their characterization of the historical transition that these pioneering writers invoked. The implication is that, even if they themselves did not benefit from its fruits, nonetheless, through their foresight and keen anticipation, these writers represented a transformation in the lives of *gens de lettres* that was no less real for being deferred into the future. But it is well worth interrogating the nature of the change signaled by this new expectation. Writers envisaged a day when they would be fairly paid for their labors. We presume their visions to be meaningful to the degree that they prefigure an actual evolution. But what if they did not? And what if the development was in fact something quite different?

Describing the late twentieth-century literary field, Robert Escarpit noted that a young novelist bringing a manuscript to a publisher with the hope of receiving a modest income of 10,000 francs for his work "has a lower chance of reaching his goal than if he had bought a lottery ticket."[9] Less provocatively, Michèle Vessillier-Ressi nonetheless confirms the view that only a fraction of writers in the contemporary period derive enough from the sale of their writings to publishers to support themselves. The majority—two-thirds, according to the data she has compiled—rely instead on an "accumulation of jobs." That is, they must hold down secondary employment that not only "pays the bills," but also, in the absence of direct earnings from publishers, might bolster the legitimacy of the individual's self-identification as an author, given that these jobs are often as teachers or critics of literature.[10] But "multiple job holding" undermines the autonomy projected in the utopian image of "living by the pen," and challenges its central association of the social identity of the writer with the fundamental link tying an individual to his or her works, expressed in the defining labor of "faire des livres."[11] Leaving aside the often very visible but statistically outlying exceptions,[12] it must be acknowledged that no writer today can really be said, without some qualification, to "live by the pen," not according to the meaning that this phrase has acquired in the historiography of early modern literary practices. And in this respect, "modern authorship" is perhaps not a whole lot different from the eclectic and, in the language of Pierre Bourdieu, "heteronomous" array of cultural, institutional, and social exchanges that defined an individual as an *homme* or *femme de lettres* in the Old Regime.[13] As Vessillier-Ressi writes, "we might ask ourselves if the amateurism which was the rule in the economy of creation of the distant past is not still a prevalent phenomenon today in the majority of cases."[14]

If not an "objective" socioeconomic regime in which writers could live by the sale of the products of their creative labors, then what do such writers as Diderot and Rousseau prefigure? What transition—if any at all—do they mark in reimagining literary practice in and through the commercial opportunities and legal rights of book publishing? The elusiveness of the shift is manifest, it seems to me, in a tendency to advance the history of authorship by always pushing the pivotal moment of authorial awakening back in time, with studies at least partly driven by the goal of establishing that the growing attention of writers to their "interests" and "rights" occurred earlier than was thought, say, in the first half of the eighteenth century rather than the second, or in the seventeenth century or earlier.[15] Such research has produced crucial insights into the interactions between writers and the publishing industry in periods overlooked by an older scholarship that figured the early exchanges with booksellers to be devoid of meaning for the lives of writers. What is less clear, though, is how persuasive they can be as accounts of "modernization" in the cultural sphere, for the risk is to assume what ultimately undermines the notion of the author as a construct of modernity: that authorship consists in a timeless potential for self-realization, merely waiting for the right individuals to stumble on the insight. The emphasis on finding an earlier originary moment might presuppose that the desire to "live by the pen" and to write "autonomously" in the sense of writing without any need for aristocratic protection is a universal ahistorical one, which only required writers sufficiently lucid and self-aware to give expression to it. The crux of the matter is then whether such clear-headed writers—as opposed to the ideal of the "author" itself—existed in a particular time, with the underlying thrust often being that prior generations of scholars, who had situated the emergence of "modern authorship" at a later historical juncture, simply lacked the knowledge and appreciation of the earlier age to see how savvy and insightful its best intellectuals really were.

There is a great deal of validity to the point. The effort to find the "first modern author" has certainly been fueled by incomplete knowledge of what comes before. One result is the ridiculous notion that early writers were indifferent to the benefits of print publication, including that of economic gain.[16] At the same time, however, observing that these *gens de lettres* had extensive and deliberate contacts with the world of the commercial press earlier than had been thought, even in the dawn of print, does not by itself demonstrate their modernity because "modern authorship" does not consist in these contacts per se, no matter how motivated, interested, or proprietary they might have been. On their own, they do not make writers modern. The causality, in fact, goes in the reverse direction; it is writers who transform their contacts with the book trade into powerful signifiers of their modernity. They do so as part of a rearticulation of their legitimacy in terms of a new but contingent vision of their social autonomy from patrons, based on an idealization of themselves as "producers" with "rights" to a livelihood from the income earned on the products of their "artistic" labors—we shall see that other ideals of the freedom of intellectuals were current, even dominant. The book trade and intellectual modernity can be linked to the extent that the new claim to legitimacy conveys an assertion of its progressiveness with respect to the "traditional" ideals that it seeks to replace, and that contacts with the book trade become the privileged testimonials to the liberation on which this legitimacy is based.

The "modernity" of the author who turns to commercial print inheres, then, in the strategic appropriation of an identity defined by this concept of independence, which projects *simultaneously* the claim to remuneration for the fruits of creative "toil" and the will to pursue a literary life outside of the old networks of royal and noble patronage. Indeed, modern authorship consists in the collapse of the two objectives into one unified motive according to which the expression of desire to be liberated from subordination to protectors becomes at the same time a demand to be compensated for literary labors, while conversely—and herein lies one of the central arguments of this study—the demand for compensation from a *libraire*, however it may be formulated and regardless of its positive or negative end result, instantly conveys a repudiation in the name of the writer's dedication and authenticity of all the personal compromises required by participation in an overindulged hierarchical leisure society.

Such a motive, and the claim to a modern intellectual self to which it gives rise, is not the reflection of a timeless longing for freedom of thought or creative control; nor does it ensue from any "natural" sense that one should be paid for the products of one's labors, whether these are physical or intellectual. The following two chapters instead locate the roots of the new vision in the evolution of the seventeenth- and eighteenth-century cultural field, and particularly in a development that might appear unrelated to the narrative of authorial modernization, namely the convergence of "letters"— identified retrospectively as "literature"—with the activities and values of a self-consciously new social elite , which appropriated "literary" writing forms—along with their writers—in assertions of its cohesiveness, brilliance, and, indeed, its modernity. Out of this intellectual and social fusion emerge familiar images of the writer as a "salon" or "court poet," who far from representing autonomy *from* elites will come to symbolize the subjugation of literature to "nonliterary" priorities in the Old Regime. Yet the articulation of a new cultural value in the language of elite sociability produces other images of the writer as well, almost as by-products, including most pertinently a view of the writer as too interested in commercial profit and too ready to pursue gain in the book trade. The image, of course, stands as a sharply devalorized view. But this should not lead us to underestimate its importance for the rising culture of *honnêteté*, in which it functions as a negative foil defining and accentuating legitimate motives and behaviors, such as aristocratic disinterest, leisure and a commitment to upholding the elegant dynamic of the group over one's own individual brilliance.

For it was to the degree that writing for economic gain in the publishing sector indicated with clarity and self-evidence the intellectual's exteriority with respect to elite social circles and his or her refusal or inability to abide by their ethical norms that rejections of commercial benefit and "professionalism" could manifest with equal transparency the personal qualities that they evoked. Part I argues that, as an institution of authorial modernization, the "literary market" has its origins here rather than in the "objective" growth of the book trade or the awakening of a long-dormant desire among *gens de lettres* for independence. We begin, in other words, with the elite socialization of writing, unfolding as a reciprocal process by which, on one hand, intellectual legitimacy was redefined to reflect the values of aristocratic sociability, with writers and their works increasingly esteemed for their refinement, polish, and ability to please in hours of leisure, while on the other hand, aristocratic sociability was reconfigured along intellectual, linguistic, and even "literary" lines. Polite conversation, wit, and belles-lettres prevailed over cruder, physical forms of interaction. Out of this dynamic, an image of the writer's autonomy gains currency. Formulated in a language of commercial enterprise and profiteering self-interest, it figures the exclusion from the elite group that the successful writer will overcome. The sociability of the legitimized writer contrasts sharply with a writer whose non-integration is indicated by an involvement in the commercial publication of his or her works.

In this process, the book trade was transformed—not as an "objective" artisanal sphere, though its real expansion is not irrelevant to our story. But more saliently it was transformed as a cultural field to the extent that it was envisioned by writers who now looked to their contacts with it as factors and conduits for their social identities as *gens de lettres*. Investing the transactions, exchanges, and outcomes defining their commercial publishing activities with a potent meaning for their lives as intellectuals, and appropriating the self-presentational spaces that were offered through the printed media, writers reconceptualized "le commerce des livres" as what Viala calls an "institution of literary life," that is, as a social, cultural, and political framework in which the plausibility and legitimacy of their "literary" identities, and of their identifies as "socialized" *gens de lettres*, would be affirmed and correlatively contested and undermined. Those writers who mobilized a commercial rhetoric as a decisive element in their intellectual self-presentation, even in a strongly negative way, could be said to have invented *literary* commerce. For they endowed this particular mode of intellectual practice with the coherence and meaning that it ultimately continues to have for us today.

Chapter 1 focuses on the seventeenth-century case of Corneille. The tragedian has often been highlighted as a precursor of the modern author for what seems a strong interest in the commercialization of his writings, reflected in his tendency to publish plays quickly and in his pursuit through administrative channels of the right to control their performance. Both moves are commonly interpreted as expressions of his aspiration for a "modern," which is to say here an anti-aristocratic, economically articulated independence. Yet it is not in the writings of Corneille that the image of his commercial savvy is to be found, but in those of his detractors who sought to discredit the popular playwright at the apex of his success. The chapter contends that in the course of the 1637 *Querelle* that exploded after the triumph of his play, *Le Cid*, Corneille became a screen onto which the anxieties of *gens de lettres* were projected as they sought to understand and define a specific category of activity—writing and publishing books—that had to be adapted to what Viala calls the first literary field. These anxieties were not so much reactions to Corneille or the doctrinal infidelities of his play. Rather, they were symptoms of a defining quandary that seventeenth-century *gens de lettres* faced, which lay in the following paradox: the rise in the status of leisure-oriented writing in elite culture allowed individuals with "literary" talent to claim a more enhanced social identity. But they could do so only so long as that identity adhered to the values of aristocratic sociability, which prescribed that, out of modesty and deference to the group, one downplay one's writing and publishing activities. As such, only by belittling their literary pursuits could *gens de lettres* benefit from the social transformation that these pursuits, valorized nonetheless by the same society that demanded their belittlement, made possible.

Chapter 2 follows the evolution of this fraught, ambivalent "anticommercial" ideal into the Enlightenment era, when it continued to impose itself as a prevailing vision while undergoing a substantial transformation at the hands of the *philosophes*. The chapter focuses on what can be called "philosophical" publishing, that is, the role of publication in the literary lives of those who constructed themselves according to the model of Voltaire. A central paradox has been noted both by eighteenth-century contemporaries and historians and critics of the period: whereas the *philosophes* are easily considered modern in their relationship to the political and religious authorities of their time, when it came to *their* intellectual property rights they refused to innovate, hearkening in their activities as writers to established Classical-era tactics of modesty, coy denial, and anonymity. But while these strategies situated the *philosophes* in a decidedly elite cultural milieu that was far closer to the literary field of Viala than to the commercial field of Bourdieu, they played a different role from similar strategies in the lives of seventeenth-century *gens de lettres*, by upholding a new formulation of autonomy. Repudiating the "douce liberté" of the leisured aristocrat as well as the uncouth self-sufficiency of a Corneille, the autonomy of the *philosophes* was defined in a complex negotiation by which writers positioned themselves between a broad public and a network of patrons. In gesturing to an abstract enlightened audience, they projected an autonomy from elites that would ground their authority as critics. These affirmations, however, drew their power as symbolic projections from the *philosophes'* proximity to well-recognized and powerful protectors who, through their support of what was becoming known as a "movement," sanctioned the grandiose self-images that such writers as Voltaire and d'Alembert presented. "Philosophical" publication was both an effect and the undertaking of this negotiation between an abstract, idealized public and a more concrete readership of elites, in the course of which the *philosophes* had to adopt contradictory and equivocal postures, or at least postures that necessarily seem as such to us.

More than a century separates Chapter 2 from Chapter 1. This is not meant at all to downplay the significance of changes that took place over the course of those years but to underscore the importance and durability of the *honnête* framework, which defined and oriented those changes, including not only the rise of the *philosophes* in the mid-eighteenth century but earlier developments as well: the novella, moralist writing, and the proto-Enlightenment scientific popularizations of Fontenelle and Bayle. I have focused on an early seventeenth-century debate—the *Querelle du Cid*—in which the evolving parameters and the polemical nature of this framework become especially clear. And by jumping ahead to the *philosophes*, I am not suggesting that nothing happens between Corneille and Voltaire, but that the figuration of the "literary market" must be understood as a direct and pointed response to the self-presentational rhetoric of a Voltaire or a d'Alembert; and that the latter cannot be understood without understanding its relation to the seventeenth-century discourse of authorial *honnêteté*, which stands both as a foil to the *philosophes'* image of themselves as socially independent critics, and as the condition out of which their assertions of independence could carry any weight.[17]

I
Literary Commerce in the Age of *Honnête* Publication

THE INVESTIGATION INTO WRITERS and the book trade in the early modern period has traditionally presented an exercise in the excavation of origins, driven by the effort to unearth "primitive" instances of what would later develop as standard behavior for writers in the commercial publishing sphere. In his survey of the economic, social, and political realities defined by the printed book in seventeenth-century Paris, Henri-Jean Martin suddenly describes a "prehistory" as soon as he turns to the question of "la condition d'auteur." The focus on authorship instantly calls up the most underdeveloped aspects of a broad phenomenon that until then had seemed remarkable for its profuseness and penetration, as well as for the complexity of its mechanisms and networks.[1] Why the pervading sense of incipience when the writer makes an appearance? One reason for such an impression, it seems to me, not only in Martin's account but in others as well, is the marked tendency to conflate a general history of writers and publication with what is really a more specific history, that of writers' moral and legal claims to compensation from *libraires* to whom they cede the rights to print and sell their works. Indeed, Martin's incorporation of the Author into his study transforms it not just into a "prehistory" but more exactly into a "prehistory of *droit d'auteur*." Referring to the payment that a writer received for the sale of his or her works, the latter term indicates not a generic but a particular contact with the book trade, one that certainly does not exhaust the range of possibilities. Nonetheless, it is characteristic of much historical work on authorship that payments are assumed to be something especially salient and fundamental.

Martin then tells this aspect of the story largely through an enumeration of the sums obtained by writers in their transactions with *libraires*[2]: Benserade's 150 livres from Sommaville for *Cléopâtre*; La Calprenède's 200 livres for *Mithridate* (also from Sommaville); Tristan's 600 livres from

Courbé and Billaine for three collections of verse (*Les amours*, *Oeuvres chrétiennes*, and *Vers héroïques*); and Scarron's 1,000 livres from Quinet for the *Roman comique*, to name a few examples.[3] Such figures have the disconcerting effect of seeming at the same time significantly low and significantly high, a fact that further underscores the nascence of the writer's "condition" vis-à-vis the book trade. They seem low to the degree that they stand out as artifacts of a distant age, elements in a life measured by a distinctly antiquated set of standards. But the payments also appear high inasmuch as we cannot help but read them in contrast to an even more primordial moment when writers received nothing at all from the printers or booksellers who put their works into circulation, other than maybe a few dozen copies of the books in question. Martin will reference this earlier moment explicitly, but it could just as easily remain implicit in its function as a powerful, ever-present myth of authorial origins. When faced with any evidence of writers being monetarily compensated for the "sale" of their writings in the early modern period, whatever the actual sums may be, we instinctively situate those transactions against a putative beginning when writers were not only unpaid but might be expected to contribute themselves to the printing costs.[4]

Moreover, the numbers always seem both highly illuminating and utterly impenetrable. They grab our attention as sharply focused glimpses into the daily lives of early modern *gens de lettres*, all the more tantalizing given the paucity of true-life documentation on such matters. But the detail, for all its banality, also reminds us of the illusory nature of the insight the numbers appear to offer. For one thing, viewed from this side of three centuries of currency changes and inflation, they strike us as alien and inconvertible. They force the question: what do they amount to in twenty-first-century dollars or euros? Yet most studies that rehearse these types of payments do not even try to establish modern equivalents for the amounts but seek to let the old numbers simply speak for themselves. What, though, can they tell us on their own? Some studies offer conversion systems, but with confusing, improbable, and arbitrary ratios they only seem to make matters worse, raising more questions than they answer.[5]

Of course, even if we could get an accurate idea of what, say, 1,000 livres from 1650 is worth in today's currency, the more basic problem remains of establishing a "real" value in terms of what it could buy at the time, thereby determining what it was worth to the writer who earned it and, with the money, sought to stake out a place in the seventeenth- or eighteenth-century intellectual field. Benchmarks have been proposed.

Viala notes that, "to make a good impression socially, one needed about 3,000 livres a year in the middle of the century, and about 4,000 at the end."[6] But this hardly offers a clearer picture than the raw numbers. After all, Viala does not specify what one would need to acquire with those 3,000 to 4,000 livres to present oneself respectably in Old Regime society. More important, such a guideline fails to get at the underlying problem. For if the figures seem opaque it is not simply due to the difficulty of knowing their values in terms of the goods and services they make accessible to aspiring *gens de lettres*, and which would be crucial for their claims to privileged cultural status. It is because such numbers tell us very little about the effectiveness of these claims in the framework of a society that was considerably less monetized than our own. We can know that with 3,000 or 4,000 livres a writer might obtain some of the basic accouterments required for a literary career in the early modern field. But the figures leave basic questions about access and legitimacy in a culture where these depended relatively more on unquantifiable assets such as personal favor, "qualité," and "politesse" too unanswered to be illuminating as signifiers of the writer's "improving" status. A writer might command important payments in the book trade, yet still be shut out of any meaningful place in the dominant social and intellectual networks. Despite the compensation—or more likely because of it—he or she might remain relatively marginalized in Old Regime literary life. The trappings of respectability might be devalorized by the very fact that they were accessed *only* monetarily and thus stand as the symbols not of the writer's *qualité* but of the opposite: ambition, presumption, and thus low stature and rightful exclusion.

The truth, in any case, is that in the context of a history of authorship the growing sums that writers earned from their publishers are really meant not to illuminate the material life to which they explicitly refer, but to propel a narrative of forward movement. That is, the numbers become meaningful less in their concrete relation to the daily lives of writers than in the extent to which they round out the image of an autonomization process marked by writers' struggles to "live by the pen." Conspicuously greater than zero, the payments are equally obviously less than what they should be, and in this sense they situate writers on a sliding scale ranging from nonpayment in a primeval past to a "fair price" projected ahead to a time when they might finally earn a "decent" living without recourse to the largesse of patrons.[7] The writer's present is thus recast as an inevitably transitional point, not just from the "objective" perspective of the scholar examining the passage of writers from patronage to market, but also from the "subjective" point of view of writers themselves, whom we assume to be driven in their negotiations with publishers by a vision of an ideal future built on a mounting frustration with their present lot as "underpaid." Their own experience draws on an ambivalent mix of hope and exasperation, which then defines the forward movement both as a psychological framework for understanding writers' engagements with the book trade, and as a moral imperative by which writers can be judged.

Yet this raises a methodological problem. For the emphasis on income seems to beg the question of what is being studied. We take for granted that the focus on payments leads to the insight that writers became more independent as they were paid more. But the interest in the amounts earned appears in fact to be an *outcome* of the very history such an analysis seeks to illuminate. The idea that the history of Old Regime writers is the history of their liberation from aristocracy would seem to dictate—rather than ensue from—the enumeration of their payments in the book trade. Put another way, the analysis of rising income, which, with a focus on the legal rights to that income, has easily been the dominant angle in understanding the role of the book trade in the lives of Old Regime writers, does not precede and summon the conclusion that the history of authorship in pre-Revolutionary France consists above all in the gradual liberation of the writer from noble society. It is, on the contrary, the initial assumption that the history of writing must be the history of the liberation of the intellectual from nobility and monarchy that yields an investigation prioritizing the growth in payments from publishers as the privileged markers of this liberation.

Two important consequences need then to be considered. The first is a mirror effect resulting from this basic homology of a particular approach to an object—the teleological focus on "progress" toward the writer's social liberation—and the object itself—the author seen as the end result of that progress. The effect is one of tautology, for in accounting for the autonomization of writers one cannot help but encounter the "modern author", inasmuch as the figure is posited from the start as the personified image of this historical process. By the same token, in describing the "condition of the author," no matter on which period one focuses, one always ends up narrating the same "progress of the writer toward independence" so long as the author is defined a priori as the pivotal agent of this evolution.[8] As such, one might argue that the "history of authorship" is ultimately the history of itself. The investigation of the rise and development of a specific intellectual figure—the author—more than anything else defines and advances a particular conception of how intellectual practices rose and developed. It is hardly a surprise then that this history tends to find its own image reflected back wherever it may be searching. Whether in the eighteenth, seventeenth, or sixteenth century, the history of authorship inevitably finds an author to be its hero.

Moreover, given this incarnation of a teleology of intellectual liberation in a single figure defined by the process, there is a marked tendency for the history of intellectual autonomization that is the history of authorship to double, in turn, as a history of *individualization*. This is the case not only in the sense referenced by Foucault in his famous essay "What Is an Author?"—which considered individualization in terms of the focalization of the sources of intellectual authority and coherence in one person[9]—but also insofar as the writing of the history of authorship has so often been drawn to exceptional figures who stand out in their precociousness and unique insight against the mass of their contemporaries, and whose lonely struggles are then considered singlehandedly to drive the narrative. In a characteristic formulation, Raymond Birn observes that Rousseau, "more than any other writer of the eighteenth century, tried to impose his work on a free cultural market. . . . In his commercial activities as in his creative life, Rousseau was rooted in criteria of understanding that were original and personal."[10]

Conversely, the history of authorship offers a paradoxical or incongruous account as soon as such transcendent cultural icons as Diderot or Beaumarchais are not its protagonists. The literary property debates of the early and mid-eighteenth century were, for instance, engaged not by forward-looking "modern" writers loudly asserting their "natural" rights but by wealthy Parisian *libraires* who sought to consolidate their privileges and extend their control over the industry. "Ironically," Carla Hesse remarks, "the argument that ideas were the property of the individual author was first advanced in defense of the monopoly of the Paris Publisher's Guild on texts whose authors were long since dead."[11] But what makes this "ironic"? Not really the specific circumstances of the literary world in the time, which do not in and of themselves imply that there was anything counterintuitive or strange about the leading role played by the Parisian booksellers and printers in the cause of intellectual property rights, or about the noticeable lack of interest of established *gens de lettres* in that mobilization. The irony ensues from the prior assumption that a pro-property argument should more fittingly emerge from the struggles and thoughts of a writer claiming those rights in an effort to maximize his or her social autonomy. Only as they are filtered through those thoughts and that heroic struggle do the rise of intellectual property and the birth of the author acquire meaning.

The Precursor's Silence

One individual through whose consciousness the "birth of the author" is thought to have been refracted is Pierre Corneille. In his long-term study of authorship as a juridical concept from antiquity into the modern age, Bernard Edelman highlights the playwright's contribution to the "consecration of the author," which begins with a moment of illumination: "the sudden insight lies in a simple formula: that the genius is free, . . . and that he owes this freedom only to himself and his own powers."[12] Bringing this insight to bear into the field of public discourse with his 1637 poem "Excuse à Ariste," Corneille sparked the polemics of the *Querelle du Cid* in the course of which "a new sovereignty of the author" was outlined. "In these debates," Edelman continues, "the eighteenth-century is already anticipated." Underscoring the playwright's precociousness, he echoes numerous assessments of Corneille's foresight. Marc Fumaroli describes Corneille's "concern for the economic foundation of the activities of the writer" as most unusual for the age. He points to a 1643 request for *lettres patentes* by which the playwright sought official control over the performance of three of his recent tragedies, *Cinna*, *Polyeucte*, and *La mort de Pompée*, construing the administrative appeal as an endeavor to protect his intellectual property rights in a time when, Fumaroli goes on to argue, "the notion itself was practically unknown."[13] Claire Carlin concurs, deeming the petition "a move unheard of at the time."[14]

For Viala, too, Corneille is a "precursor" who mobilized to "benefit from the profits that he could draw from his works."[15] To be sure, the appraisal from a 1984 article must be nuanced against Viala's much larger investigation into the commercial and legal claims of *gens de lettres* in his well-known 1985 study of the *Naissance de l'écrivain*. There Viala argues that a concern for money and property rights, especially among playwrights, was more widespread in the mid-seventeenth century than had been assumed. In this respect, Corneille stands out less as an extraordinary case for his "unheard of" claims than as a remarkably salient and illustrative one who advanced more forcefully what others were thinking: "Thus dramatists, and particularly Corneille, were the most active in asserting their property rights."[16] Still, while the tragedian's singularity is no longer quite so emphasized, it is nonetheless conveyed by the relative dearth of other examples that might more persuasively round out the impression of a broad commitment to property and payments: "Led by dramatic authors, writers acted energetically and persistently to claim their literary property rights, initiating the movement that Beaumarchais would complete in founding the Société des auteurs dramatiques and in obtaining the laws of 1791 and 1793."[17] Viala goes on to conclude, "the affirmation and practice of literary property certainly already existed, therefore, in the Classical age."[18] But as further evidence only Quinault and Racine are mentioned, although neither make as straightforward and direct a case for owning the "rights" to their texts—whether printed or performed—as that suggested by the legal recourse of Corneille's *lettres patentes*.[19]

In truth, the most deliberate, concrete, and widespread indications of a pervasive rise in the commitment among *gens de lettres* to a proprietary vision of authorship in Viala's account lie not in anything that writers such as Quinault or Racine said or did, but in the efforts of others to resist the burgeoning sense of economic and legal entitlement. The most compelling evidence is, in other words, negative not positive. Viala describes, for instance, a monarchical backlash "to the demands of authors" in a series of regulations stipulated by the Conseil du Roi between 1618 and the 1660s. Among other things, these rules forbade writers to sell their own books except through the intermediary of a *libraire*; formally abolished the older and by that time mostly abandoned custom of granting writers general privileges to their entire *oeuvre*, including to works still to be written; and supported the increasingly common practice of renewing *privilèges* upon their expiration, which strengthened the position of established publishers who had an incentive to sit on their old stock.[20] In each case, Viala argues, the goal of the Conseil was to undermine the claims of writers to payments from the book trade, channeling them instead into the state patronage system to which they were then forced to turn. In the process, of course, the administration would seem to acknowledge the intensification of those claims.[21]

Perhaps, though, the richest vein of evidence mined by Viala to show that something like a proprietary form of authorship was gaining currency in seventeenth-century France is in the proliferation of pejorative and satirical images of the literary "professional," which run through a varied cross-section of writings. Viala cites the classic lines from Boileau's "Art poétique" to exemplify the anticommercial discourse of the Classical era, which depicts publishing for personal gain and commercial reward as the sullying of a noble art.

Mais je ne puis souffrir ces auteurs renommez,
Qui dégoûtez de gloire, et d'argent affamez,
Mettent leur Apollon aux gages d'un Libraire
Et font d'un Art divin un métier mercenaire.[22]

[I cannot abide these renowned authors
Who tired of glory and starved for money
Pawn their Muse to a bookseller
And make of a divine art a mercenary trade.]

These lines are more typically invoked to illustrate a general disdain for profit within Old Regime literary culture. Viala, though, reinterprets them as an expression of resistance to profound changes that had previously taken place, according to which the writers of the time were already significantly reoriented toward the "market." They point, in other words, not to the overall low regard in which commercialized literary activities were held but to their rise as "legitimate" practices: "far from signifying that the majority of authors disdained property rights, the satire indicates on the contrary that most pursued them. His discourse is defensive inasmuch as the opposite attitude had enough power to threaten this image [of the noble writer]."[23]

Focusing less on the anticommercial gestures per se than on their mounting intensity, Viala presents a strong challenge to the assumptions of an earlier scholarship that bought too easily into the "historical myth" of the Classical-era writer's indifference to literary commerce.[24] The forcefulness and consistency of the denunciations brought by Boileau and others suggest in fact that the reality was otherwise: the book trade occupied a central place in the experiences and aspirations of seventeenth-century writers. At another level, though, Viala's analysis fails to tackle one of the key premises of the older views. For these strongly associate the commercial engagements of writers with their awakening to legal rights and economic dues, considered as a precondition to the ultimate liberation from the domination of Old Regime elites. Viala has certainly rethought the chronology of this process. While Martin's "prehistory" suggested that the consciousness of literary property in seventeenth-century literary life was present only in an incipient form, significant only as it anticipates an eighteenth-century authorial revolution,[25] Viala essentially argues that the revolution had already arrived.

But precisely in this sense his reconsideration of Classical-era attitudes toward commerce is less probing in its account of *how* the new entrepreneurial consciousness came to transform intellectual practice in the period.

Viala holds to a reading of the book trade's effect as an institution of modernization, the quintessential function of which was to incite and focalize in *gens de lettres* a desire for freedom from nobility by offering them opportunities to satisfy this desire. But Boileau's rhetoric does not support such an interpretation. The lines do suggest that commerce was a draw for writers, which, it should be stressed, was not necessarily a bad thing. In his poem, Boileau also offers a positive image of the writer whose book "is surrounded by buyers in the shop of Barbin." Commerce did present a clear danger, but not by cultivating in writers a desire for independence from aristocracy. Rather, commerce amplified their ethical weaknesses; it was associated with greed and the blindness into which such a lapse would plunge the writer, who would then lose sight of the type of writer he or she should be. In this respect, the "Art poétique" is more a wake-up call than an admonition, warning writers against their worst natural tendencies, which consist in their self-absorption, not in their desire for autonomy.

We should note, moreover, the lack of any positive portrayal of the "literary mercenary" from the time. It is notable that the proliferating negative images of *gens de lettres* who take their careers into their own hands by selling their works to *libraires* contrasts markedly with the absence of favorable or even just neutral depictions of the same phenomenon. On occasion, writers voice a wish for remuneration from a publisher, but this is never overtly connected with a longing for economic self-sufficiency, certainly not a self-sufficiency understood narrowly as the ability to support oneself without recourse to aristocratic patronage. In fact, no writer who enjoyed noble support ever wished not to have it. And those who, like Jean de Préchac in his gallant novella, *La Noble vénitienne*, own up to their venal motives in publishing do so from an entirely different point of view: "The author having lost some money playing *bassette* found the means to make up for it by publishing a book from which he recovered the best part of what he had lost."[26] Préchac's explanation hardly projects a repudiation of the dependency of letters on aristocratic society. On the contrary, through the very image of his commercialized activities, meant not to valorize his labors but to downplay the importance of his writing (he turns to the classic pejorative phrase "faire des livres" to refer to publishing), the admission places him squarely in the culture of the court, with its ludic pastimes and high-risk gambling.

In the absence of direct, positive statements associating the book trade and autonomy in the seventeenth century, literary scholars have fixed on administrative or legal records to substantiate the argument that Classical-era *gens de lettres* sought freedom through commerce. C. E. J. Caldicott explores Molière's involvement in the publication of his *Oeuvres complètes*, chronicled in "archived documents that trace the long and sad story of his conflicts with the Booksellers Guild." Specifically, he focuses on a series of *privilèges* issued to both *libraires* and the playwright in the 1660s and early 1670s. Against a tradition emphasizing Molière's identity as a court poet and a "man of letters too preoccupied with the problems of his art to care about the correction of his proofs," Caldicott paints a less familiar portrait of the writer as deeply invested in the publication of his works—"anxious about the quality of the edition"—and ready to fight the booksellers for control over the process.[27] Moreover, Caldicott asserts that the struggle was not extraneous to Molière's sense of his authorial identity, despite the typical coyness of his prefaces. Instead, it was engaged as a critical aspect of the playwright's effort to construct and control his intellectual self: "Driving the combativeness of the author . . . is a sense of his rights, and therefore an authorial consciousness."[28] This identity was, in turn, increasingly defined for Molière by the weakening of his ties to the king and the court, and by his perception of a "second career, another way of existing, according to which he would be solely in control of the future of his work." Caldicott continues, "Forged in the crucible of his solitary battles against the institutional interests of the printers, this authorial consciousness gradually assumed a preponderant role in Molière's career, up to the point where, as he pushed further along this path, he necessarily granted less importance to his relations at Court." As such, Caldicott concludes, Molière should be placed "in the ranks of the first modern authors."[29]

One is struck, though, by Molière's silence throughout this story, and by the possibility that such an interpretation of *privilèges* rests more on a series of presuppositions about why authors would be involved in the gritty details of publication than on any specific sign that the desire for "another way of existing" was what Molière's intervention into the book trade was all about. Similarly, the arguments for Corneille's modernity, in the absence of any statement from the playwright himself, have focalized around an administrative document, namely, the request for *lettres patentes* deposed in 1643. Written by a law clerk named Le Roy and corrected by Corneille, the request for the exclusive rights to "have the above-mentioned theatrical plays, named *Cinna*, *Polyeucte*, and *La mort de Pompée*, staged and represented by a theatrical troupe in whatever place in our Kingdom that he sees fit," was denied.[30] The artifact has nonetheless been seized on as evidence of Corneille's precocious conceptualization of "literary property." Assumed to reflect a heightened sensitivity to the economic predicament of writers, the request then indicates the tragedian's strong sense of his autonomy, of which his forays into the commercial publishing sphere led him to become conscious and which then drove his efforts to pursue his interests there. The *lettres patentes*—"a move unheard of at the time"[31]—thus stand out as concrete proof of his modernity.

As with Molière's *privilèges*, though, Corneille's reticence should give pause. For one thing, the *lettres patentes* can be understood in a wholly different framework, that of contemporary theater politics and the intense rivalry between the up and coming Théâtre du Marais, recently founded in 1634 by the actor Montdory, and the more established, quasi-official theater of the Hôtel de Bourgogne, which housed the *comédiens du roi*. Having quarreled with the latter, Corneille famously decided to give his plays to the new troupe, which would perform a series of his works including *Le Cid* in early 1637. The *lettres* might then be considered in light of his shifting loyalties insofar as convention dictated that once a play was in print, it was available to be performed by any theatrical company.[32] Indeed, editions of *Cinna* and *Polyeucte* appeared in 1643.[33] And with a print version of *La mort de Pompée* in press for the following year, Corneille was perhaps seeking with the *lettres* primarily to deny the performance rights to his plays to the "troupe royale" out of lingering bitterness, and in order to emphasize his changing allegiances.[34]

The examples of Molière and Corneille illustrate how central administrative records have been to arguments about the modernization of Old Regime authorship. Both highlight, too, the tendency, in making such arguments, to read certain motives and desires into things like *lettres patentes* and *privilèges* that are in reality not so self-evidently manifest in what exist ultimately as no more than signs of the writer's involvement—sometimes indirect—in the publication process. It is assumed that such documents give expression to a desire on the part of the writer for autonomy, defined specifically as freedom from dependence on aristocracy or monarchy. It is also assumed that this desire for autonomy is a natural one, which the writer had ignored or repressed in patronage relations, but which, in making the legal and economic claims the *privilège* puts forth, he or she now recognizes and embraces. Finally, it is assumed that once the natural desire for autonomy is given free rein, it will eat away at the foundations of the older order, and ultimately bring it down in order to open up a "new system" or a "new reality." Herein lies a crux of the modernization argument; the very gesture of taking out a *privilège* represents a pointed threat to the established order, and a turn to a new one.

But I would argue that such assumptions, grounded less in the peculiarities of the cases than in the logic of a prewritten "history of authorship," hide as much as they reveal about the role of the book trade in Classical-era literary life. Viala's emphasis on disparaging images of the "commercial writer" correctly calls attention to a broad awareness of the book trade in the seventeenth century that had been insufficiently valorized in earlier accounts. But when he reads those representations as purely negative reactions to a wider trend toward professionalization, Viala dismisses them as retrograde defensiveness before inevitable progress. On its own merits, the anticommercial rhetoric of writers like Boileau becomes insignificant, functioning merely as a sign of what it represses. A closer look, however, opens up an alternative interpretation, particularly when a key albeit underaccentuated factor is brought out: namely, our sense today that the anticommercial rhetoric is archaic jars strikingly with seventeenth-century perceptions that the attack on literary commerce was a "modern" cause. The pejorative view of the "professional" did indeed articulate an innovation for Classical-era observers. But the innovation was not the entrepreneurial, independent writer. It was a new cultural ideal defined against the self-interest and vulgarity of the commercial writer, and which lay in the "refinement" of letters through integration into court and noble society, and in the "socialization" of *gens de lettres* as adept participants in *le monde*.

In such a light, we might reconsider the role played by commercial publication in the lives of seventeenth-century writers in a way that better reconciles the growing centrality of the phenomenon with the apparent deepening of writers' hostility to it. For it was as it opened up opportunities for intellectuals to establish and project their associations with the privileged and powerful that the vocabulary of literary commerce entered into the discourse of literary selfhood in seventeenth-century France. And accordingly, the book trade burst into the Classical-era field not as the result of a growing desire among writers for liberation from their patrons, nor due to its objective expansion, but as it came to circumscribe a recognizable space in which writers' ties to elite society would be solidified rather than weakened. In this respect, the book trade became an institution of literary life with implications for the legitimacy of writers. Of course, it did so as a negative field. If a language of commerce was invested with significance for the self-presentation of *gens de lettres*, it was as this language conveyed the writer's distance from the "market," and as it meaningfully expressed, in the terms of reluctance, anonymity, and a refusal to profit, the writer's lack of contact with its agents and procedures. The language nonetheless became meaningful, and through it, the book trade could be envisioned as an authorial field in which literary identities could be constructed.

The Case of Corneille

The case of Corneille illustrates the transformation. The playwright was widely known—and attacked—in his own time for the attention he paid to the commercialization of his plays: "In truth, he is greedier than he is ambitious," observes Tallement des Réaux, "and so long as he makes money, he does not torment himself about the rest."[35] La Bruyère paints a similar picture: "he only judges the quality of his play by the money that it earns him."[36] Present from the earliest days of his career, such taunts established what would become an enduring image of the playwright's abiding interest in profit.[37] They also provide a backdrop of "traditional" viewpoints against which Corneille's foresight is contrasted, underscoring his philosophical and material resistance to the entrenched thinking of his age.[38] But a closer look at the anti-Corneille invective in its rhetorical context reveals a more complex situation. While the satirical images have been seized by literary history as direct reflections of a reality in which Corneille was more dedicated than others to the commercialization of his works, they can also be read as effects of a willful effort on the part of those generating them to shape—and fit into—a very different cultural reality, one defined not by growing participation in the "literary market" but by the integration of writers into an aristocratic society that for its part was becoming more intellectual and literate. Central to the articulation of this socialization process were images of exclusion from *le monde*, tendered not as proof of anything that was happening out in the world but as negative paradigms against which writers could affirm their adeptness for elegant society. Active involvement in the commerce of one's works emerged as an especially clear figuration of social isolation; and by extension, the refusal of commerce became a powerful signal of the writer's inclusion.

In fact, the most consistent theme in the attacks against Corneille was a critique of what his detractors perceived to be the playwright's strong sense of his self-sufficiency, manifest in an arrogant willingness to endow on himself the praise that he should have hoped would come from others. The abbé d'Aubignac, a persistent antagonist, castigates the playwright for his tendency to self-consecration: "this title of Great Man that Monsieur Corneille has given himself," he writes in the third of four *dissertations* written against the playwright in the 1660s.[39] Literary historians have long pointed out that the quarrel erupting after the performance of *Le Cid* in early 1637, which is generally viewed as a debate over dramaturgical doctrine, was actually triggered not by Corneille's failure to respect Aristotelian principles of tragic composition, but by his lack of modesty. Specifically, the *Querelle* was initiated by a poem Corneille circulated in the months following the success of the play, called "Excuse à Ariste," in which he celebrates his triumph, depicting it as the sole effect of his own talent. He had, in other words, no support or cabal pushing for him, but only his own merit to thank:

Mon travail sans appui monte sur le Théâtre,
Chacun en liberté l'y blâme ou l'idolâtre,
Là sans que mes amis prêchent leurs sentiments
J'arrache quelque fois trop d'applaudissements,
Là content du succès que le mérite donne
Par d'illustres avis je n'éblouis personne,
Je satisfais ensemble et peuple et courtisans,
Et mes vers en tous lieux sont mes seuls partisans.

[My work without support is staged
And each in liberty can attack or idolize it,
There, without my friends preaching their own feelings
I come away sometimes with much applause,
There, happy with the success which merit brings
I do not try to dazzle anyone with the opinions of illustrious individuals,
I please both people and courtiers,
And in all places, my verse is my only partisan.]

Corneille goes on to conclude notoriously (referring back to his verse):

Par leur seule beauté ma plume est estimée
Je ne dois qu'à moi seul toute ma Renommée.[40]

[By its sole beauty, my pen is esteemed
I owe only to myself all of my renown.]

Much of the ensuing polemic consisted in denunciations of this self-affirmation and the personal failing that it expressed. The tone was set by Jean Mairet, a rival playwright who quickly published a rhymed response taking Corneille to task for, as the descriptive title puts it, "A letter in verse, which he has published, entitled 'Excuse à Ariste,' in which, after a hundred expressions of vanity, he says about himself, I owe only to myself all of my renown." The poem begins:

I am speaking to you, Braggart, whose utter audaciousness
Has in recent days been elevated into the sky.[41]

The venomous exchange that launched the *Querelle* might be seen as incidental to the deeper issues at stake; in the words of Armand Gasté, it was a "chance cause, but a first cause."[42] Hélène Merlin, however, has recently argued that the dispute over proper comportment for writers was at the core of the debate. She inverts Gasté's reading by suggesting that it was the doctrinal questions that were secondary, and no more than a pretext for an engagement with overriding matters relating to the place of writers in an evolving court society and to a consequent redefinition of literary practice.[43] To be sure, while doctrinal matters will dominate the judgment of the Académie française, which pronounced more or less the final word in the *Querelle* at the end of 1637—and which has, in turn, deeply influenced historical representations of the affair—when another playwright, Georges de Scudéry, first raised the question of Corneille's dramaturgical transgressions in an *Observations sur le Cid* in the spring, it was in response not to Corneille's failures as a craftsman of tragedies, but to his ethical lapses as an *homme de lettres*: "when I saw that he had deified himself by his own authority; that he talked about himself as one would normally talk about others, . . . I thought that I could not, without cowardice and injustice, abandon the common cause." Otherwise, Scudéry goes on, "I am good and generous; . . . I had been happy to know the error without refuting it."[44]

For Scudéry, the questions about doctrine were subordinated to the problem posed by Corneille's immodesty, and served, above all, as part of a behavioral lesson designed to show how out of line the playwright was. Corneille rooted the celebration of his triumph in the "applause" he references in the "Excuse." Scudéry then sets out to show the weakness of the public's judgment; for the audience is ignorant of the art of theater and will be duped by a spectacle, regardless of the genuine quality of the play: "the People who judge with their eyes, allow themselves to be deceived by that sense which is, of all the senses, the easiest to fool." Only a closer and more expert examination, in light of the "principles and rules of dramatic poetry," will indicate what a play is really worth. And in the case of *Le Cid* such analysis unearths serious flaws, which Scudéry enumerates in detail: "That the subject is worth nothing at all; . . . that it lacks judgment in its construction; that it has a lot of bad verses."⁴⁵ With the public's reception delegitimized as a gauge of the play's quality, Corneille's high opinion of his own work based on this acclamation no longer has a reasonable basis, but is now revealed to be an effect of self-delusional and ungainly arrogance. Responding to the following lines from Corneille's "Excuse":

Et [je] pense toute fois n'avoir point de rival
A qui je fasse tort en le traittant d'égal,

[And I believe that I have no rival
To whom I do wrong by treating him as an equal,]

Scudéry censures the playwright for such misguided pride with a trenchant appraisal of his writing, which illustrates the inseparability of the doctrinal critique from the ethical attack:

Now as to the versification, I admit that it is the best we have seen from this Author. Yet, it is not perfect enough such that he can say himself that he is leaving the earth; that his flight hides him away in the heavens; that he laughs at the despair of those who envy him; and that he has no rival who is not highly honored when he consents to treat him as an equal.⁴⁶

It is in the context of this fierce polemic on Corneille's arrogance that the classic image of the playwright as excessively invested in the commercialization of his works takes shape, not for the first time, of course, but in an urgent and reinvigorated elaboration. The image is invoked as further proof of Corneille's ethical failing. For not only did he deign to sing his own praises, Scudéry writes, "he even had the high opinions he has of himself printed."⁴⁷ In fact, more than as additional evidence, the passage to print is rendered in anti-Corneille tirades as the straw that breaks the camel's back. It is a gesture that finally pushes Corneille over the line, whereas until that point he had merely skirted the limit. *Le Cid* pushed the envelope, yet despite its errors it could be excused. What had to be called out was the unseemly choice to print it. "This, my friend, is why you are generally blamed, not for having written *Le Cid* with all the irregularities that can be detected throughout," explains Mairet, "but only for your indiscretion in delivering it so quickly to a bookseller."⁴⁸ Another pamphleteer similarly contrasts the fatal decisiveness of publication with other less serious missteps: "You have made just two mistakes that cannot be repaired," affirms the unnamed author, "one, having your play, which was so well-liked on stage, printed; and the other, having responded to he who criticized you."⁴⁹

In particular, the anti-Corneille polemic constitutes the gesture of commercial publication in two key and interrelated ways. First, print is represented as a privileged medium for Corneille's moral failings, one that concentrates and channels his greed and self-regard, transforming them from normal everyday moral lapses into something abnormal, excessive and odious. One broadside, possibly by Scarron, denounces the "excess of avarice which made you have *Le Cid* printed."[50] Another lambastes the "freshly ennobled" playwright for projecting his renown "not by acts of valor, but by newspaper hawkers [crieurs de gazettes]," who do not just circulate Corneille's arrogance in print: "for the past month [they] have pounded the ears of everyone."[51] Second, as a conduit of his out-of-control *amour propre*, print becomes a powerful symbol for Corneille's inattentiveness to the feelings and well-being of others, and thus of the playwright's lack of sociability. Mairet criticized Corneille's rush to print *Le Cid* because in so doing the playwright repudiated his friends and their sage advice to correct his play before publishing it.[52] Further on, he represents the move as a selfish rebuke of the actors—"those who obliged you by making your Alchemy worth something"—since it denied them the chance to recoup the profits that were their due given that the circulation of the play in print opened up the possibility for other troupes to stage their own performances and compete for an audience.[53]

Consequently, Corneille's publication activities will be closely associated with a representation of his social isolation, conveyed through images of the playwright's gracelessness and outlandishness. Print thus becomes a mechanism for the transformation of the writer as a veritable monster. Jean Claveret's "modest" concession to Corneille—"I was prepared to grant that you are a greater Poet than I am, without it being necessary for you to use the voices of all the hawkers [Colporteurs] of the Pont-Neuf to announce it all over France"[54]—renders the latter grotesque by the hyperbolic valence of the adjective "all," repeated twice, and the reference to "France." He goes on to propose a deal, agreeing to believe in Corneille's singular talent as a dramatic poet, so long as the author of *Le Cid* accepts for his part, as the price of his genius, the radical deterioration of his social persona and stature; indeed, so long as he accepts his fundamental unsuitability for *le monde*, marked in a single gesture by his precipitous departure once he has sold his works:

But recognize in return that you are, in prose, the most impertinent of those who know how to speak, that the coldness and stupidity of your wit are such that your company makes one pity those who must suffer your visits, and that . . . you pass in high society [le beau monde] as the most ridiculous of all men. These are truths that will always be confirmed among the most honorable people [les plus honnestes gens] of Paris, of both sexes, where stories of your gracelessness are told that make melancholy itself laugh. You have good reason to flee as soon as you have sold your Poetic goods [denrées Poëtiques].[55]

Later admirers of Corneille would spin this by then legendary awkwardness positively as a sign of the playwright's dedication to the integrity of his work, marked by his lack of interest in the frivolities of high society[56]; and in light of this reinterpretation of his social ineptness, Corneille's equally mythologized efforts to sell his "Poetic goods" would themselves be revalorized as significant expressions of this seriousness and authorial independence. But such reasoning says far more about later ideals than about anything that might have been going through Corneille's head as he transacted with *libraires* or requested letters patent from the administration, or through the minds of his detractors as they pointed derisively to these negotiations. The discourse of the anti-Corneille forces presented a strong connection between a vision of the playwright's autonomy and his publishing activities. Yet it was a distinctly symbolic association forged by the use of images of Corneille's commercial literary activities as powerful figurations of his isolation by those who sought, indeed, to isolate him. The rhetoric does not allow us to conclude that Corneille desired this autonomy, and turned to commercial publishing in order to establish the conditions in which he might claim it. In fact, in its polemical aspect, the invective suggests a relation of influence that goes in the exact reverse direction; publishing activities do not lead to autonomy. It is instead the positing of autonomy—or the perception and imputation of a certain type of autonomy manifested in Corneille's rude and antisocial demeanor—that leads to the production of images in which publishing activities and venal motives are highlighted.

Thus, if Corneille was assailed for not having sufficiently respected his social ties and obligations, it was not because he sought to go it alone in the "market." The equation goes the other way; a depiction of the playwright seeking to earn his living commercially became current because of his failure to be integrated into *le monde*. The social isolation was prior to commerce, and had its roots elsewhere, in a natural aversion for court life and in his attachment to older forms of elite selfhood, which he would articulate against the model of the courtier.[57] To be sure, the self-sufficiency Corneille celebrates in the "Excuse à Ariste" is set against an image of the court poet who goes obsequiously from "Réduit en Réduit" looking for voices of support:

We speak of ourselves with complete frankness [franchise],
False humility does not bring one credit,
I know what I am worth, and believe what I am told of it.[58]

This is the vocabulary of a "feudal" nobility. Radically self-legitimizing, nostalgic, conscious of its vanishing preeminence, and intensely hostile to the emerging culture of the court with its communal, self-inhibiting ethos, this language is spoken in *Le Cid* by the Comte.[59] It is, in any case, hardly that of the professional author looking to make a decent living "by the pen."

Alternative New Realities of Literary Life

All this raises a key question. Given the polemical nature of the connection tying Corneille as an autonomous writer to commercial publishing, what can we say about the underlying reality of the authorial condition? To what extent, in other words, does the association forged by writers such as Mairet and Claveret point to a real "stratégie éditoriale" pursued by Corneille and characterized by an unprecedented focus on property rights and profits? Answers to the question remain speculative in the absence of any direct statement from the playwright himself. It might, though, be fruitful to pose it a little differently; that is, what reality do these images truly reflect? They are normally assumed to indicate the legal and economic reality of the seventeenth-century book trade and commercial theater, in which Corneille's participation, gauged by the 1643 "Demande de lettres patentes," was in fact intense compared to that of his contemporaries.[60] We have, however, observed that other interpretations of the "Demande" are plausible, according to which it reflects not an effort to improve the legal and economic status of the writer, but contemporary theater and court politics.[61] It is worth recalling, moreover, that the *lettres patentes* for which Corneille applied did not constitute a *privilège en librairie*, despite being incorporated by Viala and others into the type of historical account of the development of literary property in which the *privilège* is often highlighted as a key intermediate stage. "Corneille was not simply content to defend his literary property rights to printed editions; in 1643, he tried to advance them durably to the performances of his plays," contends Viala, seeming to equate the two mechanisms.[62]

Yet even granting that the *lettres patentes* might be fully comparable with a *privilège*, there are still reasons to doubt that the request was so unusual as to be "unheard of at the time."[63] Nicolas Schapira has recently shown that in fact a good portion of seventeenth-century writers, above all, "literary" authors as opposed to those involved in other kinds of writing—scientific, historical, philosophical, theological—asked for and received *privilèges* for their works in the Classical age, more than is usually assumed.[64] Studying the records of the bookseller-printer Toussaint Du Bray, who specialized in printing *nouveautés littéraires* in the early part of the century, Schapira notes that, while only 6.5 percent of his editions were protected by a *privilège* granted to a writer in the years from 1604 to 1613, between 1624 and 1633 this percentage rose to 26 percent, and by 1634–36 over half his editions had *privilèges* directly held by the author. "By the end of the century," concludes Schapira, "the *privilège* to the author seems to have become the norm"; indeed, a full ten of the fifteen *privilèges* the bookseller Claude Barbin held in 1680 had initially been requested by and delivered to *gens de lettres*.[65]

But, Schapira argues, if writers became increasingly interested in *privilèges*, it was not out of a nascent attachment to intellectual property or profits. It was instead out of a wish to enhance their reputations as *gens de lettres* inasmuch as they become aware of the effectiveness of the *privilège* in conveying royal favor. Bearing the king's seal and the approving words of a royal censor or a *secrétaire du roi*, and printed by law in every copy of the book, the *privilège* was appropriated as an especially functional medium for advertising the social, political, and cultural legitimacy of writers before a public that always remained sensitive to the decorum of authorial gestures and was predisposed to receiving a book with a high degree of suspicion toward the individual who would be connected to it as its author.[66] In his late seventeenth-century biography of Descartes, Adrien Baillet recounts that the philosopher requested a *privilège* in 1637 for the *Discours de la méthode* "to mark his love for and perfect submission to the King." Living in Holland, Descartes was eager to maintain his good standing with the authorities in France. He would in fact be embarrassed by the eulogistic *privilège général* Marin Mersenne obtained for him from the Conseil du roi.[67] Indeed, Descartes's anxiety shows, as well, that the *privilège* posed dangers if the effort to acquire it was mismanaged, for it might, in upholding an image of the writer's favor, also shed light on less admirable efforts of ingratiation and self-promotion. François Charpentier's satirical account of Martin Pinchesne excitedly reading before a circle of friends the text of a *privilège* recently granted to him, comically eager to impress them with the official esteem that it conveyed, illustrates the risk.[68]

In either case, the intersection of authorship with the *privilège* system did not manifest the professionalization of literary activities, as many literary histories assume. On the contrary, Charpentier tells another story in which Georges de Scudéry turns to the mechanism in an effort to bolster—perhaps to fabricate—an image of himself as a retired soldier devoting his idle hours to poetry rather than as a writer earning a living from his plays: "Scudéry went to Saint Germain in order to have a *privilège* issued in his name, in which he has the King say that he commanded Royal Troupes, whereas truthfully, he has never commanded any troupes other than those of the Hôtel de Bourgogne and the Marais, and a few other troupes of provincial actors."[69] The *privilège* pointed in a wholly different direction, and indeed to quite another cultural reality of which the images of Corneille's involvement in commercial publication might also be a reflection: not the slow progress of the writer toward professional independence but the evolving stakes of literary legitimacy in the 1630s, in the context of what Alain Viala called "the first literary field."[70]

This reality is characterized at least in part by two decisive developments. On one hand, we have what might be called a socialization of intellectual practices epitomized by the emergence of distinctly social qualities like politeness and *honnêteté* as essential criteria for the evaluation of writers and their works. More exactly, this socialization was an "aristocratization" of letters, with "société" understood in the seventeenth-century meaning recorded by the dictionary of the Académie française, which accentuates the pleasure of leisured interactions and the exclusivity of elite gatherings.[71] The process was thus one of the integration of writers into the networks and values of social elites, a process mediated by what Viala calls "institutions of literary life," such as the Académie, court patronage, and salons. These and other similar bodies offered privileged venues and mechanisms for introducing *gens de lettres* and their writings into "the Court and high society," where both authors and their productions would be judged according to emerging worldly criteria.[72] Charles Sorel offers an allegorical account of this "New Parnassus," describing the Muses leaving "their rustic caves for golden palaces where they frequently lived, having been received by the nobility of the age." Apollo abandoned Pegasus, "an old horse" and "hideous beast," for a stylish "Carriage."[73]

At the same time, the elite assimilation of letters was matched by a reciprocal process, a "literary" transformation and redefinition of noble society and identity. We can understand this in two ways. First is the manner described by Delphine Denis, who, in her excavation of the intellectual production of midcentury salon society—"l'archive galante"—highlights the "aestheticization" of a self-consciously rarefied community, according to which the participation of its members consists in efforts to please the others through impressions made by dress, gestures, and language.[74] These individuals become like works of art, to recall the analysis of Domna Stanton, defining themselves as objects of contemplation.[75] Yet the pleasure they offer resides in their capacity to focus the attention of others not on their own éclat, but on their beauty as a direct reflection of the excellence of the group and its dynamic. They represent its interactivity and thus its cohesiveness.

This "aestheticization" is as a result fundamentally linguistic, and not only to the degree that the charming exchanges of the group are to be perceived above all in its conversations and correspondences, but also insofar as language—indeed, *written* language—becomes the primary medium of this representation. Schapira points out that, as a site of refined social and cultural exchange, the Hôtel de Rambouillet, and by extension the "salon," is as much a discursive construct mythologized by writers who celebrated it as an actual space carved out by the marquise through architectural design.[76] In this respect, the "salon" is a rewriting of reality through the diffusion of textual depictions, often in letters but also in printed items such Madeleine de Scudéry's romances, which shape and channel the hopes, anxieties, and choices of those who then seek to situate themselves within this space. Both the "court" and the "Académie française" would circulate in printed media as the sublimated images of a "real" context, whose history they tell,[77] and which they claim faithfully to imitate—in a 1678 letter to her friend Lescheraine, Madame de Lafayette famously deemed the *princesse de Clèves* "a perfect imitation of the Court"—but whose perfection and thus authority as institutions legislating social, cultural, and intellectual norms they in fact postulate and impose. The elevation of the "court" and the "salon" as central institutions of literary life in the mid-seventeenth century would depend on this "production of belief" through writing and print in their authority to discern and elevate the good and to exclude the bad.[78]

Which brings us to the second way in which we might understand the "literary" transformation of elite identity; that is, in terms of the growing importance of writing for those who lay claim to the distinction of being noble.[79] This development grows out of a broader phenomenon: the role played by language itself as a medium of self-expression for a "modern" aristocracy that sought to distinguish itself not only from non-elites but also from a nobility identified with an earlier age, whose coarseness and vulgarity provided a countermodel against which a new elegant "salon" society oriented itself. In the early decades of the century, Rambouillet had created her "théâtre de . . . divertissements" as a kind of private refuge from the barbaric court of Henri IV: "She said that she found nothing pleasant there."[80] The refinement of the pastimes that occupied its participants compared with the amusements of the Louvre—they were the most gallant and polite, to recall Tallement—was in large part the effect of their linguistic nature; for they mobilized intellectual skills not physical dexterity, and thereby reflected an elevation of its noble practitioners who expressed themselves in elegant phrases rather than in feats of strength and prowess. Sorel registers the further development of the linguistic turn in his 1664 *La bibliothèque françoise*. Surveying works that "deal with [its] purity," he represents the ascendancy of language as a distinct innovation in elite life: "Today," he stresses, "we take those who speak French badly to be men of lowly condition and little wit." Relative to older markers of social superiority, language imposed new imperatives on those who would fashion themselves according to the cultural ethic of *mondanité*: "One must learn politeness and polish in language [la politesse du langage], as much as in composure, or in the way of dressing and in everything that appears on the exterior."[81]

Sorel emphasizes speaking; but writing was a critical part of the trend. In his treatise from 1630 on "l'honnête homme," adapted from Castiglione's Renaissance sketch of the courtier, Nicolas Faret counsels the political and socially ambitious "to develop a good writing style, including for serious matters, for compliments, for love, and for so many other subjects the occasions for which arise everyday at the court. He continues, "those who do not have this facility can never aspire to great functions [grands emplois]."[82] Faret admittedly focused on official kinds of writing—memoirs and letters—and considered belles-lettres—poetry and other "literary" forms—to be "more agreeable than necessary."[83] Three decades later, however, Molière's nobleman and would-be poet Oronte from *Le Misanthrope* would speak to the necessity of "literary" writing for those claiming a rightful place in *le monde*. Indeed, this is what the central character of the play, Alceste, really hates in Oronte's sonnet; not so much the bad verse in and of itself, but the idea that he offers it as a privileged expression of his *honnêteté*.

Monsieur, cette matière est toujours délicate,
Et sur le bel esprit nous aimons qu'on nous flatte.
Mais un jour, à quelqu'un, dont je tairerai le nom,
Je disais, en voyant des vers de sa façon,
Qu'il faut qu'un galant homme ait toujours grand empire
Sur les démangeaisons qui nous prennent d'écrire.[84]

[Sir, these are delicate matters; we all desire
To be told that we've the true poetic fire.
But once, to one whose name I shall not mention,
I said, regarding some verse of his invention,
That gentlemen should rigorously control
The itch to write which often afflicts the soul.]

Ordered to testify before the King's Marshals in a dispute that, for Oronte, has escalated into an *affaire d'honneur*, Alceste justifies his criticism by pointing out that he did not call into doubt Oronte's personal credibility as an "honnête homme" in questioning his skills as a poet; after all, what could possibly be the connection?

De quoi s'offense-t-il? Et que veut-il me dire?
Y va-t-il de sa gloire à ne pas bien écrire?
Que lui fait mon avis, qu'il a pris de travers?
On peut être honnête homme et faire mal des vers:
Ce n'est point à l'honneur que touchent ces matières;
Je le tiens galant homme en toutes les manières,
Homme de qualité, de mérite et de coeur,
Tout ce qu'il vous plaira, mais fort méchant auteur.[85]

[His verse is bad, extremely bad, in fact.
Surely it does the man no harm to know it.
Does it disgrace him, not to be a poet?
A gentleman may be respected still,
Whether he writes a sonnet well or ill.
That I dislike his verse should not offend him;
He's noble, brave, and virtuous—but I fear
He can't in truth be called a sonneteer.]

At the same time, Alceste does not hesitate to praise other activities and aspects of the courtier:

Je louerai, si l'on veut, son train et sa dépense,
Son adresse à cheval, aux armes, à la danse;[86]

[I'll gladly praise his wardrobe; I'll endorse
His dancing, or the way he sits on a horse;]

not because, it would seem, Oronte is any better at these; we have no indication at all that he is a more talented horseman, swordsman, or dancer than a poet. But for Alceste these represent traditional vehicles of aristocratic self-expression and established forms for advancing claims to social and cultural preeminence. Writing poetry, on the other hand, does not: "But, gentlemen, I cannot praise his rhyme."[87]

Signifying his preference for older practices over new and thus his outdatedness—Philinte repeatedly describes his friend as being out of touch with "the ways of the time [les moeurs du temps]"—Alceste's antipathy correlatively measures the recent nature of writing's rise as a medium for the projection of personal quality, contrasted against a set of more obviously traditional activities, with the startling ascendancy of this medium, its surging importance, further reflected in Oronte's decision to take the matter before the King's justice. Moreover, it is not only Oronte's desire to write poetry that is in dispute but more specifically, his intention to circulate the sonnet. Oronte's approach to the Misanthrope was not just about getting the latter's feedback but about securing his approbation before "going public" with his verse:

Et, comme votre esprit a de grandes lumières,
Je viens, pour commencer entre nous ce beau noeud,
Vous montrer un sonnet que j'ai fait depuis peu,
Et savoir s'il est bon qu'au public je l'expose.[88]

[Since you have such fine judgment, I intend
To please you, if I can, with a small sonnet
I wrote not long ago. Please comment on it,
And tell me whether I ought to publish it.]

In other words, the activity in question is not simply the *honnête* writing of a poem but its *honnête* publication with the requisite inscription of the act of "faire paraître" in a friendship that would compel and authorize it. And clearly what is being figured by "exposer au public" here is publication in print; Alceste's questions suggest that there is no ambiguity on this point:

Quel besoin si pressant avez-vous de rimer?
Et qui diantre, vous pousse à vous faire imprimer?[89]

[What pressing need do you have to compose rhymes?
And what on earth pushes you to have them printed?]

    Reimagined in this way, and invested with a newfound significance for the construction of an identity whose status would be a function of its positioning at the intersections of "literary" and aristocratic life, the print publication of writing was, however, defined by two problems that would fundamentally orient its seventeenth-century practice. First, in having their works printed, writers who aspired to elite social standing ran the risk of projecting not their intelligence or their ennobling *esprit*, but an arrogant belief in the enduring value of their self-expression such that it deserved the permanence of ink. The danger of publication was, in other words, the danger of publishing nothing more than one's inflated self-esteem. And indeed, central to the figuration of the "Author" in this period, as this denoted the activity of "bringing to light [mettre en lumière]" a book, was a collection of attributes that were all acute symptoms of the ethical flaw of *amour-propre*.[90] In the passage to print, the author was assumed to be driven by vanity, pride, greed, and jealousy. Thus Boileau counseled aspiring poets, "Rid yourself . . . of authorial arrogance."[91] To publish was to confront moral opprobrium, a fact that Boisrobert makes clear in the *avis* to the 1659 reedition of his *Epîtres en vers*: "I know that I have been accused in high society [dans le Monde] of not neglecting myself in the love that one ordinarily has for oneself and for one's works."[92] Consequently, expressions of modesty downplaying the merit of one's writing as well as one's role in its publication were essential. These, of course, abound in the writings of the period, and countless examples could be given. "In all ways, Reader, you are very little obliged to me. I am giving you a rather bad work, and I am only giving it to you with regret," La Calprenède affirms in the preface to an edition of his 1637 tragedy, *La mort de Mithridate*, explaining his embarrassment as an "ignorant soldier" to be distributing an unworthy text, and that he did so only once he knew that unauthorized copies, "with two thousand mistakes," had began to circulate.[93]

    Second, publication might imply that one appealed to a broader public than the audience gathered at court or in the salon, and no doubt more crucially, that one addressed this public as a stranger to it. That is, the move to print introduced an image of the writer elaborated through a sharp differentiation with the reader, one understood spatially, of course, inasmuch as publication bridged but also called attention to the distance separating the two figures. But this distance indicated another separation, which delineated against a collective of readers the solitary, isolated figure of an author who stood apart not simply in space but by talent and genius as well. The cultural logic of *honnêteté* required, however, that *gens de lettres* project their integration into groups defined by concentration not expansion, and that they offer their writings neither as vehicles of individual brilliance nor as the effects of their distance from readers but as emblems of their self-effacing participation in the collective venture of polite society.

How, though, might a medium so effective in telescoping a self beyond one's normal interpersonal networks bring the opposite result of focusing one's presence within them? Writers had recourse to a number of established strategies: they could inscribe within the work itself the elite group as intended audience and inspiration by the prefatory reference to a circle of friends for whom they had initially produced, and who then convinced them to publish the text or even took it upon themselves to do so; they could restrict the work's circulation, either by a small print run and stringent control over the distribution of copies—in his 1650 edition of Voiture's *Oeuvres*, Martin Pinchesne stresses the "few copies that were printed"[94]—or symbolically by the incorporation into the work of a system of codes, keys, or references targeted to an exclusive group of readers who, knowing the allusions, drew from the text a meaning and a satisfaction that was specific to them and denied to a wider public for whom the references remained opaque and the text frustrating; and finally, they could root the work's publication in the oral social practices of the court and the salon—or more exactly in a representation of those oral practices that conceived the printed work as derivative of and a prop to the urbane culture of conversations and group readings "à haute voix,"[95] and writing as the image of speech.[96]

The Perils and Possibilities of Print in the First Literary Field

Providing an alternative backdrop to the conventional image of Corneille as a commercially oriented writer, this other social and cultural reality was constituted by the emergence of print publication as a gesture opening up critical possibilities for aspirants seeking to mobilize their intellectual capital in the quest for enhanced social status. The opportunities had little to do with making money or exercising rights, and even less with the prospect of independence from noble society. At the same time, the alternative reality was characterized by the evolution of publishing as a tremendously fraught act, which extended fatal dangers: "printing is the pitfall [l'écueil]," wrote La Bruyère.[97] Indeed, publication appeared to subsume and intensify all the defining paradoxes of life in *le monde*: how to construct a self that would be admired for its humility; how to stand out through self-effacement before the group; and how to command attention by seeking to deflect it away.

In this respect, the act of "faire imprimer" presented to those who sought to write their way into high society, or consolidate their positions within it, the daunting prospect of a very fine line, with little separating success from failure, grace from inept self-promotion, and thus social integration from exclusion and isolation. In the *avis* to his *Epîtres*, Boisrobert affirms his modesty against those who questioned it by pointing out that he suppressed from the second edition "the praise which the most famous wits of the time lavished on the first volume."[98] But, wanting to valorize the quality of his intellect and his favorability in the eyes of eminent judges of talent, he does not suppress the reference to their existence, a fact that then seems to render the "modest" gesture heavy-handed and forced. The effort was too perceptible and as a result open to ridicule for its apparent hypocrisy. In fact, Tallement's portrait of Boisrobert will not be kind, recounting the reaction of the comte d'Estrée to Boisrobert's 1657 *Nouvelles héroïques et amoureuses*. Remembering the backlash against Corneille, and "seeing that Boisrobert spoke about these Nouvelles as of something beautiful, [the comte] took it upon himself to write a long letter in which he warns Boisrobert, without naming himself, of all the things in his book with which one might find fault."[99]

But in its postulation of such a fine line, publication also envisioned a vital way to take on the paradoxes of elite intellectual sociability; for it offered the idea of a reconciliation between the seemingly contradictory imperatives of *mondanité*. Indeed, it was conceived as a medium that was amenable to the projection of a sublimated intelligence, socialized as the ennobling quality of *esprit*. To be sure, the endeavor was more prone to fail than to succeed. Above all, it was rare that there would be consensus on an individual's self-presentation through print, and publication revealed itself to be a tremendously heated point of contestation, open to challenge at every turn. Yet if publication became a contentious affair, this speaks not simply to the profound ambivalence of the gesture in the context of seventeenth-century polite society, but also to the fact that the stakes were high and getting higher, as the act of "faire paraître [a book of poem]" was invested with significance for elite life, becoming perhaps the primary medium for advancing claims to elite social status, particularly for those seeking to base that claim on intelligence rather than blood, strength, or fortune. It is in this ascendancy, one can argue, that literary life takes shape. For the rise of print publication as a remarkably effective conduit for the assertion and reflection of social prestige represents one key index of the formation of the "first literary field," as Alain Viala defined it.

Viala describes a process by which a subset of intellectual practices— namely belles-lettres, referring to a set of creative activities identified by the fact that they are undertaken in view of offering what might be called "aesthetic" pleasure, though they are also closely tied to the pleasures of "society"[100]—was distinguished within the broader field of "letters" as they were concentrated in particular spaces—courts, academies, and salons— recognized as privileged sites for their undertaking and appreciation, as well as for the judgment of those engaged in them. According to Viala, the process was one of "autonomization." However, autonomization is a loaded and multivalent term, as we have seen, which functions at a number of different levels. It can refer to the autonomy of the "aesthetic," indicating an activity whose end is its own contemplation and enjoyment. It might also point to the autonomy of a discipline whose coherence is recognized and institutionalized, for instance, in a system of prizes or in a pedagogical program.[101] Finally, the term can refer to the autonomy of a series of practices viewed together as a sufficient basis for a distinct, coherent, and even valorized social identity, one able as such to support the individual economically and symbolically. It is no doubt this sense that Viala has in mind when he writes, "literary activity has at its disposal a certain autonomy within social structures, and possibilities of work and compensation which are specific to it."[102]

It would be a mistake, though, to understand the term here in what is certainly its more modern and intuitive signification. For the autonomy of the first literary field had little to do with freedom from the control of the politically powerful and the socially dominant. On the contrary, it was a function of the ascendancy of cultural institutions that were created at the initiative of elites and operated under their stewardship, bringing writers into their orbit rather than out of it. Christian Jouhaud has recently traced what he subtitles "the history of a paradox," according to which the "growing autonomy" of writers in the Classical age was possible only as the outcome of their growing dependence on authorities. Drawn into relationships of service with patrons and the state, they were made directly subordinate, to be sure. Yet their expanding role in the exercise of political power as propagandists and normalizers of language, as well as in the elaboration of a self-consciously "modern" elite social culture, was at the same time acknowledged and institutionalized, thereby rendering the social identity of writer not just legitimate but desirable, prestigious, and lucrative, and *sufficient*.[103] For their part, the *gens de lettres* of the period consistently conveyed a sense of their own "freedom of expression" as a direct function of their subjecthood vis-à-vis a prince, or of their subservience in strongly hierarchical relations of protection. "I am born free, and we live under the domination of a Prince who lets us peacefully enjoy an honorable license to do as we please," writes d'Aubignac, justifying the printing of his third *Dissertation* against Corneille.[104] Such "liberty" was construed as a benefit of the writer's presence in a rapport that spoke to his or her elevation and legitimacy, and thus to his or her prerogative to speak the personalized language of belles-lettres, which celebrated the self in its connections to a tight-knit and highly exclusive community of exceptional individuals. In the *éloge* to Voiture with which he prefaces his edition of the poet's *Oeuvres*, Pinchesne calls attention to Voiture's "too familiar" style in his letters and poems to nobles: "he had acquired this privilege by his habit of interacting in this way with the most noble individuals, and by the liberty that they themselves allowed him."[105]

As a result, patronage and service to political and social elites were more likely to be experienced as an opening up of possibilities for "literary" self-expression rather than as a limitation on them. And it is in this opening that seventeenth-century "court writers" located their autonomy, the most powerful figuration of which lay in an image of leisure manifesting their now enhanced standing.[106] This leisure was represented as the crucible of their writing and, in turn, transformed the writing by infusing it with prestige and cachet. Offered as a backdrop to the activities of composing epistles, poems, plays, and prose romances, it rendered the various practices of belles-lettres as credible reflections of their privileged status, and therefore as the vehicles of plausible claims to "noble" identities.[107] The "autonomization" of belles-lettres—and we could add, echoing Timothy Reiss, the invention of "literature"[108]—might be gauged by the extent to which such practices became, through the elevation of *esprit* as a marker of personal quality, *sufficient* for establishing valorized identities insofar as they were able, in and of themselves, to situate *gens de lettres* in social milieus where their ennobled selves would be recognized as such: Voiture's "facility of intellect," Pinchesne pointed out, "led him to be warmly welcomed by the highest noblemen and princes of the court."[109]

Put another way, the "autonomization" of the first literary field consisted in the process by which the activities of belles-lettristic writing and publishing, as these increasingly opened opportunities for service to political and social authorities, also increasingly afforded possibilities for individuals to represent themselves as integrated into the elite. Expressing gratitude to the Académie for its final judgment in the *Querelle du Cid*, Scudéry writes: "It is not in the mass of people nor in the cave of a loner that one must seek sovereign reason; it is where I have always found it, that is, in a society of excellent individuals."[110] By dint of their service, they were able to project themselves into a state of leisure that was at the same time a respite from the weighty responsibilities that had come with their social ascension and the underlying reality of their day-to-day existence in the upper reaches of the hierarchy. This leisure was then reinterpreted as the cause rather than the effect of their writing; it was offered as a condition that, in allowing them to "do as they please," freed them to write, with "freedom" understood not as a "lifting of barriers" but as a "privilege" or "entitlement" ensuing from their high social position. Scudéry depicts himself in his prefaces as a retired soldier having once served the king in battle but now with time to kill: "Poetry is for me an agreeable entertainment, and not a serious occupation," he writes in the preface to his 1631 tragicomedy *Ligdamon et Lidias*. "If I write verse, it is because I do not know what else to do."[111] Such a stance, of course, downplays any hint of professionalism; and as he would do in the course of the *Querelle*, Scudéry affects insouciance toward his writing, which contributes to the sense of an identity rooting itself not in any intellectual practice but in his past as a former commander of Royal troops. Poems and plays were no more than side occupations for a now idle man of the sword:

You will easily overlook the mistakes that I have missed, if you realize that . . . I've spent more years amongst arms than hours in my study, and used far more wick firing an harquebus than burning a candle; such that I know better how to arrange soldiers than dialogue.[112]

Scudéry was called out on this posturing, as we have seen.[113] But while it was challenged, the image gained credibility. In the polemics of the *Querelle*, the motif of Scudéry as a soldier who battled heroically for the common cause insinuates itself not only into his own writing but into the language of other anti-Corneille pamphleteers as well. Surprised by Corneille's attack against him, Claveret imputes it to "a remainder of pride that the arms of the *Observateur du Cid* [Scudéry] have not yet been able destroy."[114] Mairet brings the militaristic imagery into sharper focus, recounting a critical assault on *Le Cid* in which "Monsieur de Scudéry slashed twenty times with his sword into its body."[115] Against the arrogance of Corneille, Scudéry offers the model of a viable, *honnête* intellectual autonomy that was established in two moves: first, a rhetorical inversion by which Scudéry's "literary" practices are presented as the reflections of his military service and hence of his aristocratic identity, whereas it is really his "service" as a commander of troops and by extension his "noble" self that are the emanations of his writing and publishing activities; and second, the imposition of this inverted relationship into certain quasi-official discourses such as dedications and *privilèges*, and consequently onto a small but crucial public willing to buy into it—if not fully, since there were many within that public who sought to unveil the artifice of the reversal, then at least somewhat. But no doubt, this was the best for which one could realistically hope. For in the context of the "first literary field" what was at stake was less the undisputed recognition of a "literary" identity than its recognizability, and the possibility that it could be claimed and defended. Opposition not only went without saying but was in the end essential to this recognizability.

"Corneille," the Book Trade, and *Honnête* Publication

Commercial print publication became one of the first literary field's central institutions as it was perceived to open up this *honnête* autonomy to writers. In this respect, the book trade found its coherence and shape for seventeenth-century cultural life not by offering writers an escape from dependence on aristocratic patrons but in the manner of other formations such as academies and salons, that is, insofar as it offered a medium for the invention and projection of an identity that would be legitimized, valorized, and thus freed to speak by the integration of the intellectual into *le monde*. It entered into the mental landscape of writers as an "institution of literary life" to the extent that writers appropriated commercial print as a mechanism of their elite acculturation, which in the spaces of self-presentation defined by the printed text—prefaces, dedications, notes to readers, introductory letters, *privilèges*, and letters patent—facilitated the illustration of their sociability, quality, and *esprit*.

Correlatively, while we are inclined to assess writers' early contacts with the book trade as implicit, primitive, and indirect claims to "literary property" or payments, the reality is that these contacts came to play meaningful roles in the literary lives of Classical-era *gens de lettres* insofar as they were converted into devices and tropes for fashioning, controlling, and polishing their images as *honnêtes gens* before the elite public from whom they sought their consecration. Even when they expressed proprietary sentiments, Saint-Amant justified the publication of his *Oeuvres* in 1629 by indicating in the preface his fear that counterfeit copies would circulate if an authorized version did not. The gesture is open to interpretation as a "modern" claim to the ownership of his writing. It is, though, appropriated by the poet not as an assertion of his individual rights but in an effort to find and maintain that fine line between modesty and distinction that was essential to *honnête* self-presentation. Hence the deep ambivalence of a gesture offered in the end as an expression of both self-effacement and self-promotion, with Saint-Amant initially submitting his concern about pirated copies as evidence of his humility:

The just vexation that I have when I see the many small poets impudently claiming items that they have stolen from works appearing in my name, and the fear I have that some provincial bookseller would have the gall to print these items without my consent, as they have threatened to do, are what have led me to try to beat them to it [printing my poems], rather than any desire I have to acquire in this way glory.

He goes on, though, to suggest that there is in fact nothing wrong with seeking *renommée* through print. "It is a somewhat too scrupulous philosophy," he writes of the critical view condemning print publication as vainglorious and uncouth, "that not one of those who preach it would observe it if he had written something worthy of being printed."[116] Saint-Amant's tack gives his anxiety a distinct resonance, for the stakes are not determined by a writer's desire to ensure the integrity of his text as an authentic expression of his innermost thoughts. Presumed to be a "natural," defining authorial desire, the latter motive orients most understandings of the proprietary claims of intellectuals to their writings. But those of Saint-Amant are determined by a wholly different aspiration: the desire for social legitimacy as shaped by the dynamic of a self-consciously "modern," intellectualized aristocratic culture. It is in this framework that Saint-Amant's proprietary feelings are conceived and expressed: not as a constrained or embarrassed desire that would be more freely and forcefully articulated if the writer were not so held back by heterogeneous considerations of decorum, but rather as a visible, significant, powerful vehicle of affect and value, which allows the writer, though self-denigration and modesty, to lay strong direct claims to the credibility of the *honnête homme*.

The negativity of the commercial rhetoric in the self-presentation of Classical-era writers speaks less to the weakness or awkwardness of these writers' assertions of preeminence than to the complexity of the book trade as an institution that enabled such claims. In this respect commercial publication must be distinguished from those other institutions of literary life—academies, salons, and so forth—with which it nonetheless shares the twofold agenda of integrating intellectuals into aristocratic society and providing *le monde* with the venues and media for its linguistic reinvention. For while, say, the "salon" as a cultural institution points above all to a specific type of refined, intellectualized sociability into which writers sought to insinuate themselves as they pursued their renown, it also happens to describe an actual space and a real event in an aristocratic household that they might frequent in the effort. As a result, the "salon" is a relatively intuitive concept, in spite of the fact that the conflation of "worldly sociability [sociabilité mondaine]" as a cultural system with the concrete practices of elite sociability can lead to confusion.[117]

But as it is institutionalized, manifesting the rise of writing and print as social practices and vehicles of personal quality and elite status, the book trade refers, by contrast, to a space from which the writer is *absent*. It could, in fact, be argued that it is in and through the staged withdrawal of the writer from its sphere that *la librairie* can be said paradoxically to have been transformed as an institution of literary life, one in which writers might acquire recognized identities as *gens de lettres* and *honnêtes gens*, along with the autonomy to write in an ennobling leisure signaled—or even constituted—in the evocation of this disappearance: "[I] have no other goal in this work than the sole desire to please myself: for far from being mercenary, the printer and the actors will bear witness to the fact that I did not sell them that for which they could not pay me," writes Scudéry in the preface to *Ligdamon et Lidias*.[118]

In light of this, Corneille's pivotal place in the history of writers and publishing becomes more intricate; he was not just a heroic "precursor" who alone among the *gens de lettres* of the period became aware of his rights and interests as an author, and then took the initiative to act on this awareness. He also came to play an integral role in the staging of this withdrawal as a negative model: "Really, if your writings are remembered by posterity, the fruit that they derive from this will be marvelous," wrote Claveret, "but it will be in the manner that the Lacedemonians got their slaves drunk, in order to foster a horror of drunkenness among their citizens."[119] Indeed, for those seeking to affirm their absence from the book trade as evidence of their *honnêteté*, Corneille offered the stark counterexample of presence. His self-promoting rush to publish—"nobody twisted your arm to hasten you into publishing your mistakes with a royal *privilège*"[120]—and to inhabit the sphere of the book trade in order to try to valorize his identity there was elaborated as a foil against which his detractors could portray their publication activities as symptoms not of their own desire for status and fame, though of course they were this, but of their restraint and selfless dedication to the collective. In his *Observations*, Scudéry points out that, having had no intention to criticize publicly *Le Cid* despite his reservations about its doctrinal correctness, he felt obliged to make a statement only out of a sense of duty to the community of *honnêtes gens*, whose core values were assailed by Corneille's celebration of self: "I thought that I could not without injustice and cowardice abandon the common cause."[121] Claveret, too, plays up his gracious reluctance to get involved through a sharp contrast with Corneille's eagerness to jump into the fray: "I am not happy that a remark so unfavorable to you must come from my pen, and that I am reduced to this shameful necessity of circulating my letter by the same means that you used in order to sell [débiter] your attacks."[122]

Corneille's presence in the publishing world, not as an objective "reality" but as the emblematic figure of an overly strong personal investment in publishing, and therefore of an authorial arrogance and singularity that the *honnête* writer had to avoid, is ultimately what, in the context of the *premier champ littéraire*, "commercialization" denotes. It develops, in other words, as a polemical articulation of the self-interest and vanity of writers, to the degree that these moral attributes are rendered particularly visible and readable in their engagements with the commercial production of their writings. It makes sense that writers who emphasized their reluctance to publish in upholding their *honnête* integration into *le monde* would be remembered for their resistance before a mounting outside force. But in positing the commerce of letters as an "objective" phenomenon existing independently of its repudiation by *honnête* writers, such an appraisal obscures the fact that resistance to the book trade was, paradoxically, the framework in which *literary* commerce took form in the seventeenth century as a viable, which is to say, a conceivable albeit illegitimate authorial mode.

These writers would, by the same token, also be remembered for their attachment to "old-fashioned" practices, attitudes, and values; correlatively, their "anticommercialism" would become one of the identifying traits of their archaicness. Yet this brings to light a historical contradiction, in the context of which the following chapters will situate the formation of the "literary market." For in the 1630s it was Corneille who, as a bad example, pointed not to the future but to the past, and it was his adversaries who fought beneath the banner of modernization. Those who attacked Corneille for his publishing activities did so not out of respect for tradition but in the name of a progress represented in their minds by the reciprocal integration of writers into aristocratic society and intellectualization of court culture.[123] The abbé d'Aubignac criticizes the playwright for not being up to date with current tastes. He chose violent and fantastic subjects such as that of Oedipus, which might have pleased an audience from an earlier, more vulgar age, one still plunged "in that old ignorance which [Corneille] had up to this point found indulgent toward his first mistakes," but which no longer amused the polite society of midcentury: "it is better to adapt oneself to one's time when one wants to please," he writes, warning Corneille to conform to the "values of our century."[124] In this reversed dialectic, "commerce," too, rather than "anti-commerce," is associated with being behind the times. Corneille's "eagerness to profit" functions in the *Querelle* much like his "thirty years of schooling" or his crude Norman patois, namely as the sign of his backwardness.[125] Underscoring editorial activities that manifest this lack of *honnêteté* inasmuch they give expression to his vanity and unbridled self-importance, "commerce" indicates not Corneille's prescient transcendence of the domination of *lettres* by nobility but the fact that he has yet to enter into this transformative relationship with elites. It places him at the beginning of a process not looking ahead to the end. Described by Mairet as a "clerk's move [pas de clerc]," his involvement in publication points to an older humanistic model, to an older, coarser nobility that would have better appreciated his out-of-date subjects, and indeed to an earlier time whose real coherence consists in the simple fact that it precedes the elegant fusion of social and linguistic practices that lies at the heart of the new social system of *mondanité*. Far from a future independence, Corneille's interventions into the book trade, played up in the polemical writings of his enemies, designate a "prehistory" against which the court elites and salon poets of midcentury would articulate a sense of their own progressiveness.

What is more, this alternative narrative inverts the causal relation between commerce and modernity that is normally posited by the account of the heroic precursor asserting rights. In a standard telling, the expansion of literary commerce induces modernity by offering *gens de lettres* the material conditions for their social liberation. Commerce in this view operates as an external force that bends and alters the "traditional" practices, attitudes, and institutions of Old Regime literary life according to its own logic. In the confrontation between patronage and the book trade, it is almost always assumed that the latter, in opening up the space of the "literary market," undermines the former as the opportunities extended by commercial print draw writers away from their rich and powerful sponsors, toward new liberated modes of authorship.

But the story that seventeenth-century writers tell of their own transformation suggests a different sequence, according to which commercialization is not a cause but an effect. As it erupts into the *Querelle*, for instance, "commerce" is not an objective driving force of change, but a subjective valuation reflecting the social and intellectual evolution that is the institutionalization of the first literary field. In this respect, "commercialization" is not the result of the mounting interest of writers in commercial payments and property rights, as Viala argued.[126] Rather, it is the expression of a new kind of social judgment of *gens de lettres*, articulated in the diffusion of images of writers according a disproportionate place to their concrete, motivated involvement in publication. Tallement rehearses in detail the terms of a contract that Jean Chapelain received from the bookseller Courbé for *La Pucelle*—3,000 livres plus 150 copies including "several which, because of the paper and the binding, cost 10 écus and more." Commerce surges into the world of letters in this portrait, but not because Chapelain was in fact more involved than other writers in the sale of his works to publishers, or involved in a way that others had never been. Rather, it bursts in as a transparent and powerful signifier of negativity, invoked to complete what is already a critical portrait of an individual whose stature and reputation Tallement wants to undermine.[127]

Finally, it is worth spelling out what is implicit in this analysis, since it will be central to what follows in the next chapters. Literary commerce is not only the effect of a social judgment; it is also, by this same token, the invention of that in the name of which the judgment is pronounced: namely, the cultural ethic of *mondanité*. And in this respect "literary commerce" does not refer to a natural, instinctive, or primal phenomenon. The tendency, though, in studying the historic role of publication in the evolution of literary practices has been to construe "commercialized" gestures—the demand for direct payment in exchange for works or the claim to property rights—as the manifestations of "true" desires expressive of the fundamental nature of the Author. By contrast, "anticommercial" moves—refusing payment or neglecting rights—are considered to be affected and constrained gestures reflecting incidental desires, such as those for recognition from social and political benefactors, desires assumed to be functions more of the contingent circumstances in which the writer operates than of anything essential to the nature of writing and Authorship. As a result, writers "automatically" move into the market of their own free will once they have the chance, but they enter into patronage relations only because they have to, for lack of an alternative. Commerce is then associated with "liberation" inasmuch as it is considered to furnish writers with just such a possibility, thereby allowing them to act on those defining drives, which had been repressed and disfigured by a symbolic order imposing on literary life a decorum seen as "artificial" since it reflects "nonliterary," heterogeneous ideals and values.

In the discourses of seventeenth-century literary selfhood, however, the opposition of "true" to accidental desires is exactly inverted. Here, "literary commerce" points to a disfiguration, not of the author, to be sure, but of the social function of the *homme de lettres* as imagined within the cultural configuration of *le monde*. And the desire for property rights and *droits d'auteur* are neither "true" nor "natural" but are the constructs of this symbolic order. Rather than discovered, they are invented as possible modes of writing and literary selfhood, which, driven by authorial self-interest and impoliteness, will offer a counterpoint to legitimacy. This symbolic constitution of "literary commerce" will be critical for *gens de lettres* of the eighteenth century, for as we will see, they turn to *la librairie* less for the economic and legal conditions of a social liberation that they will hardly find, but to position themselves vis-à-vis elite society, either within it following patterns inherited from the Classical age or outside of it, according to newer ideals that will root the legitimacy of writers in their sincerity, seriousness, and devotion to truth. It is the argument of this book that the "literary market" as a cultural field grows as much out of the seventeenth-century investment of the "commerce of letters" with meaning for the identity and authority of the intellectual, as out of the economic development of the publishing industry.

2

The Paradoxes of Enlightenment Publishing

THE PARAMETERS OF *HONNÊTE* PUBLICATION are defined in Classical-era debates such as the *Querelle du Cid*, and subsequent developments in the intellectual field must be understood in their light, including the formation of the literary market. Of course, with its commercial aspects and its decidedly non-elite denizens, the market seems far removed from the social spheres in which an ethic of *honnêteté* prevailed on writers. I suggest, though, that the essence of the literary market lies precisely in its constitution as a field of *honnête* publication, which is to say that it evolves first and foremost as a space for the symbolic legitimization of *gens de lettres* rather than for their economic compensation. In this sense, despite its lead role in a narrative underscoring the radical shift by which writers became "independent" from aristocratic patrons, the market is actually historically continuous with the refined spaces circumscribing seventeenth-century literary life. It develops more than it breaks with a "traditional" view of the cultural field as a system upholding a particular type of social prestige rooted in intelligence and writing. And if the market does represent a shift, it is not because it advances the concept of "autonomy" per se, which, as we have already seen, was no less integral to the valorization of intellectual selfhood in the "first literary field," but because it formulates a specifically new figuration of autonomy in the language of economic self-sufficiency; the writer became autonomous insofar as he "lived by the pen." This image of freedom was, in turn, a function of a new conception of legitimacy, defined in a repudiation of the very same aristocratic sensibility in which this particular story of the birth of the modern writer first takes root.

In order to better understand both the broader continuity and the particular transformation that the literary market represents, we turn to the vision of *honnête* authorship to which the writers who, in a sense, "invented" the market were reacting. We turn to the *philosophes* who stand as dominant figures in the mid- to late eighteenth-century intellectual world. These well-placed and visible *gens de lettres* established leading models of intellectual practice not simply for their contemporaries who aspired to lives in letters, but for the modern era. Nicole Masson considers Voltaire to be a "'prototype' of the modern intellectual."[1] In reality, of course, they embodied a set of intellectual conventions that were heavily indebted to the aristocratic patterns identified in debates such as the *Querelle du Cid*, even as they adapted these patterns in the effort to valorize their own activities as autonomous critics. The fact remains, though, that writers such as Voltaire and d'Alembert were pointedly targeted by those who sought to make a rejection of elite culture and sociability an integral element in a new ideal of literary legitimacy, for they identified the *philosophes*—with attention to the latter's cultivation of elites—as especially representative of a corrupt and outdated system.

But while of interest to critical contemporaries, it is striking that the authorial field as envisioned by the *philosophes* in their contacts with the book trade has remained something of a non-topic in literary histories of the Enlightenment. Conversely, the history of writers and publishing in this period has focused much more on obviously nonphilosophical figures, that is, individuals who, by their own positioning or by the maneuverings of others, have come to be identified *against* the group of writers recognized at the time and still celebrated today as the *philosophes*. Rousseau, of course, presents a clear example; as do the "hacks" who inhabited the "literary underground," so influentially described by Robert Darnton. Indeed, it seems that those down and out types are specifically defined by the two attributes: their exclusion from the intellectual circles of the *philosophes*, for one, and their dependence, as an outcome of their cultural and social isolation, on commercial publishing activities, for another. We might add Diderot to this list, for he stands as an especially notable protagonist in the history of writers and the book trade in the Enlightenment. To be sure, Diderot was much better integrated into the world of the *philosophes* than either Rousseau or the *pauvres diables* of the literary underworld. Yet his role in this history is normally granted in spite of this inclusion. He is pivotal not as a *philosophe* but to the extent that he was never quite wholly able to assume that identity, constrained as he was both by the memory of his early years writing in relative obscurity for profiteering *libraires* rather than rich and powerful patrons, and by his continued close involvement with bookselling milieus as the general editor of the *Encyclopédie*. Diderot thus plays a leading role in this history to the extent that, as Darnton observes, he "never fully extricated himself from Grub Street."[2]

There is a compelling reason for why the book trade as perceived through the eyes of the *philosophes* has remained an elusive object of study. Their publishing practices do not present a familiar image of that field but seem to jar with established notions about who the *philosophes* were and what they stood for. Historically, these writers have been valorized as the heroes of change and modernity, yet their choices in the publishing sphere appear at first glance to hearken back to patterns inherited from the polite writers of the seventeenth century. They were neglectful of their intellectual property rights, and, far from trying to maximize their revenues in an effort to live independently of patronage, "by the pen," they were more concerned to project their *honnête* disinterest in the manner of the court and salon poets of the Classical age. As a result, their publishing practices tend to present stumbling blocks, and the attempt to characterize the *philosophe* as a cultural formation confronts them as paradoxical or anomalous phenomena not easy to incorporate into the standard account of the *philosophe*'s birth as a "modern" figure. Nicole Masson grants that, although a "prototype," Voltaire nonetheless "does not yet have an idea that one can or should live by the pen."[3] Likewise, Jules Bertaut is stymied by the incongruity of the same writer's silence on his rights and dues: "It is a curious fact that Voltaire, normally so determined to profit and who knew so well how to defend his own interests in all his endeavors, . . . did not show the same combativeness when it came to his literary interests."[4]

The publishing practices of the *philosophes* need, in other words, to be rationalized. Either their role must be clarified within the larger philosophical project or they need to be downplayed as extraneous to that project since they reflect not the real thinking of the *philosophes* but the material and intellectual constraints under which they labored. In the latter sense, Bertaut surmises that payments from publishers were not yet high enough to engage Voltaire in what surely was the lost cause of literary property rights and *droits d'auteur*: "No doubt, he calculated that the benefit was middling, and that it was not worth the efforts that he would have to apply."[5] This is not a ringing endorsement of Voltaire's choices as a leading author of the Enlightenment, but the statement justifies the writer in light of the underdeveloped state of the publishing industry.[6] Jacques Douvez, on the other hand, examining Voltaire's livelihood and seeking to contextualize his publishing strategies with respect to both his fortune and his mission, considers his negligence not just understandable given the state of the book trade, but entirely consistent with a movement that conceived of its objectives largely in the dissemination of new ideas to a public whose reading had always been tightly controlled. Voltaire may well have shown little interest in payments and rights, but, as Douvez reminds us, "his goal was philosophical battle; he thus had to win the favor of booksellers."[7]

Still a third alternative, of course, is not to attempt any kind of explanation at all of the ostensibly incongruous publishing activities but to acknowledge, insofar as they were not chiefly oriented toward maximizing the writer's autonomy from elites, that the practices were compromising. They speak to the collusion of writers like Voltaire and Duclos with the established hierarchy, exposing, in contradiction to their own claims, their choice of status and prestige over any true commitment to equality and fairness. Already in the eighteenth century, Simon-Nicolas-Henri Linguet, a disbarred lawyer turned journalist and polemicist, in a response to the book trade reforms of 1777, scathingly attacked the "so-called *philosophes*"—he refers specifically to d'Alembert and Marmontel—for ignoring the debate and neglecting "the property of their creations. All the while they bow at the feet of the most contemptible people in order to obtain puny pensions."[8] Linguet, about whom much more will be said in the course of this investigation, had already positioned himself as a fierce adversary of the "encyclopédistes," and was especially hostile toward d'Alembert who, he felt, had denied him a seat in the Académie française in 1764, effectively blocking his entry into the inner circles of Enlightenment-era literary life and frustrating his ambitions. This view would, however, be taken up by a series of twentieth-century scholars with no personal axe to grind, yet who would call for a comparable reassessment of the conventionally heroic image of the *philosophes* in light of an attachment to elite culture that, among other ways, was manifest in their choice to disregard their intellectual property rights and authorial dues in favor of "traditional" forms of income and support, including patronage and court sinecures. Darnton is perhaps the most famous and ruthless in his reevaluation of the *philosophes* as "mandarins fatten[ing] themselves on pensions," arguing that "Duclos, Voltaire, and d'Alembert urged their 'brethren' to profit from the mobility available to them in order to join the elite. Rather than challenge the social order, they offered a prop to it."[9] But he is not the only historian to postulate that the *philosophes* were far more rooted in the traditional values and practices of the Old Regime than has generally been admitted.[10]

Articulating conflicting judgments on the place that should be accorded to the *philosophes*' publishing activities in the larger scheme of their intellectual project, these three options nonetheless share a common assumption that the activities presented stark inconsistencies with the project, as well as with a fixed ideal of intellectual selfhood that the *philosophes* are broadly considered to have forged. Standard to most histories of eighteenth-century literature, the ideal is predicated on two moves: first, writers of the period became *philosophes* in their pursuit of an agenda driven by a critique of conventional ideas and established institutions in the name of a pragmatic and humanitarian rationalism; second, in undertaking the critique, these *philosophes* lay claim, through a series of characteristic gestures—rejecting patronage, increasing their mobility across Europe, and resorting to strategies of subterfuge in the publication of their writings—to autonomy from the social, political, and religious authorities under whose tutelage writers had long labored. In his early twentieth-century study of Enlightenment-era *hommes de lettres*, Maurice Pellisson highlights the processes by which the latter became "more and more independent," and in the process became "more capable of directing the public [l'esprit public]."[11] Masson renders the move toward autonomy as a similarly defining aspect of the new intellectual paradigm embodied by Voltaire, whose career can be read, she argues, "as the conquest of independence for the man of letters."[12] Darnton, of course, counters such rhetoric with a more sober assessment of the *philosophes'* indebtedness to social elites, apparent in their reliance on connections and patronage rather than "sales of books."[13] But in emphasizing these ties as a shortcoming—as a failure to "challenge the social order"—Darnton ultimately reveals his own beholden-ness to the very same ideal of the *philosophe* as a fundamentally independent figure.

The examination of the publishing practices of the *philosophes* in light of a predetermined conception of who these writers were, claimed to be, or indeed failed to be has, however, produced only limited insights into the logic of these practices. It can hardly be said to have generated a clear understanding of what publishing books meant to them. This is an arresting blind spot, though, given the importance that the writers themselves accorded to the activity. When in his 1787 *discours de réception* to the Académie, Claude-Carloman de Rulhière, a man imbued with the spirit of the Enlightenment, marked the "general revolution . . . in letters and morals [moeurs]," he did so with a recitation of those moments when the great leaders of the movement broke through, around 1750, as the authors of major works thought to have had a profound effect on a readership whose eyes were then opened onto new ways of thinking; Montesquieu with *L'Esprit de lois*; Buffon with his *Histoire naturelle*; and Voltaire with plays and early writings on the English philosophers. Rulhière's brief history stands in stark contrast to the inclinations of those recording intellectual progress in the Classical era, who as we have seen were more likely to emphasize as turning points the creation of a salon or the cultivation of certain urbane ethos at court. The publication of a book was in the seventeenth century not seriously recognized as a significant moment, either for the culture as a whole or for the individual seeking renown as an *homme d'esprit* within that culture. By contrast, the *philosophes* were decidedly authors, and their history is, as Rulhière told it, the story of their publications.

At the same time, though, the philosophical embrace of book publication cannot be adequately explained by juxtaposing the choices and activities of Voltaire or d'Alembert against the Classical-era paradigm of the disinterested court poet, despite the fact that the rejection of the leisured amateur of letters would be incorporated as a central element in the *philosophes*' self-presentation. The story is more complicated, for as Darnton shows, the *philosophes* did not reject the social dimension of writing, or its capacity to integrate individuals into aristocratic networks. They undertook those gestures that remain challenging to modern sensibilities for their apparent subordination of the intellectual objectives of authorship to the "traditional" imperatives of politeness and *bienséance*. Refusing profits and intellectual property, the *philosophes* circulated their works in fine editions as gifts to social and political luminaries. Rousseau and his followers would turn to writing as a pointedly nonsocial or even antisocial act by which one gave voice to an "authentic" self defined against a corrupt "civilized" self that had been disfigured by the compromises of life in *le monde*. Yet for the *philosophes*, what was at stake was not the integrity of an inner nature, but a distinctly social preeminence constructed *within*—not outside—the established, albeit evolving hierarchy of the Old Regime.

In fact, this is really the anomaly unearthed by the publishing practices of the *philosophes*. They bear witness to the rising importance of writing and publishing for a claim to authority that, in its critical inclination, was firmly rooted in an image of the writer's independence from social and political elites. But for all that, they do not mark a patent shift from elite sociability as the dominant mode of intellectual activity toward a new paradigm that, whether in a professional or proto-romantic vein, was in any case starkly opposed to the ethos of aristocratic sociability. To the contrary, they speak to the *philosophes*' persistent elite orientation. But if their publishing practices muddy the conventional image of the *philosophes* as "autonomous," a more direct focus on these activities, rather than less attention, is essential to clarifying the problem, I would argue. Accordingly, this chapter proposes a new approach to the matter, which inverts the traditional perspective on philosophical publishing. Rather than examine its paradoxes in light of a fixed notion of who the *philosophes* thought they were and what they thought they were doing, it instead revisits the very concept of the *philosophe* as a specific model of literary identity in light of the underlying logic of their activities in the book trade. In so doing, it draws on Christian Jouhaud's and Alain Viala's argument to "take seriously" the very concept of "publication" as a salient point of access allowing for "ANOTHER historical perspective" on the central concepts and categories of early modern literary history.[14] The sticking point here involves one such concept: that of autonomy, which is what seems to be problematized by the publishing activities of the *philosophes*. However, instead of either ignoring these practices or writing off the *philosophes* themselves for their hypocrisy, a more nuanced study of their engagement with "publication" may show that the lack of clarity actually lies in our understanding of the position that they sought to occupy vis-à-vis monarchs and nobles, and thus of the "autonomy" to which they lay claim, and on which they sought to construct themselves. After all, in the cultural field of the Old Regime, as we have seen, "autonomy" was a complicated, ambiguous notion. It is, above all, one that should not be identified with its modern connotation of a radical severing of the writer's social, political, and economic ties to the powerful and the privileged.

Indeed, as their writings consistently attest, the *philosophes* never imagined themselves outside of their interactions with social and political elites. Their vision of themselves as independent and critical writers was rooted in a reconceptualization of these relations, rather than in a repudiation of them. Specifically, philosophical selfhood lay in an inversion, according to which the writers of the Enlightenment no longer worked for the entertainment of royalty and aristocracy in their idle hours. It was instead a reinvented elite, won over to *les lumières* and wholeheartedly devoted to the triumph of reason and good governance, that mobilized their power and prestige not for their own ends but to serve disinterestedly the *philosophes* and their campaign. The publishing practices of the latter find their logic in this reimagining of the cultural field. They function as mechanisms of the social inversion in and through which the *philosophes* set out to define themselves as the advisors and friends of princes. As such, they are integral rather than antithetical to the "autonomy" on which they alleged their identities as writers to be based. In this respect, far from signaling a rejection of the sociability of the seventeenth-century *homme de lettres*, the autonomy of the *philosophe* can be considered, in a way, as an even stronger claim to the social integration and ascendance which underlay the transformation of the writer in the courts and salons of the Classical era.

Helvétius's *Privilège*

One curious, ostensibly opaque, yet potentially illuminating sequence in the history of Enlightenment publishing occurred in 1757–58, when Claude-Adrien Helvétius did something quite unexpected. Having retired from a lucrative post as a tax farmer and moved to his chateau at Voré, he composed, under the influence of Voltaire and the British sensationalism the latter had made fashionable, a philosophical treatise. Helvétius would certainly have known his work to fall within the purview of a new kind of critical inquiry that sought to challenge metaphysical orthodoxies and moral conventions against considerable resistance. The patterns of publication for such writings were, moreover, long established, with recourse to foreign *libraires* or clandestine printing in France being the two clear options. Nonetheless, Helvétius took the most unusual step of submitting his manuscript to a censor as a first step in applying for an official *privilège* from the Direction de la librairie. It was an astonishing move, matched only by the equally extraordinary outcome: the censor gave the green light, issuing his *approbation* on March 27, which opened the door for the *privilège* to be granted on May 12.

This marks the beginning of what would blow up as a major scandal in the cultural history of the Enlightenment.[15] Once the *privilège* was obtained, Helvétius arranged for the work to be published by Laurent Durand, who was an officer in the Paris Guild and an associate of the *Encyclopédie* publishers. The printing of *De l'Esprit* began in the summer of 1758. Word soon got out, though, that the book might pose difficulties. The print industry was closely monitored by inspectors, one of whom, Charles-Alexandre Salley, having managed to peruse the manuscript in the print shop, warned the current director of the book trade in late June of the "peculiarity [singularité] of the work."[16] Charged with overseeing all the aspects of the commercial publishing industry in France, Guillaume-Chrétien de Lamoignon de Malesherbes was in fact a famous friend of the *philosophes*. He was mostly sympathetic with their agenda and remained a long-time advocate for restraint in censorship. He was, though, also a conscientious administrator concerned for the integrity of his office, and no doubt believed that little was to be gained either by the *philosophes* themselves or more generally by writers and booksellers from any kind of controversy. He therefore ordered the printing of *De l'Esprit* stopped and took the unusual measure of having the work reexamined by a second censor who proposed a series of suppressions involving passages too transparently critical of the Church. Helvétius readily complied with these cuts, and the printing was resumed.[17]

De l'Esprit became available on July 27, provoking an instant outcry beginning in the camp of *dévots* at court, gathered around the queen. Jean-Baptiste-Antoine Suard recalls in his *Mémoires* being in the antechamber of the dauphin soon after the work was published, when the latter burst out of his apartment with a copy of the book, exclaiming that he was going to show the queen what Helvétius, a *maître d'hôtel* in her retinue, was printing.[18] The outrage spread to the Parlement, the Jesuits, and the Sorbonne. Malesherbes at once ordered Durand to suspend sales of the book, and under mounting pressure, he had the *privilège* revoked by an *arrêt du Conseil* hastily signed by the king on August 11.[19] Helvétius was forced to make a series of retractions, as demanded first by the queen, to whom he was personally attached through his family and court post;[20] then by the Jesuits who deemed the first retraction to be insufficiently repentant and far too self-justifying;[21] and finally by the Paris Parlement whose firebrand *avocat général*, Jean-Omer Joly de Fleury, had made a mission of curtailing the proliferation of "encyclopedic" writing. The *philosophe* was dismissed from his position in the queen's household. And while some contemporaries were actually surprised by the leniency with which he was treated—for instance, he was saved from imprisonment or exile by the intervention of powerful court allies such as Madame de Pompadour and the duc de Choiseul—Helvétius was shaken enough by the episode never again to publish; *De l'Homme* appeared posthumously in 1772.

Two significant aspects of the affair can be retained, each allowing it to be interpreted in a markedly divergent way. First and no doubt more familiarly, the episode has come across as an emblematic and powerful illustration of the plight of the *philosophes* in their struggles against reactionary forces in the Old Regime. Indeed, if the event has passed into literary history, it is above all as it has been integrated into a broader story about the increasing repressiveness of the 1750s and early 1760s, when various factions were beginning to perceive and denounce the dangers that an emerging group of writers appeared to pose, articulating in the process the group's cohesiveness as a rising movement, party, or "sect." The attacks were underway in 1752 when the first two volumes of the *Encyclopédie* were suppressed following the scandal unleashed by the heterodox Sorbonne thesis of the abbé de Prades, who was a contributor to the edition. In the years to come, opposition to the "encyclopedists" would take hold in numerous venues including among the *dévots* at court, among the Jesuits at the *Journal de Trévoux*, in Parlement where Jansenist sympathies always ran strong, and in "anti-philosophical" journalism and pamphleteering, where writers such as Fréron and Palissot found a platform. From as early as Duvernet's 1786 biography of Voltaire, the retelling of this mounting hostility has accorded a central place to the mobilization against Helvétius and *De l'Esprit*, proffered as evidence of the darkening climate.[22] Indeed, the affair often stands as a "critical date" or a threshold opening onto a whole sequence of markedly repressive responses.[23]

In this view, the affair plays into a conventional understanding of the *philosophes* that construes their intellectual lives as a function, first and foremost, of censorship. That is, *philosophes* by definition said what was not supposed to be said, and thus for them writing and publication were in essence direct clashes with the authorities enforcing the limits of what was permissible to say. In this sense, their prison stints, arrests, burned books, and years on the run mark their ascendency just as surely as their bestsellers, academic seats, and theatrical triumphs.[24] Belin considers Helvétius a martyr to the encyclopedic cause for having borne the brunt of the government's heavy-handed efforts to muffle dissent.[25] David Smith's account of the *affaire* is subtitled "A Study in Persecution," which underscores a heroic dimension of the philosophical enterprise by portraying Helvétius as a writer who, for the modernity of his ideas, suffers the antagonism of the conservative institutional interests entrenched at court, in the Parlement, and in the Church. Of course, Helvétius was also a retired *fermier général*, sitting on an immense personal fortune that had allowed him to withdraw to his country estate. His family attachments to the queen provided him with the coveted position of *maître d'hôtel ordinaire*, and thus credibility and access at the court. This is not to minimize his "persecution" throughout the summer, fall, and winter of 1758–59. The pursuit was indeed relentless, continuing far beyond several points at which it might have been abandoned, say, at the moment of the revocation of the *privilège* in August or of the initial public retraction soon afterward. And it is clear from his correspondence that, in particular, the possibility of exile was a visceral and terrifying one for Helvétius, especially in light of how much he had to lose. We can track a series of desperate letters from September and October in which Helvétius expresses his fear of the impending censure of the Sorbonne, the continued opposition of the dauphin, and a mounting sense that he was going to have to flee.[26]

However, such a representation of the affair skips over a number of salient elements. Ann Goldgar discusses the historiographical commonplace of depicting the trajectories of Enlightenment writers exclusively in terms of their head-on confrontations with authorities, arguing that it obfuscates the real complexity of their relationships with them, a complexity that was in fact at the core of what it meant to be a *philosophe*.[27] The paradigm of expression versus repression, she contends, is inadequate for understanding what, for instance, the institution of censorship represented at the time, especially if we recall that many eighteenth-century writers sympathetic to the philosophical cause themselves became censors. As the function was integrated into the royal administration, and separated from its traditional base in the Faculty of Theology of the Sorbonne, the post of censor opened to qualified *gens de lettres* for whom it represented an attractive option. After all, being a *censeur* brought legitimacy along with a supplementary income. In turn, philosophically inclined censors approached their charge less with an eye to ensuring Catholic orthodoxy than with a concern for assessing the utility of a work and improving its style and argumentation. They thus conceived of their role in an increasingly positive rather than a purely negative way.[28] Conversely, the *philosophes* cannot be defined exclusively by the illicit and insubordinate nature of their writing. This is not to suggest that articulating critical views in a repressive environment was not an essential aspect of philosophical discourse. Far from it. But as we shall see, there was more to it, for even at its most dissenting this skeptical discourse required a certain conventionally established legitimacy—affiliation with an academy or the "friendship" of a grandee or monarch—to be viable as "philosophical" expression and avoid being discredited as purely insurrectional. Chartier underscores the "paradoxical link, in the eighteenth century, between the new definition of the man of letters as a fearless practitioner of the philosophical spirit and the respect for the most traditional forms of patronage that was still necessary."[29]

In the case of Helvétius, the persecution narrative minimizes a number of significant details, including the author's personal investment in the social hierarchy of the Old Regime as a courtier and former tax farmer, along with his evident desire to hold onto the status that he enjoyed, and which was jeopardized by the publication of his treatise. It also, not unrelatedly, plays down the central fact of the *privilège* itself, even though Helvétius's request for the official protection of his work was integral to how the *affaire* unfolded. In fact, the *privilège* is also what opens up the episode to an alternative and contrary interpretation of it as a quite singular occurrence, one that must be distinguished from, rather than assimilated with, the other instances of repression from the same period. For indeed, among the books regularly listed in historical accounts as the objects of the mid-eighteenth-century crackdown, *De l'Esprit* was the only one published with a *privilège du roi*, with the obvious exception of the *Encyclopédie*. But the *Encyclopédie* is another story. At the outset, the project was the initiative not of the *philosophes* but of a group of publishers who planned a modest—and inoffensive—translation of Ephraim Chamber's two-volume *Cyclopaedia*, which had appeared in England in 1728. It was then to the *libraire* André-François Le Breton and his associates that the *privilège* to the *Dictionnaire raisonné* was initially granted in December 1745, as a standard protection of a business venture, almost two years before Diderot and d'Alembert signed on as co-directors in 1747. The dynamics were, therefore, rather different.[30]

In fact, observers were more struck by the uniqueness of the *De l'Esprit* episode as conveyed by the *privilège* than by its capacity to typify a broader pattern of repression. In August 1758, Charles Collé observes, "the most peculiar aspect of his adventure is that the work was printed with the approval of the king."[31] Joly de Fleury writes in similar terms to Malesherbes in early August: "What is truly peculiar is that on the only copy that was shown to me, I saw the approval of a censor on whose good faith the *privilège* was accorded." He adds, "This circumstance does not, however, prevent me from urging you to stop the sale of the book," implying that the *privilège* was a mitigating factor in the prosecutor's zeal to denounce *De l'Esprit*.[32] The reality, though, was otherwise. Joly de Fleury could of course not dismiss the *privilège* in his correspondence with Malesherbes, given that the permission had been issued by the director's office. There seems little doubt, though, that his campaign against the work was spurred by the official nature of its publication, which, as it seemed to indicate a massive failure in the administration's surveillance system, made a strong response from the Parlement all the more imperative, especially in light of the long-running power struggle between the Crown and the Paris Parlement over who got to exercise control over the print trade, and more broadly over the latter's "traditional" role as a "depository and interpreter of the fundamental laws of the Kingdom."[33] Joly de Fleury advises Malesherbes the next day to "make an example in order to ensure that the censors are more careful."[34] It was, in turn, a view quickly shared among writers sympathetic to the Enlightenment that Helvétius's recourse to privileged publication offered an unnecessarily conspicuous pretext to a more concerted attack on the *philosophes*, while tying the hands of those like Malesherbes who sought to protect them. Grimm writes in considerable anger:

Philosophy will long suffer the effects of the almost universal uproar that this author has unleashed with his work. And for having too freely written a book of bad and false morality, M. Helvétius will have to reproach himself for all the difficulties that those sublime and lofty geniuses who still remain will have to face, and whose destiny was to enlighten their fellow men and to spread the truth across the earth.[35]

This view of the *affaire* as a unique and unusual event jars with the first not only in its focus on the *privilège* but also in its central depiction of Helvétius, who, rather than the defiant *philosophe* taking on the authorities, plays the role of a writer dutifully submitting to their procedures. His letters to Malesherbes call attention to his conscientiousness: "I have thus fulfilled the formalities to which all citizens are subject. You feel that you must deprive me of these same citizens' rights by making me submit to a second censor. I am not complaining, and I will agree to it," he writes on July 4 after Malesherbes raised the prospect of a second round of censoring.[36] The discrepancy presents something of a challenge to scholars; not only are the circumstances of Helvétius's decision to pursue a legal rather than a foreign or clandestine route difficult to ascertain, but the overall picture is one that does not fit so well into the broader account of the Enlightenment as a struggle to speak the truth against a repressive regime. One line of thinking, focusing on the details of how Helvétius negotiated the censorship process, maintains that the writer's decision to request official approval reflected not deference to the authorities but an even bolder and more audacious ruse than the standard dissimulating techniques of the *philosophes*.[37] Specifically, with the connivance of his friend and associate Charles Le Roy, Helvétius found a pliable and distracted censor, one Jean-Paul Tercier, who was a close friend of Le Roy's and enjoying a successful career as a civil servant (*premier commis*) in the Ministry of Foreign Affairs. Tercier was preoccupied with his administrative duties, and moreover, as a specialist in political writings rather than philosophy, he was in any case not qualified to judge the arguments advanced by the treatise. Nonetheless, Helvétius and Le Roy managed to overcome his initial reluctance and convince him to take on the job, even getting Malesherbes to help pressure the nervous official.[38] They then fed him the manuscript at irregular intervals, in small fragments out of the order in which they fit together in the book. Tercier would later claim he saw "neither the thread nor the principles of the work," but, trusting his friend Le Roy, as well as Malesherbes who had personally requested his services, he signed off on the text without apparently getting much of a handle on it.[39]

The account offers a plausible explanation of how the censorship process unfolded, though it reveals a strange discomfort with Helvétius's role and an investment in seeing Le Roy as the real brains behind the subterfuge, the "villain of the piece," perhaps because the plan was in the end so ill-conceived and reckless, with dire consequences for the philosophical movement as a whole.[40] The analysis, however, does have blind spots. For one thing, such machinations were not as unusual as it indicates. Véronique Sarrazin argues that they were in fact the norm; she points to the *affaire* not as an extraordinary manipulation of the system, but as an example of exactly the kinds of negotiations that were regularly taking place between writers, censors, and the Direction de la librairie in the eighteenth century.[41] Moreover, with its emphasis on scheming and deception, the account also raises as many questions as it answers. For instance, how could Tercier have been so fooled? He was, it would appear, an able administrator with no overly strong ties to the philosophical movement. He had also been advised to pay special attention: "I had warned him to be careful of the work," Malesherbes writes to Joly de Fleury.[42] Notwithstanding the fact that he saw it only in fragments, did he really have no notion of what the work contained? Pierre-Michel Hennin, who worked alongside Tercier in the Ministry and wrote a brief report on the episode, contends that he surely had some idea.[43] It has been suggested that the censor did not actually read the manuscript: "I assure you that he neither read nor understood *De l'Esprit*," the comte de Bernis, minister of foreign affairs, wrote to Joly de Fleury in defense of his employee.[44] But Collé disputes this: "it is not for lack of having examined and read it with great attention. He knew the text so well that the next day, when the *affaire* broke out, he immediately wrote a short memoir justifying his actions, which contained in two pages such a precise summary of the work that one cannot doubt that he had it very present in his mind."[45]

Above all, though, it is the central question that continues to burn: why did Helvétius make the request in the first place? For Le Roy's influence still does not explain why the *philosophe*, "who knew very well that his book was not of the type to be approved by a censor," and who had initially expressed reluctance to go that route, was persuaded to change his mind, despite the fact that, as Collé again reports, "All of his friends had begged him on their knees to have it only printed abroad."[46] Two possibilities are implied; either he was convinced that the plan would work or he was so blinded by the enthusiasm of Le Roy that he let himself be dragged along.[47] But both seem far-fetched. We can assume that Helvétius was well aware in the late 1750s, after Voltaire's English exile, the imprisonment of Diderot, and the controversies around the early volumes of the *Encyclopédie*, of the dangers of philosophical publishing.[48] At the same time, we have little reason to believe that someone as concerned as Helvétius with his stature in *le monde*, and who had acquired for himself a good position and a reputation, would have let himself be so managed by Le Roy.

Helvétius's decision remains difficult to grasp, I would argue, so long as we attempt to understand it through the initial assumption that the primary purpose of submitting his work to the censors was to deceive and evade the authorities by taking them on in a bold and conniving way. In truth, though, there is nothing to suggest that Helvétius considered the publication of his treatise as a wholly defiant or rebellious act. And it may, in fact, be more accurate to conclude that his decision to publish through official rather than unofficial channels indicates that he must have felt it to be, in some ways, a viable thing to do. The venture might provoke ire, to be sure. Helvétius must have felt, however, that he had at some level *legitimate access* to the medium of print, even for such a project as *De l'Esprit*. Some evidence substantiates the hypothesis. His personal credibility as a *maître d'hôtel* would certainly have bolstered his expectation that he would not suffer the same fate as less reputable and less protected writers like Diderot.[49] Moreover, Helvétius had by now read the work at court, where "it had been very graciously received," according to Suard.[50] That he would, consequently, approach the *privilège* as a validation of his previously established socially strong position and of his embeddedness in *le monde*, rather than as an ingenious and devious scheme, is reflected in La Harpe's view of the legal publication of the treatise "with so much confidence," as the upshot of Helvétius's "vain and unfortunate aspiration for celebrity"—an aspiration that should be understood in social rather than purely intellectual terms, as a desire for elevated status and renown. Indeed, Helvétius was known for his status seeking and willingness to put his writing skills at the disposal of his self-promotional efforts. La Harpe recalls an anecdote according to which Helvétius developed scholarly interests when he saw Maupertuis at the peak of his popularity, surrounded by a "circle of women." He writes: "Helvétius was struck by the glamor and the pleasures that a scholar, a man of letters might owe to his celebrity; he resolved at that moment to acquire them for himself."[51]

This is not to suggest the directly contrary view that Helvétius, in asking for official approbation, betrayed the intellectual mission of the Enlightenment by preferring to mollify the authorities he was supposed to be defying. For it is clear that he was intent on fulfilling the role of the *philosophe*, and sought to articulate and disseminate a critical perspective that he knew would appall the agents of tradition. When Malesherbes brings up the need for a reading by a second censor, Helvétius replies in a sardonic Voltairean manner, "I hope that you have not put me in the clutches of a ridiculous theologian, since there would be no way to print anything at all but children's primers."[52] Rather, the point is to illustrate the degree to which the official publication of *De l'Esprit*, in a basic way, eludes the old oppositions—between expression and censorship, resistance and submission—that have been so critical to interpreting the intellectual practices of the Enlightenment. If the *privilège* request at the center of the story has been difficult to interpret, it is because the gesture fails to situate the writer in a clear fashion, placing him on both sides of the intellectual divide simultaneously as he spoke out against established beliefs *and* acquiesced to the authorities invested with the task of defending those beliefs. Moreover, it suggests, in its recklessness, that he did so without much of a sense that there was a fundamental conflict between the two moves. Or more exactly, he was cognizant of a potential conflict, which he took pains to avoid. But he believed that the *privilège* and the philosophical project of *De l'Esprit* could coexist. Not completely peacefully, of course. He surely anticipated resistance. But he did not imagine that the tension would so dramatically push matters to a breaking point, and thus be so catastrophic for his reputation as both an *homme du monde* and an *homme de lettres*. In this respect, the central quandary that the incident presents to us in trying to understand it better is less how he thought that he could have gotten away with such an extraordinary ruse, than how he thought that it might have been reasonable and legitimate to apply for official protection for his emphatically philosophical work.

The incident therefore raises new kinds of questions, the answers to which will be essential to casting the configuration of the *philosophe* in a new light, particularly inasmuch as the *philosophe* always incarnates an ambiguous position as both prototypical intellectual outsider *and* consummate Old Regime establishment insider. We can and should ask how the *philosophes* articulated criticism in the context of surveillance and repression. But we must also investigate the factors that led them to feel authorized to do so, and the ways they reconciled their will to critique with their desire for recognition—what they called *considération*—within a traditional order whose hierarchical nature they ultimately did not question. In fact, what the *privilège* entails is a shifted framework that is no longer defined solely by the problem of freedom versus censorship, but also takes into account the evolving definitions of cultural, social, and intellectual legitimacy that underlay the emergence of the *philosophe*. For *philosophes* did not become *philosophes* merely by attacking old ideas and timeworn institutions. They also made claims to credibility and recognition that were viable and accepted, leading to academic seats and prestigious positions at court, as well as social integration within *le monde* and the "friendship" of monarchs and princes, distinctions that they received not in spite of their critical inclinations but because of them. To this unlikely fusion of insiderhood and outsiderhood the publishing practices of the *philosophes* were crucial. It is largely through them, I argue, with recourse to *honnête*, self-effacing gestures inherited from an earlier age, that the writers who would successfully assume the identity of *philosophe* rendered palatable and legitimate their critique, thereby allowing them to maintain the elevated social status and distinguished positions that were essential to being and remaining a *philosophe*. Yet it is also through their publishing activities, in projecting themselves as the authors of "serious" books, which fearlessly propagated penetrating critical insights, that the same writers forged an intellectual credibility that was rooted in their courage, in their independent voices, and in their steadfast commitment to truth and reason, an authority that was pointedly articulated against the too eager to please literary practices of seventeenth-century court culture.

What Is a *Philosophe*?
Autonomy and the Intellectual in *Honnête* Society

We have, of course, studied the *privilège* in Chapter 1. A commercial cession granting one or more individuals—either publishers or writers—provisional exclusive rights to print and sell a particular work for a specified time in a specified place, it has in literary and cultural history most often been associated with questions of "copyright" and "literary property." And it does indeed seem to have been the mechanism around which the movement for intellectual property rights coalesced in eighteenth-century France, when booksellers, who since the seventeenth century had been receiving longer and longer *privilèges* to works along with the ability to renew those *privilèges* on expiration, argued for the logical extension of these practices, namely the recognition of their permanent rights to the works on the basis that they had "bought" them directly from writers, and that, therefore, they owned them just as one owns anything that one buys with one's private resources.[53] As Roger Chartier, Carla Hesse, and others have noted, however, the connection between the *privilège* and intellectual property was an accidental and arbitrary one. In principle, the official exemption had nothing to do with protecting property rights. It was grounded in the belief that there was no such thing, and that only the grace of the king could legitimize such a private, individualized claim to an idea and to its articulation in a piece of writing.[54] As late as 1777, when the book trade regulations were reformed in six articles promulgated by the Royal Council, the official position of the French state remained that the *privilège* ensured no right of ownership whatsoever. Article five reads: "His Majesty has acknowledged that the privilege is a grace founded in justice."[55]

Moreover, as we have seen, recent studies by Nicolas Schapira contend that the *privilège* has historically played a quite different role from that of guarantor of ownership rights, certainly in the lives of writers if not of *libraires*. Rather than affirming a natural, proprietary link between a writer and a work, the *privilège* was instead appropriated by *gens de lettres* as a particularly effective mechanism for mediating their images before an elite, refined public of aristocrats and *honnêtes gens* who were especially sensitive to the decorum of authorial gestures. The *privilège* offered a way to address what I argued in Chapter 1 emerged as one of the defining tensions of Old Regime literary life, arising from the parallel development of a social ethic of *honnêteté* as a prevailing value system against which literary activities, works, and identities were judged, on one hand; and of writing and publishing as increasingly valorized media for advancing claims to social distinction, on the other. The tension ensues from the fact that while *honnêteté* calls for self-effacement and deference before the group, writing and publishing tended to convey the opposite: arrogance, vanity, ambition, and separation from the community. The *privilège* allowed writers to negotiate this tension by opening up a new medium in which they might, in the very act of publishing, project an image of themselves as socially integrated and enjoying the king's favor, since it was issued in the monarch's name. It enabled individuals to counteract one of the great dangers of publishing, to be defined by the activity as a "professional," or worse, as an "Author." Ironically, given its ultimate connection with debates about literary property rights and "professionalization," the *privilège* was one of a series of paratextual devices that helped fix the primary identity of seventeenth-century writers as amateurs, *gens du monde* who engaged in writing and publishing not in order to earn a living, but to pass the time nobly, entertaining an elite group of friends.

Such a reading of the *privilège* takes us deep into the culture of the Classical era, to be sure. Nonetheless, the motif of a conflict between authorship and sociability, of a possible split between an intellectual self constructed in study, writing, and publishing and a social self constituted through polite interactions at court or in salons, continued to haunt literary life in the eighteenth century. The famous *Encyclopédie* definitions of "gens de lettres" and "philosophes" make clear that the "socialization" of letters was no less a decisive aspect of their viability and progress—and the lack thereof no less a peril—for Enlightenment-era observers than it had been in the previous century. Both entries pointedly set out to justify those engaged in intellectual pursuits against older preconceptions of the poet or philosopher as a withdrawn, solitary and uncouth figure. In contrast, they highlight the polished manners and "sociability" of the "modern" man of letters as a determinate characteristic, to the point where the importance of such attributes is fully equal to that of any purely intellectual category, such as learning: "It is one of the great advantages of our century . . .: the spirit of the age has made them for the most part as apt for high society as for their studies; and it is in this respect that they are far superior to those of previous centuries," writes Voltaire in his entry on "Gens de lettres."[56] The article dedicated to the "Philosophe" perhaps even more firmly grounds enlightened intellectual activity as much in a commitment to society and social participation as in the search for truth and knowledge through study.

> Our *philosophe* does not believe himself to be an exile in this world; . . . he wants to find enjoyment with others: and to find it, he must provide it: thus he tries to be pleasant towards those with whom, by chance or his own choice, he lives; and at the same time, he finds what pleases him: he is an *honnête homme* who wants to please and to be useful. . . . Feelings of probity enter into the mechanical constitution of the philosophe as much as the light of intellect. . . .[T]he notion of a *malhonnête homme* is as opposed to the idea of the *philosophes*, as is stupidity.[57]

It should be emphasized, in turn, that the references to *honnêteté* and *plaisir*, along with Voltaire's invocation of *le monde*, drawing as they do on the vocabulary of a seventeenth-century aristocratic ethos, leave hardly any doubt that the sociability in question is that of elites, modeled on the refined, leisured, and idealized exchanges of high society.[58]

More evidence of the degree to which elite socialization remained perhaps the most pressing matter for those probing the condition of writers in the eighteenth century can be found in two significant reports from the time: Charles Duclos's chapter on *gens de lettres* in his *Considérations sur les moeurs de ce siècle*, published in 1751, and Jean le Rond d'Alembert's "Essai sur les gens de lettres et les grands," which first appeared two years later. Both situate the problem in light of the gradual *mondaine* assimilation of writers, presented as a critical factor for understanding the specific nature of modern literary life. Duclos states: "In the past, men of letters, devoted to study and separated from society and the world [séparés du monde], when working for their contemporaries, thought only of posterity. Their habits [moeurs], full of candor and harshness, had no resonance with those of society." But *gens du monde* would acquire a taste for letters, and seek out the company of those who cultivated them. *Gens de lettres* for their part "were drawn into society," resulting in an interpenetration of the previously disconnected worlds. In line with seventeenth-century commentators, Duclos considers the evolution to be a decisive and beneficial exchange around which a new and superior culture took shape: aristocracy grew less coarse and more cerebral and linguistic; at the same time, "literary" practices became more polished and respectable, both in their elegant style and through their association with the privileged and the powerful. He concludes:

Everyone has gained by this contact. *Gens du monde* have cultivated their taste and discovered new pleasures. *Gens de lettres* have equally benefited. They have found protection and consideration; they have perfected their taste, polished their intellect, softened their habits, and acquired knowledge of numerous things about which they would not have learned from books.[59]

In his "Essai," d'Alembert begins with the same historical dynamic: "nobles begin to seek not only works. They also endeavor, at least out of vanity, to offer to talented individuals marks of their esteem, often more self-interested than sincere." Meanwhile, "ripped from their solitude, *gens de lettres* were sucked into the whirlwind of society."[60] His language makes clear, of course, that he does not share Duclos's celebratory agenda. He may recognize the gains that *gens de lettres* drew from their association with elites—"The first benefit that *gens de lettres* discover when they venture into society is that their merit is, if not better known then at least more celebrated"—but a qualified, suspicious tenor pervades the "Essai," suggesting that there is another side to the story of the integration of writers into noble society: "It is an experience . . . which can be useful so long as one does not stay there for too long," advises d'Alembert.[61] In this respect, he paints a more familiar image of the *philosophe* as a voice of skepticism toward a nobility obsessed with its own pleasures and glory, who chafes at his subordination before this group. John Pappas highlights d'Alembert's revolt against his dependency, playing up the philosopher's disgust at the *éloges* Voltaire continued to shower on nobles and monarchs despite his independent wealth: "It is indeed the humiliation that the man of letters must endure in his relationship with nobility that deeply offends d'Alembert."[62] In a similar reframing, Darnton, normally so focused on unearthing ways in which the establishment *philosophes* ingratiated themselves with elites, nonetheless sees in the "Essai" a "declaration of independence for writers and writing."[63]

Thus, like Duclos, d'Alembert presents the integration of writers into elite society as the key factor in his survey of literary life in the mid-eighteenth-century. It was, however, not in order to valorize the opportunities that this evolution opened up in an emerging "climate of *honnêteté*" for writers to become respected, rich, and famous.[64] Instead, he sought to characterize the threat that the development posed to what he correlatively defined, in the very process of spelling out the danger, as the purpose and "integrity" of intellectual practices. Dinah Ribard describes d'Alembert's hostility to "la mondanisation des lettres," which, she argues, represents a dissolution of the coherence and forcefulness of intellectual activities as they are appropriated by socializing elites. In becoming no more than instances of leisured interaction, these activities lose their edge, power, and critical vigor.[65] Accordingly, one of the central goals of the "Essai," which no doubt goes far in making it identifiable as a "declaration of independence," is to distinguish clearly what can legitimately be called "philosophie" from other types of discourse, which, though potentially also serving as vehicles of *esprit philosophique*, are nonetheless driven by a foreign logic, that of high society interactivity: say, *jeux d'esprit* or salon conversation.

In the effort, d'Alembert emphasizes various characteristics of *la philosophie* that allow it to be sharply differentiated from the languages of elite intellectualized pastime. For one, abandoning what is undoubtedly the fundamental tenet of aristocratic culture as it had been theorized since the seventeenth century, namely the principle of *plaire*, he posits instead the precept of what can be called "not offending, if possible": "Whatever care that I have taken with this writing to speak the truth in the least offensive way possible, without weakening it, I doubt that it will have the good fortune to please everyone."[66] The difference is critical, for essential to *plaire* is the imperative to calibrate one's expression and behavior to one's audience; and to be what Faret called, in his 1630 treatise on *honnêteté*, supple.[67] *Plaire* implies, in other words, pleasing everyone and knowing how to please varied audiences. By contrast, d'Alembert underscores his doubt that his text will please all. In so doing, he downplays social agility in favor of a consistency figured as the writer's steadfast commitment to "tell the truth" no matter what. It is also to impose, following La Bruyère, a hierarchy to the traditional duo of *plaire et instruire* according to which pleasure is now subordinated to utility: "the first duty of Philosophy is to instruct, and it is only by instructing that it can please," d'Alembert writes in the *avertissement* to the second edition of his *Mélanges* from 1758.[68]

As an articulation of this dedication to utility, *la philosophie* must then orient itself toward a larger public, one whose bearing and importance is almost always measured against the smallness and exclusivity of the *mondaine* coterie, now construed as the symbol of self-interested, frivolous myopia. "One should not limit oneself when writing to a small circle of friends or of obliging flatterers; one must either offer one's work for the world to see [se produire au grand jour], or at least work as if one ought to present oneself in such a manner. Woe to any work whose author seeks only to pass the time, or to be praised by five or six individuals who, in any case, were sure to approve the work before they had read it," d'Alembert cautions.[69] Indeed, Helvétius calls for precisely the same turn in *De l'Esprit*—"whoever wants to know exactly what he is worth can only learn this from the Public, and must, as a consequence, expose himself to its judgment"—likewise defining the new audience in opposition to "private societies [sociétés particulières]." Ostensibly, the latter refer to communities defined by a particular rather than a universal interest.

The distinction, however, is more pointed inasmuch as the particular interest in Helvétius's account is invariably identified with the desires of the idle upper crust: "in order to present to private societies the ideas which are the most agreeable to them, one must throw oneself into the whirlwind of high society [le tourbillon du monde]."[70] The rarefied spaces of aristocratic sociability were at one time viewed as the most propitious spheres for the discovery of universal truths about human nature and society— La Rochefoucauld's *Maximes* posit a seamless, and from our perspective paradoxical passage from the small coterie to general insight: the stylized, self-consciously exclusive behavioral patterns of the smallest segment of French society offers an unproblematic template for an investigation into "l'homme." The *philosophes* were, of course, operating in similarly restricted, privileged contexts. The fact remains, though, that central to their claims to philosophical authority was a direct repudiation of these rarefied milieus, which now come to symbolize an intellectual parochialism against which the expansiveness of the *philosophes*' thinking becomes most apparent: "To what ends do our frivolous conversations serve a philosopher if not to shrink his intellect and to deprive him of excellent ideas, which he might otherwise acquire through meditation and reading," asks d'Alembert.[71]

These qualities—seriousness, dedication to truth, and universality of perspective—underlie a new image of the intellectual elaborated in opposition to that of the *bel esprit* who, seeking integration into the court or salon, aims to please a gathering of elites. The *philosophe*, by contrast, will do what he can to make the truths that he tells as palatable as possible to such a group; but he will not distort or obfuscate them in the cause of amusing its members or saving them from discomfort or boredom. *Philosophes* are sociable inasmuch as they are sensitive to aristocratic decorum and civility. They are loath not to please. Yet sociability is not an end in and of itself. At best, it is a means to an end; but the intellectual objective is always exterior to the cultural logic of *mondanité*, which remains focused on its own gratifications, whereas the *philosophes* eye a higher prize. "It was not in the Hôtel de Rambouillet that Descartes discovered the application of algebra to geometry," asserts d'Alembert.[72] As a result, in the pursuit of their goal, *philosophes* will, if need be, abandon their pleasing demeanor; they are not beholden to it. "The great man ... is ... only slightly [foiblement] motivated by the desire to please them [*gens du monde*]," observes Helvétius.[73] In a self-portrait from 1760, d'Alembert sums up this provisional sociability, describing himself both as polite and as someone who does not care whether others see him as such. He pleases in that he is not tiring or "pédantesque," but he does not seek to please, and in the end, does not care whether he does or does not do so. This, d'Alembert notes, makes him an imperfect *habitué* of the salon because, in the name of honesty, he can certainly be uncivil and unpleasant.[74] In fact, the *philosophe* always calls attention to a *potential* to be rude. The ostentatious refusal to guarantee his politeness signifies his dedication because if he does engage *le monde*, it is only out of his natural generosity and respect. It is not because his credibility depends on finding approval there. Philosophical publication, I would argue, finds its logic as an articulation of this potential, whose valence lies in its dual significance as both a credible threat—the *philosophe* really was believed to have it in him to buck social decorum in the name of truth—and an essentially unrealizable one—the *philosophe* could not actually be rude without abandoning any plausible claim to the identity of *philosophe*.

Writing, Books, and the Authority of the *Philosophe*

For the rise of the public in opposition to the spaces of aristocratic sociability as a legitimizing institution calls to light another key factor. That is, while the media defining the "court" or the "salon" are, above all, instances of personal interaction, with conversation being the archetypal form, those defining the "public" are necessarily writing and its circulation in print. The gesture of "exposing oneself to its judgment," evoked by Helvétius, essentially refers to the publication of the works of the individual who seeks recognition as a *philosophe*. There are not a lot of other ways to understand "s'exposer." In fact, all through their accounts, both d'Alembert and Helvétius closely tie the trajectory of the *philosophe* to the circulation and reception of his *ouvrages*.[75] So much so that we might venture to consider the concept of the "Public" as ultimately a means for referencing less a new audience, than a new medium, and a shift away from an intellectual self-presentation through personal contacts and social exchanges toward one exclusively rooted in study and the writing of works communicating the insight derived from study. All the more when we consider that, while in the rhetoric of the *philosophes*, "public" appears to reference a markedly different collection of individuals with respect to *le monde*, the truth is that the groups actually consisted of more or less the same set of social and political elites, with the difference lying not in the constituency of the readership/audience but in how that constituency was accessed, whether through the immediacy and transience of face-to-face contact or the permanence of printed writing.[76]

In any case, writing and publishing were integrated as essential components of the philosophical model of intellectual selfhood, and in a way that was quite different from the seventeenth century. I argued in Chapter 1 that, while the authorial trajectory of the Classical-era writer was fundamentally determined by the increasing importance of writing as a social practice, it was, at the same time, no less centrally defined by the need to deny the importance of writing as a social act defining one's identity in gestures of self-effacement and modesty. By contrast, the *philosophe* openly appropriated writing as a tangible sign of the fact that, while he circulated in *le monde*, he was not of it. For by writing books he indicated that he was motivated by distinct priorities and objectives, not that of pleasing, which makes it tempting to posit a reversal in values vis-à-vis earlier times. Against the seventeenth-century effort to collapse one's intellectual identity as defined by writing into a larger social identity constructed through polite interaction, we now witness the ascendancy of the Author over the *homme* or *femme du monde*. This by no means constitutes an outright rejection of *mondanité*. It does seem, though, to present an inversion of the older justificatory relationship between writing and socializing, for unlike the *beaux-esprit* of the Classical age, the *philosophes* did not rationalize their activities as writers in the light of their sociability by offering their poems, plays, and stories as efforts to entertain friends or patrons. They ceased to vindicate their productions as the effects of leisure. Rather, it was their participation in *le monde* that now demanded explanation; and this, they justified in terms of an underlying philosophical mission, which was accomplished through the publication of their texts. D'Alembert suggests variously that *gens de lettres* who ventured into noble society did so not to be "civilized" but to find a less jealous judgment than that offered by peers—"they are judged by another tribunal than that of their rivals"—or to observe in order better to depict human nature in a "work of imagination"; or alternatively to instruct those elites genuinely interested in the progress of *lumières*.[77] The reasons may be diverse, but constant is the preeminence of an intellectual project fuelled by talent and dedication, and realized in important books. It is, moreover, a project that the cultivation of elites served rather than the other way around. The *philosophes* enlisted nobles and monarchs to empower their writings; they did not write in order to befriend monarchs and nobles.

The inversion was, of course, implicit in the evocation of the latent rudeness of the writer, who could abandon a civil demeanor yet remain a *philosophe*. He could not, however, abandon the intellectual integrity to which his "oeuvre" was a monument. It also finds its representation in images of the failure of the writer in *le monde*. Such images recur as a striking motif in d'Alembert's "Essai," where the notion of the writer's inability to please an elite group is central to the legitimacy of his philosophical project, insofar as to succeed inevitably means to cater to the frivolous whims of aristocrats seeking not truth but a reflection of their own prestige. He highlights the bad judgment of nobility, warped by pride and egoism: "is it surprising that they cannot perceive any real difference between works or between men? The man of letters who sees them and flatters them the most, however mediocre he might be, is for them the best of his kind." Failure, in this view, measures the universal bearing of the writer's activities, which refuse to be defined by the narrow interests of a tiny, self-absorbed audience. In addition, it underscores their long-term significance, affirmed in contrast with the ephemeral nature of "works of society [ouvrages de société]." Failure comes as a consequence to manifest the writer's greatness; in the "crowd [foule] of small societies and tribunals," it is "great geniuses [who] are ripped apart by those unworthy of reading them."[78]

A similar picture emerges in Helvétius. The seriousness that transforms a writer into a *philosophe* is discernable not in triumph but defeat: "The *philosophe* who lives with petty nobles will be a ridiculous imbecile in their society."[79] To illustrate the point, he refers to none other than Pierre Corneille, whose genius can be gauged not only by the sublime majesty of his tragedies, but also by his gracelessness in refined society. For if he was "insipid . . . at high society dinners [dans nos soupers de bonne compagnie]," it was due to his detachment from "the small details that make up the everyday interaction of *gens du monde*," and due to his orientation toward larger and more profound truths, occupied as he was with "reflections that, pertinent to man in general, belong to and please humanity."[80] We have come a long way from the days of the *Querelle*, when Corneille was assailed for the poor figure that he cut at court and, significantly, for his willingness to appeal to the "Public" through print.

The experience of failure will, in turn, be central to that of autonomy, at least once the *philosophe* grasps the implications of his bad reception. Evoking the sight of "great geniuses" scorned by "small societies," d'Alembert writes, "such a spectacle, seen through the eyes of a clear and calm reason, will be more than sufficient to console the true philosopher for the deprivation of much frivolous praise." Surging up inside the individual, the sense of tranquility elevates the writer above the present circumstance, and fuels his feeling of untouchability: "Similar to a formidable sovereign, inaccessible to attacks because of his superiority, he will see beneath him and far away, barbaric hacks tearing each other apart after having tried vainly to cause damage on the frontiers of his State."[81] The language of elevation, built on an exorbitant political claim—the writer was no longer the servant of a sovereign but was himself a king—could not contrast more starkly with the participatory, self-submerging immersion paradigm of the previous century.[82] The resulting autonomy will, of course, be consistently upheld by the *philosophe* as a defining attribute of his identity: "his love for independence goes as far as fanaticism," d'Alembert declares in his self-portrait, "to the point where he often refuses things that would be agreeable to him when he imagines that they could be the source of some type of constraint, which is what made him say to one of his friends, justifiably, that he was a *slave to liberty*."[83]

However, the hypothesis of a reversal in values, according to which the authorial self dominates the social self in the *philosophes'* assertions of their credibility, encounters a problem, which is that it is, at its core, a pure fantasy, belied not by a Duclos-style pro-*monde* discourse with which it seems, at first glance, to be in contradiction. In fact, Antoine Lilti shows that the philosophical apology of *mondanité* is rooted in the same defense of utility and autonomy underlying d'Alembert's hostility to elite society. The difference between d'Alembert's rejection of "petty societies" and, say, the abbé Morellet's embrace of salon conversation consists not in a fundamental disagreement over the place of the *philosophe* in noble milieus, but in the degree to which each conceives that the social practices of elites have or have not adapted to incorporate and facilitate purely philosophical objectives. Morellet defends conversation not as a source of pleasure but as a medium of critical inquiry; "the specificity of this appropriation," argues Lilti, "is to emphasize the utility of conversation, thus breaking with the aristocratic ideal of a ludic and disinterested practice."[84] D'Alembert, by contrast, invokes an older elite society, which continued to be characterized by leisure activities and noble *amour propre*. The distinction is important, to be sure. But it does not problematize a shared vision of the *philosophe* whose authority pertains in his dedication to "serious" issues and general truths that transcend the frivolity and insular expectations of a traditional aristocratic audience.[85]

The fantasy is instead belied by a reality in which no one who claimed to be able to exist outside of the social framework of *le monde* and retain the intellectual credibility that made the *philosophe* recognizable as such ever actually did so. The potential for social outsiderhood, which writers such as d'Alembert and Helvétius were firmly determined to assert for themselves, was never realized. "The *salon* held the monopoly of first publication," Habermas has observed, "a new work, even a musical one, had to legitimate itself first in this forum." As would Daniel Gordon and Dena Goodman in his wake, he emphasizes the particular eighteenth-century actualization of the salon as a space for "free" and serious intellectual inquiry: "In the *salon*, the mind was no longer in the service of a patron."[86] However, the monopoly of the salon points equally to the inescapability of its polite, elite, hierarchical social norms. And inasmuch as this domestic venue became the "home" of philosophical inquiry, *philosophes* never were rude, not in such a way as to ensure their exclusion from the social fixture. They were not disrespectful toward those who, as elite hosts or guests, imposed on the space their status and preeminence.[87] Nor did the *philosophes* ever "fail" in the manner they imagined in their writings. None was identified as an imbecile or as insipid; and certainly, none suffered the vicious assaults on his civility that Corneille had endured a century earlier.

Rather, those who could viably claim the distinction of being a *philosophe* inevitably conformed, more or less, to the mold of *gens du monde*. They were by all accounts witty, polite, and pleasant. Helvétius was, according to La Harpe, "a man of gentle manners [moeurs douces], pleasant society [société aimable], and kindly character [caractère bien faisant].... [A]n *honnête homme*, a man of wit and talent."[88] D'Alembert, at first glance, seems not to fit the pattern so well. The marquise du Deffand's portrait of him shows that, with no parents overseeing his upbringing and just a "common education," not to mention with his formation in the world of science and mathematics rather than in that of belles-lettres, he could seem brusque and off-putting: "he was not equally well judged by everyone."[89] Nonetheless, in a letter to Voltaire, she portrays him as "the most *honnête* man in the world, who has a good heart, an excellent mind, much probity and good taste in many things."[90] Ronald Grimsley's account of d'Alembert's early years suggests a more straightforward integration into high society via the salons of Geoffrin and Deffand, and the Sceaux court of the duchesse du Maine, with whom the young *philosophe* developed a close relationship.[91] Marmontel recalls that d'Alembert stood out in the social circle around Geoffrin as "the most cheerful man, the most animated and the most amusing in his cheerfulness." Against Deffand's portrait of d'Alembert refusing to abandon the gruff mien of a scientist, Marmontel notes that, "with the vibrant and pleasant demeanor that this man, who was so bright, deep and solid, used to adopt, he made us forget the philosopher and scholar in him and instead appreciate only the likable man [l'homme aimable]."[92]

This is not to deny the critical or adversarial nature of *philosophes*, or to suggest that they were, in reality, ingratiating and sycophantic in their social exchanges with elites. They were not, and we must take seriously the "emancipation" that the *philosophes* enjoyed in the salon, and the resulting forcefulness of their intellectual inquiries.[93] It is, however, to underscore that their contrarian stances, critical drives, as well as the "freedom" of which these were the product, were not, in spite of their threats, to become manifest in any kind of disagreeable or impolite demeanor. Whether or not d'Alembert shocked *mondains* with his frankness and simplicity when he first appeared in their midst, the truth is that once he was established as a *philosophe*, those traits were instantaneously sublimated and transformed into affable ones that spoke precisely to his *mondaine* integration. For, ultimately, being esteemed in elite society remained an imperative for the writer aspiring to be a *philosophe*, not only in his person, moreover, but in his writing, too. La Harpe contrasts Helvétius's *De l'Esprit* with La Mettrie's *Homme machine*, observing that the works offered similar ideas but whereas the latter seemed "coarse [grossier]," the former contained "art," "restraint," and "charm [agrément]."[94] In this sense, not only was *mondain* pleasure critical for the success of a book, but we can also see that such pleasure was not antithetical to philosophical critique. Far from it. The salon culture in which the philosophical movement took root evolved to demand an increasingly probing and irreverent discourse. But it did so as part of its investment in elite sociability, not as a departure from it. The culture of *mondanité* was thus committed to the idea of the *philosophe* as a congenial figure, who with *moeurs douces* would contribute to rather than detract from the enjoyment of elegant interaction.[95] Writers incorporating an adversarial or antisocial aspect into their behavior and works were by contrast never acknowledged as *philosophes*. And correlatively, those *gens de lettres* unwilling or unable to maintain the distinction of being a *philosophe* paid for it with fierce attacks on their civility, which characterized them as unpolished eccentrics or unruly rogues. We need only think of the example that Rousseau furnishes us in this respect.

The authorial self/social self hierarchy was, it would then seem, not quite as inverted by the *philosophes* as they let on in their texts. Does this mean that they were hypocrites? Darnton asserts as much in juxtaposing d'Alembert's 1753 "declaration of independence" against the arc of his career, in the course of which he basked in his relations with high society and embraced the hierarchical bodies that institutionalized those connections, including the salon and the Académie française: "He defended the academy's mixture of *grands seigneurs* and writers. And he emphasized the role of courtiers, as experts in the realm of taste and language, in a very elitist Enlightenment."[96] To be sure, the problem posed by the perception of a sharp disjuncture between what the *philosophes* said about themselves in their published writings and how they actually behaved in society was duly noted by eighteenth-century observers, who marked the inconsistencies, for instance, between the deferential posturing of Helvétius during the debacle of *De l'Esprit* and the strident voice that he had adopted in the treatise: "The more his book is bold and strong," wrote Collé, "and the more he seems to project an independence and an unbridled love for what he believes to be the truth, the more his weak and feeble behavior showers him in ridicule, and presents a cruel contrast between his sentiments and his actions."[97] Similarly, if La Harpe described Helvétius's "gentle manners" and "pleasant company," it was not to celebrate the latter's conviviality, but to advance his *Réfutation* of the notorious book by emphasizing the contradiction between the tone of the text and Helvétius's politeness: "he seemed to present a sharp contrast with his book . . . which struck everybody."[98]

The suggestion of hypocrisy, in other words, picks up on hints from the period. Yet to focus on hypocrisy is to misconstrue the central dynamic of philosophical identity. As it unravels in the course of Helvétius's affair, the identity is undermined not by the discrepancy between social and intellectual selves per se, but by the visibility of the incongruity. In fact, philosophical identity was from the beginning constructed in and through such a contradiction, when *gens de lettres*, formed in the patterns of the elite socialized intellectual practice inherited from the Classical age, made strong claims to being something other than old-style court poets. The writer became a *philosophe* insofar as he was able to inhabit the contradiction in such a way as to render it imperceptible. The claim to being something new was, if not wholly believed on its own merits, then at least accepted by an audience that was in a position to legitimize such a claim and the intellectual identity based on it, which means, of course, an elite, symbolically powerful audience. This audience can, in a sense, be said to have indulged the *philosophes* in their self-stylizations as independent and critical, knowing that their fashionings were true only to the degree that their *mondains* and grandee readers who constituted this public deemed them so.

At the same time, by continuing to orient themselves toward a readership of *les grands*, the *philosophes* allowed those powerbrokers who chose to align themselves with the movement—the Malesherbes, the Pompadours, the Richelieus, the Luxembourgs, along with the Fredericks and the Catherines—to bask in the prestige, celebrated by the *philosophes* themselves, of their membership in a new kind of political and social elite, which was valorized by its progressiveness, reason, disinterest, and its embrace of letters not out of arrogant pride or self-glorification but for the sake of intellectual, social, and political advancement.[99] It is significant, even as he casts general doubt on the ability of nobles and princes to judge and support letters, that d'Alembert never fails to incorporate exceptions to the rule into his text, often in asides or footnotes, tendering glimpses of an enlightened elite in which those aristocratic readers sympathetic with his project might be able to discern facets of their own reflections. They might perceive themselves explicitly: Frederick for one is praised at great length, not for being noble but for being unlike the typical noble: "Above all prejudice, this monarch only distinguishes men by their merit. Light and truth, so necessary and so hidden from the majority of princes, yet which he loves and knows because he is worthy of them, are fruits of the noble and wise liberty which he grants to letters."[100] Or the connection might be forged in a more abstract way. The 1759 *avertissement* to the "Essai" highlights a device by which d'Alembert calls on aristocrats to oppose or support his discourse as they either react angrily to its caricature of the generic ignorant nobleman or identify sympathetically with the enlightened outlier. The preface then valorizes the latter choice as the effect of personal quality; identifying with the exceptional aristocrat is proof of one's "merit": "Has he attacked or even named anyone? This is what matters to individuals. Has he not expressly acknowledged that there were exceptions to the general picture that he has painted? And one is thus in one's right to feel oneself exempted from this picture if one deserves to be."[101] Read in this manner, the text effected a complex exchange, which far from undermining the relationship between writer and elite reader, intensified it, enhancing in the process the defining quality of each: the aristocrat's "disinterested" support lent credence and force to the writer's claim to independence and seriousness. Correlatively, the lofty status and authority of the noble was reaffirmed in and through the image of his or her generosity and larger-than-life focus on the big picture at the expense of any personal, self-serving gain.

Moreover, reflecting the discrepancy between a reality in which *philosophes* were beholden to processes of social legitimization in the hierarchical framework of *le monde* and an idealization of themselves in writings that depicted them as existing outside of those processes, the contradiction, in turn, calls attention to the fact that philosophical selfhood was predicated, above all, on a credible claim. Accordingly, d'Alembert's analysis of the condition of writers probes much less the underlying structures of literary life than the characteristic rhetorical moves and conventions that regulate social interactions between *gens de lettres* and those in a position to consecrate them. His "declaration of independence" does not rest on an argument for change in the objective organization of the literary world. He does not call for an end to patronage in favor of an alternative system nor mobilize, say, for literary property legislation. The "declaration" is no more than the word would suggest; it is a strong avowal of belief in the autonomy of writers vis-à-vis the nobility, which is then to play out in the elite social arena. Writers are called upon to assert their freedom simply by behaving in accordance with their belief in it, and conducting themselves in their interactions with aristocracy as if they, as the authors of books serving the greater good and the cause of truth, are entitled to their respect. As an example, d'Alembert urges his colleagues to withhold their tributes to nobles in order to offer them only to those protectors deemed worthy. In this way, by force of his rhetoric, not to mention by deploying a shrewd publication strategy, the *philosophe* upends the hierarchical structure of the relationship, seizing the power to confer distinction on nobility rather than submitting to the reverse.[102]

But the *philosophe*'s claim to authority, legitimacy, and autonomy based on his activities as a writer and publisher of critical texts had no credibility on its own. Its credibility lay instead in a prior legitimacy established not by publication but in a more standard Old Regime way: by the writer's integration into high society through personal connections and a mastery of the behavioral and linguistic codes of *le monde*, even as these codes evolved to embrace a more and more critical and "serious" tone. The prior integration enabled *gens de lettres* to acquire key markers of cultural distinction—pensions, prizes, academic posts, as well as friendships with princes and other elites—that opened up possibilities for weighing in and participating authoritatively in debate. It was this initial projection of legitimacy that allowed the gesture of publishing "serious" works to be construed and mythologized, retrospectively, as that on which the *philosophe*'s authority really rested. As Lilti recounts, Edward Gibbon pointed to his *Essai sur l'étude de la littéraire* as his "best recommendation" and the secret to his success in Paris. In truth, though, it was the fourteen letters of recommendation he was able to present on his arrival there that ensured not only his success, but his ability to assert that his success was based on his work, and as such to assume the identity of *philosophe*.[103]

The order was then reversed. *Sociabilité mondaine* was not incidental to the intellectual lives of *philosophes*. It was a necessary first stage for anyone who sought an identity as a *philosophe*. The paradox of philosophical selfhood, however, lay in the fact that one only became a *philosophe* to the extent that this identity was subsequently perceived to predate one's appearance in *le monde*, and thus to be wholly unrelated to it. Or more exactly, the *philosophe*'s consecration came when his identity as an intellectual was viewed as the a priori condition for this social integration, which resulted when enlightened *mondains* and nobles called for his presence in their midst. The image of worldly and princely demand for the *philosophe*, of course, only further ratified the latter's assertion of independence. In a short autobiographical memoir, d'Alembert recounts how Catherine the Great had asked him to come to Moscow to tutor her son: "D'Alembert refused to do it. The empress insisted, and pressed him again by a letter written in her own hand." He cites the letter in a footnote, which renders both her polite but urgent insistence and his continued intransigence, thereby further underscoring his autonomy.[104]

This is also ultimately the story that the marquise du Deffand tells in her portrait of d'Alembert; he was a scientist and a solitary *homme de lettres*, immersed in the study of the ancients, before he one day "appeared in *le monde*," where he eventually imposed his presence on wary *mondains* by the force of his "disinterest," "wisdom," and "true merit."[105] It is the narrative that d'Alembert himself weaves into the "Essai," evoking an a posteriori entry into elite society as a scientist already formed by learning, followed by a hasty exit: "Torn from their solitude, writers find themselves caught up in the whirlwind of high society. . . . It is an experience that I have had, and which can be useful so long as one does not stay there for too long."[106] Of course, as the son of one of the great *salonnières* of the early eighteenth century, abandoned to be sure, yet provided for, d'Alembert came of age in the same context of *mondanité*—in the same salons of Mme Geoffrin and Mme du Deffand, as well as in the academic culture with which these salons were contiguous—as *mondain* apologists such as Duclos, Morellet, and Marmontel. Furthermore, the implication that he had by 1753 left the life of aristocratic socializing behind him is a distortion, to say the least. But it is a fiction that d'Alembert's contemporaries were willing to buy into, not to mention his historians and biographers. Accounts of d'Alembert's life, like those of other major Enlightenment figures such as Voltaire, tend to repeat the *philosophe*'s own assertions, echoed by contemporaries who were invested in d'Alembert's identity as a *philosophe*, that, though he carried himself there with perfect skill, propriety, and civility, he was not of *le monde*.[107] He was not a product of this elite sphere, and did not cater to its pleasures.

Helvétius, by contrast, failed to pull this off. In the wake of the publication of his treatise, the contradiction between his social and authorial selves was made apparent not only by his devout former protectors at court who highlighted Helvétius's uncivil abuse of his status, but also by his natural allies who downplayed the importance of *De l'Esprit*—"His book is about no more than those poor and useless philosophical truths which do no harm to anyone," wrote Voltaire[108]—while attacking his carelessness in publishing it so brazenly.[109] Unlike d'Alembert's *franchise*, Helvétius's audacity was not connected to a deep-seated philosophical ardor but was believed to emanate from a distinctly worldly ambition: "his only passion,"

Collé notes, "is to be seen as the greatest writer of his century."[110] In its visibility, the contradiction rendered invalid any claim Helvétius made to an intellectual authority grounded in a prior dedication to progress, truth, and the greater good. Far from it, he was unveiled as a fraudulent *philosophe* whose interest lay only in his own social success, where indeed it had been from the beginning. Highlighting how much *De l'Esprit* merely responded to prevailing fashion "in that frivolous world" where "the name philosopher . . . was first becoming fashionable," La Harpe writes that the contrast between Helvétius and his book,

> makes one wonder first of all what might have pushed an *honnête homme*, a man of wit and talent, to circulate [débiter] with so much confidence a mass of paradoxes, in which the faultiness of the reasoning is as easy to demonstrate as the odiousness of the implications. It is impossible to identify any motivating cause other than that vain and unfortunate ambition for celebrity, which corresponds perfectly with what we are told about the initial circumstances that pushed Helvétius towards a literary career.[111]

In the end, d'Alembert and Helvétius came out of an identical sociocultural world in order to claim the identity of *philosophe*, but only the former successfully convinced his public of the priority of his dedication to serious critical inquiry, and thus of his fundamental nature as an intellectual who only passed through society, drawn there not by ambition for fame but by the interest of its members who demanded his presence and by his own generosity in trying to educate them. Helvétius, by contrast, never managed to subordinate or hide the truth of his identity as an *homme du monde* who turned to philosophy as a dabbler, an eighteenth-century Oronte who sought no more than to enhance his prestige and appeal.

The Nature of Philosophical Publication

That Helvétius was ultimately undermined by his decision to print and circulate his work with the *privilège*, a move driven not just by his desire as a writer for official legitimacy but by his sense of entitlement to it, illustrates just how critical publishing practices were to the success or failure of the balancing act between social integration and intellectual independence that was at the core of philosophical identity. It is in this specific framework that they need to be understood, which means, for one thing, that they cannot be considered apart from the question of who the *philosophes* were. Their decisions in the book trade cannot be dismissed as incidental or extraneous, no matter how out of synch with other elements of the discourse of *philosophie* they might seem in their apparent failure to take on the conventions of Old Regime publishing—the lack of literary property rights, nonpayment of writers, and surveillance. At the same time, though, these practices should not be seen to invalidate the basic claim to autonomy and credibility on which the philosophical self was constructed. For far from contradicting the claim they were in fact crucial to an assertion of intellectual independence that did not repudiate the relationship of the writer to the aristocrat but endeavored to reinvent it. In this respect, if Helvétius was undermined by the *privilège*, it was not because the request for it reflected either an excessive compliance with censors or ill-considered resistance to them. Rather, it was because the gesture of asking for the official license to publish constituted a dramatic mismanagement of his self-presentation as an *homme de lettres* by forcing an expression of approval—in the name of the king—from theoretically sympathetic social and political elites that they could not, however, offer without compromising their own credibility and stature, especially once other factions weighed in against the work. Confronted by the queen and Joly de Fleury, Helvétius's allies at court and in *le monde*—Malesherbes, Madame de Pompadour, and the duc de Choiseul—were faced with a choice between the hierarchical cultural order of *mondanité* and the intellectual discourse of *philosophie*. Yet the success of *philosophie*, with its powerful but nimble critical penchant, had from the beginning rested on the prospect that such a choice would not have to be made. As Helvétius allowed his self-image to degrade in a glaring contradiction between the *honnête homme* with *moeurs douces* and the brazen author of *De l'Esprit*, the choice, rendered inescapable, proved not just detrimental to the reputation of the writer, but menacing for the philosophical movement as a whole, which could survive in the absence of neither the wholehearted support of sympathetic elites in Paris and at Versailles nor the plausibility of its critical and independent voice.

For his part, as Dinah Ribard points out, d'Alembert was positively transformed by the 1753 publication of his *Mélanges de littérature, d'histoire et de philosophie*, a collection that first offered to readers his "Essai sur les gens de lettres," along with his *Discours préliminaire* to the *Encyclopédie*, which had been well received when it first appeared two years earlier in volume one.[112] Mme du Deffand marked the change in d'Alembert's persona in a letter to the latter, noting that he had broken out of the world of mathematics with the circulation of the "Essai," and that she would despair, "if you would shut yourself away with your geometry."[113] The *Mélanges* thus records his shift from scientific into "literary" matters; and interestingly, d'Alembert highlights the distinction between "belles-lettres" and "géométrie" in the "Essai" just as he takes leaves of one field for the other. Significantly, the distinction consists in the social orientation of the former "agreeable sciences," which seek a public and cannot be conceived to fulfill their purpose unless they find some measure of approbation with it. By contrast, the success of geometry lies in its own inherent correctness, a quality that persists even in the absence of any ratification—or perception—by readers. It makes sense to study geometry on a deserted island, d'Alembert contends, but not to write poetry.[114] To the extent, then, that his transformation as an intellectual is mediated by his turn to "belles-lettres," it is also at root a turn to society. Paradoxically, though, he becomes a *philosophe* inasmuch as this move into *le monde* is articulated as a rejection of society and of the overriding imperatives of worldly sociability and elegant affability: "Be a philosopher," Deffand continues, "and do not be troubled about appearing as such; let your disdain for men be sufficiently sincere to deprive them of the means and the hope of offending you."[115]

Unlike Helvétius's *privilège*, such a rebuff is digestible to a rarefied audience of *mondains* and *grands*, who are invited to participate in his serious and frank discourse as exceptions to the rule of aristocratic self-interest and ignorance: "whoever is jealous to acquire and conserve the esteem and confidence of the public must support [ménager] the writers of his nation," d'Alembert writes in the *avertissement* to the 1759 edition of the *Mélanges*.[116] The hostility that he is repeatedly described by Deffand and by the *philosophe* himself as inciting in nobles offended by his text and scandalized by his too forthright demeanor, rather than recording any actual break in his relations with elites, registers in fact a deeper integration into their midst by giving those *grands* who choose to be sympathetic with his undertaking a negative model of haughty outmoded aristocratic self-absorption against which to define their own transcendent "modern" roles as Enlightened rather than traditional protectors. When Frederick II arranges a pension of 1,200 livres for d'Alembert in 1754, he dispatches a note to the latter offering the explanation, "The pleasure and satisfaction of bestowing marks of my esteem on a man of merit are the only motives which have led me to establish the pension that I have granted to you."[117]

Whether Frederick self-consciously patterned his patronage on the models developed by d'Alembert in his writings, or whether the "Essai" instead monumentalized Frederick's gestures, the important point is that publication operated a key mediation of the relationship in all of its deep complexity, conveying but also constituting the *philosophe*'s autonomy and sociability, as well as the intellectual prestige of a new enlightened elite. Frederick goes on in the above-cited letter to emphasize at once both d'Alembert's freedom and his close ties to the king, both of which are validated in and through the patronage exchange: "I ask for nothing from you other than the continuation of the attachment that you have shown me in your letter."[118] Indeed, for the *philosophes*, publication was more than anything else an effort to unite the two ideals of autonomy and social integration in such a way as to render them indistinguishable or at least, non-contradictory. The one did not invalidate the other; and a gesture toward elite integration—offering a book as a gift to a patron[119]—could at the same time viably articulate a claim to autonomy, even if the book was, say, the *Traité sur la tolérance*.

The *philosophe*'s work was thereby invested as an ambivalent sign. It was, on one hand, to manifest his dedication to "spreading light," and as such accentuated his extrication from the oral exchanges of *le monde* and his independent turn toward a broad reading Public that he accessed through print. On the other hand, the work was to mediate an image of his *honnêteté* as an *homme du monde*, and to strengthen his ties to the socially and politically prominent. It should, moreover, be pointed out that while the work directly expressed the former in the *philosophe*'s strident voice and critical views, it articulated the latter negatively by projecting a distance between the *philosophe* and his writing, partly, for instance, through the work's anonymity and the author's disavowals. Voltaire was, of course, famous for relentlessly denying authorship of a large portion of his texts, and in particular those "philosophical" works—the *contes*, satires, and polemics—with which he would be most closely identified: "his mania is to write always, to publish always, and then to disavow what he has done," reads a 1766 entry from the *Mémoires secrets*.[120] The pattern is often viewed as a self-protective maneuver in a literary field under constant surveillance. In fact, the denials did not radically dissociate him from the writings in question so much as they articulated, in one equivocal gesture, both the possibility that he could have written them and the reality that he did not. This, in turn, enhanced his stature as a *philosophe*, which was grounded in his public identity as the producer of a certain type of unconstrained, probing discourse, by acknowledging and thereby validating the suspicion of his authorship, as well as by establishing his underlying sympathy with the work: "I am not its author," he writes to Damilaville in 1763 as the *Traité sur la tolerance* begins to circulate, "but I am, as you know, interested in this work, solely on humanitarian principles [par principe d'humanité]."[121] At the same time, the denial, asserted in the face of the possibility that he could have written the work, also enhanced his respectability as a self-restrained *honnête homme*, who, unlike the "real" author of the work to whom he invariably points, refused to cross the line into incivility and revolt. Voltaire provided endless images of this *honnête* moderation in epistolary and journalistic disavowals that imputed his works to fictionalized alter egos, in contrast to whose transgressions Voltaire's own image, while clearly remaining that of a daring writer intent on taking on society's prejudices and unreasonable superstitions, nonetheless remained well within the boundaries of acceptable comportment: "It is a certain M. Desmal, a man of much intelligence, who wrote *L'optimisme ou Candide*, and who, even more than I do, makes fun of fools," he writes to his Swiss friend Elie Bertrand in 1759, thus in the same year as the second edition of d'Alembert's *Mélanges* and one year after Helvétius requested his *privilège*.[122]

Philosophical selfhood was rooted in this effort of synthesis, I have argued. Much about the publishing practices of the *philosophes* can be understood in this light, and correlatively, philosophical selfhood can itself be greatly illuminated by taking "seriously," in the language of Jouhaud and Viala, the publishing activities of writers who were able to appropriate for themselves that identity.[123] The most successful *philosophes*, writers like Voltaire or d'Alembert who were easily recognized as such both in their own time and later, were those who were ultimately most able to pull off the double act, and convince an elite public in and through their activities as writers of both their basic intellectual independence and of their *honnête* sociability. By contrast, efforts to discredit the *philosophe*, and to undermine his legitimacy and authority as an intellectual, almost invariably probed the incongruities between the *philosophe* as a writer and as an *honnête homme*, indeed precisely the convergence celebrated in the *Encyclopédie*. On one hand, the efforts might reveal his claims to autonomy to be inconsistent with, and therefore a negation of his status as an *homme du monde*, much in the manner of the *dévot* mobilization against Helvétius, which upheld the strength and freedom of the voice conveyed in *De l'Esprit*, but construed these qualities as a disrespect and a license that called into question the author's suitability for life at the court and in *le monde*.

However, another antiphilosophical approach would take shape, one that will occupy us in the chapters to come. Rather than the *philosophe*'s strident critique, this view took his sociability and his will to please elites as fixed variables in light of which his claims to intellectual autonomy, and therefore his claims to know and to be entitled to propagate the truth, were compromised. From this vantage point, the claims of such writers as d'Alembert and Helvétius to both independence and elite sociability were untenable. A friendship with a monarch or an official post at the court was in acute tension with the writer's assertions that he produced with no thought to pleasing elites and no desire for personal advancement. Moreover, for those who advanced this perspective, endeavoring as they did to define a new intellectual identity predicated on the irreconcilability of authorship with *mondanité*, the publishing activities of the *philosophe* stood out as stark, unpleasant symptoms of this hypocrisy. They inaugurate in this respect a tradition of suspicion.

Our purpose in the next part is to trace the formation and rise of this new perspective, which linked a certain type of personal involvement in the commercial publication of writings, an authorial involvement that would be signified through various tropes of the literary market such as "literary property," "droits d'auteur," and "exploitation," with an ideal of sincerity that, in turn, was defined in opposition to a "selling out" almost exclusively conceived in the image of aristocratic sociability. If the *philosophes* showed no interest in literary property rights or *droits d'auteur*, it was not because they were too rich or well-connected to have to worry about such things. It was because "literary property," as a claim not simply to a legal right but to a particular intellectual identity, sent out a signal about who the writer was and where he was situated, that they were not interested in broadcasting. For as we shall see, "literary property," and more generally, the commercialization of the work, vitiates its value and meaning as a polite social act. When d'Aubignac justifies his harsh attacks against Corneille, he points to the fact that he had acquired the playwright's works in the book trade, and thus he was freed from the constraints of civility that would have restricted him had he received the books as a gift:

When one gives me a book as a gift, I consider the affection or at least the civility of the Author, and this consideration of propriety and even duty obliges me by gratitude to say only good things about what I read in it, and not to say anything about things that I do not like, if I cannot excuse them. But when a book is sold publicly, and we only acquire it at a price, it is our belonging, and each can do with it as he or she pleases; it is no less abandoned to the judgment of the public than to the liberty of purchase.[124]

In this respect, the following chapters tell a story that is not about the dawning consciousness of "natural" rights but about the rhetorical appropriation of an already constituted vocabulary—the vocabulary of "literary commerce"—and its investment with an entirely new value. The "hypocrisy" of the *philosophe* is inseparable from the "sincerity" of the modern, proto-Romantic Author, just as the *philosophe*'s "indifference" to intellectual property rights and income from the book trade cannot in the end be disconnected from the Author's highly self-conscious representation of himself as inextricably caught up in the commercialization of his writings, whether in a positive sense as a literary entrepreneur or in an undoubtedly more enduring and poignant negative image as the exploited victim of rapacious and greedy *libraires* and a philistine public. These are in any case two side of the same coin. And both possibilities mark the turn away from the cultural field of the Old Regime and into what is increasingly understood to be an *alternative* intellectual field: the "literary market."

PART II

THE LITERARY MARKET: THE MAKING OF A MODERN CULTURAL FIELD

Reconsidering the Alternative

Accounts of the literary market in the eighteenth century have typically hinged on the struggles of writers to support themselves in what David Pottinger characterized as the "primitive business conditions of the *ancien régime*."[1] Specifically, this history accentuates two key movements: first, the intensification of writers' struggles for economic "independence," which sparks a growing consciousness of their "rights" to payments from publishers for their works; and second, the development of the book trade as gauged by objective external factors such as an increased demand for printed reading material and rising prices paid to *gens de lettres* for their manuscripts. It is easy to see how the two developments are interrelated; higher levels of remuneration from booksellers spur writers to become more aware of their rights and dues, while an orientation toward commercial success leads them to seek, demand, and create opportunities to profit in a growing print industry. What the exact relations of causality may be, though, is not so salient in this analysis. For the question is peripheral to understanding a process—the formation of the market as an institution of literary life and intellectual modernization—that was, at bottom, driven neither by the growth of the book trade nor by the awakening of *gens de lettres* to their rights, but by the appropriation of a specific vocabulary of intellectual self-presentation in an effort to conceptualize, articulate, and impose a new ideal of literary selfhood over and against older ideals, by opposing that which appears most to define the latter: their rootedness in the values and practices of aristocratic sociability.

More significant for our purposes is the fact that standard accounts of the market tend to emphasize its exteriority with respect to an established Old Regime cultural field that was defined in and through its contiguity with dominant social and political structures such as the court and the noble household. The literary market, by contrast, is made up of mechanisms, motives, and individuals that pointedly come from elsewhere, and functions by a logic that is external to the world of elites. The underlying desire for independence to which writers awaken and which fuels their struggles for rights and payments is, in its individualism and seriousness, quite foreign to, for instance, the social bond of the patronage relationship and its orientation toward reciprocal duty and leisure. By the same token, the development of the commercial publishing sector unfolds decidedly outside of the aristocratic framework of the "first literary field," in its association with agents who have little or no connection to the cultural and political establishment, indeed by agents who come to be characterized by this fact: provincial or foreign printers and booksellers who operated in an underground trade employing dissolute hack writers to generate a mass of "unofficial" titles, all of which lack the imprint of the official censors. These books, moreover, are aimed at a broad new readership spread across the provincial towns of France and Europe rather than concentrated in Parisian salons.[2]

In this perspective, the literary market takes form as a distinct *alternative*, transforming the eighteenth-century literary world by starkly dividing it into "two systems of remuneration," with a "still-present patronage" now facing an ever-expanding "market regulated by supply and demand."[3] The history of the author, in its emphasis on intellectual liberation from nobility, develops then as the story of a passage from one system to the other, or more exactly of the increasing inevitability of the passage inasmuch as the alternative of the "market" becomes, with the book trade's growth, more viable and more visible. Indeed, the market emerges not just as any alternative but as a more and more obvious one, to the degree that it directly appeals to and cultivates in the writer what are presumed to be "natural" desires for independence that patronage had constrained. Of course it does not necessarily satisfy these desires. In fact, the defining experience of the market will be their frustration; yet the frustration nonetheless formulates an essential articulation of the writer's efforts—even as they fall short—to pursue and project a "truer" authorial nature.

Whatever might be compelling about this story, though, it cannot be said to root itself in anything that the writers of the time were seeing or saying; for there is really no reason to believe that seventeenth- or eighteenth-century *gens de lettres* perceived "literary commerce" as so clear an "alternative," certainly not in the way historians such as Roche and Martin have tended to construct the opposition. To be sure, Roche does situate the "two systems" in an "ambiguous climate," and it might be tempting to consider this ambiguity as somehow closer to the perception of early modern writers confronting a commercial sector that was not yet very developed. Still, it is hard to shake the sense that the haziness to which Roche points has less to do with the difficulties that writers might have encountered in discerning the contours of the "market" within a field dominated by "patronage," an endeavor that would have to presuppose some initial intuition of a meaningful opposition between the two institutions as separate "systems," than it has with the possibility that these writers were not thinking about "literary commerce" in such terms at all. The ambiguity, in other words, lies not in the inchoate state of the eighteenth-century literary field but in a historical disconnect residing in the fact that what seems to us an obvious way of conceptualizing the early growth of the book trade—in terms of an emerging alternative to patronage—was apparently not self-evident to those who experienced the development. The truth is that they were more "instinctively" drawn to an array of other models for understanding the expansion of commercial publishing, none of which acknowledged the viability of an intellectual career pursued outside the framework of the "traditional" field. Moreover, if the trend as the century progresses is toward less ambiguity, the reason is not that conditions in the literary world became clearer to writers by conforming, as the book trade grew, to their preconceived notions of "patronage" and "market" as opposed self-governing systems. Rather, I would argue, their perception of these conditions evolved in order to become more like our own. In other words, the ambiguity dissolves to the extent that we slowly discern the roots of our own "modern" understanding coming to the fore, eclipsing what will then always appear to us as "archaic" views of writing and publishing; archaic inasmuch as these activities are not ostensibly connected to an affirmation of the writer's social and intellectual freedom from aristocratic influence.

As a "system of remuneration," identified as such by writers who turn to it precisely as an "alternative" to patronage, the literary market is the product of this shift in perceptions. It takes form as a function not of the development of commercial publishing as an alternative to noble patronage, but of an increasing tendency to interpret commercial publishing as such an alternative. What propelled this view? I argue that it was not, in and of itself, the "objective" growth of the book trade. Rather, the book trade became the literary market to the degree that it was perceived through a mounting exasperation among a distinct group of writers with life in the established cultural field, which led these writers to see in the opportunities offered by the print industry possibilities for escape rather than social integration. Rooted in the eighteenth-century expansion of the intellectual field and an ensuing increase in the viability of what can be considered "mediocre" careers—undistinguished yet durable, and as such able to sustain but not satisfy literary aspirations—the frustration drove new definitions of literary identity that were valorized in opposition to older visions. Against the sociable, pleasing wit of the salon habitué, the new claims underscored earnest dedication, authenticity, and seriousness, qualities that were then manifest in a distance from the world of elites that writers studiously maintained and inevitably highlighted in their self-presentations. Asserting their physical remove from the effete world of court and salon as a sign of their moral detachment from its ethos of frivolous amusement, the "literary market" would become a visceral figuration of this symbolic distance. Perhaps it was the most important image of it. For if the market has in the long run offered a powerful explanatory model for describing the modernization of writing and authorship in the dying years of the Old Regime, it is partly due to the degree that we have accepted its credibility and significance as an articulation of this "dissociation" and of the sharp break with previous ideals on which the new claims turn.

The goal of Part II is not to question the importance of "commercialization" as a process that drew writers away from the "first literary field" of the Old Regime into a newer one formed around the publishing industry, but to probe the nature of this transition. Our sense of it has tended to rest on a central mystification, namely that the process began with writers in a state of semiconsciousness, having little notion of the book trade, and no investment in its opportunities or outcomes. It is precisely this lack of investment that comes to define the beholden-ness of the early modern *homme de lettres* to the Old Regime social and political order, as Alain Viala suggests in his reinterpretation of Boileau's famous warning against transforming poetry into a "mercenary trade."[4] The turn to commercial opportunities marks, then, a kind of illumination in which the awakening of intellectuals to their rights and dues manifests a deeper *prise de conscience*, when writers assumed full responsibility for who they truly were and who they should aspire to be: socially independent, useful contributors to the public good, serious workers, and authoritative judges of right and wrong, just and unjust, good and bad.

But we have seen that the writers of the seventeenth century were hardly unconscious of or uninterested in the opportunities extended to them by the commercial book trade. They did not ignore this "system of remuneration." They were invested in its outcomes; the assumption that they were not is based on a confusion according to which the affirmation of a particular vision of social autonomy from elites as the defining trait of intellectual identity in the eighteenth century is conflated with the discovery of a timeless ideal of artistic freedom as a universal essence characterizing the Author. The latter, by this line of thinking, is assumed to represent a fundamental, transhistorical archetype of intellectual practice, its most perfect and "natural" form whose history would be the struggles of those aspiring to this ideal against the social and political constraints that long forced them to deviate from it. Certainly, eighteenth-century intellectuals who decried the "disfigurement" they had to endure in their relations with social elites cultivated the myth of the universality of their conceptions of authorial autonomy, in the light of which earlier writers, or contemporaries who failed to adapt to this emerging ideal, were to be recast as subservient, suspect, and discredited. These "modern" writers, who self-consciously constructed themselves in and through a break with the past, might, in this sense, be said to have drafted the first script of their own history.

Classical-era writers were, however, no less committed to autonomy, a fact that we appreciate only so long as we take the concept not in the contingent sense of a rupture with nobility but in a more general and no doubt useful meaning, according to which "intellectual autonomy" refers to the social condition in which an individual could lay claim to an identity based on "intellectual" activities—more precisely, writing and print publication—without coming across as ridiculous or unseemly in so doing.[5] It is undeniable that writing and publishing independently of nobility and its cultural imprimatur was both ridiculous and unseemly in the seventeenth century, which explains why the "paradox" of literary selfhood in the early modern period consisted in the fact that the autonomy on which the identity was based lay in a greater proximity with elites instead of the opposite.[6] It is hardly surprising, of course, that the necessary recourse to noble sponsorship would deeply inflect the nature of the participation and investments in the book trade of "premodern" or "archaic" writers who sought to cultivate this proximity rather than distance themselves from elite circles. Such a motive, however, does not render meaningless or nonexistent these investments, or imply that the writers were unaware of the "real" benefits of commercial publication.

Instead, it changes the nature of the story that needs to be told. For if accounts have often traced the awakening of writers to their "true" interests as autonomous intellectuals, I suggest that the real story lies in the shifting ways that autonomy, as the social condition out of which an individual claimed legitimacy as an intellectual, was understood, represented, and affirmed. The rise of the literary market, in this view, presents above all the story of a transformation in the self-conception and self-presentation of writers. Their contacts with the book trade acquire a certain resonance in this respect, becoming meaningful experiences of the "market" not as they reflect the expansion of opportunities for writers to support themselves, but as they are believed to offer increasingly effective signals of a break with noble society on which writers sought to stake their legitimacy. In this perspective, Part II pursues what might seem an inverted approach to the role of commercial publishing in the history of authorial modernization; for it argues that commercialization was central to this history not as its "objective" driving force but as an effect or an articulation of a discursive shift. I am less interested in how the growth of the book trade opened up new career pathways for intellectuals seeking to become "modern" by freeing themselves from the tutelage of nobility, than in how, in their efforts to validate a new intellectual legitimacy rooted in a vision of social autonomy conceived in anti-aristocratic terms, they turned to a preexisting language of "literary commerce" that had been forged in the polemics and quarrels of the seventeenth and eighteenth centuries. This language of authorial self-interest, legal rights, and economic dues was adopted and transformed as a preferred vehicle of intellectual self-presentation to the extent that it highlighted the "commercialized" writer, defined not by social connections but by rights and dues, as an outsider, and thus as untouched by the compromises of life in elite circles. In the process, the book trade was transformed as a privileged space, indeed, as a "literary market" where new and *alternative* possibilities allowed writers to construct revalorized identities for themselves in and through their engagements with the economic and legal realities of Old Regime publishing.

Part II focuses on two of these engagements, one concerned with economic payments, the other with legal rights, though of course the two problematics are at a basic level interwoven. Chapter 3 analyzes the classic motif of "living by the pen." Often mobilized to invoke the economic foundation of the writer's intellectual liberation, in the polemics of the Enlightenment era the image conveyed at first a distinctly negative impression of a writer's lack of symbolic capital from any kind of protection or patronage. "Vivre de sa plume" was not triumphant autonomy. Rather, it indicated morally dubious ambitiousness as well as a position into which one fell—or was rhetorically consigned—when one failed to acquire, or lost, the kinds of indicators that normally conveyed personal credibility in the early modern cultural field: a pension or a position in an elite household or academy. As an affirmation of intellectual independence, the claim to "live by the pen" was built on this semiotics of exteriority and lack of recourse. As such, it had little to do with writers' actual abilities to support themselves economically by writing. In fact, the image of "living by the pen" was generally summoned with the presumption of the inevitable failure of the endeavor—this accounts, as we shall see, for the vast majority of eighteenth-century (as well as contemporary) references to the topos—the goal being to project authorial poverty as proof of the writer's heroic refusal to cater to decadent elites. No matter, in turn, that this "poverty" had as little correlation as the myth of self-sufficiency to the real circumstances of the writer's existence, which was almost certainly more comfortable and viable than alleged. Positing the writer's economic and social misfortunes, and postulating them, moreover, as a massive symbolic success, "living by the pen" seeks, in its most meaningful formulation, to transform the mediocrity of the nonprivileged writer's literary life.

While the self-presentational topos of "vivre de sa plume" focalizes attention on the writer's relations, or lack thereof, with elite protectors, Chapter 4 turns to rhetoric that sought to invest with significance the writer's interactions with the book trade, and in particular with its principal representative, the publisher. Central to the theorization and construction of the market, the elevation of this invariably fraught relationship, in and through which writers valorize their spirituality and transcendence, is explored in the debates on literary property prevailing in the second half of the eighteenth century, spearheaded, as we have noted, by the publishers of the Parisian guild, but which enlisted Diderot, Linguet, and others. We would tend to assume that "literary property" indicates an exercisable legal right from which *gens de lettres* hoped to profit. But their rhetoric depicts it as a far more ambiguous concept, conveying less a "real" claim to property rights than the denunciation of the inevitable theft of the products of the writer's labors, which results from the latter's inaptitude for commercial negotiation, as well as from the essentially unsellable nature of the literary work as the emanation of the writer's "thoughts" and "soul." In this respect, writers wielded claims to "literary property" in order to distinguish their writings absolutely and qualitatively from straightforward commodities. Paradoxically, therefore, as a self-consciously hopeless assertion, the idea of intellectual property rights advanced a pointed rejection of the commercialization of literary life, a rejection through which the literary market took shape as a negative space in which the presence of writers there, established through images of their victimization and exploitation by booksellers, played up their inexorable foreignness to its crass self-interested logic.

Finally, a short Chapter 5 focuses on Rousseau's correspondence with his publisher, Marc-Michel Rey, and explores the intense anxiety with which writers then entered into contact with their booksellers. It is through the prism of this anxiety, which elevates the writer/publisher relation as a crucial nexus defining the new cultural field of "modern authorship," that their turn to commercial publishing would in fact articulate a rejection of it, and that the book trade would in the process be transformed as the market.

3
"Living by the Pen": Mythologies of Modern Authorial Autonomy

ONE ESPECIALLY POIGNANT EVOCATION of the passage into an alternative field lies in the image of "living by the pen." The motif recurs in historical writing as a shorthand reference to the escape of writers from patronage into the freedom of the market.[1] The reality itself—of Old Regime writers supporting themselves from publishing income—has, however, proven difficult to ascertain, and scholars narrating the transition have found themselves trying to account for what are at best understated gestures of embrace, which, in their silence, ambiguity, or complexity, fail to broadcast any obvious rationale. They thus call for an interpretation from the historian that is invariably open to contestation, and in this respect are like Corneille's *Demande de lettres patentes*. Corneille's request can be viewed as a product of his desire to establish independence from his court patrons by trying to make his living commercially as a self-sufficient writer. But the project does not in itself entail such a reading, and the *Demande* can just as plausibly be viewed in other ways, say, in terms of the politics of theater troupe rivalries in the 1640s—in any case, in ways that do not emphasize any deliberate move away from aristocratic protection into the book trade, let alone the significance of such a transition for Corneille's own sense of his identity as a dramatic poet.

Moreover—and here, the Enlightenment-era field presents itself more in continuity with the seventeenth century than in a break with it—it is always easier to discern unfavorable representations of the writer's proximity to the book trade than positive ones. Indeed, as with the Classical age, if a "turn to commercial publishing" stands out as a significant transitional moment in the history of eighteenth-century writers, it is initially to the degree that such a phenomenon is depicted in a markedly negative light, which aims not to valorize the shift as part of a struggle for greater autonomy, but to discredit those *gens de lettres* who would be associated with the move. This chapter begins with the polemical roots of the concept of "living by the pen" in the pamphleteering of the *philosophes* in the 1750s and 1760s, as they confronted increasingly vociferous opposition. In acerbic diatribes such as Voltaire's satirical poem "Le pauvre diable," the image conveyed a strongly negative vision of literary outsiderhood, one that played up the outsized ambitions and the failures of their adversaries, partly in an effort to legitimize their own problematic integration into *le monde* as dedicated and talented intellectuals, rather than as *gens d'esprit*.

This will provide a context in the second half of the chapter for better understanding how "living by the pen" then develops as an affirmative trope for later writers, for whom the example of the *philosophe*—especially the latter's sociability—will stand out as a countermodel against which they endeavor to define themselves: not as reluctant socialites but through a more complete repudiation of *mondaine* sociability, as outsiders having no contact whatsoever with the corrupt cultural world of elites. In this respect, "living by the pen" does not articulate a direct, concrete (insofar as it is economically based) shift away from patronage into the market. For in truth, writers who claimed the social autonomy of the market invariably remained reliant on patronage to a greater or lesser degree, and no eighteenth-century writer can meaningfully be said to have "liberated" himself from that dependence; they all ultimately lived what from our vantage point seem hybrid lives based on a mix of commercial and noncommercial pay. Yet the image advances a profound *moral* rejection of *mondaine* culture by writers who would never live the rejection quite as they affirmed, but who nonetheless defined a rigorous new intellectual stance in opposition to the superficiality and hypocrisy of the d'Alembertian claim to "liberté."

Enlightenment Polemics and the Struggle to Make a Living

In the 1750s, as the *philosophes* faced the mounting criticism and official repression that we explored in Chapter 2, a new literary protagonist enters the stage: the *anti-philosophe*, playing the role of emblematic adversary both to specific projects such as the *Encyclopédie* and to the intellectual and cultural movement of the Enlightenment as a whole. There has been a good amount of recent interest in this figure and in the "counter-Enlightenment" that he represents.[2] The present chapter, however, focuses on the crystallization of the type, less as an actual writer bringing a real agenda into the intellectual sphere, than as a caricature in the propaganda of pro-Enlightenment polemicists such as Voltaire, Morellet, and Diderot, who, in responding to their critics, set out to define them in pointed ways. In particular, the *philosophes* pressed an ethical attack that sought to connect their opponents' hostility to Enlightenment ideas with a repertoire of graceless manners, including a deluded ambition to succeed despite their utter lack of intelligence and talent, which they imputed to the *anti-philosophes* in mocking accounts of their struggles to make a living as writers.

The *anti-philosophes* were thus not merely wedded to religious orthodoxy but in their commitment to traditional views, they were unveiled as blustering, pompous, and self-righteous. When Jean-Jacques Le Franc de Pompignan, a provincial magistrate, president of the Montauban *cour des aides*, and a poet and playwright, seized the occasion of his reception speech to the Académie française in March 1760 to deliver a startling attack on the fashionable new *philosophie* and its proponents, Voltaire hit back with a series of prose and verse rejoinders that sealed an image of the new academician as a witless nonentity, "full of arrogance and verbiage," whose grandstanding before the Academy was all the more ludicrous coming from a man who had never produced anything worthwhile: "When one does not distinguish one's age by one's works, it is a strange audaciousness to disparage one's age."[3] Moreover, not only were the *anti-philosophes* insufferably self-important but their sanctimony proved hollow. Two months after Le Franc de Pompignan's speech to the Académie, Charles Palissot's comedy, *Les Philosophes*, was staged by the Comédie française, causing a sensation for its ruthless characterizations of prominent intellectuals such as Rousseau, Diderot, and Helvétius.[4] In response, the abbé Morellet circulated a pamphlet in the guise of a preface to the play, in which Palissot is depicted as he awaits inspiration, hearing a voice that directs him to attack "what we call Philosophers" so that one day piety will conquer intelligence: "And in assigning positions in the Académie," intones the voice, "we will not ask about the works of Candidates, but about who their Confessor is, and we will put a collection box and a fount at the door of the chamber, and acceptance speeches will be Sermons against *incredulousness*."[5] Who, though, is this second-rate playwright to undertake such a crusade? Morellet proceeds to evoke Palissot's dubious personal history of theft, slander, and debauchery: "you stole a cashbox that had been confided to you," says the voice, as it runs down a lengthy list of Palissot's *friponneries*; "you made of your house a place of ill-repute [un mauvais lieu]." Ironically, the record of malfeasance is now transformed as the very source of the moral authority out of which Palissot's power to condemn emanates. The voice continues:

when the refuse of your life will have been sorted through, it will be stunning to discover that you suddenly became the Apostle of morals and the Defender of Religion, and it will be asked how a man without Religion or morals or integrity dared speak of integrity, morals, and Religion, and you will answer that faith covers a multitude of sins, and it is better to be a rascal than a non-believer, and to be villainous than a Philosophe.[6]

Most important for our purposes, however, is the propensity of the *philosophes'* polemics to show the *anti-philosophe* as a writer who was caught up in a hopeless struggle to make a life for himself in the world of letters. He was, in other words, a nobody desperately trying to become a somebody, with no more than questionable results and prospects to show for it. Morellet's preface opens with Palissot contemplating his poverty—"I had no money"—and searching for the secret of success: "oh, who will give me the eloquence of Chaumeix, the light touch of Berthier, and the profundity of Fréron," he asks.[7] These are ridiculous questions, of course, intended not to be taken seriously but to mock three critics of the *philosophes* scarcely known for their eloquence, lightness, or depth.[8] But they also emphasize Palissot's anonymity, while conjuring up both his ambition to be famous and the inevitability of his continued failure given the terrible models that he chooses to emulate. Similarly, if his satires against Le Franc de Pompignan do not adopt such rhetorical strategies—after all, the latter was a more established figure—Voltaire's attacks on other critics of the *Encyclopédie* do follow the pattern. When the Comédie française agreed to perform *Les Philosophes*, Voltaire decided in response to have the *comédiens* put on his own play, *L'Ecossaise*, which, at that point, had only been staged at his Ferney estate. The play included a character who was transparently based on a central figure in the anti-*Encyclopédie* movement: the journalist Elie-Catherine Fréron. Transformed as Frélon in the printed version[9]—an amalgam, of course, of the journalist's name and the French word *félon*—the character is a scurrilous, backstabbing type who spends his time in a café where he trucks in calumnious writings: "I'm already earning a little by speaking ill." Above all, his introduction into the scene hinges, in the manner of Morellet's Palissot, on the concomitant images of his obscurity and his ardent desire for celebrity, though in a contrast to the forlorn questioning that Morellet attributes to Palissot, Frélon's frustrated ambition plays out in his bitterness at the success of others. As the curtain rises on act I, we find him bristling as he reads about these good fortunes in the paper: "What distressing news! Favors [des grâces] have been accorded to more than twenty people! And none to me!"[10]

Voltaire will develop at length the portrait of the *anti-philosophe* as a writer defined by his vain struggles to find a meaningful position in the literary world in a 1760 verse satire called "Le pauvre diable."[11] This piece has come to characterize the very type of the hopeful but unestablished writer in the second half of the eighteenth century, the "poor devil" driven by a fierce desire to succeed even though his ambition is not grounded in what had, throughout the early modern period, always been necessary attributes for those asserting a social identity rooted in intellectual activities: wealth, connections, social skills, and of course, talent.[12] The ambition was instead shown to be built on air as the product of fantasy and pretension. Or it was an illness contracted from reading, which convinced the individual to want to establish himself as an "author":

J'étais sans bien, sans métier, sans génie.
Et j'avais lu quelques méchants auteurs;
Je croyais même avoir des protecteurs.
Mordu du chien de la métromanie,
Le mal me prit, je fus auteur aussi.

[I was without fortune, a trade, or genius.
And I had read a few miserable authors;
I even thought that I had patrons.
Bitten by a mania for verse,
The sickness took hold, and I became an author as well.]

The poem then probes the disastrous consequences of the stark discrepancy between the character's feverish aspiration and any realistic expectation that he might make it, recounting the *pauvre diable*'s endless failures in his attempts to establish himself. In turn, these failures are consistently tied to his involvement in anti-philosophical campaigns. He is hired by Fréron to write articles for the latter's journal, "with the hope of a salary," and gains a reputation "for [his] slander [infamie]." He next meets Le Franc de Pompignan, who takes the young author—a fellow native of Montauban—under his wing, offering him a "tragic masterpiece" that he had composed, *Zoraïd*, to read to the actors of the Comédie française; but the *pauvre diable* is rebuffed by the jeering troupe. Finally, he decides to become devout and present himself at Versailles as a "moral author"; yet not only does he fail to be received but even the lackeys at court laugh at him. An endless string of obstacles and humiliations leads the would-be author into paralyzing self-doubt—"What must I do next? Where am I? And who am I supposed to be?"—at which point he stumbles on the narrator of the poem, who asks him how he came to such a state. After listening to the story, Voltaire's interlocutor shows him, and by extension all those targeted by the rhymed polemic, an acceptable way out when he encourages the *pauvre diable* to abandon his literary dreams and take on instead the kind of position—as a porter—the sheer banality of which, as a "way to make a living," pointedly highlights the fanciful nature of the individual's earlier authorial desires. In so distilling the essence of the poor devil character into the base pursuit of gainful employment, which any job would in the end satisfy, the satire unmasks the sheer illegitimacy of his lofty cultural ambitions.

Of all the philosophical caricatures of their critics, though, it is Diderot's portrait of the nephew of Rameau—the self-proclaimed leader of a troupe comprising "All the fallen poets . . ., also the despised musicians, unread authors, hissed actors," among other victims of the cultural field[13]—which is the best known and most celebrated, undoubtedly because it is also the most complex and multifaceted. *Le Neveu de Rameau* was composed in the wake of the mobilization against the *Encyclopédie* that brought about the revocation of its *privilège* by Malesherbes in 1759. As its chief editor, Diderot, of course, found himself as the center of the controversies and had been singled out by Palissot in his satire.[14] He thus began his text, which recorded a conversation between the renowned composer's nephew and a figure referred to as "Moi," in the early 1760s.[15] To be sure, unlike Voltaire's and Morellet's satires, Diderot's was not offered as an explicit contribution to the debates since, as with much of his later writing, he opted not to publish it.[16] Nonetheless, it reveals the basic patterns of the other broadsides with its central definition of the nephew in terms of his efforts to survive. In fact, Diderot pushes the topos further by characterizing this "survival" not just as the scrounging for recognition and remuneration, but more fundamentally as the satisfaction of brute, primal hunger: "His first care on arising in the morning is to ascertain where he will dine; after dinner, he ponders supper."[17] The metaphorical appetite for success is translated as a raw physical craving, the initial rhetorical effect of which is to invert a system of preferences on which *gens de lettres*—and though he is a musician, we can include the nephew in this group—have traditionally sought to base their authority: their ennobling willingness to put an intellectual quest ahead of the base desire to be well housed, fed, and clothed, and thereby to suffer for their art.

But the nephew argues for the opposite. When "Moi" proposes a classic formula for undertaking "great things"—"It would be better to shut oneself up in a garret, eat a dry crust, drink plain water and try to find oneself"—he replies, "it is not in the order of things not to always have something to eat."[18] It may be tempting to chalk such a statement up with similar assertions from the period disowning the clichés historically invoked to devalorize letters as a profession. D'Alembert, for instance, qualifies his moral elevation of authorial poverty by arguing that writers do not *need* to be poor. In fact, there is no reason why they should be denied the same payoffs as those in other *états*: "why," he asks, "should a man of letters not have the same right to opulence as so many useless men?" Yet, he points out, they have a responsibility not to fear poverty: "I say only that they should not dread it," he explains in an effort to reconcile intellectual dedication and material ease.[19] Diderot's text offers no such resolution. The nephew's statement undermines his legitimacy as an *homme de lettres* by wholly identifying his activities and, indeed, his "literary" persona as a whole, with his desire to satiate his appetites. For the nephew is not struggling to survive in order to devote himself to letters, subordinating his comfort and security to the lofty goal of discovering and communicating truth. On the contrary, he devotes himself to intellectual activities in order to survive. In fact, he turns to them as a relatively *easy* way of making it compared with other options in an evolving field affording increased opportunities for "making a living" to those willing to trade on "literary" skills as writers, tutors, librarians, or secretaries, and amenable to the conversion of those skills into the social capital required for access into the households of the rich and powerful—the nephew insinuates himself into that of the financier Bertin. There, along with conversations, readings, and performances, meals were invariably served.

If we hesitate to put the nephew in the same category as the *pauvre diable*, it is due to the complexity and depth of the character, compared with the one-dimensional cartoon that Voltaire sketches. Ultimately, though, it is less that the two figures are so fundamentally different than that they do not function rhetorically in their respective texts in the same way. The figure of the poor but ambitious devil who is ready to do anything to get ahead serves as a foil against which the authority of the philosophical voice is articulated in a polemic that does not simply discredit adversaries but also expresses the preeminent stature of the philosophical perspective in the literary world. Voltaire's interlocutor, who can easily be conflated with Voltaire himself, is a self-assured, authoritative judge of talent. Calmly leading the *pauvre diable* to the realization that he would be better off as a porter, and in fact by offering him the position which happens to be in his own household, he is able to identify and impose an unambiguous distinction between authentic *gens de lettres* and those who merely pretend. The "oui-da monsieur," with which the formerly aspiring poet submissively agrees to the job, thus registers a definitive return to what is at once an intellectual and social order; the authority of the philosopher/head of the household is acknowledged by the now domestic laborer: "I will obey without retort to my master, / as a good porter should."[20]

"Moi," on the other hand, reacts very differently to the spectacle of the nephew insofar as his attention is drawn not to what separates him from the outrageous personality, but to what he, and indeed everybody else, secretly shares with him. Asked by his interlocutor what he has done since the last time they saw each other, the nephew replies: "What you and I and the rest do, namely, good and evil, and also nothing. And then I was hungry and I ate."[21] Later, as the nephew performs his famous pantomime, it is "Moi" who perceives the connection between the contortions of the nephew's dance and the behavior of all interdependent, socialized humans: "Really, what you are calling the beggar's pantomime is what makes the world go round."[22] He attempts to rescue the *philosophe* from the generalization by, like d'Alembert, emphasizing the intellectual's capacity for sacrifice and self-denial. Able to suppress his material needs and, therefore, not dependent on anyone else, the *philosophe* stands as "one human being who is exempted from the pantomime."[23] This may or may not be convincing. The fact is that it comes across as something of an afterthought and does not seem to be offered as the central truth of the dialogue. In this respect, purveying what is no doubt its key insight into human nature and society, it is the nephew whose authority is reinforced by the text more than the *Moi*, who pales before his companion, even though he is at the same time obviously meant to be the voice of the established, well-respected *philosophe*. The nephew's sardonic references to him as "monsieur le philosophe" or, more extravagantly, "monseigneur le philosophe" function as an ironic echo of the *pauvre diable*'s subservient "oui-da." Far from affirming the yawning gap that separates the socially prominent, well-off narrator from his lowly interlocutor, the phrases instead collapse the distance.

Yet, if Diderot's ambivalence makes for a more interesting read than "Le pauvre diable," the truth is that Rameau's nephew is a projection of the same polemical move underlying Voltaire's poor devil and Morellet's Palissot, that is to say, the attempt to delegitimize the adversary by depicting him in terms of his struggles to make a living. We should note, however, that while these polemics formulate a clear notion of "living by writing," they do not exclusively identify their targets with the book trade. Instead, the *anti-philosophes* stand out by the eclectic nature of their literary lives. The *pauvre diable* sets out on many paths through an array of cultural and social institutions in the hopes of finding success, including journalism, the Comédie française, and the court. So does the nephew, who also takes on a series of odd jobs, most infamously as a sham teacher of music. Neither is especially focused on making money through the sale of his productions to publishers, whether writings or compositions, and both eagerly enlist the protection of elites. They are not, in other words, satirized in the same fashion as Corneille when the latter was hit more specifically with a reputation for seeking profits in the marketplace as a way of highlighting his arrogant repudiation of the court. Philosophical propaganda cannot really be said, then, to have envisioned commercial publication as an "alternative," even a dramatically devalorized one, to the established intellectual field that was organized around the sociability of elites.

However, this discourse works out a nexus of key ideas. For one, it thematizes the *anti-philosophes'* exclusion from the valorizing cultural spaces of the Old Regime field by pointedly associating this dislocation with a driving ambition to succeed, which calls attention to their exclusion and, in turn, guarantees it, as their feverish efforts of self-promotion ultimately disqualify them for *mondaine* integration. At one level, their ambition points to the obstacles that initially block advancement, which are, ultimately, their personal deficiencies, including their lack of talent, protectors, and resources. At another, it weakens their claims to legitimacy by compromising their motives and highlighting their self-interest. In this sense, it is the desire to be integrated into the cultural field that prevents their integration, a paradox figured in images of the *anti-philosophes'* hapless tendencies to undermine themselves. The motif, for instance, of their fawning efforts to ingratiate themselves with protectors underscores the unbridgeable chasm separating them from the elites whom they address. Rameau's nephew, constantly eyeing ways to serve the powerful, is allowed by a *grand seigneur*'s coachman on occasion to spend the night on a bed of hay next to his horses.[24] More than anything, such a "reward"—coming moreover not from the patron him or herself, but from a subordinate—points to the unrewardability of its recipient. And if they do obtain protection, it is by extravagant flattery, which discredits both writer and the patron moved to support him. In a satirical dossier from 1762 entitled *Anecdotes sur Fréron écrites par un homme de lettres à un magistrat qui voulait être instruit des moeurs de cet homme*, Voltaire relates how the journalist's circular, *Lettres sur quelques écrits de ce temps*, was suspended for an article on Ninon de Lenclos then reauthorized after Fréron "groveled before Solignac, a secretary to the King of Poland and like him [Fréron], an ex-Jesuit."[25]

But if groveling is the most prevalent trope in the rhetorical association of ambition and social exclusion, images of literary commerce figure prominently as well. In the *Anecdotes sur Fréron*, Voltaire goes on to describe his adversary's treachery toward both his collaborator at the *Lettres sur quelques écrits de ce temps*, the abbé de la Porte, whom he forces to agree to unfair terms—"in doing a quarter of the page, I want to be paid as if I had done a half of it"—and the publisher of the paper, Duchesne: "He secretly struck a deal with the bookseller Lambert; and neglecting his agreement with Duchesne, he withdrew the sheets from the latter." "There is a printed *mémoire*," Voltaire continues, "in which Duchesne complains about Fréron's deceit."[26] The actual situation was murkier than this. Duchesne's published reply appears not as a "mémoire," which might imply that the *libraire* had taken legal action against Fréron, but as an *Avis* printed in the thirteenth installment of the *Lettres*. What is more, the text does not actually accuse Fréron of any dishonesty, but more prudently offers Duchesne's regret at Fréron's decision to take his periodical to a competing publisher, Lambert, while expressing the hope that the journalist might return in the future to Duchesne's print shop. In fact, François Cornou argues that Fréron was entirely justified in turning to Lambert since, he contends, Duchesne's terms—"typical evidence of the tyranny exercised by publishers towards authors"—were cutthroat.[27] In any case, the point is not whether Fréron's behavior vis-à-vis his publisher was honorable or not, but the salience of Voltaire's distortion of history, which highlights his recourse to the thematics of commercial activities as an effective way of underscoring Fréron's desire for self-promotion. Or more exactly, Voltaire's invective, in turning to the language of the market, postulates this desire as the driving force of Fréron's literary life, upholding it as a raw and primary urge, which can as such then exhaustively explain his involvement in letters. As a writer, Fréron was thus defined by literary commerce.

Raw Commerce and the Sublimation of Reality

In a discussion of the phenomenon of *mécénat* in the early modern period in which he distinguishes the practice from other types of clientelistic or service-based relations between intellectuals and elites, Daniel Roche emphasizes the alchemistic power of the noble patron who, by his magnanimity rather than any self-interested motive, deploys his resources to "protect" a writer as a "magician who transforms real capital into symbolic capital."[28] This protection might take the form of a gratification or a pension bestowed on the writer, the primary value of which consists not in the economic worth that it stores—in reality, such tokens offer relatively small amounts compared with other sources of remuneration—but in the prestige it conveys as a sign of the writer's favor with the aristocrat. This overshadowing of the "real" by the "symbolic" exemplifies, Roche argues, "the reign of euphemism in the relation of intellectuals to money," inasmuch as its principal operation is to stylize an underlying reality—a base one in which writers must earn income to feed themselves—through a discourse that extirpates such banality from the system of cultural practices by representing its agents as driven only by noble ideals: the glory of producing great works, on one hand, and the generosity to support such endeavors, on the other. Indeed, Roche argues that patronage, as an "objective reality," is inseparable from a discourse that constantly imputes such motives to writer and protector, obfuscating any other possible reasons for the enterprise as a whole.

Roche's own argumentation, however, rests on a similar association of the real and symbolic whose articulation he is analyzing. His assumption is that, while glory and generosity are situated in the realm of stylized discourse, the intellectual's "relation to money" is a nondiscursive "raw" truth that the language of patronage then endeavors to veil. Yet the polemics of the *philosophes* against their enemies illustrate that, as with the case of Corneille, writers' contacts with money are just as stylized and overdetermined, no matter how "raw" they might appear. The "reality" of these contacts, consisting in the participation of *gens de lettres* in interactions whose logic is narrowly identified with the imperative of self-interest, material benefit, and personal profit, is no less inseparable from the representation of this reality in texts and images that establish value systems and impute motives than is, according to Roche, the "objective reality" of patronage. To be sure, a key difference lies in the oppositional nature of the relation between discourse and reality in the case of commerce. For the writer's "relation to money" is almost always the effect of a decidedly negative polemic. In contrast with the hyperbolic, encomiastic language of patronage, such "anti-idealization" might well be what gives early modern depictions of writers and money a distinct impression of "realism." But this is misleading, for the negativity is most certainly not a gauge of the transparency of the discourse with respect to the "real lives" of the writers involved.

At the same time, the cases of Corneille and the *philosophes* must be differentiated according to the distinct stakes driving the respective polemics. For in laying claim to their status as *gens de lettres*, Corneille's critics played up their civility and aptitude for life in *le monde*, which they defined against Corneille's uncouth arrogance as this was projected in images of the playwright's singular focus on his commercial success. For their part, the *philosophes* advanced a more complex claim to legitimacy. Certainly, they undertook to integrate themselves into a polite society that had evolved directly from the court and salon culture of the seventeenth century. They sought intimacy with social and cultural elites; but the intellectual authority by which they gained acceptance into high society was not envisioned in terms of their ability to please such a refined audience by their wit and grace. Rather, it was conceived on the basis of a philosophical autonomy that was defined against the increasingly discredited principle of *plaire*, yet which remained polite enough to be accepted anyway—even embraced—as a critical voice by at least an influential enough segment of those same notables whose social and political worlds were targeted in philosophical discourse.

Philosophical authority was, in other words, the effect of a fragile balancing act. It rested, as we saw in Chapter 2, on the intellectual's ability to define himself in and through a discrepancy between what he said and what he did, on the basis of a claim to autonomy from elite society, the credibility of which was, in fact, rooted in the *philosophe*'s prior acculturation in *le monde*. It rested, too, on his ability to mask this discrepancy, precisely with the rhetorical and social skills that he denied having: his knack for mobilizing behind him an audience of the privileged and the powerful, not despite his willingness to critique but *because* of it. Signaled by the *philosophe*'s incorporation into such institutions as the salon and the Académie, the embrace by elite culture of his critical voice established him as a recognized intellectual whose "seriousness" resided in his willingness, as an outsider with no stakes in *le monde*, to unleash his talents against authority and tradition. It figures, then, that those who would take on the *philosophes* as their opponents would do so not only on ideological grounds by calling attention to their materialism, irreligion, or anti-authoritarianism, but also by probing this inconsistency and bringing into the light of day the true elite social foundation of an authority asserted to be fundamentally nonsocial and non-elite.

Thus, in Palissot's satire, as well as being amoral, relativist sensualists, the *philosophes* are portrayed as vapid flatterers preying on the modish obsessions of *femmes du monde* who treat them like stars. Their "authority" consists, first, in their audacity to interpret such accolades as meaningful emblems of consecration: "Believing themselves to form a Court with admirers," says the principal character Damis, as he observes with bemusement the philosophical takeover of the household of Cydalise, a pretentious would-be salonnière who is also the mother of the women with whom he is in love.[29] They then seize for themselves the right to judge on such a categorically false basis. Simon-Henri-Nicolas Linguet, writing in a 1764 text against philosophical "fanaticism," highlights the hollowness of the independence that was to substantiate the *philosophes*' rhetoric. Rejecting the latter's professed readiness to endure poverty and isolation—"they vainly applaud themselves for their disinterest"—he renders them as hypocrites: "men who, having been able to make a happy life and to free themselves of all the responsibilities of Society, elegantly perorate on the ways in which others must shoulder them," and implores them to cease eulogizing "the solitude that they seem to want to protect, and the disinterest for greatness that they affect so extravagantly."[30]

The *philosophes*' legitimacy thus hung in the balance, for it was rooted in an autonomy from social elites that was not, in and of itself, an objective reality but was an image of a reality that had to be imposed both in the face of circumstances that did not necessarily conform to it—namely, the *philosophes*' relations with elites—and over the increasing objections of "adversaries" who were only too eager to expose the conhadiction. It was, therefore, as an essential part of the rhetorical effort to make this independence "real" that a discourse of literary commerce assumed a central place in the vocabulary of the *philosophes*, hence not only in order to discredit their critics for their ambitiousness but also in order to rationalize their own identities as *gens de lettres* who operated almost entirely in the social arena of *le monde*. Invoked as a motive, money highlighted the profundity of the gap separating the writer from his goal of integration into the cultural field. Furthermore, money did not just inscribe his exclusion, but foregrounded his efforts to overcome that exclusion. These, however, did not valorize the writer. On the contrary, as they manifested a desire for payment, the writer's efforts to succeed were inevitably desperate and outlandish, and invariably drove him into dishonest and degrading behavior. Hence they underscored the unreasonable, even aberrant quality of an intellectual aspiration that was ready to buy its success with flattery or with the money earned through hucksterism. We can recall in this light the nephew's infamous lesson to his son on the significance of gold: "Gold, gold is everything; and everything, without gold, is nothing."[31]

Pointed images highlighting "le rapport de l'intellectuel à l'argent," to quote Roche, served to show, then, that the writer's social exclusion was in the natural order of things. If he was at all focused on earning money in order to succeed, his failure was, by this very fact, inevitable and well deserved. By contrast, the absence of money, as it was variously emphasized in the self-representational discourses of the *philosophes*, whether in the noble posturing of a Voltaire refusing to accept payment or in d'Alembert's assertions that he would rather be poor than stoop to flattery, projected the legitimacy of the *philosophes*' inclusion. Not that they wanted to be there. Ostensibly, they did not. Nonetheless, their presence was merited. It was not forced by extravagant efforts but was "naturally" rooted, on one hand, in the depth of their insights and in the inarguability of their talents as purveyors of these insights—"Oh, if I only had your talent," says the nephew to Moi—and on the other, in the demand generated by their intellectual qualities with a rarefied public whose self-conscious exclusivity was increasingly expressed in its enlightened taste for philosophical critique. If the *philosophes* engaged elites, it was in spite of themselves, not because they had tried to get there or sought to please its gatekeepers. They were, as d'Alembert and Duclos had observed, "sought out." And in the face of this unasked-for high society interest, the *philosophes* could express a studied, coy reluctance, which served to emphasize further their pretense to being outsiders to *le monde*. "Don't think I speak well. I can only tell the truth and, as you know, that doesn't always go down," Moi responds, assuming a complicated but characteristic position as both socially integrated and socially inept.[32]

Against the countermodel of the nephew, with his outsized ambitions and his ridiculous money and food obsessions, such a pretense, contrary to reality and as wide open to criticism and mockery as it might be, could nonetheless at least seem a plausible claim to intellectual identity. And as I have been arguing throughout, it is the plausibility of such an assertion rather than its absolute veracity that is key, which is to say its ability to prevail over competing or conflicting claims. By the same token, if a wave of writers, adopting Rousseau as their hero, imposed a new ideal of literary identity rooted in a stark vision of the writer's social dislocation and formulated against an image of the well-heeled and now "hypocritical" *philosophe*, it is to the degree that such an image became more persuasive to an audience increasingly likely to digest the assertions of legitimacy on which it rested. The believability of these claims rested largely on the symbolic power of images conveying the writer's involvement in the commercialization of his texts, appropriated, more than invented by intellectual outsiders as familiar signals of their distance from elite culture. "Living by the pen" is an expression—and a mechanism—of the rhetorical shift.

Living by the Pen: Social Autonomy and Commercial Publication

"Wanting to be independent, I relied only on my pen," declares Jacques-Pierre Brissot in the opening lines of the *Mémoires* that he wrote as he awaited the guillotine. Meant to underscore his commitment to the three ideals that inspired his writings—a love of glory and humanity, and a hatred of despotism—the statement purports to establish his credibility as he undertakes in this critical final hour the apology of his life in letters and politics. But the simplicity of the image is deceptive, loaded with a history that inflects it in a specific way. In the polemics of the *philosophes* the motif presented itself as a thematization of the inaptness of their critics for a respectable place in the world of letters. In "Le pauvre diable," Voltaire describes Fréron as having "on his pen . . . founded his cuisine."[33] This is hardly how the concept has been invoked by Old Regime cultural historians for whom "living by the pen" signifies the ability of writers—"finally"—to live off of the sale of their writings to publishers after centuries of underpayment or nonpayment in the commercial sphere. "Living by the pen" has consequently been viewed as a generally positive phenomenon. At one level, it projects the "liberation" of writers from their economic reliance on patrons, and thus, in the manner indicated by Brissot, their assumption of a newfound intellectual autonomy. At another level, it refers to the ascendancy of writing as the basis of a real profession, in a constructive sense, as a respectable, legitimate way to earn a "decent living." None of this is implied by Voltaire's satire of Fréron, nor by the broader characterizations of the "unfortunate species that writes in order to survive [qui écrit pour vivre]" in his *Questions sur l'Encyclopédie* and other texts.[34] In such discourse, the essential qualitative distinction emphasized is, as we have seen, less between a commercially and patronage derived income than between a literary activity driven by ambition versus one valorized by disinterest. Moreover, if this language does establish the former distinction as well—in that the ambitious writer is more inclined to accept the easy revenues of commerce while the disinterested writer, playing a wholly different game, is more likely to draw on the support of a prestigious patron—it is clearly not in order to celebrate the freedom that comes with a market-based compensation against the humiliating constraints of having to please a protector for a pension.

It is, instead, used in a much more negative sense to evoke not greater opportunities for the writer to be supported in his activities, but fewer. To describe a writer as "living by the pen" in the mid-eighteenth century is, in most cases, to evoke the obstacles that blocked his advancement in the cultural field, and his failure to acquire something more legitimate. Commercially derived income was in its essence a fallback. We can see this in the files of the police inspector Joseph d'Hémery, who between the years 1748 and 1753 compiled dossiers on over 500 active *gens de lettres* working in Paris. Among the myriad details that he recorded, along with age, height, and current address, he noted, in many cases, how they earned their keep. Most of the *gens de lettres*, by a long shot, were supported in the standard ways for the time, as Darnton points out in his well-known study.[35] They enjoyed posts at court, in the Church, or in aristocratic households where they might be tutors, secretaries, or librarians. They were the beneficiaries of pensions, and many forged their way as lawyers. Given the preponderance of what we might call noncommercial livelihoods—livelihoods that do not hinge on selling works to publishers—Darnton argues that the market is "conspicuous by its absence" in the files, and there is a great deal of truth to this. But it should be noted that the market is not entirely missing. In fact, a handful of writers are reported by the inspector to support themselves through the sale of their works, generally with a variant on the expression "vivre de" or 'live off," and it is worth exploring in some detail how this condition was described by an attentive observer of eighteenth-century literary life.

In one representative case, d'Hémery's dossier on a twenty-eight-year-old lawyer from Senlis named Gaillard records that "at present, lives off his works."[36] This observation seems straightforward enough, but the use of the expression is actually weighted with unsuspected meaning. For in the world portrayed by d'Hémery's files, a writer did not simply "live off his works" as a matter of innocent choice or as the effect of opportunities.

Far from it, this circumstance was invariably represented as the outcome of an unlucky trajectory according to which the writer in question had either fallen out of a more established position or been locked out of one from the beginning. As it turns out, Gaillard is in the first category. If he "lives off his works," it is only after a series of short-lived stints in more "official" posts. Thus he was a librarian at the Collège des quatre nations but quit that position when Voltaire found him a job as a "tutor of children." He did not last long in this capacity: "he only stayed there for six months," d'Hémery notes, after which point—*à présent*—"he lives off his works." A writer named de la Barre from Normandy follows a similar route in d'Hémery's files toward reliance on income from publication. Originally "holding a position as a *Controlleur de l'extraordinaire des guerres*," de la Barre had to sell this office due to unspecified "misfortunes . . . such that he now finds himself in ghastly poverty." As a result, with no other resources to fall back on, "he has given himself over wholly to La Billiot"—a Parisian *libraire*—"who supports him [qui le fait vivre] and for whom he produces from time to time small works that La Billiot sells."[37]

D'Hémery's references to the phenomenon of "living by the pen," scattered as they are, show nonetheless consistently a condition characterized not by the writer's resolve to make a "decent living" but in a sense the opposite, by the impossibility of doing so. "Living by the pen" was a last recourse. In a dossier on the two brothers Parfaict, "gentlemen" who "have no wealth," d'Hémery's observation that the would-be novelists and playwrights "only live off their works [ne vivent que de leurs ouvrages]" bolsters the image with the restrictive negative construction "ne . . . que": they do not live, except off their works.[38] Indeed, throughout the inspector's files, reliance on writing for the book trade consigns one, above all, to a qualitative void. In this sense, the "literary market" takes shape not as a field of potential autonomy for the writer but as a space defined by lack of distinction. It emerges discursively as a way to conceptualize a literary career that is not supported by prestige-endowing income and connections. Conversely, a writer who acquires some kind of gratification or finally lands a reputable post in an aristocratic household or with an official journal no longer lives by the pen. In an update to the file, d'Hémery records De la Barre's reintegration into the fold of the Old Regime cultural field: "M. Bouyer found for him a small appointment [commission] at the Gazette de France, with M. des Meslée."[39]

There has been much discussion of the eighteenth-century market as a space defined by its absorption of writers who had been excluded from more respectable prospects. Such a conception has fueled two interrelated accounts regarding the evolution of the literary field in this period. The first focuses on a demographic crunch according to which a growing number of aspirants to what Duclos called "considération" found themselves in greater competition for the limited positions that would lead to such distinction. Though these positions—academic seats, salon memberships, sinecures as tutors, secretaries, or librarians in aristocratic households—were also increasing in number, they were doing so at a decidedly lower rate.[40] The result was an exploding population of ambitious *gens de lettres* who were frozen out of the pathways to cultural prominence. One outcome, as Darnton's influential work on the "Literary Underground" has forcefully argued, was an intensifying bitterness among excluded writers toward those occupying the coveted posts, as well as an acute sense of the uncrossable divide separating insiders from outsiders, a dynamic that, in turn, played a large role in the ferment leading up to the Revolution, whose protagonists would largely come out of the ranks of the angry and marginalized intellectuals.[41] The second narrative follows from the first, when those excluded *gens de lettres*, with nothing to fall back on but the "menial work available in the Enlightenment print trade," then constitute a pool of desperate laborers for profiteering publishers to exploit.[42] Darnton writes, "while the mandarins fattened themselves on pensions, most authors sank into a sort of literary proletariat."[43] Roche adopts the same charged language, describing the formation of a "proletariat of parasites who dream of higher destinies," with the essential point being that those writers who came to depend for their livelihood on what they could earn by selling their wares to booksellers fared very badly.[44] As a holding pen for *littérateurs* who, "lacking positions and pensions," were not able to gain a foothold in the eighteenth-century cultural field, the literary market evolved as a space in which they were inevitably abused and descended into crushing poverty.

There is, of course, good reason to accept that life in the eighteenth-century market was not very comfortable, a view that becomes apparent in the dossiers of the inspector. François-Vincent Toussaint, "a lawyer in the Parlement who does not practice," comes to depend on the sale of his writings to publishers, and this leaves him in difficult straits: "He works a lot for publishers, which means that he is not so well off [il n'est pas trop a son aise]." But d'Hémery's imputation of causality in the entry might be misleading. He suggests that Toussaint's poverty is the result of his dependence on the book trade. This may be the case with the writer in question, but it would be a mistake to generalize from the one instance, and assume that dependence on publishers, in and of itself, invariably entailed poverty. D'Hémery's files depict another young Norman who specializes in works of criticism: "He sells them himself," reports the inspector, "and only lives off this [et n'a que cela pour vivre]."[45] But here the deprecating "ne . . . que" is deceptive since the writer in question is none other than the abbé de la Porte, the one-time associate of Linguet, who would become notorious for his widely disparaged yet extremely profitable publishing ventures. Grimm's *Correspondance littéraire* estimates in 1769 that de la Porte earned about 5,000 to 6,000 livres a year as the producer of varied print-trade products such as compilations, almanacs, and travel journals.[46] Seven years later, Pidansat de Mairobert upped that figure to around 10,000 to 12,000 livres.[47] These sums were easily competitive with the most generous pensions that writers might hope to obtain either from the state or through other noncommercial, prestige-oriented sources.[48]

To be sure, d'Hémery's report was from twenty years earlier, and certainly the younger de la Porte, in his early thirties and having recently quit the Jesuits to make a life for himself in literature, was faring less remarkably well in those early days. According to Pidansat de Mairobert, the abbé left the Compagnie "naked as a worm."[49] Still, the disparity between what seems an unmistakably positive trajectory through the market and the decidedly negative articulation of the abbé's exclusive dependence on book trade income in d'Hémery's papers—"il n'a que cela pour vivre"—remains striking. For one thing, success came relatively quickly to de la Porte. He may have entered the fray with next to nothing, but he did not spend too many years toiling in indigence. At about the time that the inspector was recording his impressions around 1749 or 1750, de la Porte enjoyed a modest breakthrough with a work of criticism entitled *Voyage au séjour des ombres*, published in 1749, with re-editions in 1751 and 1753, and mentioned by d'Hémery himself in the dossier.[50] For another, even at the height of his successes, de le Porte continued to be scorned as a literary nonentity who inhabited the outer fringes of the Enlightenment-era cultural field. La Harpe's 1780 obituary in his *Correspondance littéraire* conveys the derision: "The abbé de la Porte died a short time ago yet his death did not receive much more attention that did his life." La Harpe continues, "however, he was a man who published many books."[51]

De la Porte's file calls for more precision in defining the eighteenth-century book trade as an authorial field. To begin with, it suggests that we be more careful in distinguishing from "real" poverty defined by actual material deprivation, a symbolic poverty resulting not from a dearth of income or necessities, but from a lack of prestige. Moreover, inasmuch as this symbolic poverty is so often figured by images of material want—recall the nephew's hunger—it suggests as well that we take special care to distinguish from real poverty a representation of real poverty that is not a transparent window onto the writer's destitution but a sign of his exclusion within the networks of the Old Regime cultural world. Images of want and need, mobilized to identify the writer's *symbolic* poverty, do not necessarily imply *economic* poverty. And while d'Hémery's "il n'a que cela pour vivre" sounds as if it describes de la Porte's financial hardships, the phrase actually records a lack of stature that is, in fact, not inconsistent with a comfortable living earned by writing. Similarly, Voltaire's representations of Fréron as a writer who "scribbled on paper for money" and "was dying of hunger" would seem to mark the journalist's struggles just to make ends meet, an impression that is further reinforced by the shadowy demeanor of Frélon in *L'Ecossaise* lurking in cafés and complaining about his lot—"I barely make enough to live on"—and indirectly, by the troubles of the *pauvre diable*.[52] But the truth is that, notwithstanding the rhetoric, Fréron was not poor by any reasonable measure, and although he would be tainted by debt-related difficulties that were the result of his profligate spending, he made a "decent living," enjoying healthy receipts from subscriptions to the popular *Année littéraire*. He built himself a country house outside the gates of Paris, and was known for the lavish dinners that he would give: "he received people with the luxury of a tax-farmer."[53]

Accounts that underscore the indigence of writers who found themselves more dependent than others on publishing income have, then, undoubtedly been too quick to accept at face value eighteenth-century depictions of authorial poverty that were born not of the desire to give an objective picture of the "real" conditions of writers in the book trade but of polemics aimed at orienting perceptions of these conditions, and above all, of the *philosophes*' campaign to discredit those who opposed their agenda and claims to authority.[54] In the process, such accounts have, if not missed entirely, then certainly downplayed as inessential or anomalous the basic truth the stories of de la Porte and Fréron illuminate, namely the rising viability of constructing a more or less comfortable life in letters without recourse to extensive elite support. They thus indicate the opposite of what they are usually thought to show, which is the impossibility of a "decent" life in an intellectual field thought to be radically divided between those with and without protection and positions. D'Hémery's files then require us to nuance our earlier conclusions. For they ultimately portray the "market" not simply as a place with no distinction, but more exactly as a place with no distinction that could nonetheless support continued literary activity; that allowed writers with no patronage and no connections to go on writing and publishing, and in so doing laying claim to the prestige of an *homme de lettres*, even as they lacked the markers conventionally expected for such assertions. In fact, the market allowed writers to construct entire careers in these conditions. Those of Fréron and de la Porte were not only lucrative but long, durable, and productive. La Harpe's sneering comment that de la Porte published "a lot of books" is obviously proffered as a nullification of the latter's identity as an intellectual. But at some level it is a paradoxical slight, resting on the fact that de la Porte was able not just to publish works, but to publish a huge number of them. The opportunities were there, even as he lacked the symbolic payoffs. His entry in Michaud's *Biographie universelle* counts, in addition to his copious journalistic work and his many compilations, 16 titles appearing between 1749 and 1777.[55] The entry for Linguet, who figures prominently in Darnton's "Literary Underground," includes 53 works alongside his periodical writings, spanning thirty-two years, of which 46 were published prior to 1789.[56] Another important outsider, Louis-Sébastien Mercier, boasts a bibliography of over 120 items written in the course of half a century.[57]

This sustainability was the result of two factors, the first being the simple truth that the possibilities were out there, even if the prevailing rhetoric tended to conceal them. Nonetheless, the length and productivity of such careers as those of Fréron, de la Porte and Linguet point to a surge of prospects rather than a lack thereof. These writers are hardly evidence of the "proletarianization" of unpensioned writers sinking into desperation, but, as Elizabeth Eisenstein and other critics of the "Literary Underground" thesis argue, they illustrate the existence of a midlevel field of opportunities in which *gens de lettres* who were not destined to occupy positions of prominence could ply their trades anyway, and for considerably more than a minimal, starvation-level wage. They could in fact lead "relatively secure" lives based on the earnings from their unglamorous labors.[58] Eisenstein stresses the abundance of opportunities for gainful employment, especially abroad in the cities of northern Europe such as Amsterdam, London, and Brussels, and in what Darnton called the fertile crescent running along the northeastern border of France, an area in which typographical societies serving the market for French-language books were clustered just out of the juridical reach of the French authorities. Such options, Eisenstein argues, allowed "writers who never got pensions [. . . to avoid] sinking into the Parisian lower depths." As journalists, editors, translators, popularizers, and compilers, and as authors of innumerable historical, scientific, philosophical, polemical, religious, and imaginative works, they "propagated the Enlightenment without starving or turning to crime."[59]

The second factor is at once less and more obvious: more because it would appear to go without saying, but less because, compared with the tangible and well-rehearsed developments that can broadly be identified as the growth of the book trade, its effect has been less appreciated. This is quite simply the willingness of these writers to avail themselves of the new possibilities described by Eisenstein and others. It is the critical variable, though, whose effect determines in a more profound way the formation and evolution of the literary market. For to suggest that the development of the book trade and the demand for literary labor is the key factor for the history of the market is to write this history in terms of a tipping point. That is, writers "live by the pen"—or at least endeavor to do so—at a precise moment when the book trade becomes lucrative enough to make such a thing viable. But as we have seen, this moment turns out to be desperately elusive. Its historical coherence as a point in time is undermined by two apparently contradictory facts: first, the existence of lucrative opportunities in the book trade from the earliest days of the printing press, of which writers were well aware and whose benefits they indeed did seek to maximize through savvy, commercially driven behavior, even in the "prehistory of *droit d'auteur*"; and second, the failure of most writers today to "live by the pen," manifest in the widespread need to supplement their publishing income with revenues from other more profitable activities such as teaching, journalism, and criticism.[60] Both facts problematize not only the conventional placement of the "tipping point" in the eighteenth century, but more significantly, the very notion that there existed such a pivotal moment in the history of authorship.

In this respect, the transition from patronage to the market, which has emerged as a powerful signifier of "modernization" in literary practices, must be sought elsewhere: not in the increasing availability of opportunities to make money by writing, nor, we might add, simply in the readiness of writers to cash in on those opportunities, a phenomenon that can be discerned in earlier times. The transition lies in a more complex mental evolution, by which the willingness to go on is not just a willingness to avail oneself of commercial prospects but also a willingness to lay claim to the privileged identity of an intellectual with nothing to show in support of the assertion other than the outcome of these efforts, namely a record of published writings. The transition to intellectual "modernity" lies in the writer's willingness to present himself as an *homme de lettres* based on, rather than in spite of, what in principle were nonvalorized activities, and as such based on the writer's total *dependence* on the book trade. Moreover, if it seemed to place the writer squarely in the book trade, this willingness was in fact not directly about the publishing industry per se. It was instead about a new attitude toward outsiderhood embraced as the foundation of an emerging ideal of legitimacy, one formulated in strident opposition to the model of the socially beholden insider exemplified by the *philosophe*. This new attitude impelled the individual seeking credibility to proclaim rather than conceal his connections with and investments in commercial publication. If the shift seems to indicate a move into the market, even in a physical sense—suddenly we see the writer in the book trade—in truth, his presence there is the effect of the integration of these connections into his self-presentation as a key factor of his legitimacy.

Failure, Poverty, and the Menace of Respectability

Essential as it is, the willingness to "live by the pen" has eluded probing analysis because the traditional emphasis on the growth of the book trade as the key determinant presumes that it goes without saying. Such a conjecture rests on the parallel assumption that eighteenth-century writers "naturally" preferred the independence of the marketplace to reliance on aristocratic protection, which, it is further assumed, they experienced negatively, as a need to adjust, alter, or disfigure their writings in the demeaning effort to please a benefactor. Accordingly, when it was possible to support themselves with income derived from publication, they are assumed to have chosen the "freer" alternative without thinking twice about it. We have seen, however, that eighteenth-century discourse on literary life hardly reflects the notion that the writer's willingness to "live by the pen" was a default posture merely waiting for the right circumstances in which it might be adopted. The most consistent representation of this "willingness" lay in the image of a stubborn, deluded choice made by the luckless hack who continued to devote himself to letters despite repeated failures to reap any of the rewards or achieve any of the goals that would justify such dedication, and despite the availability of other more "practical" or "reasonable" options for employment. The choice to go on was, in other words, viewed as a decidedly aberrant one. It was the effect of blind, irrational persistence, dramatized as illness by Alexis Piron in his 1738 comedy: "la métromanie" referred to a feverish addiction to poetry.[61] "The sickness took me," the *pauvre diable* had explained to his interlocutor in Voltaire's satire, describing his propensity to pursue career options leading to penury, abuse, and anonymity over not wealth but the comfort and security attainable by a more sensible, clearheaded course.

Linguet develops what seems a similar diagnosis in a pamphlet from 1768 entitled *L'aveu sincère ou lettre à une mère sur les dangers que court la jeunesse en se livrant à un goût trop vif pour la littérature*: "Tell me, what is the life of a man of letters? What can he expect from his efforts, if not an unbearable obscurity?"[62] At one level, Linguet's text takes up the *pauvre diable* theme in accentuating the futility of literature as a livelihood, which means as compensation for the lack of symbolic and financial capital. For "young people born into an obscure condition," who must "attend to the well-being [le repos] of their families" and who then turn to letters as a means of enhancing their status and income, the prospects are grim. Channeling Voltaire, Linguet defines his goal to steer impressionable youth toward more respectable and remunerative activities. Mercier echoes the sentiment in the *Tableau de Paris*: "the most deplorable condition is to cultivate letters without personal fortune; yet this is the lot of the great number of *littérateurs*; they are almost all doing battle against fate [aux prises avec la fortune]."[63] He too exhorts that one avoid the literary path that he himself followed: "he who does not find himself freed from need [au-dessus du besoin] must be wary of wanting to earn his living by the pen [fonder sa subsistence sur la plume]."[64]

To be sure, if this cautionary discourse takes up the motif of the hopelessness of letters as an "état," it does so from a significantly different vantage point, which is that of sympathy rather than scorn for the struggling writer. Indeed, Mercier chastises Voltaire, who, "instead of making fun of poor writers in his *Pauvre diable* might have done better to bring them relief with a part of his wealth."[65] In fact, Voltaire could be generous toward literary newcomers if he deemed them worthy combatants in the battle against *l'infâme*. That, however, is less the issue than Mercier's self-conscious positioning in opposition to the *philosophe*'s contempt for the outsider. For underlying the gesture is an entirely new claim to credibility. Voltaire's admonitory portrait of the *pauvre diable* served to legitimize intellectually the *mondaine* integration of the *philosophe* through a representation of the effortlessness of the latter's social inclusion, in contrast with the ridiculous flailings of the mediocre marginal writer. By contrast, Linguet and Mercier show the exclusion of writers to reflect positive attributes, even as it is similarly figured by their struggles to make a living. Thus the outsiders of the literary sphere are in Mercier's view valorized as "modest, studious men of merit" by the same prodigious efforts that for the *philosophes* manifested their mediocrity.[66] Moreover, they are valorized not just by the efforts themselves, but by their fruitlessness, which no longer signifies the writer's lack of talent but translates an even more extraordinary dedication in impossible circumstances. The exorbitant struggles of the marginal writer evoke a heroic readiness to forfeit all security, comfort, and reputation for the literary project, a sacrifice that then certifies his virtue as the linchpin of a new identity: "if he escaped all the traps and conserved his dignity as a man of letters," notes Mercier, "he will be able to say boldly to his compatriots: *I had the courage that comes with a love for virtue.*"[67]

Illustrating in Voltaire's satires a disconcerting lack of lucidity in one who kept writing and publishing despite repeated rejection, the willingness to go on now emanates from the singularity of an individual who brought to his intellectual undertaking an uncommon devotion, one measured by the extent of the deprivation that his own commitment ultimately forced him to endure: "The poverty of the man of letters is, undoubtedly, a title of virtue," writes Mercier.[68] If it is tempting to see a parallel with d'Alembert's elevation of poverty and failure in his "Essai sur les gens de lettres," we are in fact dealing with two entirely different figurations of the refusal of self-interest as a gauge of intellectual credibility. D'Alembert's rallying cry for writers is rooted in confidence and pseudo-aristocratic detachment. It projects a courageous dedication to the truth, but the dictum records a potential more than an actuality. Urging the writer not to fear loss, d'Alembert of course assumes that the writer has something to lose. In addition, as we saw, he is quick to point out that advising resoluteness in the face of potential poverty is not tantamount to insisting that writers must be poor. On the contrary, he embraces the notion that *gens de lettres* have every right to enjoy the rewards of their endeavors without this necessarily undermining their honor or the value of that work.

For Mercier, by contrast, the writer's poverty represents not a possible loss but a dispossession from the beginning. It is most decidedly not an articulation of stoic indifference to the pleasures of an exclusive society in the midst of which he finds himself, but is the effect of a primary and permanent exclusion from that milieu. As such, the valorized writer's condition consists not in hypothetical poverty as proof of his detachment from worldly entertainments, but in an actual, viscerally real want. And more than anything, perhaps, it is this concrete and pressing *reality* that the exorbitance and futility of the marginal writer's efforts are designed to underscore, especially as evoked in stark opposition to the actual ease of the *philosophes*' lives and thus to the underlying *nonreality* of their difficulties, as well as to the galling pretense of any claim otherwise: "What a difference it makes to cultivate letters as does M. de Voltaire," writes Mercier, "with a hundred thousand livres of income, rather than having to do battle with the most pressing needs and to fall back on one's misfortunes, when one should enjoy a free mind [un esprit libre], liberated of worry, to abandon oneself entirely to the meditation of one's art."[69] Brissot similarly affirms in his *Mémoires*: "Helvétius and Montesquieu were rich, and did not draw any income from their important productions. It was easy for them to spend the time necessary in order to make them perfect."[70] Highlighting the facile posturing of the *philosophes*' self-presentation—it is, of course, easier to live *as if* one does not care about money when one has plenty of it—as a way of accentuating the ineluctable fact of their own crushing poverty, such declarations establish their superior dedication as intellectuals; they project a more profound rejection of self-interest in the name of truth, and thus a deeper virtue and a more genuine authority to speak out in its name.

The problem, through, is that self-professed marginal writers did not, in fact, live any less "as if" than did the *philosophes*. They, too, formulated their claims to legitimacy and authority out of a critical gap that lay between what they asserted about themselves in their writings and the conditions in which they actually lived and wrote, even if the nature of the discrepancy was different. For if the "reality" of the lives of Mercier, Fréron, Linguet, and other marginals was not defined by their integration into the most valorized elite networks, nor was it shaped by crushing poverty and exclusion, as we have seen. Rather, it was characterized by precisely the kind of "decent living" that it has long been argued was impossible for writers to attain in this period, which is to say by a degree of respectability and material comfort, generally enabled by the protection of particular nobles. Such writers may not have been fêted by European monarchs or invited into the salons of fashionable Parisian society. They spent time in the Bastille (as did Voltaire) and found themselves displaced, on the run, and living abroad outside the reach of French authorities. But this did not mean that they were destitute. Their failure to reach the summits of literary life in Paris as stars in high society salons, privileged confidants of kings and empresses, or academicians did not relegate them to complete anonymity and misery.

In fact, it would be absurd to conclude that it did, for how could they have continued to foster and express ambitions without some kind of platform of modest "success" from which to do so? Utter failure would, it seems, be tantamount to utter silence: a lack of access to publication, no income, and a *real* as opposed to a proclaimed decision to give up and move on to something else. But it is a moderate success—defined not by glory or celebrity but simply by an ability and willingness to continue writing and publishing—that stands out as the effective cause behind their self-presentations as intellectuals confronting dire poverty, not actual poverty itself. Ironically, then, it is their modest success, their adequate, sustainable results, that allowed them to go on producing images of their failures and of the unsustainability of their lives, images destined not to paint an accurate picture of their careers but to legitimize careers that were in the end short of spectacular, and as a result, in desperate need of valorization.

Mercier writes in his chapter on Authors from the *Tableau de Paris*: "in their lifetimes, they are left in indigence."[71] Writers railed against this condition by asserting their rights to a respectable living from their labors—Fenouillot de Falbaire asks in a pamphlet attacking the abuses of the Parisian booksellers against *gens de lettres*: "Like the bee that nourishes itself from the honey that it creates, why can the man of letters not find his livelihood in the works that he produces? The most common artisan, without protection, help, or intrigue, in his trade lives off the labors of his own hands. Why do labors of intelligence, works of genius, not provide the same advantages . . . ?"[72] But this was, in a sense, a ruse aimed at distracting from the fact that they increasingly were earning "decent livings" from their "labors of intelligence," perhaps as decent as they might earn in another professional field. Voltaire's caricature of the author turned porter was misleading, willfully so, of course, given the polemical spin of the poem. More typical would be Linguet's attempts to establish an *état* in law when he felt that he was getting nowhere as a writer. His fallback was not a position of subservient labor. In 1764, he became a *stagiaire* in the Parisian bar in training to become a lawyer.[73] He would notably take on the case of the Chevalier de la Barre before Voltaire became interested in the young nobleman from Abbéville who was tried, tortured, and executed in 1765 on dubious charges for blasphemy.[74]

In Linguet's own account, his career change represented a critical turning point; several of his biographers cite a letter to a friend in which he describes his decision as a dispiriting, albeit sensible, but in any case pointed turn from a life of grandiose literary aspirations—"I gave the ten best years of my life to the pursuit of fantasies [chimères]"—to stability and propriety:

"A family above reproach, a highly esteemed father, and a glimmer of talent assured me of a respectable rank. . . . I was mad to disdain and run away from it." He goes on to characterize the transition as a concession to the hard social and economic reality of the need to "be something": "I have never respected the trade of lawyer, but I will do it because one must be something in life; one must earn money, and it is better to be a rich cook than a poor and unknown scholar."[75] This last phrase, of course, echoes Voltaire; and no less than the *Pauvre diable*, it stylizes rather than transparently depicts the shift from letters into a "real job." Little actually changes between Linguet's life as a writer and his life as a lawyer. He is not saved from dire poverty since he was never victim to it. Above all, as Levy points out, the activities themselves that constitute the alternative pathways are hardly distinguishable: "The decision was not that clear-cut. The lawyer remained a man of letters, *malgré lui*."[76] Lawyering was an extension of, not a break in his intellectual trajectory. Far from rescuing Linguet from the disappointment of letters, it offered an opening that, in the face of his unfulfilled expectations, allowed him to go on writing, publishing, tackling philosophical causes, and fashioning an identity for himself as an *homme de lettres*, even as he claimed to have left this life behind him.

This is a key point, although it is not always intuitive in the case of marginal writers, since the self-justificatory function of their discourse of abandonment stands in opposition to what the discourse itself says. That is, the dramatization of material renunciation serves to valorize the refusal to give up in the face of a danger that was, in fact, not represented by the poverty depicted in their writings but by the banality of their lives as second-tier workaday *littérateurs* without much distinction or prestige, something that they do not evoke. But the increasing viability of literary banality is undoubtedly one of the defining dilemmas of eighteenth-century intellectual life, sensed as such by Diderot, who has Rameau's nephew rage at "being mediocre" rather than destitute.[77] The fundamental issue facing the expanding population of writers who failed to "make it" was not the brute struggle for survival but the effort to distinguish their nonvalorized activities on the basis of which "survival" was becoming easier and easier. The topos of authorial poverty was integral to the effort to invest these activities with a symbolic value that they lacked. "This indigence is honorable," asserts Mercier. For it transformed their unremarkable exteriority—an exteriority that was in fact a manifestation of their unremarkableness—into a sign of their profound integrity and independence: "proof, at least, that he has never debased either himself or his pen. Those who have sought and obtained pensions cannot say as much before their conscience."⁷⁸ Such qualities lent credence to the claim to significance that was always implicit in the act of publication. In the face of failure and its ensuing hardships, the writer's dedication showed that he had a privileged access to the truth, which in turn justified his writing and its monumentalization in print.

Conversely, if images of poverty were appropriated as crucial mediations of the acts of writing and publication, analogous in a way to seventeenth-century references to pressure from friends, so too the acts of writing and publication—in the "pure," nonsocial, non-elite form figured by the topos of the "market"—became one of the most recognizable and compelling signs of an intellectual's knowledge and virtue. To be sure, the latter wrote and published because he understood the nature of things; his insights validated his books. But the causality could be reversed: an individual was transformed as an intellectual to the extent that he wrote and published his insights. That is, the very fact of presenting his ideas in the form of a book rendered them more substantial and more penetrating. Authorship began in this respect to formulate its own justification and, in the framework of a new cultural field, was able to bestow legitimacy on people, activities, or ideas, whereas in the seventeenth century, as we saw, it was authorship that needed to be valorized through its association with people, activities, and ideas able, in turn, to endow the literary pursuit with a social respectability that it did not have.⁷⁹

Paul Bénichou traced the rise in this period of the writer as a moral leader who stepped into the vacuum created by the decline of the Church as a source of spiritual authority.⁸⁰ Clearly, the outsiders of the late Enlightenment were ardent believers in such a conception of the writer: "If despotism has been civilized," affirms Mercier, "if sovereigns have begun to fear the voice of nations, to respect this supreme tribunal, it is to the pens of writers that we owe the new restraint [nouveau frein]."⁸¹ The implication of the thesis, though, goes beyond the secularization of traditional authority or the continuation of a spiritual authority in lay form, for it evokes as well the emergence of distinctly new gestures and rituals as the guarantees and conduits of moral authority. It was, after all, the writer who seized the ascendant position, not the lawyer, doctor, or politician. That we take the substitution for granted is certainly an indication of how powerful the *sacre de l'écrivain* was. But when Mercier asserts, "the infraction of justice is an injury against the human race; this is why every Author worthy of the name feels sharply the wrong that is done to his fellow-man; he cannot tolerate it," it is worth recalling that this was not simply the elevation of a certain type of individual, but also of the practices that defined the type as an Author. In this light, the "advice" that marginal writers extended to young aspirants, which they themselves failed to heed, can be seen for its complexity. It was never intended to dissuade anyone from embarking on a life in letters but identified—or more exactly, conceptualized and affirmed—the singularity of the enterprise. For only writing—authorship—embracing the universal in its orientation toward the "public," produced a self-generating value such that its undertaking, on its own, even in the face of failure and the public's indifference, brought credibility to the individual.

Writing for the Market

Much like Classical-era writers, the self-professed marginal writers of the Enlightenment, in conceiving and depicting their transcendence, had recourse to anticommercial language that played up their disinterest. The valences of the articulations, however, could not be more divergent. For the *gens d'esprit* of the seventeenth century, nonpayment, reflecting their leisure and noble disdain for commerce, projected their integration into elite circles. But the image conveyed the opposite for the outsiders of the eighteenth century: their autonomy from such aristocratic spaces. This might at one level seem counterintuitive inasmuch as we have come to expect the "independence" of the writer from nobility to be associated with a growing ability to earn a "decent living" from the direct sale of works. But Brissot's *Mémoires* suggest a different relation between earnings and autonomy. Having begun with the declaration cited earlier—"Wanting to be independent, I relied only on my pen"[82]—he will not go on to evoke the earnings on which he might then build a livelihood. Far from it. He proceeds by insisting on his exploitation and poverty: "no author has, I believe, shown as much disregard for his own private interests as I have shown for mine. I sold at a very low price, and was barely paid the half of what I was owed, normally through arrangements that finished by ruining me."[83] The *Mémoires* are replete with accounts of his misfortunes in the book trade. Describing a series of brochures that he composed in the early phase of his literary career, he writes: "I approached a bookseller who promised me [a good price], but did not keep his pledge, and who sold and kept everything.[84] And if he does recall the thousand livres that a *librairie* paid him in 1781 for a ten-volume *Bibliothèque philosophique des lois criminelles*, it is in order to point out that "the printing costs absorbed two thirds of this sum, and the other third was never paid to me."[85]

Dwelling on such experiences, Brissot's auto-mythology conjures up a more convoluted link between intellectual and financial autonomy, with the former resting not on the emerging reality of the latter but on the latter's ultimate failure to take shape as a reality. This is at once a failure *tout court*—writers never did earn enough to live off their works—and a *relative* failure resulting from the postulation of an ideal case against which the current reality would always be perceived and depicted as an injustice: not only are writers not paid, but in light of the fact that they should, in principle, make money from their literary labors, this was now wrong and the writer's subjection to this travesty elevated him. Brissot's "ne . . . que"—"je ne me reposais que sur ma plume"—certainly responds to the inspector D'Hémery's nullifying "ne . . . que" with a positive declaration of autonomy and moral resolve. But this self-affirmation is not rooted in his ability to earn a living without the support of patrons. It is rather out of his inability to do so that he asserts an independence from nobility that was less of a socioeconomic nature—he did not need their support—than of a moral and symbolic character: he did not cater to them; he did not aim to please and amuse them out of base self-interest. Underscored in turn by his subsequent miseries in the book trade, such a refusal marked his seriousness and sincerity, and his authority to speak out.

Brissot's self-portrait also raises another issue, which is that the relation between intellectual and financial autonomy, even in the inverted model posited in his *Mémoires* whereby autonomy ensues from failure, does not exist in "reality." The foundation on which the intellectual's autonomy is constructed is not comprised of the "real" conditions in which the intellectual operated, but of an image of those conditions that inevitably diverges from the reality. For the truth behind Brissot's claim to independence was of course not his utter lack of recourse to "traditional" means of support. As Eisenstein and Frederick de Luna show in their responses to Darnton's account of Brissot as a hack-turned-spy, he was not wanting for meaningful connections and associations.[86] Nor did the truth lie in his abuse at the hands of publishers who cruelly exploited his disinterest and lack of commercial savvy. Darnton's study of the correspondence between Brissot and the publishers of the *Société typographique de Neuchâtel* reveals that the latter were mostly patient and supportive, while Brissot strategized and schemed in order to maximize his personal benefit, understandably so, of course, but in a manner that was quite inconsistent with the self-portrait that he would sketch in the *Mémoires*.[87] We might add, moreover, that Brissot's own self-glorifying invocations of his failures in the book trade, while downplaying his publishing activities, nonetheless point straight at them, as well as at the modestly positive results that undoubtedly made the efforts worth pursuing. He laments that he was only paid half of what he was owed. This is bad in absolute terms, but in the context of the Old Regime publishing world, such a result was no doubt far more mitigated. It suggests in any case that Brissot earned *something*. And if he got mired down in dire financial straits—Brissot spent a spell in 1784 in the London debtor's prison[88]—this had to do less with commercial print directly which consistently offered him openings whether or not these were the kinds that he wanted, than with his own economic mismanagement.

Ultimately, the "reality" underlying Brissot's vision of his independence was the lack of a clearly valorized position in the Old Regime literary field. His support from elites, while enough to keep him attached to the promise of a literary life, was not sufficient to claim on this basis the privileged identity or authority of the *philosophe*. At the same time, his mixed outcomes in the book trade facilitated rather than impeded the choice to continue writing. But no more than his membership in the provincial Châlons Academy, they did nothing to sanction or glorify the choice. If anything, these experiences simply highlighted the decision to go on writing as a perfectly rational one, and hence as a thoroughly ordinary one that could not distinguish him in any way. When Rousseau writes in the *First Discourse*, "He who will be a bad versifier or a subaltern Geometer all his life would perhaps have become a great cloth maker," it is the reasonableness of the second-rate literary life that he laments, the fact that it made perfect sense for a young aspirant like Brissot, who possessed the cultural capital of an education, a respectable family background, and connections, to write rather than devote himself to more "useful" endeavors.[89] This is the "reality" of Brissot's intellectual life: not isolation but the possibility of writing as a "professional," yet without any acclamation, and thus with nothing to answer to his expectations of soaring success. For to be sure, Brissot brought stratospheric hopes into play: "It was a love of glory which, as of the age of nine, drove me to work at night in my bed . . . . I unceasingly had, before my eyes, the image of those great men who had made themselves famous by their writings, and I wrote."[90]

All those who entered the literary field did so, and as a result, literature was transformed as an all or nothing game, even if the actual outcomes offered by the literary field made a middle-ground result eminently plausible. But for those who pursued a life in letters, it was as the uncle of the aspiring poet Damis described it in Piron's *La métromanie*, in response to his nephew's exasperation at his continuing anonymity on attaining an age when Corneille and Racine had already become celebrated:

Et ne sçais-tu pas bien qu'au métier que tu fais,
Il faut, ou les atteindre, ou ramper à jamais?[91]

[Do you not know that, in the enterprise that you undertake,
You must either attain their heights, or grovel forever?]

In such a worldview, how could one process the modest success that was ultimately the experience of these writers; how could they understand their own ability to continue with unremarkable work? The irony is that what Rémy Saisselin described as "the intermediate levels on which the writer might find a modest place" fostered the bifurcated expectations that denied the existence of such middle levels.[92] This "middle ground" allowed the lofty hopes of writers to take root, develop and mature over time by allowing them to continue identifying themselves as "writers"—as *écrivains* or *hommes de lettres*—despite the lack of symbolic support for such a self-identification, and in the face of the increasingly salient possibility, as time passed, that the support would never come, and that this was not a temporary, early career anonymity but an entrenched professional predicament.

As a conceptualization of literary life, "vivre de sa plume" expresses the attempt to understand this new experience in its complexity and ambivalence as the coexistence in the *littérateur* of grandiose hopes and hopelessness. And in this sense, the motif has little to do with the livelihoods of writers. It is instead the endeavor to invest with meaning a position that was defined neither by financial autonomy nor by exploitation but by a symbolic null born of the writer's inability to be integrated into privileged circles and by a creeping lack of hope in the possibility of eventual inclusion. "Living by the pen" is consequently a type of rhetorical device that shapes rather than reflects the writer's literary life. It does so first by obfuscating any connections that he might have with elite patrons which, while essential to his durability as an intellectual in the Old Regime cultural sphere, also played up his relative insignificance. Brissot's position as secretary in the Chancellery of the duc d'Orléans suggests that he was probably not the pathetic, seething hack that Darnton has made him out to be. But it also shows that he was just as far from being the next Voltaire. And second, to the degree that the trope of "living by the pen"—both in the rhetoric of Old Regime writers themselves and in the discourse of their historians—ultimately refers to the failure actually to make a living by writing, the device further valorizes outsiderhood by projecting the writer's moral authority in images of commercial exploitation, which accentuate his sacrifice, disinterest, and virtue.

If, finally, in order to "live by the pen," writers turned to the "literary market," this does not mean a simple turn to the book trade in order to find a more independent income, at least not in the sense indicated by Roche or Martin when they describe the Enlightenment field as divided into two coexisting "systèmes de rémunération."[93] Such a schema understates both the extent to which writers had already from the earliest days of printing been heavily involved in the commercial publication of their writings and the degree to which they remained dependent on patrons and noncommercial revenues well into the new typographical regime. The passage to the "literary market" should instead be seen as an effect of the reconceptualization of the cultural field in such a way that the symbolically empty, commercially oriented midlevel positions of outsider writers would now be reconfigured as the most meaningful nodes around which the field as a whole would be constructed, with these writers' distance from *le monde* highlighted by their contacts with the print trade, and as we shall see in the next chapter, with its primary emissary, the publisher. More than any move toward actual economic self-sufficiency, the writer's turn to "commerce" formulates and advances a claim to independence from elite society, whose power builds on images of his suffering in the book trade, the latter now circumscribing a battlefield in which the writer's sincerity and dedication clash brutally with the mercantile interests of greedy printers and booksellers, yet in which these qualities are, in the very process, articulated. This reconfiguration generates the "literary market," not as an underlying cause of the intellectual autonomy of the "modern author," but as one of its essential rhetorical effects.

4
Economic Claims and Legal Battles: Writers Turn to the Market

As an institution of literary life, the market normally enters into the purview of historical analysis in one of two ways: either as envisioned through the entrepreneurial moves of writers who wake up to their "real" interests as authors and, repudiating their ties to patrons, stake claims to the economic dues and legal rights in the book trade that will then allow them to become independent professionals, or as perceived through the exploitative treatment suffered by writers when they are sucked into a commercial system in the process of taking over all aspects of an increasingly "commodified" cultural sphere. To be sure, the two narratives are equally familiar yet offer what appear to be contradictory images of the "literary market," on one hand, as a field of social liberation and intellectual actualization, and on the other, as a dystopia of conflict and disharmony that imposes on the writer the bleak choice of stark impoverishment or "selling out."

These divergent images might be reconciled chronologically with the postulation that a utopian "market" was experienced by writers in an initial moment when they were first freed from their dependency on protectors only to discover subsequently the new and ever more cutthroat constraints of the commercial publishing world. In this respect, the "market" wherein the historian might discern "the conditions of a possible independence for men of letters" was a transitional space, prevailing only in those few decades during which *gens de lettres* were able to imagine for themselves greater autonomy vis-à-vis aristocratic society through the commercialization of their activities, yet continued to have to adapt to a patronage system that still determined realistic possibilities and outcomes.[1] By contrast, the negative image of the market as a sphere of exploitation presents a more forward-looking model, with hints of Romanticism and beyond. Pierre Bourdieu finds in the downtrodden "society of writers and artists" studied by Robert

Darnton a precursor to the alienated culture of mid-nineteenth-century Bohemianism, though "on an undoubtedly much smaller scale."[2] And Darnton himself suggests that the underpaid hacks of the "Literary Underground" were indeed the forebears of the struggling poets who would later be "romanticized" by Balzac.[3]

Of course, Darnton is better known for his spatial and sociological account of the good and the bad markets, which was rooted in his bifurcated vision of an eighteenth-century literary world sharply divided into high and low camps: those with connections, sinecures, and pensions versus those without. In this view, the commercialization of intellectual activities as an experience of dispossession and psychological fragmentation—rather than of liberation and autonomy—was associated with those who "fell" into a life of menial, poorly remunerated labors in the book trade as a result of their failure to secure a place in the established field.[4] In both the temporal and spatial accounts, though, the market is assumed to be an *objective* entity. One turns to it or is enveloped by it; one passes through its phases or is tracked into one or another segment of it. The fact remains that the market is out there in the real world, existing as a viable possibility and a genuine "alternative."

Yet this is, I argue, to conflate the market with the book trade, and to ascribe features to the latter that more precisely define and characterize the former. Certainly the book trade existed "out there." It had for centuries, during which time writers were perfectly aware of its presence, of its being "out there," and of its viability as a source of revenues and possibilities for the circulation of their writing. They had been turning to it as consistently as it had been intruding into their own varied activities. It is, in this respect, something of a mystification to suggest that the patronage system—as a "system of remuneration"[5]—was distinct from or opposed to commercial publication inasmuch as it was, of course, through the commercially published book that a dedication assumed its value as the signifier of a protector's favor.[6] As such, the book trade had always offered tremendous opportunities to writers, not to those seeking to establish their independence as professionals "living by the pen" but to those who looked to construct their intellectual identities through the cultivation of prestige-endowing associations. Such motives explain the vast majority of cases when writers turned to *libraires* in the Old Regime, even into the Enlightenment when publishing for traditional forms of esteem—and to establish one's *honnêteté*—remained the overriding paradigm. Voltaire's dealings with his booksellers—richly documented in an extensive correspondence with them that reveals his deep engagement in the publication process[7]—were essentially oriented by the desire to nurture his contacts with the privileged and the powerful, whether the *philosophe* was chastising the publisher for mistakes or delays in printing or strategizing about how and where to circulate copies.[8]

In such a framework, however, the book trade was engaged neither as a utopia for writers nor as the contrary, for it was simply not invested with this kind of cohesiveness, autonomy, or power over their lives and reputations. It was a subfield, a system of remuneration, to be sure. Writers accepted payments from publishers throughout the early modern period, and no doubt they valued the compensation as important to their livelihoods.[9] But the book trade was not by this fact an alternative; it did not in and of itself offer writers *another* way to make a life in letters. Consequently, it could not present especially definitive constraints on their identities as intellectuals. If the publishing process was fraught—as we have examined in Part I—it was not the same fraughtness that would characterize a more modern permutation of the cultural field in which, for instance, the difference between publishing and not publishing becomes determinate for the status and success of the writer. Indeed, we can find countless Old Regime examples of individuals whose identities as *gens de lettres* were fully acknowledged without their putting any writings at all into circulation in the form of printed books.[10] Mercier notes with irony that members of the Académie française hardly even put pen to paper at all: "for whom is the academic chair [le fauteuil académique] appropriate?" he asks. "For any man who no longer wants to write."[11]

The "alternative" was presented not by commercial publication in and of itself, but by the literary market, which, I have argued, should not be strictly identified with the book trade. The market took shape to the extent that commercial publication was conceptualized and engaged by writers as *sufficient* means for constructing a valorized intellectual identity. To claim the authority and status of the intellectual, it was enough, in other words, to write and publish a book so long as that book was presumed to communicate faithfully the innermost thoughts and insights of the writer. This, in turn, was a function of a redefinition of what a valorized intellectual identity was. It was no longer defined through the social integration of writers into elite social networks based on their ability to please, which rested on their suppleness and attention to the desires of their aristocratic interlocutors. It was instead rooted in the opposite, namely in the distance that writers were able to maintain from monarchs and nobles, and thus in their autonomy from them which, as it highlighted their disinterest, affirmed their commitment to the truth, and the honesty of their works.

It was to represent this distance that writers turned not so much to the book trade per se but to a charged, commercially inflected rhetoric that invoked their contacts with the book trade as central to their intellectual identities, and which had been increasingly thematized since the seventeenth century. Those Classical-era polemics, as we have examined, had articulated a strongly negative association between publishing activities and literary outsiderhood. Of course, now writers turned to this language not in order to discredit others for their antisocial arrogance or to play up their own *honnêteté* as *gens de lettres* who did not pay attention to their financial interests. Instead, they wanted to appropriate for themselves the outsider position that writers had previously sought desperately to avoid.

This is how the market took shape, refracted through the shifting expectations of writers who staked their legitimacy on their cultural and social exteriority as a clear and forceful signifier of their authenticity as well as of their commitment to the ideals of truth and justice. The present chapter explores the market's formation as a new theorization of the cultural field, which reflected less the actual experiences of *littérateurs* in the book trade, than their efforts to conceptualize and articulate the autonomy of the writer from nobility as a "modern" vision of intellectual authority. Due no doubt to the complex, indirect relation of image to reality, the literary market emerges in convoluted, ambiguous, and often contradictory ways. Certainly, its coherence as an institution of literary life is more obvious to us today than it was to the *gens de lettres* of the Old Regime, who even in their pronounced hostility to it remained beholden to a cultural world oriented not around the commercial exchanges of the print industry but around the practices and values of an elite social and political world. The resulting confusion has been a source of frustration for scholars who regret the absence of less equivocal statements and behaviors from writers, which would come in one of two recognizable if opposed gestures: either writers insufficiently embraced their economic interests as authors and failed to engage the book trade in a lucidly entrepreneurial way,[12] or else they insufficiently repudiated the economism of the publishing sector, adopting in the end the unsatisfactory stance of choosing to publish commercially yet neglecting to assert forcefully their dues and rights. Thus they allowed themselves to be exploited by profiteering publishers, while failing to denounce the exploitation and, more generally, failing to articulate in response a coherent rejection of the commercialization of literary life.[13]

However, it is precisely this lack of clarity that is key. It will present our running theme; for such "confusion" actually leads us into the central dynamic of the emerging market inasmuch as its source—from our vantage point—lies in the prevalence of considerations that, for their relentless focus on elite cultural life, come across as archaic. Yet these considerations suggest a deeper unity beneath the discrepant and ambiguous views of writers who stood before literary commerce. The underlying coherence of the eighteenth-century market remains elusive if we assume that it lies exclusively in the convergence of what we take to be "natural" desires for authorial independence with expanding commercial opportunities, which would then suggest that the story of the market is to be found either in the "professionalization" of writers as free-agent income-earners or in their "exploitation" by merchants and in the "commodification" of their writings. In fact, the market is about shifting definitions of autonomy as an effect of the effort to rethink intellectual authority in its imbrications with "society"—the latter still to be understood in its Old Regime meaning, referring above all to the world of social elites and to its central dynamic of exclusivity and individual aspiration for inclusion. In this respect, the "market" is first and foremost an engagement with "traditional" mechanisms of cultural consecration—traditional inasmuch as they posit a strongly positive association of legitimacy with social integration and ascendancy—in an attempt to consider, depict, and assert new ones that pointedly repudiate such a correlation, and thereby idealize the intellectual through a valorization of this figure's distance from and imperviousness to *le monde*.

Incomplete as they may be, we can nonetheless discern for our purposes the two angles to this eighteenth-century effort to think the "market," one that can be characterized as "economic," and which interrogates the "traditional" socially oriented paradigms of intellectual selfhood and legitimacy through the articulation of an image of the writer as a "professional" defined by entitlements to payment and the holding of intellectual property rights; and another that is properly "anti-economic," highlighting instead the heroism of the writer who resists the commercial pressures of the marketplace, not as an entrepreneur but in a deeply moral refusal that plays up the purity of the writer's motives against the corruption of commercial pressures. These angles, in turn, correspond to two disparate views of the cultural sphere, of the "market," and of the autonomy on the basis of which the individual stakes a claim to authority and credibility as an intellectual. They also correspond to a traditional contrast between two types of "modernizing" writers in the framework of the eighteenth-century field, exemplified by Diderot's embrace of "professional" authorship and by Rousseau's repudiation of "the trade of authorship [le métier d'auteur]."[14] Such an opposition presents a useful way of accessing the question of how literary life evolved in the Enlightenment era as *gens de lettres*, faced with what they perceived to be the failures of the traditional consecrating institutions, sought "alternative" ways to valorize themselves and their activities, but only if we remember that it is in the collapse of this opposition that the "reality" of these evolutions—the reality of "modernization" and "commercialization"—is to be found. The fight for "literary property" is an evocative point of conceptual confusion and therefore presents an opening for understanding the invention of the market.

The Publishers' Case

If the "anti-economic" view, with its emphasis on exploitation and the resistance to "selling out," has offered a more enduring vision of how intellectuals engaged commercial publication in the modern era, it is by contrast the "economic" paradigm that has been more pressing in studies focusing on "modernization" in the Enlightenment-era intellectual sphere.[15] With notable exceptions—Darnton's studies of the "literary underground" come to mind, along with the scholarship that it has influenced—the transition from patronage to market has most often been conceived in terms of claims to rights and entitlements advanced by self-possessed individuals making rational choices about how best to pursue their activities. The shift ensues, in other words, from a lucid reorientation toward commerce rooted in the writer's estimation that the "autonomy" offered by opportunities to publish commercially is preferable to dependence on a protector, with all the personalized obligations that such a relationship entails, above all the need to modify the work a priori in order to cater to the protector's desires. Diderot warns in his 1763 *Salon* that "one must never command anything from an artist." He goes on to articulate a key association between the market and a vision of artistic independence figured by the possibility of bringing a "ready-made" product to the public, one that had been created prior to any contact with the consumer in the free space of the studio where only the artist's genius and talent directed the operation: "when one wants a painting in his own style [de sa façon], one must tell him: 'create a painting for me and choose yourself the subject that suits you,'" adding, "it would be better and quicker moreover to buy an already completed work."[16]

The story taps into a powerful modern mythology of authors as defined by their freedom and singularity. We have, however, seen how few instances there actually were of French writers who indeed took their destinies into their hands in this way. The entrepreneurial and proprietary spirit is difficult to localize in the context of the eighteenth-century French cultural field, at least inasmuch as such a spirit might be manifest in an embrace of commercial activities. As a result, the account of a turn to the market in the form of claims to rights and dues has proven difficult to flesh out in its details.[17] Another hurdle lies in the fact that the most strident mobilization in the name of property rights was undertaken not by writers seeking independence but by booksellers in pursuit of a separate agenda. What is more, as some commentators have noted with palpable unease, these champions of property rights in eighteenth-century France were not just publishers, but the most established booksellers of the Parisian guild, who engaged arguments with central authorities about the nature of the *privilège*.[18]

I have already discussed at some length the *privilège en librairie*. It was, of course, a mechanism dating from the first years of the printing press that bestowed on its holder the exclusive rights to publish a work in a given place and for a specified, limited duration.[19] Traditionally, the *privilège* was viewed as a *grace*; that is, it granted temporary rights meant to help the *libraire* recoup his investment in an industry notorious for its high costs and risks—presses and paper were particularly expensive materials. The seventeenth-century chancellor Pierre Séguier defined it as a "exception to common rights [dérogation du droit commun]," in exchange for which the publisher agreed to abide by corporatist quality standards—the *privilège* normally stipulated that the book would be printed "with good paper and good type"—and more important, no doubt, to respect political and religious authority. In the eighteenth century, the *privilège* was accompanied by an *approbation* signed by a censor who had read and, with a few possible suggested changes, approved the work.[20]

Against this view, a markedly different one gradually took hold among the publishers of the guild, according to which the publisher's exclusive rights to print and sell a work did not derive from the king's grace. The guild members argued instead that these rights followed from a transaction with the work's author by which they were transferred in the form of "property rights" to the *libraire*, who held them until he or she, in turn, decided to sell them. Louis d'Héricourt, a lawyer for the Parisian guild, addressed a "Mémoire" to the Garde des Sceaux in 1725 in which he argues that: "it is not the *privilèges* granted to booksellers by the king that makes them owners of the works that they print, but solely the acquisition of the manuscript, whose author transmitted his property to them by means of the price that he received."[21] In other words, the *privilège* ratified what was already there, since the publisher's rights to the work—to do with it as he or she pleased—were anterior to their official acknowledgment. The king did not grant them by his grace or favor, and certainly could not then take them away: "the sovereign himself, as a consequence of his own laws, finds himself happily powerless to take away the *privilèges* that he grants to a bookseller who owns a manuscript."[22] Indeed, he could with no more legitimacy curtail the publishers' entitlement to these "veritable possessions" than he could expropriate other freely and legally acquired belongings, the rights to which he was compelled by justice and natural law to protect rather than curb: "whether land, houses, furniture or other possessions of whatever type they may be."[23] It was, in fact, in the name of this justice that permanent *privilèges* with no expiration date had to be mandated, bringing to a logical endpoint the seventeenth-century trend that saw both the duration of the *privilège* and its propensity to be renewed on expiration steadily increase. For the temporal limits that had traditionally been written into each one were now revealed to be an arbitrary, unjustifiable exercise of royal power.

Central to the *libraire*'s argument was a conception of the writer's relation to his work as a fundamentally proprietary one. If the publisher could claim property rights to a work based on the fact that he had purchased it from its writer, it was to the extent that the author had the right as the work's owner to do with it as he wished, including cede the rights to its reproduction and circulation in print. For its part, the right of cession was rooted in the labor that the writer had applied in accordance with a conceptualization of property that, following Locke, characterized the literary work as "the fruit of a labor that is personal to him, and which he should have the freedom to use in whatever way he sees fit."[24] Later, when the guild attacked the 1777 book trade reforms, which aimed, among other things, at curtailing the dominance of the Parisians, another pro-guild lawyer named Cochut deployed similar rhetoric in a 1778 "Requête au roi." Referring to authors, he argues that "literary productions are the fruit of their sleepless nights [veilles]: they [authors] are the ones who give them existence. They therefore have a greater right to them than one has to land acquired in an ordinary way."[25]

In these polemics, moreover, the discourse on the author's labor produced more than an abstract philosophical concept in logical support of the publishers' arguments. It also outlined a concrete image of the Author as a respectable professional who worked hard to make a living and support a household, and who thus deserved to have his efforts adequately rewarded. If the author had the freedom to do with his work as he pleased, d'Héricourt adds, it was in order to procure for himself, "in addition to the honor for which he hopes, a profit that provides for his needs and even for the needs of those who are attached to him by blood, friendship, or gratitude [reconnaissance]."[26] Such sentimentalized language, aiming to foster a sympathetic connection with the figure of the author, was a far cry from an earlier age when the guild publishers would complain to the authorities that *gens de lettres* expected to be paid at all. Traditionally, of course, writers were paid merely in free copies.[27] Their growing presence as active agents in a publishing industry that, well into the eighteenth century, was still mostly occupied with the publication of works whose authors had long gone, was hardly embraced.[28] Responding to public criticism that publishers were charging too much for books, André Chevillier countered in his 1694 *Origine de l'imprimerie* that it was the fault of authors "who, having extracted a considerable sum from the bookseller," force the latter to raise his price. Appealing to the kinds of prejudices against authorship that we explored in Chapter 1, Chevillier adds that he considers this "behavior, in my view, hardly dignified for a man of letters who, when he composes, should be motivated only by a view of the public good."[29] The argument for permanent *privilèges* advanced by the eighteenth-century guild was, by contrast, grounded in a call to pay authors more, not less, and in the premise that this constituted an honorable and necessary payment, which, far from undermining the dignity of the work, was in fact a precondition for it: "To put these great men in a state to apply their talents toward the good of the society to which they found themselves attached either by inclination or by nature," writes d'Héricourt, "it is necessary that they can draw from this precious industry benefits that are proportional to the importance of their labor."[30]

Indeed, behind the publishers' arguments lies the key premise that writers *needed* the book trade, and that without its payments they could not fully function as intellectuals. D'Héricourt contends that without an unrestricted transfer of rights pursuant to the sale of a work by a writer to a publisher, "the work of a man of letters becomes useless to him since it remains forever in his possession."[31] This might seem an obvious remark to present-day sensibilities, but we must recall that in the framework of *honnête* publication, as it continued to prevail in the period, there was nothing self-evidently valorizing about having a work published commercially. It certainly did not make one an *homme de lettres* even if the work sold many copies.[32] Conversely, a work that was not ceded to a *libraire* was hardly useless. To assert that it was is vastly to underestimate the importance of other "publication" possibilities, such as readings before a salon gathering or the Académie française, or circulation of a manuscript through the social networks of *le monde*.[33] In this respect, the elevation of the author/publisher transaction in all its "non-euphemized" raw economic reality opposed a traditional devalorization of writer's dealings with *libraires* as incidental. Now in the form of a *droit d'auteur*, the payment became meaningful not only as an effect of justice, but symbolically, as a sign of the individual's ability to assume a positive intellectual identity, while the other forms of recognition on which even semi-successful writers could count in the eighteenth-century literary field appeared to vanish from the frame. Pensions, gifts, and prizes do not count for anything in the construction of an authorial life, according to the publishers. On this point, the guild *libraires* and self-conscious outsiders such as Mercier and Linguet were in agreement. Of course, the latter rejected "measly pensions" as part of their broad repudiation of an elite culture in which the *homme de lettres* was forced to acquiesce to its whims and frivolities.[34] The publishers by contrast had no complaints with *le monde*. They took a different tack in elevating commercial pay over traditional income, identifying its ability to signify success—and the stature of authoritative intellectuals—with the contribution that the market payments made to writers' capacity to cater to their material needs, considered at an individual and a household level.

Put another way, the *libraires* assumed the author to be an effect of "professionalization." One became an author to the degree that one lived off the income derived from the activities of authorship. As a result, not only was this income invested with meaning as that which allowed an author to function in society, but what then became especially salient was the *amount* of these revenues. A quantitative correlation between success and payment from *libraires*—more money equals greater success and thus a stronger claim to the identity of author—again seems an obvious point to underscore in an age of bestseller lists. But the idea deeply rethinks the writer's relation to money. Conventionally, it was the provenance of compensation—and specifically the status of the person who paid it—that counted, far more than its amount. A small gratification from the king was clearly a more important reward than a larger one coming, say, from a low-ranking hometown notable. Of course, noncommercial revenues had, on the whole, never brought in a lot of income to writers, which hardly mattered since the real worth of these payments lay in the prestige that they conferred, and in the degree to which they projected the social integration of recipients and their *honnêteté*.[35] Opportunities to become "établi" with a position in a noble household or a more regular, substantial pension would ensue. But with *droits d'auteur*, the sum was paramount. Insofar as success in an activity is gauged by one's ability to earn a living by it, this makes sense. It was not important which *libraire* paid 2,000 livres. What mattered was that 2,000 livres was a hefty sum that would allow a writer to devote him- or herself in a dignified manner to the vocation. And the writer was all the more dignified by the payment as it increased.

A new calculation emerges to account for the status of the author in the cultural field, which compares the earnings of the writer from sales of his works with his cost of living. D'Héricourt established the ideal equivalence, arguing that a writer needed "a profit that provides for his needs."[36] In fact, the computation will reach beyond the *libraires*' polemics to play a noticeable role in the engagement of such figures as Diderot and Rousseau with the book trade, and thus in their conceptualization of the "literary market" as a sphere of intellectual autonomy and selfhood.[37] It has, in addition, been highly influential for the history of authorship, which, as we have seen, has always gravitated toward accounts of the augmenting sums earned by writers as relevant measures of their ability to "live by the pen."[38] Scholars such as Alain Viala have tried to apply the calculation to those who operated in a noncommercial patronage system.[39] I have suggested the difficulties of the endeavor, but it is worth adding that, unlike the focus on payments from the print trade, this latter arithmetic has no Old Regime precedent. While Diderot and Rousseau certainly did compare the money they earned directly from their writings with their material needs as individuals and heads of households, there is little indication that writers not oriented toward the "market"—say, seventeenth-century court-based *gens de lettres* or the *philosophes*—ever did so.

That especially forceful arguments promoting not just literary property rights per se but a sympathetic vision of authors, their hard work, and their legal entitlements to payments would be advanced by publishers rather than by writers themselves has presented something of a dilemma given the overriding historical tendency to view publishers as obstacles in the march of writers toward their "economic" liberation. All the more so inasmuch as the publishers in question were part of an Old Regime patriciate appealing to the king to enhance their long-established favors. Carla Hesse highlights the particularity of this development in France, where, in contrast to the situation in England or Germany, "the author was a creation of the absolutist police state, not the liberal bourgeois revolution."[40] To be sure, there is no denying that the *privilège* represents a deep collusion between its holders and the royal authorities. It should however be acknowledged that there is also pragmatism at work here, with the *privilège* standing as the obvious mechanism in place that *privilège*-holding publishers could appropriate in order to advance feasible claims to "property rights." Hesse presents "absolutist police state" and "liberal bourgeois revolution" as a stark ideological choice, but in claiming permanent *privilèges*—a claim, it should be remembered, that was never indulged by the crown[41]—the publishers themselves were choosing not so much "absolutism" as market control and monopoly profits. These happened, of course, to be a hybrid function both of their favor with the absolutist administration and of what appears to us as a "liberal" regime of strong property rights.

This pragmatism points to what might be a bigger source of discomfort among scholars with the argumentation of the *libraires*, which is less its ideological complicity with the regime than in its raw instrumentality. The image of the author that they proposed was positive, but it was driven at all points by unbridled self-interest. D'Héricourt maintained the urgency of the fair compensation of *gens de lettres*. But it was ultimately because this payment designated the author's ratification of the deal by which he ceded his work, and as a consequence signified the inviolability of the publishers' rights. After all, it is "by means of the price that he receives," d'Héricourt stressed, that the author legally transferred ownership to the *libraire*.[42] His push for better remuneration of authors reflects not a concern for their well-being but a desire to underscore the legality of the transfer; the more the publishers paid, the more unassailable the acquisition had to be. Furthermore, if the guild lawyer emphasized the importance of paying *droits d'auteur* by describing with much pathos the difficulties that authors endured when publishers could not remunerate them well, there can be no doubt that the *libraires* had much to gain from the idea that authors had no other recourse than the book trade. As Birn points out, while d'Héricourt advocated for the rights of the author to deal freely with his work in order to maximize his benefit, he failed to denounce the regulation that prohibited authors from selling their own works, forcing them to negotiate with a publisher in order to see their writings in print. As it would happen, some of the strongest authorial involvement in the cause of literary property in eighteenth-century France will be contextualized by precisely the struggle between writers and publishers over the right to sell books.[43]

The author was, in this sense, not so much an ideological construct of the state as a rhetoric ploy designed to bolster the *libraires*' argumentation in favor of permanent *privilèges*, as well as to win sympathy for their cause from administrators who were more likely to be moved by the struggles of *gens de lettres* to contribute great works to the nation's patrimony than by the "hardships" of the well-heeled guild members in their efforts to pursue even more profits. But while this instrumentality seems to be at the root of much of the scholarly unease regarding publishers' leading role in the defense of authorial rights, the fact is that the concept of an author's legal and economic rights is *always* a rhetorical ploy; no less so, I would emphasize, when writers themselves articulate it. The assumption is generally that writers engaged the cause more "sincerely"; hence, their various interventions into the debates—whether through writings or legal cases or otherwise—have a greater import and more significantly drive the transition into a modern "system of remuneration." Yet this is to misunderstand the nature of the discourse on literary property. For in truth writers were no more interested in literary property in and of itself than were publishers, which is to say that they were interested in it only indirectly, and to the extent that it presented an effective vehicle for advancing a claim to something else. When they take up the cause in the eighteenth century, the struggle does then not become more "authentic" or more "genuine," though the rhetoric driving the interventions of authors into the debates certainly aims to give this impression—and to be sure, the "sincerity" of their involvement becomes a fundamental aspect of the persuasiveness of their arguments. Instead, the cause is oriented in a different way, not toward the economic strength of guild publishers, but toward the legitimization of new writerly comportments reflecting the new antisocial, anti-elite ideal of the intellectual as a singular hero.

Rights and Exploitation: "The Writers of Low Literature" Make Their Case

The unease among commentators regarding the *libraires*' initiative-taking in the debates on literary property also, of course, translates dissatisfaction with the engagements of writers who did weigh in on the issue, engagements that stand out as convoluted at best, especially compared with those of their more entrepreneurial counterparts in early modern England or in late eighteenth-century Germany.⁴⁴ With the *philosophes* taking no interest in the matter, the issue played out in two ways. Some have emphasized the role assumed in the debates by "scorned members of 'low literature'" or "second-rate writers" without favor or pensions, who, coming to depend on what they could earn from "hack" work, were more attuned to their interests in the marketplace.⁴⁵ Alternatively, the cause was taken up by one *philosophe*, namely Denis Diderot, although in an ambiguous and frustrating way. In 1763, at the behest of the syndic of the Parisian guild, he composed a letter—first published in the nineteenth century under the title *Lettre sur le commerce de la librairie*—addressed to the royal administrator in charge of supervising the publishing industry, which formulated an appeal for authors' economic rights. But writing as a spokesperson for the guild, Diderot's overarching goal was not ultimately to promote the well-being of authors but to advance the arguments of the guild for permanent *privilèges*, the publishers having calculated, concomitant with the strategic elevation of the figure of the author in their rhetoric, that it might also be beneficial to have one actually plead their case. Diderot complied.

With such instances to draw upon, it does not seem surprising that the transition of French writers into the market, as this might be told through an account of their claims to property rights, has been a difficult story to tell. But this is partly because the questions have been framed in such a way as to render it so. For the narrative is recounted generally in response to negative interrogations, whether these are openly posed or not, and as a result it often unfolds in the form of a justification that assumes what is being queried is not quite right. Éric Walter's question following his observation that it was minor writers rather than reputable *philosophes* who mobilized for literary property rights—"are they not at the same time authors, thus producers of cultural goods, and writers, that is, more than entertainers, but creators of meaning?"—conveys not simply the logic of the division of intellectual labor into high and low, but also a sense of its unsatisfactoriness, its need for explanation. With his question, Walter implicitly confronts another: why did better writers—writers who were more articulate, smarter, with more resources, authority, and greater access to media—not get involved? Similarly, critics keen to uphold Diderot's *Lettre* as a significant contribution to the theorization of "literary property" in eighteenth-century France have had to face a different but no less vexing uncertainty: why did he not directly advocate in favor of authors' property rights rather than do so merely as the "paid propagandist" for the publishers, and therefore under the cumbersome baggage of their agenda?[46]

Yet it might be illuminating to flip things around. Instead of asking why writers failed to engage more forcefully or more effectively, or indeed at all, the literary property debates in eighteenth-century France, we might, in contemplating the situation of the *homme de lettres* in the period, wonder why they would have. The former questions have dominated studies of the Enlightenment-era intellectual, in part because the answer to the latter one is assumed to be self-evident. If Voltaire had become a strong advocate of literary property rights, we would not ask why. Of course, he did not, and we are preoccupied with understanding this choice inasmuch as it jars with our expectations of him. What held him back? What distracted him from this essential fight? Correlatively, it is perhaps even clearer why Diderot, with far less wealth than Voltaire, would have become a pro-property advocate. What, then, prevented him from offering his *Lettre sur le commerce* independently of the guild publishers, as a free-standing, pointed defense of the legal and economic rights of *gens de lettres* rather than as apology for a cause that was not directly his own?

The questions are, however, badly posed. Probing the motivations of writers who were operating in the framework of *honnête* publication, they assume that claiming property rights was a natural thing for them to do because, it is further assumed, they naturally desired to be free of their dependence on royal and aristocratic protection. But this does not begin to get at the complexity of writers' engagements with the Old Regime book trade through the emerging concept of "propriété littéraire." In fact, no writer who inhabited the cultural field of eighteenth-century France wanted to be "liberated" from the patron or the sinecurial position that ensured his or her livelihood; and writers who indulged the discourse of autonomy from nobility through involvement in the literary property debates did so not in order to free themselves from their protectors. Rather, from a position in which patronage was not as forthcoming as they hoped, and in particular, not sufficient to substantiate a strong claim to intellectual distinction, they engaged in a rhetoric of economic autonomization in order to valorize and project—indeed, to postulate—their a priori lack of aristocratic support, the "fact" that they had never so demeaned themselves. Writers who rejected patronage never really turned away "protection." Instead, they sought to disguise and repudiate a condition in which they were not protected enough, which implied invariably that they were protected to some degree.

There are, of course, significant differences between the involvement of the minor writers in the literary property debates and that of Diderot. Indeed, they initially stand in opposition to each other as anti- and pro-publisher, respectively. But they had in common a more important goal than that of situating the author vis-à-vis the *libraires* as enemy or friend. Namely, through an image of the author as a holder of legal rights and economic entitlements, they shared the goal of articulating intellectual outsiderhood in a symbolically meaningful way. The point was, in this respect, not actually to exercise those rights or cash in on those entitlements. Ultimately, it was to play up the opposite: authors were not just holders of rights; they were holders of rights that were invariably denied them. They were defined as economic agents, but ones whose economic nature consisted in their susceptibility to exploitation rather than in their entrepreneurial capacity to "live by the pen." They were "workers," integrated into the labor market as agents whose production demanded recompense; yet this income would never be commensurate with intellectual efforts that, in their tirelessness, profundity, and deep connections to the being and soul of the individuals undertaking them, were unlike any other form of labor. Writers were, in other words, workers just like any other. But they were also fundamentally distinct. And whether it was mostly publishers who were targeted for failing to acknowledge this distinction or administrators in the *Direction de la librairie*, it hardly mattered.

Perhaps this is clearest in the case of minor writers, figures such as Linguet or the playwright Fenouillot de Falbaire, both of whom wrote strong pro-property tracts. Their writings were shaped by context, with perhaps the most important framework being that of the lawsuit brought against Luneau de Boisjermain by the guild publishers in 1769–70. Luneau was a scholar and a teacher whose writings consisted primarily of pedagogical works, including a *Discours sur une nouvelle manière d'enseigner et d'apprendre la géographie* from 1759 and a *Cours d'histoire universelle* from 1765. In 1767, he prepared and had printed a critical edition of Racine's plays, which he then decided to sell himself. This went strictly against the ordinances of the French book trade, as stipulated by the *Code de la librairie* in 1723 and 1744, which allowed only licensed *libraires* to sell books, and the guild took action, suing him and seizing his stock. A belated subscriber to the *Encyclopédie*, Luneau responded with his own countersuit against the publishers of that work, who happened, of course, to be leading members of the guild—Le Breton was both a major investor in the *Encyclopédie* and the syndic of the guild—claiming that they had cheated subscribers by expanding the final edition well beyond the eight volumes originally announced in the 1750 prospectus, with a concomitantly steep rise in the price of the work.[47]

Luneau was an unlikely hero for those seeking to defend a heroic vision of the author against the degradation inflicted by the *libraires*. And his case was no less improbable as a catalyst for mobilization in favor of literary property rights. For one thing, he was sued not as an author selling an original work but as an editor. And in any case, the publishers were not contesting Luneau's "ownership" of his edition but defending their turf by opposing his involvement in a commercial activity for which he was not certified. Yet when Linguet was engaged as Luneau's lawyer, and Fenouillot pamphleteered against the guild publishers, they articulated some of the most direct and forceful, if not the most sophisticated arguments for intellectual property rights to emerge in eighteenth-century France. In fact, they appear to us as direct and forceful primarily because they were oriented directly at the *libraires*, who were constructed in the polemics as the problem to be confronted. In sharp contrast with, say, d'Héricourt's focus on the state as the obstacle to the adequate payment of writers, here it was the publishers who were denying authors their due, and against whom the latters' rights then had to be asserted. Such an argumentation reflected—or shaped—a broader impression of the case. If it seems an obscure one today, at the time the trial was a veritable *affaire* publicized in numerous venues. The *Mémoires secrets*, in particular, reported on the proceedings, extending, in its strong sympathies with the defendant whose troubles were seen to be emblematic of a larger dynamic, a view of the legal wranglings as a shameful illustration of the systematic abuse of writers by *libraires*: "A private affair, which has become almost a general dispute between *gens de lettres* and publishers, bears reporting," reads the entry for October 20, 1769.[48]

The demonization of the *libraire* points, in a way, to the real work being done. Clearly, Linguet's or Fenouillot's involvement in the debates was not about "liberating" themselves and their colleagues from their elite patrons, none of whom would have felt especially constrained in this regard. It was instead an effort to legitimize positions in the cultural field that, as we saw in Chapter 3, were defined not by the utter absence of elite protection, but by the inadequacy of such support—in quantity and quality—to establish these writers as more than secondary though viable players. It follows therefore that if these writers turned to the literary property polemics, it was not about the money, even if the claim to a fair compensation for their labors was the foremost argument they advanced: "The most common artisan . . .

in his trade lives off the labors of his own hands. Why do the labors of intelligence, works of genius, not provide the same advantages . . . ?" Fenouillot had asked.[49] However, as evidenced by their ability to make their literary lives endure, their crisis was at bottom not an economic but a symbolic one. They endured and made a living, but they did so in a middling, unimpressive way. They lacked the legitimacy to be more, and by laying claim to their "rights," it was this intellectual credibility—not their livelihood—that they were seeking to advance.

Accordingly, the claims of these writers to compensation in exchange for their labors were not driven by the hope that they would be paid. In fact, it would be more accurate to assert the contrary: their claims to payments and legal rights had really no aim other than to expose to public outrage their lack of remuneration and legal dispossession. At first glance, they echoed the *libraires*' rhetoric, not only in decrying the inability of writers to make a living from their activities, but in assuming that they should be able to do so without recourse to patronage. The "most common artisan," Fenouillot notes, who, in contrast to the writer, was able to live off his toil, did so "without protection, help, or intrigue."[50] But now the evocation of nonpayment brought into focus an image of the writer as the victim of the *libraires* rather than as an ally, an image that would run as a central theme in the pro-property polemics of the minor writers, which cast the publishers as ferocious tyrants. The first lines of Fenouillot's *Avis* read: "Since the art of print was invented, publishers have always reaped almost by themselves the fruits of the nightly labors [veilles] of the studious man."[51] Linguet's *Mémoires judiciaires* in defense of Luneau similarly denounce publishers as "insatiable despots," who appropriate what does not belong to them and thereby consign authors to a "ruinous slavery."[52] They are "the same as those tyrants who do not want their subjects to be able to proclaim that, during their lifetimes, they enjoyed a single moment of liberty, and who mark them with the withering seal of servitude."[53]

The claim to literary property was thereby formulated out of a position of weakness and extended as a cry of the dispossessed railing against injustice. It is hard to determine whether such a tactic helped the specific case in question. The *saisi* of Luneau's stock was ruled illegal in the end, to be sure, and the defendant was duly compensated for the damages he incurred to the tune of 100 écus. The judgment, however, seems not to have really confronted the question of proprietary rights per se, or for that matter, the well-being of *gens de lettres*, and was instead based on the irregularity of the procedures that the publishers had followed in confiscating Luneau's books. For their part, the guild managed to have Linguet's "injurious statements" suppressed, which suggests that the "exploitation argument" was perhaps not what cracked open the case.[54]

But as a self-presentational strategy, the assertion of victimhood was more effective, highlighted by the *Mémoires secrets* in its reports on the legal briefs of Linguet and the pamphlets of Fenouillot. The circular offered detailed summaries playing up both the exploitation at the center of the Luneau affair, and the representativeness of the case as a window onto the condition of the writer. As a result, Luneau's suit became a symbol for something much larger: "The cause of M. L de B is therefore that of all men who think, and who write," affirmed Fenouillot.[55] It was transformed as it came to thematize the broader, underlying dynamic of a cultural sphere that was becoming radically divided between writers and *libraires*, and defined by the mistreatment of the former by the latter, now playing the role of "leeches [sangsues] who gorged themselves pitilessly on the blood of authors."[56] In this framework, the exploitation defense was less about trying to get a particular result than about an effort to ennoble authorial activity and invest it symbolically, with the harshness of literary life evoked in order to emphasize the dedication and disinterest of writers who, despite being robbed by publishers, devote themselves anyway to the pursuit of truth. It is, of course, this selflessness that imbues with a sense of authenticity the authorial identity of a writer who "sends away disdainfully those little merchants who want him to work for their store." For, had he been "dominated by a love for money" and a desire for material comfort, he would have found something else to do: "he would not have entered the literary field [le champ de la littérature]," concludes Fenouillot.[57]

The writer's scornful dismissal of the merchant, though, should be understood in its complexity. For despite an impression to the contrary, there certainly is contact with the commercial sphere. It is articulated negatively, as contempt or outright rejection. Or it is formulated in vague terms that downplay the writer's willingness to deal with *libraires* in order to represent the contact as an unwanted imposition from the outside: "Circumstances, chance, necessity sometimes forced very esteemed men of letters to work for these merchants, and to submit to being paid piecemeal for immortal works."[58] Such insouciance or stylized neglect should not blind us, however, to the critical importance of these commercial contacts—in their negativity—as some of the most significant media for a compelling, plausible projection of the writer's selflessness. For while there is a strong willingness on the part of the writer to reject the commercialization of his work, the fact is that there is an equally strong willingness to depict this commercialization in images of exploitative treatment and underpayment, images that render authorial contacts with commerce as a dramatic clash of values in which the economically rational, profit-maximizing goals of the bookseller are pitted against the non-economic, altruistic priorities of the writer. The publisher, of course, easily wins the commercial game as he takes full advantage of the writer's indifference or inaptitude: "This is how publishers, proud of their wealth and believing themselves to be superior to those who labor for them, quickly turned themselves into the tyrants of all men of letters, who were forced to use them in order to sell their works."[59] But in its ruthlessness the publishers' "victory" is actually a massive symbolic triumph for the writer, whose pure motives are articulated and affirmed.

Such was the nature of the "exploitation" suffered by writers in the cultural field as the field was reimagined in the property rights discourse of the minor writers. What they advanced was not, in this sense, a "traditional" vision of exploitation, which would consist in the domination of the strong over the weak rather than in the dissimilarity of motivations underscored by Fenouillot. Correlatively, the source of this exploitation lay less in the actual circumstances of the interaction between *libraire* and writer—that is, in the relative strengths or weaknesses of their positions as rich or poor—than in the credible imputation to the opposing protagonists of these divergent motives, which suggests, therefore, that it was not about the motives themselves but about the persuasiveness of their representation. That Luneau comes across as a heroic defender of literature speaks precisely to the question of this effectiveness, for whether or not the professional pedagogue's legal response to the seizure of his valuable stock can be considered heroic at all, it is something of a stretch to see it as heroism in the defense of *literature* or even *authorship*—we should recall that the case in question revolved around an editorial enterprise. All things considered, he corresponded very little to the mythologized author persecuted by but courageously resistant to the *libraire*, as this figure would be celebrated by Fabre d'Eglantine in the character of Clar from his 1787 play *Les gens de lettres*, or more famously, by Vigny in his highly popular 1835 play, *Chatterton*.[60]

Of course, no living author even remotely fit such a mold. But this is exactly the point. The incongruity of the elevation of Luneau and his legal battle with the Parisian publishers illustrates more than anything else that the interventions of "minor writers" into the polemics on literary property rights had little direct connection with the reality of their engagements with the publishing industry for the simple reason that they were not driven by this reality but by another: the effort to render credible a new kind of intellectual identity, reflective of outsiderhood and rooted in the sincerity, seriousness, and dedication of the writer. As with the *philosophes*, these personal qualities were valorized against the old paradigm of *plaire*; writers were sincere, serious, and dedicated to the extent that they refused to amuse leisured elites. But these qualities were also defined against the *philosophes*' gravity insofar as they were apparent only through the negative but highly visible integration of writers into the commercial sphere, which played up an authorial independence from elite culture that the *philosophes* could not plausibly claim. The latter could assert moral independence based on the importance of their objectives expressed in their rejection of *mondain* frivolities. But with their official positions, pensions, and friendships with the high and mighty, they could hardly declare the more radical independence conveyed by the burning need to make a living and by a visceral hardship in opposition to the hypothetical poverty advocated by d'Alembert. Such images cut at the heart of the philosophical compromise with *la société mondaine*, transforming its underlying *bienséance* into the height of hypocrisy. Signified by the material ease of the *philosophes*—"What a difference it makes to cultivate letters as does M. de Voltaire with a hundred thousand livres of income"[61]—this hypocrisy in turn offered a countermeasure against which the profundity and honesty of the new intellectual could be evoked.

Thus, if the "minor writers" formulated their arguments for literary property rights out of a position of weakness, it was because they had constructed their position as "weak," at least from a market perspective. Their claims to be "underpaid" by vicious publishers ultimately say little about the details of their transactions with *libraires*, or about the character of the *libraires* with whom they dealt. Instead, they speak to a rhetorical inversion which invests the money that they are *not* being paid with a poignant meaning. At one level, then, the minor writers follow the arguments of the guild publishers, subscribing to their postulation of an exclusive symbolic connection between direct earnings from the sales of manuscripts and a recognizable authorial identity. But in the case of Linguet or Fenouillot the relationship is far more ambivalent. The earnings from sales do indicate the tireless efforts of writers, which point to their dedication and integrity for shunning the demeaning support of protectors. But they can convert this economic value into symbolic value only to the extent that they do not in the end receive the payment that is their due. It must exist as a virtuality that does not become real, and indeed cannot become real. In fact, there is no intention in any of the polemics that it would do so.

Herein lay the irony of the mobilization for literary property. It was driven less by the desire actually to gain that right and benefit economically from its recognition than by the desire to highlight its "manifest theft" by publishers.[62] In its charged significance, "literary property" exists only in this expropriation; and in this respect, it does not represent a natural right to which *gens de lettres* awaken; it is not out there in the world waiting for writers to claim it in their progress toward independence. It went the other way—a new vision of authorial autonomy, defined against the *honnête* social integration of the *philosophes,* came first. Literary property offered an articulation of this autonomy, not as a reference to the economic independence of the freelance writer but as it figured a commercial dispossession that pointed to the intellectual's selflessness—he was too disinterested to fight for his economic benefits—and his seriousness: he remained dedicated to his philosophical project despite its unprofitability. These qualities then defined his commitment, integrity, refusal to sell out, and as a result his faithfulness to his own insights. The writer claimed literary property rights only to the extent that such rights were always already stolen because only insofar as they were stolen did they then reflect upon his credibility and transcendence.

Consequently, there is no meaningful call from its "literary" defenders for reform of the system, which is surely one reason why the pro-property texts of the minor writers have not made a great impression on historians. Oddly enough, given his hostility to its publishers, Linguet's proposals almost exactly mirror those of the guild. He certainly does not think beyond the *privilège*. Referring to the economic entitlements of authors, he notes, "to effectuate this equitable restitution, we do not need to innovate with the regulations of the book trade; it is not a matter of destroying them, or even changing the laws." His main goal is simply to reorient the debate in order to recast the *libraires,* who might have been seen as strong allies in the fight for literary property rights, into the undisputed role of obstacle to their fair recognition: "It is only necessary to precisely fix their meaning [that of the regulations], and to limit the usurpations of publishers. It is essential simply to assure for men of letters the prerogatives that time, their inattention [*négligence*, implying their disinterest], and the greed of their enemies [publishers] have still not take away."[63] Fenouillot de Falbaire takes things in a somewhat different direction, calling on *gens de lettres* to form a "typographical society" as a way to bypass the publisher: "to help themselves mutually in the printing and sales of their works."⁶⁴ This may seem like the outlines of a more constructive solution. But in the end the plan is vague and utopian, and with its first appearance on the forty-fifth page of a forty-six-page pamphlet, it is clearly not offered as the centerpiece of a brochure that, much more in line with Linguet's legal *mémoire*, is overwhelmingly given over to denunciations of the systematic abuse of writers by publishers.

Diderot and the *Lettre sur le commerce de la librairie*

In contrast to the minor writers, Diderot's engagement with literary property seems less rhetorical, more direct, and more pragmatic. There is no grandstanding or heated denunciations. The *Lettre sur le commerce de la librairie* instead offers a more intricate analysis of Old Regime publishing and of the *privilège* system by which it was regulated, one that was finely attuned both to the history of the industry and to the subtleties of its present dynamics. It is also, of course, a text written by an established figure in the intellectual world in the form of a personal letter addressed to the preeminent administrator in charge of the French book trade, Antoine de Sartine. Paradoxically, no doubt, it is the very strength of the position from which Diderot weighs in on the topic that has been at the root of the preponderantly negative reception it has received. For if Diderot had the ear of the *directeur de la librairie*, it was because he had been asked by André François Le Breton, the powerful syndic of the guild and, as one of the editors of the *Encyclopédie*, Diderot's employer at the time, to help the publishers make their case for permanent *privilèges*. That Diderot took on the task, and argued for literary property rights not as an independent intellectual speaking truth to power but as a "paid propagandist" for the guild has strongly devalued the *Lettre* in the eyes of many critics, who consider it to be a derivative, philosophically compromised dispatch. Darnton dismisses it as a rehash of "old arguments about maintaining quality by restricting production."⁶⁵ He echoes Henri Falk's earlier view that in the *Lettre* Diderot "was content to dress up in a lavish and ardent prose the somewhat feeble argumentation" of the booksellers.⁶⁶

There is no denying that Diderot was brought into the job as a "propagandist" for the Parisian guild with his primary focus on their campaign. And whether or not he was actually paid for the effort, he did have a working relationship with Le Breton and his associates, and much to gain by helping them; as Falk puts it, "almost all the authors of the eighteenth century lived in Paris and . . . needing the Parisian publishers in order to make a living, they supported their claims."⁶⁷ More complicated is the question of how this might invalidate his involvement in the literary property debates. Was it because, unlike Linguet and Fenouillot, he was sympathetic rather than hostile toward the publishers? Diderot's conciliatory tone accounts for some of the problem, but the notion of a *libraire*/author alliance in the struggle for rights was, as we have seen, not a ludicrous one at a time when the real problem, it could be argued, was the refusal of the state to recognize anything other than the *privilege* as a grace from the King. Moreover, it was not necessarily absurd for Diderot to be drawn in good faith to the image of the writer as put forth in d'Héricourt's 1725 mémoire, a text that was among the materials provided to him by the guild *libraires* as he prepared his statement.⁶⁸ Diderot was comfortably in the philosophical camp by the early 1760s, of course, but he had put in some years "working for a living" by selling his writings. After the break with his father in the late 1740s following his marriage to Antoinette Champion, Diderot himself affirms that he was "forced to work and to draw an income [tirer part] from [his] work," which he did, he goes on to explain, by turning "entirely towards letters."⁶⁹ Thus if anyone was in a position to associate the *philosophes'* elevation of the intellectual's "serious" work—aimed not for the pleasure of elites but for the edification of the Public—with the *libraires'* conceptualization of authorship as based on direct remuneration for that work, it would be him. Indeed, Diderot draws on his own memory in reproducing the publishers' symbolic valorization of such compensation as a clear marker of the distinct qualitative transformation of an individual into an *homme de lettres*: "one must have been in my place, in that of a young man who for the first time receives a modest return on a few days of meditation; his joy cannot be understood." The higher price received for a second manuscript has nothing to do with the lower risk presented by a better known writer—"the rise in commercial value of his second production has no relation to the decrease in risk"—for instead it measures his mounting legitimacy, which is finally consecrated in a third deal that affirms the writer's triumphant assumption of the identity of Author and consequently his autonomy: "At the third success, it is over. The author may have written a bad treatise, but he will do it more or less as he pleases."⁷⁰

It is, though, not just his support for the publishers that puts off critics. More saliently, the problem of Diderot's associations with the guild lay in the fact that the mobilization of the publishers for permanent *privilèges* was not merely a drive for literary property rights per se, but an effort to extend their monopoly control over the industry, as exercised through the mechanism of the *privilège*. In the *Lettre*, therefore, Diderot betrayed "his own liberal principles" by becoming an apologist for an archaic, corporatist industrial policy.[71] Yet the *Lettre* itself does not frame the argument in this way. Nor did d'Héricourt's *Mémoire*, for that matter. But the *Lettre* distances itself even more pointedly from any pro-guild advocacy, beginning very quickly in the second paragraph of the text as Diderot outlines his objectives:

Je vous dirai donc d'abord qu'il ne s'agit pas simplement ici des intérêts d'une communauté. Eh! que m'importe qu'il y ait une communauté de plus ou de moins, à moi qui suis un des plus zélés partisans de la liberté, prise dans l'acception la plus étendue, . . . qui ai de tout temps été convaincu que les corporations étaient injustes et funestes, et qui en regarderais l'abolissement entier et absolu comme un pas vers un gouvernement plus sage.[72]

[Let me tell you right away that it is not simply a question here of the interests of a guild. Ha! What does it matter to me that there be one more or one less guild, me, who has always been one of the most zealous advocates of liberty, understood in its broadest accepted meaning, . . . who has always been convinced that guilds were unjust and harmful, and who would consider their complete and absolute abolition as a step towards a wiser government.]

The "à moi" stridently marks Diderot's separation from the publishers' monopolistic agenda. Instead, he asserts that while the guild might rally in the name of outdated market control, he has a completely different goal, a fact to which he regularly calls attention throughout the *Lettre* with similarly emphatic, self-referential language that always rhetorically sets the *philosophe* apart from the guild's old corporatist logic: "Ah! Destroy all the guilds [communautés]; return to all citizens the freedom to exercise their faculties according to their inclinations [leur goût] and interests; abolish all privileges, even those of publishing, I agree to it. Everything will be fine so long as laws covering contracts of sale and acquisition remain in vigor."[73]

Diderot in fact argues that the guild's ideal of market control is in conflict with its objective of establishing a new system based on permanent rights. In his view, the latter represented the end of the *privilège* regime insofar as the *privilège* was a mechanism of favor by which a preferred few were granted special prerogatives by the king. To acknowledge permanence based on natural, inviolable rights of property was, by contrast, to turn away from such a system, and open up those "prerogatives"—now viewed as "rights"—to anyone who had the ability and means to avail themselves of them. Anyone could own property, of course, so long as they had acquired it in a legitimate way: through labor or trade. And if they owned property, they could not reasonably be denied the freedom to do with it as they pleased, according to the argumentation of the guild lawyers themselves. Diderot turns the argument against the publishers by distinguishing between the traditional *privilège*, on the basis of which a "communauté" might define itself, and a *privilège en librairie*, which should not have such an effect. "These concepts are so conflated in your mind that you have trouble separating them," declares Diderot, pointing out the misleading nature of the use of the term "privilège" in reference to the second legal form. For the publisher's *privilège* is essentially different. Inasmuch as it codifies a Lockean conception of property, it conveys not the limited favors enjoyed by a protected group but general rights exercisable by anyone. Diderot thus evokes a free trade in works with access to publishing determined not by any special dispensation or licensing but by the willingness of the individual to make it happen. No doubt, as a "propagandist," he does not drive the point home, but he certainly brings it into the light of day in various asides and digressions that, in ostensibly upholding the guild's cause, actually raise hypothetical alternatives that undermine the corporatist system. "If everyone had the freedom to open up a bookstore on the rue Saint-Jacques, the acquirer of a manuscript would be no less its real owner, and as such, a citizen protected by laws, while the counterfeiter remains a robber to be pursued with all severity," he writes, explaining the illegitimacy of piracy, but in the process conjuring the image of an open, unrestricted market in cultural goods.[74]

Sympathetic readers of the *Lettre sur le commerce de la librairie* who have sought to validate Diderot's participation in the literary property debates in the face of all the criticism he has received are at their most persuasive when they point to these small barbs aimed at publishers and the guild in particular, which the latter then cut out when they reworked the text into an official form to be submitted to Sartine.[75] And there is no denying that, for a defense of an "Old Regime patriciate," the *Lettre* offered some harsh rhetoric about the Parisian publishers: "the booksellers' guild is one of the most destitute and disparaged; they are almost all beggars [des gueux]," Diderot points out in one soon-to-be-deleted passage; "Cite me a dozen out of all 360 [members of the Parisian guild] who own a change of clothing, and I will show you that of the twelve, the wealth of four has nothing to do with their *privilèges*."⁷⁶ There is obviously strategy behind such language, as Diderot seeks to validate the publishers' claims by evoking the enormously difficult conditions of their trade. What is interesting, though, is his framing of the argument. For the guild, the question of intellectual property was rooted in a vision of an industry that was sharply partitioned between themselves and provincial publishers. D'Héricourt begins his mémoire by asking, "if it would be just and equitable to grant provincial *libraires* the permission to publish books which belong to the Parisian booksellers."⁷⁷ Indeed, from the perspective of the *libraires*, the argument for property rights was in a large part driven by their sense of entitlement as a long-favored elite; for them, literary property, even as a "natural right," was also a function of their loyalty and dedicated service to the Crown.⁷⁸

This is the subtext undermined by Diderot's negative images of publishers. D'Héricourt made the case in the name of *libraires* who were struggling valiantly to apply "their talents for the public good [l'utilité commune]."⁷⁹ By contrast, Diderot's *Lettre* offers an account of their abandonment of this struggle. His early excursus into "the history of the laws" basically amounts to an exposition of the process by which the great Renaissance printers—Estienne, Morel, "those rare men who will forever be remembered in the history of printing and letters"—ceded the business to "incapable men who had none of their talents."⁸⁰ The question becomes that of how the book trade came to be populated by "so many inept editors of large and small books, so many journalists, so many adapters and simplifiers, so many mediocre minds that are occupied and so many able men who are idle," which, in turn, represents a marked shift in the analysis from the objective business conditions onto the behavior and character of the publishers confronting these conditions.⁸¹ Diderot emphasizes the cravenness of the publishers as entrepreneurs, whether counterfeiters eager to cash in on the labor of others or more important, legitimate publishers who no longer had the bold vision and courage to take on the ambitious projects that were the hallmark of the great humanist printers. If the book trade is so rife with mediocrity, "it is the effect of the indigence of the publisher, who is deprived by counterfeits . . . , and faces the impossibility of undertaking an important but slow-selling work."⁸² Later in the *Lettre*, Diderot pursues the point, arguing that without the protection of the *privilège* as a permanent right, the stock of the *libraire* will lose its value. And in the absence of a "solid stock [fonds]," there is "no more credit, no more courage, and no more enterprise."⁸³

Ultimately, the decline of the print trade is encapsulated by the publisher's loss of his entrepreneurial spirit. This is a recurring theme in the *Lettre*, which more than anything else tells the story of the loss of the *libraire*'s nerve. The text develops the narrative of a "discouraged profession" whose members are increasingly not up to the risks that the industry presents.[84] These were of course sizable; publishing required "considerable advance payments" relative to other trades because the press was an expensive technology and costs for materials—above all the paper—were high.[85] The upfront expenses entailed large press runs so that the per-copy price would not be too exorbitant: "it would be impossible to sell a work at a reasonable price without running a certain number of copies."[86] Yet the eighteenth-century book trade remained a small market in what were still luxury goods, the consumers of which were drawn from a narrow, well-off elite of Old Regime notables, professionals, and administrators.[87] As a result, there was an endemic risk to the business of publishing books. Diderot's particular angle, distinguishing him sharply from the guild lawyers, was to make the response of publishers a critical measure of their mission and success.

Moreover, Diderot's argument reflected not only an elevation of entrepreneurial acumen in his analysis of *la librairie*, against the guild's emphasis on their traditional preeminence. It also pointed to another crucial shift. For if risk for the publishers represented an economic quandary defined entirely by the problem of earning profits despite small markets and the prevalence of piracy, in Diderot's account, it raised not so much a purely economic as a cultural or "literary" problem. The ambitious projects that humanist printers had the courage to undertake were not impressive for the economic rewards that they reaped. Their value lay in their long-run cultural significance. Conversely, rather than in their unwillingness to go for the big money, the spinelessness of contemporary *libraires* was expressed in their reluctance to devote resources to "scholarly works and works of a certain quality," choosing instead to do business in "common, everyday works" that carried a more certain immediate commercial payoff.[88] Perhaps it is in this respect that Diderot dedicated himself to "old arguments about maintaining quality," to recall Darnton's critique,[89] not as a defense of guild regulations per se, but as an effect of the cultural orientation of his examination, which intersected with a common conflation for the time of material and intellectual excellence. That is, he upheld the guild quality regulations not because he cared about them, but to the extent that he presumed the material quality of a book to lie in an organic, synergistic relation to its nonmaterial aspects; because indeed, in Diderot's world a great book invariably took an appropriate form as an expensive folio with fine type and binding.[90]

Be that as it may, if risk became a problem in Diderot's analysis, it was to the extent that he considered the more difficult but more worthwhile choice to be a work of literary merit rather than of economic value. The big payoff for the *libraire*, in his estimation, was not to make a bundle with a high-stakes gamble, but to produce a writer whose eminence might one day rival that of Corneille, Voltaire, Bayle, Moréri, Pliny, or Newton. The safe option was to pick a work that was wholly reducible to its identity as a commodity, one that would never be more than a vehicle to turn a profit. Thus, beneath the short- and long-run alternatives, and the low- and high-stakes bets, the choice was really between literary and commercial value. In this sense, Diderot's *Lettre* envisions the book trade as an arena in which the opposition of economics and culture hardened and played out. The dynamic imposed itself on the *libraire*'s stock with its division into quick- and slow-selling editions, and on works themselves, which came to be starkly categorized by the binary as economically viable but culturally worthless or the reverse: highly valuable to the culture but impossible to sell. Publishers were craven to the extent that they abandoned the latter product for the former. For Diderot, their risk-averseness produced not low profits, but uninteresting and insignificant writing.

The growing importance of "literary property" in the eyes of Diderot reflects the mounting relevance of this discrepancy. And as such, if his involvement in the polemic was solicited by the publishers, his engagement with the problem was driven by a distinct agenda: the promotion of a noneconomic value—great works and great writers—through the commercial market. Unlike other apologists for literary property, Diderot does not conceive of this question in terms of a necessary antipathy. He seems, idealistically perhaps, wedded to the possibility that the economic and the noneconomic might be reconciled, and that the true purpose of *la librairie* to promote "works of a certain quality" and their Authors might be achieved through the well-directed business practices of the publisher, so long as these are supported by clearheaded regulations, including the recognition of permanent rights in intellectual property. He does, however, fundamentally conceive of the book trade, in its particular logic, to be defined by the tension; much like Fenouillot or Linguet, it is through the tension that he understands "literary property" as a way of highlighting not the economic value of the writer's work—indeed, de la Porte's compilation labors posed no problem to the publisher seeking only instant financial return—but its transcendence with respect to pure economic valuation; the fact that the work was something qualitatively superior and thus inherently difficult (though for Diderot not yet impossible) to evaluate commercially. Herein lies the specific rationale of the book trade, entailing, as Diderot points out, that we cannot "apply the principles of the manufacture of textiles to the publishing industry."[91] Moreover, to the extent that the economics/culture clash reflects, above all, the integration of the writer into the book trade, it is also what transforms the latter into the "literary market."

Correlatively, Diderot and the minor writers share a same view of the writer's work. It is, on one hand, like the artisan's work in that it is, precisely, *work* not pastime. It produces use-values not entertainment, and hence is entitled to compensation: "Everyone . . . receives money as the price of their troubles, as salary for their work; and you want the class of men of letters to be solely excepted from this general and necessary order," writes Fenouillot.[92] But the writer's work is at the same time essentially distinct. As such, in the argumentation of Diderot, the Lockean labor theory is transformed, for it now points not merely to the time and physical efforts of the writer who undertakes the duties of his profession, but to his very being, his soul, in an embellished image of the writer's "nighttime efforts" that reveals, philosophically and lyrically, a property that was in the end utterly *unlike* other kinds:

quel est le bien qui puisse appartenir à un homme, si un ouvrage d'esprit, le fruit unique de son éducation, de ses études, de ses veilles, de son temps, de ses recherches, de ses observations, si les plus belles heures, le plus beaux moments de sa vie, si ses propres pensées, les sentiments de son coeur, la portion de lui-même la plus précieuse, celle qui ne périt point, celle qui l'immortalise, ne lui appartient pas? Quelle comparaison entre l'homme, la substance même de l'homme, son âme, et le champ, le pré, l'arbre ou le vigne que la nature offrait dans le commencement également à tous, et que le particulier ne s'est approprié que par la culture, le premier moyen légitime de possession? Qui est plus en droit que l'auteur de disposer de sa chose par don ou par vente?[93]

[What is the good that a man can possess, if a work of intellect, the unique fruit of his education, of his studies, of his sleepless nights, of his time, of his research, of his observations, if the most precious hours, the most beautiful moments of his life, if his own thoughts, the feelings in his heart, that part of him which is the most cherished, which never perishes, and which immortalizes him, does not belong to him? What comparison can we make between man, the very substance of man, his soul, and the field, the meadow, the tree or the vine that nature initially offers to everyone equally, and that the individual only appropriates by cultivation, the first legitimate means of possession? Who has a greater right than the author to transfer his work by gift or sale?]

Ironically, it is precisely the specificity of literary property, its rootedness not simply in the physical labors of the author but in his intellect, thought, and being, that renders this "belonging" unsellable and thus impossible to remunerate. "The works of a man of letters can no longer be compensated with money," writes Mercier.[94] After all, what price can be put on the character and insight of the writer? Any figure instantaneously demeans its real value and reconverts it into something banal, an "everyday" volume conveying no insight, no soul, and no character. What had to be asserted, nonetheless, was the principle not just that writes should be paid for their toils, but that no one deserved more to be paid for such sublime efforts than authors, though ultimately no one was paid less.

Rejecting the Market: Commerce and Cultural Value

In the end, the orientation of writers to the book trade through claims to literary property and economic entitlements conjures a vision not of entrepreneurial writers but of writers as failed entrepreneurs. They are defined by their integration into the economic field: by their labor and rights to compensation for that labor as well as for the utility that their efforts produce. Yet they are at the same time defined by the fact that they never actually exercise those rights or pocket the earnings; that their work is in its essence unlike "normal" work; and that the utility and contribution of their writing, immeasurably greater than that of most laborers, are however not recognized in their age but only, if they are lucky, much later by posterity when they are no longer around to benefit: "In this supposedly enlightened century," observes Mercier, "arts and trades [les arts] are never remunerated other than inversely to their utility.... The wages of a brilliant coachman or an excellent cook are twice that of a good tutor, even if his name is J. J. Rousseau.... While during his lifetime, the Author will not have been compensated."[95] Diderot similarly asks: "how many authors have only attained the celebrity that they deserved a long time after their death? It is the fate of almost all men of genius; they are not understandable to readers in their time; they write for the following generation."[96] In its broad strokes, the image is timeless, but for the writers of the late eighteenth century eager to transform their social marginality into something more meaningful, its force drew on the resonance and power of images of difficulties in the commercial sphere. Their coming-before-their-time aspect was most compellingly conveyed in the evocation of unsold books languishing in the stock of a *libraire* or of authorial defiance to the publisher's domineering efforts to alter the writer's work in catering to current tastes.[97] Which means that only inasmuch as the work was commercialized did its essential resistance to commercialization, and all the distinction that went with such a refusal, become clear.

Authorial anticommercialism was, in its essence, an outcome of a "turn to the market," which consisted, as we have seen, in the incorporation of images of commercial involvement into the writer's self-presentation in order to project his alienation from commerce. The writer pointed to an engagement with the publishing industry in order to highlight a repudiation of it and transcendence with respect to it. It is in the inextricability of the opposed movements into and out of the book trade that the "literary market" takes shape. The complete assimilation of the writer into the book trade, on its own, did not establish the latter as a true literary field. Voltaire in fact envisioned such a comprehensive commercialization in a well-known letter from June 1733 addressed to an unidentified royal officer. In it, he pursued what might be called an economic benefits approach to the administration of *la librairie* that anticipated the later arguments of Malesherbes against excessive regulation based on the wealth and economic dynamism that the book trade, considered purely as an industry, represented for the nation's economy: "the thoughts of men," writes Voltaire, "have become an important object of commerce."[98] Above all, censorship should be minimized; Voltaire's call for "freedom of the press" is what has made the text famous.[99] Censorship ensures orthodoxy, but in the process, Voltaire points out, it drives business out of the country. This presents a trade-off, which administrators had traditionally not weighed with enough lucidity: "Dutch booksellers have earned a million a year from the intellect of the French," he asserts, and while a bad novel might, from a moral perspective, merit suppression, pragmatically, it helps a whole series of people live off their productive capacities.[100]

Voltaire spells out the economic beneficiaries of press freedom, including, but only as one among many others, the author: "The novel sustains [fait vivre] the author who wrote it and the bookseller who sells it, along with the foundry worker, and the printer, and the papermaker, and the binder, and the pamphlet peddler [colporteur], and bad wine merchants, to whom all of these bring their money."[101] At first glance, such language seems to manifest a thoroughly economic orientation in its striking equivalence of literary activity with other artisanal and mercantile trades. In truth, it is exactly the opposite. The text's unproblematic integration of the writer into the business of book publication expresses a decidedly *non-economic* view of letters, in that the precondition of such a seamless integration is a firm belief that this business, in the end, had nothing to do with the intellectual's credibility and moral authority, and that, by the same token, intellectual legitimacy was entirely unaffected by the writer's fortunes in the commercial sphere. The economism of Voltaire's "Lettre" reflects the conviction that the credibility of the *homme de lettres* would be established elsewhere, in the salons of *le monde* or through personal relations with monarchs and potentates. In any case, only by excluding the possibility that the publishing sphere might be a battleground for the legitimacy of writers could Voltaire survey it and, from this perspective, see no constitutive tension or clash of agendas between writers and *libraires*. For there was nothing in the business of books at stake that was not of an economic order; Voltaire merely recognizes the fact.

It is when the credibility of the writer and "literary" value are introduced as factors into the production process that the book trade becomes the "literary market," as it becomes a cultural field in which intellectual legitimacy hangs in the balance. This, I suggest, is what fundamentally integrates the writer into the market, even as this integration is conveyed through a negative language that articulates the rejection of all commercial interest on the part of the writer, making the economic-benefits view of Voltaire unthinkable. The market, after all, calls forth a new type of rejection, not the aristocratic haughtiness that continued to be the dominant modus operandi of writers dealing with publication in the eighteenth century, the purpose of which was to project their *honnêteté* as socialized, non-professional *gens de lettres* with little at stake in the print trade.[102] In its magnified anxiety and its postulation of a primary, intense clash in values between the economic and the literary or cultural, the new rejection instead invoked authorial proximity to commercial publishing, situating the writer squarely within the book business, but as an outsider to it and a stranger to its rationality. In so doing, it also rendered the economic nature of the publishing industry essential. As the writer constructed an identity, legitimacy, and spirituality through a self-conscious insertion into the fierce battle over values that publishing came to imply, the book trade was reconfigured in decisive ways.

Pierre Bourdieu's influential conceptualization of the "literary field" highlights the negative reactions of writers to what he presumed to be the objective commercialization of the literary world in the Second Empire. The model endeavors "to understand the experience that writers and artists had of the new forms of domination to which they found themselves subjected in the second half of the nineteenth century," he writes, adding, "the reign of money was everywhere affirmed."[103] Against this incursion of pitilessly economic priorities into the cultural sphere, writers envisioned an alternative field in a point by point repudiation of economic rationality, defining for themselves "an inverted economic world" in which their commercial failures signified success. Inhabiting this countercultural, antibourgeois space, the writers were then "freed" from the pressures of the market: "The symbolic revolution by which artists freed themselves from bourgeois demand by refusing to recognize any other master than their art had for effect to make the market disappear."[104]

We might, though, invert Bourdieu's hypothesis and argue that "commercialization" takes shape as an effect rather than a cause of the valorization of "anti-economics." The book trade has an objective reality, of course; it would be absurd to suggest otherwise. But we should not assume that this reality corresponds to the often charged, polemical rendering of the publishing industry in terms of the rawness of its economic rationality, which is so often to be encountered in the overdetermined texts of writers or, for that matter, in the investigations of scholars who have been especially influenced by these writers. The image does not go without saying, for it was the outcome of a discursive effort. Nothing better illustrates this rhetorical transformation of the print trade than the negative caricature of the *libraire* as a profiteer. Publishers became markedly devalorized figures in the eighteenth century. Not that they had enjoyed an especially high status in earlier times. In the seventeenth century, though, they were dismissed not as ruthless pirates but as lowly artisans defined by the service that they performed. They were as a result objects of scorn. But publishers were also suitable recipients of the generosity of writers, particularly insofar as the latter lay claim to a noble identity, and in the effort, sought to convey their contacts with *libraires* as expressions of their aristocratic magnanimity. Molière satirizes such gestures in *Les Précieuses ridicules* when the valet Mascarille, playing the role of an aristocratic *bel-esprit*, affirms that he has had his madrigals printed merely to help out his publishers: "It's beneath my dignity to print; but I do it for the sake of the book-sellers."[105] The latter might be uncouth, inept, inelegant, and ungracious. They were certainly merchants, driven by a base desire to make money. However, before the eighteenth century, they were rarely "pure merchants," to the extent that the "pureness" of their mercantile natures was conceived to be a travesty of their vocation as printers/booksellers.[106]

It was in the eighteenth century that they became "pure" merchants. The characterization was widespread, prevailing even among officials in the administration such as Malesherbes, whose liberal approach to overseeing the book trade entailed a view of the publisher as a thoroughly economic actor. This was not so much for Malesherbes a slight as a way to oppose the choking guild regulations, which for instance required publishers to be "adept in Latin" and to know how to read Greek—excellent rules for forming a humanist scholar but of scant relevance in a modern print industry in which Classical books were no more than a niche market.[107] But for writers seeking to construct their legitimacy as intellectuals, the image had another currency. An early pamphlet from 1725 by Pierre-Jacques Blondel set the tone with a description of the publishers of his day as "men solely preoccupied either by their profits or their pleasure."[108] Fifty years later, the image had not lost its power: "Publishers in France devour all the revenues from the books that they produce. Thus they almost all make quick and prodigious fortunes, which should no longer surprise us," writes Fenouillot. "Most live in luxurious houses with expensive furniture."[109]

Was it true? To what extent had publishers become narrowly commercial in their motivations and initiatives? No doubt, measuring the eighteenth-century *libraire* against the Renaissance printer, as observers of the time did, was apt to highlight significant changes in the profession. The publishers of the Enlightenment were clearly not humanists. But did this signify that they were, as a consequence, cold-blooded profiteers with no interest in the intellectual aspects of book publishing? The rhetoric of anti-*librairie* writers indicates that they were. Having highlighted the avidity of publishers focused on nothing but economic gain, Blondel describes them as "lacking knowledge and for the most part education." They are, he continues, "ignorant and unlettered men."[110] Yet publishers were more complex multifaceted characters than this suggests. Of course, they were not solely driven by lofty objectives, and certainly they were prepared, in the conduct of their trade, to sacrifice philosophical or ideological consistency, as Darnton has shown in his studies of the correspondence of the Société typographique de Neuchâtel.[111] But from mixed and flexible motives, it does not then follow that *libraires* were driven *only* by the profit motive conceived in all its rawness, ready to do whatever necessary in order to amass a fortune and live a life of luxury. By most indications, publishers were not led to abandon so completely their intellectual interests, even as their commercial activities became more sophisticated and remunerative. To some degree, they were always able to assume complex, dual identities as "men of letters" and "businessmen." Elisabeth Eisenstein cautions against an "either/or approach" to Enlightenment-era publishers, which presumes that if they were not a scholar-printer in the mold of Robert Estienne then they must have been ruthless sharks willing to do anything for a buck: "they are miscast when assigned one or the other single role," she affirms.[112]

I would suggest that the transformation in eighteenth-century France of the publisher as a *pur marchand* who was by nature hostile to any deviation from a rigidly economic agenda, and thus hostile to cultural value and to the writers who advanced it, had much more to do with the reconceptualization of the cultural field in terms of a constitutive tension between economic and literary values, than anything else. In this respect, the publisher as a "bloodsucker" was the outcome rather than the cause of the writer's self-presentation as "exploited." The *librairie* became a "tyrant" not on the basis of any concrete mistreatment of the writer, but to the degree that the publisher was conceived in terms of an exclusively economic disposition, which then inevitably appeared to take unfair advantage of a writer who was, at the same time, being redefined in terms of an equally complete lack of commercial savvy. The *libraire* exploited the writer not by being dishonest or ruthless, but merely by trying to make money at all, which is to say by the logic of a commercial orientation. Fenouillot wants to show "how publishers, proud of their wealth and believing themselves superior to those whom they make work, quickly made themselves the tyrants of all men of letters." His illustration, though, does no more than point vaguely to the business arrangements into which writers entered with publishers seeking to buy their manuscripts, as if the development in and of itself entailed the conclusion of economic tyranny: "Circumstances, chance, necessity sometimes forced very esteemed men of letters to work for these merchants, and to submit to being paid piecemeal for immortal works, and they made for the publishers immense profits."[113] The evocation of bookseller gains, always in comparison with the pittance paid to recognized "great" writers, would be incorporated as an integral element in this binary rhetoric. Fenouillot, for instance, goes on to note the 100,000 francs that the seventeenth-century publisher Michelot made off of *Les caractères*, while La Bruyère took home a measly 100 écus. But it is the example of Le Breton and the millions he and his associates pocketed from the *Encylopédie* against the few thousand livres paid annually to Diderot for his years of tireless editorial labors to which the anti-*libraire* polemicists return: "as long as he worked for them, M. D*** only received a modest honorarium of 2,500 livres a year, which was to provide for his livelihood; he now only has annuities of *200 pistoles* left. Meanwhile, it has been shown that the Publishers have earned more than two million," objected Fenouillot.[114]

If the literary market resulted from the conceptual transformation of the book trade as a cultural field in which "literary" rather than economic values were the chief product, it was also as it was incorporated into the model of the literary market that the publishing industry became a cutthroat world ruled by a relentlessly economic logic. In truth, these were two facets of the market, and both worked to advance literary value. The rhetoric of exploitation might sound like the account of the subordination of the great to the mercantile. But in reality, far from reflecting the objective abasement of the writer to the greedy publisher, such discourse articulated the writer's transcendence since in its essence, the publisher's utter economic domination of the intellectual would become one of the clearest, most resonant, most persuasive, and most durable signs of the latter's basic qualitative superiority. It underscored the gulf that from "a trafficker who sells" and a "subordinate merchant" fundamentally distinguished the Author as "a man who thinks and who invents,"[115] thereby constituting this gulf as a believable premise in the minds of readers who would buy into its objective reality, and as a consequence, into the reality of the writer's difference, singularity, and credibility as a moral guide. The intellectual authority of the new outsider-writer took shape in the eyes of this developing public, a public often identified with the readers of Rousseau, surely because Rousseau, to whom this study turns in the next chapter, put on one of the most compelling performances of sacrifice and victimhood.[116]

5
The Reality of a New Cultural Field: The Case of Rousseau

THIS STUDY HAS UNDERSCORED the discursivity of writers' engagements with the book trade, examining their efforts to "live by the pen" and their denunciations of "exploitation" in the commercial sphere as arguments for a new vision of intellectual legitimacy rather than as transparent accounts of their lived experiences dealing with publishers. I am not, however, suggesting by this emphasis that these experiences were not meaningful or indeed *real*. If the appropriation of a charged language of stolen rights and abuse was above all a rhetorical move meant to cultivate belief in a new paradigm of authorial credibility, this should not then lead us to conclude that the discourse was nothing more than cynical posturing. The *philosophes* depicted their critics as hypocrites faking their way up the slopes of Parnassus—we might recall Morellet's mock preface to Palissot's *Les philosophes*, in which the author of the play hears a voice that, after describing his scurrilous past, urges him to become "the Apostle of morals and the Defender of Religion."[1] In the final chapter, we will associate the rhetoricity of the literary market with a far more complex psychological evolution, one that should not be reduced to the scheming ambitiousness of the *anti-philosophe*, nor for that matter to the raw anger of the *raté*, emphasized by Darnton and illustrated in the figure of Rameau's nephew.[2] The framework is instead that of an emerging and ultimately characteristic authorial anxiety, which concentrated on print publication once that process was embraced by writers as the essential and exclusive conduit for the projection, through a work, of a legitimized intellectual identity; and thus once the book trade as whole was approached as *the* field in which such an identity would be constructed and affirmed.

The rhetoric of the market was "strategic," though, as understood by Pierre Bourdieu, meaning that the turn to a legal and commercial language of authorial selfhood was driven by an intuitive "practical sense" or "feel for the game," which was neither purely rational calculation on the part of writers nor an entirely unconscious "natural" urge, but a drive that lay somewhere in between the two.[3] It is clear in any case that the development of the market as a cultural field owed not just to writers' investing their commercial pursuits with a new value against the symbolic dearth that had typified these activities in the framework of *honnête* publication. It also owed to the anxiety through which writers then experienced the book trade, to the degree that they grew convinced of the importance of the economic/cultural bifurcation as an essential trait of the literary field. If a "modern" intellectual identity builds on an experience of frustration with mediocrity, the market takes form when the dissatisfaction with one's middling place in the cultural field metamorphoses into an anxiety about the publication process, expressive of an increasingly *real* belief that negotiations with publishers indeed were critical moments in which success or failure was at stake, and as such really were battles in a larger war over cultural value and legitimacy. In a way, the anxiety was the psychological underpinning of the inexpressible happiness about which Diderot fantasized in his *Lettre*, when describing the writer's first payment from a *libraire*: "his joy cannot be understood."[4] Both responses assume the fundamental significance of the transaction, and assume that everything hung in the balance.

Put another way, the rhetoric of the market was, paradoxically, an effect of writers' sincerity; though not the profuse sincerity advocated by Rousseau and his disciples, but a more basic earnest engagement with reality that drove the substitution of a representation of an unambiguous outcome—say, outright abuse of the innocent writer at the hand of an avaricious *libraire*—for the inevitably more equivocal truth. For outsider writers desired the representation to be true, and felt that it *should* be so. Their sense of legitimacy—and hence their willingness to pursue careers despite the less than impressive nature of the outcomes that they experienced—were based on the premise that their perceptions of the cultural field as resting on a set of clear oppositions (commercial versus anti-commercial; insider versus outsider) were actually more "real" than the murkier facts of the eighteenth-century literary world. The rhetoric, however, aimed less to obfuscate an accepted reality in a cynical or hypocritical way, than to deny the complexity, while playing up a more simplified concept of the "market" as a description of the "truth" of the field, in which the writer's place was defined by unambiguous choices between currying noble favor or dedicating oneself heroically to the truth, and between selling out or suffering for one's art. It was in other words a question of neither deliberate deception nor self-delusion but of a good-faith, "sincere" effort to illuminate a system that was lived in convoluted ways, yet whose principles were firmly believed to be transparent. By this very fact, of course, the rhetoric of moral clarity was also shaped by a strong sense of the discrepancy, and of the resistance that the "real world" offered to the edifying visions of writers who lay claim to an authoritative understanding of things. It was haunted by the awareness that what writers affirmed to be true—say, the purity of their motives, for which, as would Rousseau, they paid dearly by their exclusion from established social circles and their exploitation in the book trade—clashed with an objective world that did not always accord this "truth" much credence. In their refusal to conform to the view the "real world" had of them, these writers might be confirmed in their superiority, at least in the eyes of those predisposed to see in such recalcitrance a noble commitment to ideals. More menacingly, though, the discrepancy also underscored the actual ambiguity of their own motives, which were neither entirely pure nor wholly disinterested but were reflective of the overarching complexity of a literary field in which ultimately no hard and fast distinction between commercial, social, and intellectual interests could be made; a field in which one motive invariably implicated the others; and where businessmen were, as publishers, always to some extent also men of letters, and men of letters always entrepreneurs marketing their writings and identities. And all were connected to the social field through ambition and a desire to be recognized and respected by an increasingly literate public with a mounting interest in books along with greater resources—money, time, education—to devote to them.

In this respect, the rhetoric of the literary market did indeed refer to a *real* turn to commerce. The market articulated a reorientation experienced as real by writers and for us understandable as such. The new reality, though, consisted of a transformation in expectations reflecting not contacts with the publishing industry where none had previously been, but an intensifying visibility to those contacts that no doubt made it seem as if the writer was caught up in commerce for the first time. Yet such an image points less to an unprecedented engagement with the book trade, than to efforts rooted in the disappointment of less-than-successful writers to advance an alternative ideal of intellectual credibility, which would convert their mediocre positions—signaled by their inability to close the distance separating them from the *mondain* focal points of the Old Regime field, such as salons and academies—into transcendent ones signified by the very same distance, figured now to reflect their integrity and autonomy. Incorporated into the heart of their self-presentations, this distance was evoked in writers' avowed desire to speak to a broad public, a move that was, in turn, concomitant with a shift away from the socially oriented media of the traditional field—oral readings, conversations, correspondence, and manuscript circulation—to that of commercial print. For with its paratextual devices for addressing an abstract readership and its potential for a wide geographic dissemination, print was especially able to affirm and sustain an image of the writer's repudiation of high society coteries in favor of a more significant and universalizing audience.[5] Indeed, the market reflects the elevation of print as the exclusive media for the projection of authorial quality.

Of course, the *philosophes* had also presented themselves as the writers of important books rather than salon conversationalists or court poets. But they also maintained close rapports with the elites whom they considered to be their most important audience. They could therefore offset the robust assertions of autonomy that defined their textual voices and grounded their credibility as intellectuals with *honnête* behavior outside the textual interaction, which projected not their liberty but their social dexterity and likeability: as it would turn out, d'Alembert was "merry," "animated," and "amusing."[6] Absent in his writings, these qualities were widely attested and enabled his continued *mondaine* integration and hence his viability as an establishment intellectual. The writers of the "literary market" could not, however, sustain such an ambivalent posture because they had no countervailing possibilities. The elite social field was not an option for them. Not that it was entirely closed off; we have seen that it was not. But it was open to them only as a space in which their secondary status as midlevel writers would be highlighted. Consequently, the stakes of publication dramatically changed since there was no other framework in which these writers could project their excellence other than through a textual exchange that was mediated exclusively by a printed book. Their qualities were, as a result, no longer external or partly external to the publication process, but entirely internal to it. Indeed, their preeminence and their intellectual credibility were, in the minds of these writers, its *only* meaningful output and, conversely, only the publication process could manufacture these values. Rooted as we saw in a viscerally "real" rather than a rhetorical social isolation—that is, in an isolation and poverty constructed as a "real" experience against the "hypothetical" poverty of d'Alembert and the *philosophes*, though it was, of course, just as rhetorical—the transition into the book trade was, by the same token and in spite of its discursivity, a "real," lived experience, as was, moreover, the literary market, which would then be conceptualized as the concrete, coherent, and autonomous field into which the writer shifted when he or she turned away from elite society and its pleasures.

The Stakes of Publication: Authorship as Anxiety

Manifest in an increasingly acute anxiety through which the book trade, as a field for authorial self-actualization, was engaged, the "reality" of the literary market surges forth in Rousseau's correspondence with his Dutch publisher, Marc-Michel Rey. Specifically, it is discernable in a characteristic gesture of those letters: namely in Rousseau's strong assertions of authority *within* the publication process, which forwarded a claim to a preeminent position vis-à-vis the publisher and his agents in the name of authorship: "If it is ever permitted to touch the text of the author against his will," Rousseau affirms, rejecting a change made by one of Rey's correctors, "it must at least be to make the work more perfect."[7] Lest we take such an assertion too much for granted, we should recall the degree to which Rousseau made the rejection of the various forms of cultural distinction a central feature of his intellectual autobiography. The *Confessions* offer many examples: he refused a pension from the king in appreciation for his 1752 opera *Le Devin du village* and a sinecure at the *Journal des Sçavans* obtained for him by Malesherbes, about which he wrote: "With it, I entered into a lettered society of the first order."[8] He consistently underscored his desire to be seen in the eyes of a public of Parisian *salonnières* and intellectuals not as a *philosophe* or *homme de lettres*, but as a humble copier of music, "earning ten *sols* per page by his work."[9] In his letter to the Archbishop of Paris, Christophe de Beaumont, following the latter's long condemnation of *Émile* and *Le contrat social*, Rousseau ironically takes issue with Beaumont's reference to him as a *philosophe*: "I have never aspired to that title, to which I acknowledge that I have no right; and I am surely not renouncing it through modesty."[10] Moreover, Rousseau had enjoyed success in the book trade, and certainly could have posed as a "professional author" as a way of accentuating his lowliness against the social pretensions of Parisian intellectual elites. Yet quite to the contrary, when it came to interacting with printers, correctors, pressmen, and *librairies* over the publication of his writings, Rousseau insisted on the recognition of his authorial status as an inarguably superior one to theirs.

Not that this was an original stance to take. Rousseau was actually adhering to a well established hierarchy in the discourse of pro-property polemicists who long argued that publishers were subordinate to writers not just from a symbolic perspective but from a commercial one, too, as agents within the production process. "It seems that in a right order, the Publisher is made for the author and not the author for the Publisher," wrote Blondel in 1725.[11] As a polemical flashpoint, the exploitation of writers was at a basic level an attack on the *libraire*'s refusal to acknowledge this priority and a reassertion of the right order according to which the author was preeminent. In the opening report on the trial of Luneau de Boisjermain, the *Mémoires secrets* praised the stand of his lawyer, Linguet, against "the tyranny exercised by publishers towards men of letters, of whom they should be no more than their laborers [manoeuvriers] and their sellers [colporteurs]." The entry adds that Linguet "brings them back to the respect and the subservience that they [publishers] owe to authors."[12] Such a perspective diverges strongly with the Voltairean economic-benefits view, which, as we studied in Chapter 4, conceived of writers in the book trade as one among a series of equal agents contributing to the production of a book. Now authors assume a primary place in the sequence, radically so because they are taken to be not just the most important source of value, but the sole source, occupying a singular position on the basis of the irreplaceable factors that they apply to the undertaking: their thoughts and insights. These and only these are the elements that make the book significant and valuable, not the efforts or time of the pressmen, printers, or correctors. Consequently, the latter play an exclusively negative role in the manufacture. Unable to add any value to the product, they can only subtract it, either by introducing modifications—any change traceable to the laborers of the publication process was obviously a bad one[13]—or by making mistakes, either way, by doing something to alter the writer's text, thereby distorting its communication in the book, making the latter worthless as a conduit of the writer's vision. The ideal function of the workers is then to be as unobtrusive as possible, and to focus all their energies on ensuring that the work was not compromised in the process of its transformation. Their job, in this sense, was to accept and defer to the authority of the writer, and in so doing, to help constitute it.

That was, at least, the writers' view of their position in the book trade. In the real world, of course, the arrangement was not so self-evident. Far from it. As a result, inseparable from their sense of superiority was their need constantly to assert it. Rousseau's self-affirmations might, in this respect, be contrasted with the sense of preeminence that was also expressed, not surprisingly, in Voltaire's letters to his Genevan publishers, Gabriel and

Philibert Cramer. Certainly, Voltaire did not feel any less superior to his *libraires* than Rousseau. Unlike the latter, however, Voltaire did not directly defend his paramount position in direct assertions of it but articulated his superiority in coy expressions of insouciance, sarcasm, and playfulness, which had the effect of conveying his untouchability. Voltaire had little at stake. Or more exactly, one of the primary goals in his publishing activities was to project just how little he had at stake, and in so doing to project the stability of his identity as a socially integrated, politically connected *philosophe*. His reactions to his publishers' mistakes offer a case in point; they can be alternately amused, exasperated, or stern, but his sternness is that of the self-possessed aristocrat disappointed by a mediocre service rendered. His responses are tinged with dry ironic reprimand: "*Pucelle* is rife with mistakes; my works bristle with them. . . . My dear brothers, a little more attention and care," he berates his publishers as they are printing his burlesque epic in 1762.[14] A year later, reading the proofs for the *Traité sur la tolérance*, he adopts a similarly sarcastic tenor, "Monsieur Cramer has not sent the final proof O. There were a lot of mistakes on it. It would be sad if they had been printed."[15]

Voltaire's composure underscores, through contrast, Rousseau's feverishness in a corresponding position, confronting his publisher's errors: "The correctness of the work that you will print is more important and more worrying to me than I can tell you," he writes to Rey with the printing of the *Lettre à d'Alembert* getting under way in the spring and summer of 1758. In a striking counterpoint to Voltaire's haughty nonchalance, Rousseau's responses to the blunders that he uncovers in the proofs were explosive and hyperbolic: "the mistakes are getting more frequent," he complained in June, "and if this continues, the end of the work will be unrecognizable." We might think that Rousseau is describing a massively botched job; in fact, the letter goes on to mention only five minor typos, including an unapproved hyphen in *grand-maitre* and a missing *s* in *celle*, which referred pronominally to *moeurs* rather than *vie* as the typesetter had mistakenly surmised.[16]

Moreover, like a nobleman scolding his tailor, Voltaire is primarily concerned by the impression that he will make; thus his attention is drawn more to physical than textual details, consistent with Darnton's vision of the "typographical consciousness" of the early modern age. "Seven mistakes in the preface of *Jeanne*; several pages with ink so white that they are not readable; it is the fault of the printers," he chastises the Cramers in 1761, in reference again to *La Pucelle d'Orléans*.[17] On another occasion, after seeing the proofs for the *Lois de Minos* in 1773, Voltaire objects to the quality of the characters, "the enormous size of the capital letters takes up too much paper and makes the volume unbearably thick."[18] Undoubtedly, the focus on the material imperfections of the end-product reflects Voltaire's vision of the reception of the work by a readership that knows him already, knows what he stands for and what he means. His principal concern was, in other words, to meet established expectations, or rather to affirm the established nature of those expectations, the fact that, as an influential *philosophe*, he had appropriate expectations to meet. Of course, more than anything else, this meant not disappointing those elite readers with whom he never failed in his letters to the Cramers to posit a preexisting rapport, and whom he knew to be in a position to ratify his claim to stature as an intellectual. Discussing some notes he wants to add to the *Lois de Minos*, Voltaire declares: "the whole thing will comprise a small volume that will be of interest to *honnêtes gens*, and notably to the King of Sweden, the King of Poland, the Empress Catherine, and Frederick [King of Prussia]."[19] Indeed, perhaps the most consistent logic driving his interventions into the publication process was that of gift-giving. His letters show an unremitting concern that the copies he plans to send to his intimates in high places be of a suitable quality with fine paper and binding. And he is content for corrections to be done by hand in these special volumes.[20]

If the mistakes of publishers invite assertions of authority on the part of both Voltaire and Rousseau, the former's interventions were rooted far less in his relationship to his text as its author than in his status as a *philosophe* with a valorized, socially determined position in the cultural field to defend. And while he seems to care little about the transmission of meaning—Voltaire never appears worried about any of the mistakes distorting the sense of his work—Rousseau, for his part, hardly ever says a word about typeface, paper, or ink quality. His concerns are centered exclusively on meaning: "a mistake, a misinterpretation or a misunderstanding are capable of ruining everything," he wrote in 1764, "The crucial thing is the exactness of the correction."[21] Voltaire's experience of publication was shaped by his desire to control and prop up his image as an *homme de lettres*; Rousseau's was oriented by a conviction that what was at stake was his authority as the mind behind the work. His relationship to the work itself, as its author, was paramount.

This is what he set out to defend as a publishing writer, an endeavor that, on one hand and in a manner analogous to Voltaire, was less the protection of a preexisting state of affairs—the idea that Rousseau entered the publication process with a preestablished authority to direct it—than the postulation of its preexistence, signaled by the embattled demeanor that he assumed in his correspondence: he had to forge this authority and impose it on those who, as they converted his writings into books, did not necessarily buy into it. Rousseau thus adopted aggressively defensive stances, always for instance pushing for a faster print schedule.[22] So did Voltaire, of course, but the latter did so out of concern about keeping his esteemed readers waiting.[23] Rousseau sought to minimize the time to press during which modifications might be introduced into the text or a counterfeit version might begin to circulate: "After eight months, this work, which was supposed to be ready in six weeks, is yet to appear . . . I am warning you that if your edition is not available in Amsterdam before the first of July, you will see one in London by the first of August," he writes to Rey who was printing the second *Discours* in 1755.[24] In addition, he put up fierce resistance to any revision suggested by the proofreaders, including the rectification of patent errors: "They must follow my manuscript exactly, the spelling, the punctuation, even the mistakes, without trying to correct anything," he declared as part of the terms for ceding the rights to *La Nouvelle Héloïse* in 1759.[25] When Rey noticed in a passage from the *Lettre à d'Alembert* text that "tour" should read "tort" and made the change, Rousseau thanked the publisher but only with extreme reluctance, adding: "I would prefer that you leave them [my mistakes], rather than make corrections that are not in the manuscript, because it is impossible for you to distinguish with certainty the mistakes that escape me from those that I want to leave in the text."[26] Such apprehensive gestures spoke to the writer's sense of his deep connection with his work as the sole source of its meaning. The book in turn had value only to the degree that it maintained the connection and offered its eventual owner the opportunity ultimately to peer directly into the mind of the author. The writer's objective in the publication process was therefore to preserve the relationship, and to ensure that the work, in its transformation from manuscript to book, remained conducive to the type of reception of his text—in which a reader perceived the moral figure of the author—that Rousseau theorized in a lengthy meditation entitled *Dialogues: Rousseau Juge de Jean-Jacques*.

Written in 1776, at the height of Rousseau's paranoia, the *Dialogues* stage a conversation between a character named "Rousseau" and an interlocutor referred to as "le François" about "Jean-Jacques."[27] The latter figure is the author of Rousseau's works and is shown in the text as the target of a coordinated campaign of vilification, which has succeeded in imposing on the general public a view of Jean-Jacques as "the most dissolute, vilest decadent who could exist."[28] Reflective of his generic appellation, the Frenchman adheres to the conventional wisdom despite not having known Jean-Jacques personally, and more important, not having read a word that Jean-Jacques ever wrote. The dialogues then play out Rousseau's long efforts to convince the Frenchman to change his mind, an endeavor that hinges on his ability to persuade the latter to examine the relevant books "for himself": "read for yourself the books in question," he implores, "and based on the dispositions which this reading inspires in you, judge that of the Author when he was writing them."[29] After much resistance, the Frenchman finally consents. He reads the writings, which certainly leads him to the "real" Jean-Jacques. Indeed, he finds more; as a function of Jean-Jacques's goodness, the Frenchman discovers a whole new way of seeing the world. His encounter with the true character of the author opens onto a vision of moral clarity; the two reading experiences are, in fact, inseparable. The author's individual truth is manifested in the power of his vision: "I found in them [the works] ways of feeling and seeing that distinguish him easily from all the writers of his time and most of those who preceded him."[30] That the works are the fundamental conduit for this discovery of ethical insight through an interpersonal communion is underscored by the Frenchman's refusal, after having read them and in spite of the urging of Rousseau, to meet the writer in person. There is no need for such an encounter since the Frenchman has, in reading the works, seen all that he needs to see.[31]

The Author, now in the guise of a moral visionary who reflects back onto the reader an idealized image of his or her own potential for virtue, takes form in this exchange, which develops as a communion between two souls mediated by the text, the function of which is to present as transparent a window as possible between them. Correlatively, for Rousseau, authorship becomes above all the distillation of the individual's unique moral essence into a writing that would convey this essence to a reader. Such a communication, however, rested not simply on the writer's desire and willingness to pour himself into his work as brutally honestly as he could. It lay as well in his ability to guarantee the work's transparency as a conduit of his vision. That is, the exchange, which was constitutive of the author, required that the writer convey two distinct messages: on one hand, his personal qualities, which legitimized his vision as profound and authoritative, and on the other, the credibility of the transmission of those qualities and the vision that they valorized. The two are easily conflated since they both reflect on the writer's sincerity. But the first reflects the sincerity of his dedication and seriousness in the pursuit of truth, and thus the clarity of his insight. The second indicates the reliability of the author's communication of this insight, which is to say his trustworthiness as a writer circulating his vision in a text. The precision is important for the first message assumes that what the reader finds in the book corresponds directly to the thought and intention of the individual to whom the text points; the second does not, and thereby raises the question of the individual's engagement as a writer in the transcription, printing, and publication of his thoughts.

The fact, then, is that Rousseau's transcendence as an Author—rather than as another type of cultural luminary or intellectual leader—relied not merely on his sincere and disinterested writing, as described in the *Dialogues*: "the intrepid and bold language of a writer who, consecrating his pen to the truth, does not seek the approbation of the public and who is placed above the judgment of men by the testimony of his heart."[32] It consisted no less in an ability to impose himself on the publishing process in such a way that the name Rousseau attached to the title page of his books served as a firm guarantee that the words printed in them precisely reproduced the "intrepid and bold language" in which the reader was to discover the authorial figure, and conveyed nothing else. The writer/reader connection envisioned in the *Dialogues* was radically abstracted from the actual, tangible processes by which a reader gained access to Rousseau's thoughts. After his perusal of the works, the Frenchman imagines Jean-Jacques as "an inhabitant of another sphere where nothing is like it is here."[33] But the abstraction of the image—the fact that there was no concrete social context for the exchange such as a salon or a bookstore, or at best, the context remained highly stylized as, say, "nature" or "another sphere"—was belied by an awareness that the reader would have accessed the writing in a much more prosaic way. The exchange by which the reader acquired the book in order to read it, purchasing the end-product of a complex and prolonged artisanal and commercial process that was open to all kinds of delays, pitfalls, and interventions, stood in sharp contrast with the literary exchange idealized as a communion of souls. The name of the author effectively had to obfuscate or deflect attention from this contrast. Indeed, the authority of the figure lay in the capacity to do so.

To be an author was to inhabit the uncertainty generated by the discrepancy between ideal and real. The discrepancy, in turn, outlined a new authorial space that was defined by the opposition between the ethereal intellectual plane where writer and reader communed and the artisanal and commercial system which, in reality, brought the writer and reader together not just in a spiritual bond but in one that was built on a banal economic exchange, by which the latter bought the former's book. More exactly, the authorial space, which was ultimately the literary market, took shape as the idealized sphere of writer/reader communion but only to the extent that it was envisioned by the writer (and by the reader) through a strong sense of his or her embeddedness in the commercial book trade, and therefore through all of the anxieties and fears that this sense of embeddedness produced. In this respect, the market is a fundamentally hybrid field because it is at one and the same time an idealization of the literary world in terms of abstract spiritualized encounters and an affirmation, at a psychological level, of its nuts and bolts mechanics as a field rooted in the publishing industry, and thus undergirded by economic priorities and interests. It is, more precisely, a manifestation of the inseparability of these two orders; yet also of their increasing semiotic divergence, wherein lay its tension and singularity.

Writers had of course always contended with the difference between real and ideal. The Hôtel de Rambouillet as it was celebrated in writing by *gens d'esprit* was obviously not identical with the actual social space in which they regularly encountered their patrons and fellow *gens de lettres*. There was, though, a basic homology underlying the eulogistic transformation of the cultural space, which, whether as a sublimated image or as a concrete event, remained a sphere of aristocratic social interaction. The *philosophes* presented a more complicated scenario, given their avowed hostility to a salon audience that was also their main readership. Texts such as d'Alembert's "Essai sur les gens des lettres" affirmed an oppositional relationship between an intellectual activity imagined to be geared toward a nonexclusive, universalizing public and the social framework of *le monde* in which the *philosophes* actually operated. The elite readers of the *philosophes* were, however, not so foreign to the writer/reader exchange posited in the works as the conventional wisdom, upholding the *philosophes'* unremitting hostility to the aristocracy, would have us believe. For, as we saw in Chapter 2, these works systematically incorporated exceptions to the rule of an uncultured, dissolute, and self-absorbed nobility; as a result, noble salon readers could find themselves in these works, celebrated in their role as an enlightened, exceptional elite that had transcended the traditional corrupt behavior of its caste. In this way, a certain continuity was established between an ideal field envisioned in the text—one in which the authority and the autonomy of the *philosophe* were a self-evident, acknowledged fact—and the actual social arena in which the writing was circulated and read—in which the authority and autonomy of the *philosophes* was also a fact, not as a self-evident truth, but as an effect of the desires of a self-consciously progressive elite readership eager to enhance its stature through its enlightened protection of letters.

It is undeniably one of the more significant aspects of the "literary market," and perhaps a hallmark of its specific modernity as a model of the literary field, that the relationship between real and ideal that it postulates is not one of continuity and gradation. The abstract, idealized spaces of writer/reader communion, imagined in works destined for a pointedly nonelite, nonsocializing readership, are not "better" versions of the places in which these encounters really take place. They are radically different. And as a figuration of the intellectual, the author constructs him or herself in and through the radical nature of this difference, with, in a sense, a foot in each world. In the process of self-actualization and self-presentation, the dissimilarity of the book trade and the cultural field is, moreover, transformed as a direct and elemental opposition, which it is not "objectively." Objectively, the book trade is a complex, multivalent space amenable to profit maximization *and* the pursuit of cultural value; it is characterized overall by the generally operative intermingling of the two motivations. But in the mind of the writer laying claim to the new legitimacy of the Author—the outsider who turns to print publication in a repudiation of the traditionally sociable literary activities of the *mondain* field—the book trade was a much simpler space, regulated by the single logic of pure commerce. The simplification, moreover, had little to do with the actual activities and agendas of those actors who inhabited the world of the commercial press but was a behavior imputed to them in the emerging framework, which rested in part on a rigid identification of the publisher's interests as relentlessly and exclusively economic. In their then inevitably painful losing clashes with such self-interested, cutthroat, and materially focused agents, the disinterest and commitment to transcendent moral values defining the new authors could only become clearer.

The Author and the Publisher

The conception and experience of publication as an epic battle fought over the substance of the text—not over its physical aspects but over its meaning and value in the eyes of readers—did not ensue from the increasingly domineering nature of publishers endeavoring to dumb down the text in their search for lucrative sales, as the anti-*librairie* discourse of literary property rights would have it. It resulted from a reconceptualization of intellectual legitimacy against an established paradigm based on the writer's elite social integration. Now the author was defined in terms of interiorized, nonsocial, indeed even antisocial personal qualities that would be projected exclusively through the published work, with the work pointing no longer outside the frame of the text, even if obliquely, to the social and political associations of its writer, but exclusively to the presence of the mind and soul of the writer manifest within the text itself—to his most personal thoughts, as Diderot had put it; to the sentiments of his heart and the purity of his motivations; in other words, to everything that defined the writer in his goodness and singularity as an individual with a profound, unique, morally clear vision of the world. Envisioned as a ruthless commercial field run by vicious sharks, the literary market was, by this fact, the field in which socially isolated writers could, in images of their struggles against *libraires*—whether the polemical battles of a Linguet or a Fenouillot in favor of literary property or the psychologically driven disputes of a Rousseau with his publisher—transform themselves as ethereal figures inhabiting "another sphere."

At one level, all this bears witness to the commercialization of literary life in the eighteenth century, yet only so long as we understand the process not in reference to changes in the objective circumstances of the book trade, though these certainly have an impact, but as a function of an evolution in mentalities, by which writers turn to commercial print with a mounting expectation that it offer an *essential* medium of self-presentation rather than the ancillary one, upholding and enhancing an image constructed elsewhere. At another level, though, the rise of the literary market as a cultural field represents a *decommercialization* of the book trade, a fact that seems counterintuitive in light of the market's conceptualization of the publishing world as a relentlessly profit-maximizing one. But such a view should be placed in historical perspective. For in the "traditional" imaginary of the Old Regime the book trade was always a thoroughly artisanal sphere. Its agents were never expected to be anything more than tradesmen rendering a service, with whom the socially superior writer would have an appropriate relationship. The correspondences of the seventeenth century, in those rare cases where they point to such a thing at all, manifest little substantive interaction between writers and their *libraires*, beyond the formulaic discourse that such a socially asymmetrical commercial relation would entail.

Albert Schinz observed about Rousseau's letters to Rey, "we are aware of no more precious documents . . . to help us know the real Rousseau."[34] Such a statement would be unthinkable about seventeenth-century writer/publisher epistolary exchanges, which in any case have generally not been well preserved.[35] The contacts that these letters would register are in fact more likely to be encountered indirectly, surfacing, say, in the correspondence between a writer and an intermediary, often a friend and hence a worthier interlocutor, who had been dispatched to negotiate with the *libraire* on the writer's behalf. For instance, Guez de Balzac's interactions with the Elzevirs, the Dutch printing family in charge of publishing *Aristippe* in 1652, come to us via his letters to Valentin Conrart, who, as a *secrétaire du roi* in charge of issuing privileges from the 1630s to the 1650s, was often called upon to play a mediating role between *gens de lettres* and *libraires*.[36] It is to Conrart that Balzac voiced his concerns about the Elzevir edition, given that a copy was meant for Queen Christine of Sweden. Despite the high-stakes patronage, his qualms remained, nonetheless, polite and restrained: "Even though I am not that happy about the Leyden edition, I do not want to be uncivil [*faire d'incivilité*], and I have written to Messieurs les Elzevier the enclosed letter that I am submitting to your usual courtesy."[37] Most important, authorial views on the publisher in the seventeenth century did not conceive of the latter as a callous or exploitative profiteer, even though they recognized the economic raison d'être of the *libraire*, especially in that classic gesture of *honnête* publication which articulates a magnanimous concern for the publisher's profits: "It's beneath my dignity to print; but I do it for the sake of the book-sellers," Mascarille had affirmed in a line from Molière's *Précieuses ridicules* cited earlier.[38] The would-be noble poet acknowledges the economic orientation of the publisher, without then demonizing it as an abdication of a greater moral vocation; for the seventeenth-century *libraire* was not expected to have such a vision. Guez de Balzac would not doubt that his publisher did not share his intellectual priorities, at least not entirely, and this thought would not give him a moment's pause. For even with its inevitable failure to correspond with the writer's agenda or hopes, the publishing process was not by its commercial nature assumed to present a serious threat to the latter. Print publication certainly presented dangers, which we explored in Chapter 1, but they were not related to the mercantile orientation of the profit-maximizing *libraire*.

At first glance, eighteenth-century nostalgia for the great humanist-printer of the Renaissance registers the commercialization of a cultural sphere in the process of being overrun by "pure merchants." What it actually records, though, are the evolving expectations of writers who turned to the agents of the book trade for more than a provision of artisanal labor and commercial possibilities to circulate their texts. The nostalgia expresses the sense of a need for a more profound involvement by *libraires* and their employees in the process of cultural production—as it was consummated by the writer/reader exchange envisioned in the *Dialogues*—to the extent that writers increasingly considered the book trade to be a critical field of authorial self-presentation, not ancillary to the traditional social field of literary life but the alternative to it. Enlightenment-era publishers had not become more money-obsessed and cutthroat than their forebears. Rather, the standards against which their activities were gauged had shifted. The anxieties of Rousseau symptomized the changed norms. They did not just express his deep conviction of being an outsider to a process that he desperately sought to control. They also articulated his desire that the commercial agents of the book trade with whom he dealt—and above all, the publisher who emerges as the pivotal figure—would see what was at stake, that they would read him in the manner of his idealized reader, or at least understand the meaning of his reader's profoundly moral experience. They would then tend not just to the mechanical aspects of their job as artisans and businesspeople, but devote equal attention—or more attention—to its intellectual or "literary" dimensions, as well. Indeed, Rousseau's letters to his publishers convey that the latter function was vastly more significant than the former, and ultimately defined the "real" significance and value of their labors.

From a tradesman, the publisher was to be transformed as a different kind of participant in the literary project. He became an ally who, as Immanuel Kant described the publisher's role in a 1785 article on counterfeiting, worked "in the name of" the author to "bring [the author's] discourse . . . to the awareness of the public."[39] As such, he served the author in a moral rather than a purely professional capacity, with the relationship between them no longer that of a socially embedded individual seeking service from an artisan, but a more complicated and fraught one defined by confidence, trust, and friendship. "I attached myself to Rey with a veritable friendship," writes Rousseau, recalling in the *Confessions* a pension that the publisher had set up for his wife Thérèse Levasseur in 1762, in the wake of the condemnation of *Émile* and *Le Contrat social*, during a bleak period of mounting isolation and illness when he began to anticipate his own death.[40] His glowing praise for the *libraire*—"the only one that I have always been able to praise"—reveilingly overlooks the latter's shortcomings as an actual printer to accentuate instead Rey's personal qualities as more decisive: his honesty, generosity, and trustworthiness: "In truth, we often argued over the execution of my works; he was absent-minded; I was bad-tempered. But as far as the relevant questions of interest and procedure go, even though I never signed an official contract with him, I always found him to be very correct and acting with complete integrity."[41]

In the framework of the literary market, we see take form a new kind of relationship between writer and publisher, the novelty of which lay not in its commercial rationale but in the opposite: its remarkably intensive, personal nature, with the bookseller called on to transcend his tradesman/artisanal identity and professional detachment in order to throw himself fully into the effort not just of producing the writer's work but of constructing and upholding the preeminence and purity of the author's cultural identity. In 1764, Rousseau instructs Rey to print a series of letters "written from the mountain," which formulate a defense of the writer following his condemnation by the Petit Conseil of Geneva: "You will have to stand up to the bad will of certain people," he writes, "and you will have to pay extraordinary attention to the printing."[42] Commentators emphasize the striking intimacy of the Rousseau/Rey association. The publisher not only assumed the role of protector to Thérèse, but named Rousseau as godfather to his daughter.[43] In the preface to his edition of the Rousseau/Rey letters, Johannes Bosscha described the relationship as "more intimate than is normally that between a writer and his publisher," a view echoed by Schinz and Elisabeth Eisenstein.[44] Ernst Cassirer noted in his classic study that Rousseau's "misanthropy grew out of a genuine and deep feeling of love, out of the yearning for unconditional devotion and an enthusiastic ideal of friendship."[45] Accordingly, the flip side to a relationship so grounded in the writer's desire to enlist the publisher as a friend worthy of his trust was the propensity for crises and dramatic failures of nerve, in the throes of which the writer would impute to the publisher sinister motives which, seen from a neutral perspective, could never be discerned. We might surmise, adapting Cassirer, that the very personal nature of the relationship as one of trust and confidence was paradoxically one key prism through which the sinister, odious publisher took shape in all of his permutations, including the publisher as ruthless exploiter.

We close with an illuminating episode from the fall of 1761. It concerned not Rey this time, but the Paris-based publisher Duchesne, who for the stunning sum of 6,000 livres had acquired from Rousseau the rights to print *Émile*. During the autumn, Duchesne had been slow furnishing Rousseau with the proofs of his treatise on education, and the writer's growing unease was exacerbated by a series of unexplained events: when some proofs finally did arrive, Rousseau saw that they covered early parts of the text which he had already corrected. Yet no galley proofs were forthcoming, though he had sent back the revisions. Most mysteriously, Rousseau learned that Duchesne had dismantled some of the galleys from the early parts of the edition, delaying the final edition by several months, according to the writer's own guess.[46] He recalled that Duchesne was associated with another publisher named Guérin, who, as it would happen, was also a well-known champion of Jesuit causes. Racked by illness, Rousseau began to perceive the outlines of an unlikely conspiracy, which he relayed in a letter of December 1761 to his friend Paul-Claude Moltou:

Those are the facts; here are now my conjectures. One does not throw six thousand livres into the river simply to suppress a manuscript. I am presuming that my declining health has led those who have taken hold of my manuscript to gain time and delay printing until after my death. Then, master of a work that no-one will be able to inspect, they will change it and falsify it at their will, and the public will be very surprised one day to see a Jesuit doctrine published under the name of J. J. Rousseau.[47]

The distress associated with a possible Jesuitical hijacking of his manuscript consumed Rousseau for about six weeks, during which time both the director of the book trade, Malesherbes and a prominent aristocratic ally, the duchesse de Luxembourg, did everything that they could in order to placate him with the results of their surprise visits to the print shop: "I spoke to [Duchesne] him about your book," Malesherbes assured him, "and he answered me with such an air of innocence and seeming so unable to imagine why you would have complaints about him, that I admit to you that if his goal was to fool me, he succeeded."[48] Despite these reassurances, though, Rousseau was only calmed in late December when he finally received from Duchesne eight galley proofs: "I am opening my eyes with a shudder," he wrote contritely to Malesherbes: "For the past six weeks, my behavior and letters have been nothing but a string of iniquities, follies, and impertinences."[49] The episode was passing.[50] Its effects would linger, however, illustrating an experience fundamental to the formation of the literary market, whereby the writer's efforts to control the publication of his works symptomized, in their feverishness and heightened anxiety, the fragility of his confidence in the process, as well as in the publisher who was in charge of it.

In 1773, Rousseau would abruptly break with Rey in a fallout evoked in the *Confessions* by an elliptical note added to the manuscript page on which, years earlier, he had sung his publisher's praises: "When I wrote this, I was far from imagining, conceiving, and believing the frauds that I would later discover in his printings of my writings, and which he was forced to acknowledge."[51] The nature of these "frauds" has been difficult to determine. Rousseau became suspicious when Rey, on request, sent him a copy of *La Nouvelle Héloïse*, a text that he claimed in these later years was the only one of his works that he still had any desire to reread. Expecting a copy from Rey's original 1761 print-run, Rousseau was surprised to receive "a very different edition" and initially assumed a mistake on the part of the *libraire*. He was soon dismayed though to learn that the book, indeed, was from Rey's own printing, a discovery which then led him to conclude that Rey was in the business of circulating the same sinister, "falsified" versions of his writings as the enemies against whom he had been railing in such texts as the *Dialogues*; and Rey did so, Rousseau presumed, under the same nefarious influences: "All of them," he wrote, referring to both Rey's and all other "falsified" editions in a 1774 statement in which he sought to disavow publicly every reprinting of his writings, recognizing only first editions as authorized, "were done on the same model and according to the same directions."[52] All communication between the two ceased at this point.

If the precise details of the rupture have remained elusive, it is because much of the pertinent correspondence has been lost, in particular, Rey's responses to Rousseau's accusations. Schinz speculates that Rey had sent a copy of the second rather than the first edition of the novel, which included some changes that the author had himself approved.[53] The revisions were done during the turmoil of 1762–63, with Rousseau on the run following the banning of *Emile* and the *Contrat social* and the warrant for his arrest; thus he had been prevented from seeing the final version in print.[54] Bernard Gagnebin pushes Schinz's hypothesis a step further, postulating that Rousseau had received a subsequent reprinting of this second edition in which a number of errors had been fixed and fifty-five notes removed.[55] Did Rousseau notice the alterations but then fail to recognize them for his own improvements to the work? In the end, the question is impossible to answer with any certainty. What seems clear, however, is that Rousseau's repudiation of Rey was not based on a reasonable perception of fault by the publisher but reflected a crisis of confidence in him, the panicky nature of which was underscored by the overall benevolence of Rey's disposition toward the author throughout their long association: "perhaps no more was needed for Rousseau to feel deceived by the publisher," writes Gagnebin, noting the fragility of the mental state of a writer who had almost never been badly treated by his publishers.[56]

Characterized as he always is by these kinds of episodes, Rousseau will also always seem a singular example. But in his singularity he can also be viewed as a kind of limit-case, revealing by the very extravagance of his reactions something quintessential about the experience of those writers who, in an Old Regime cultural field increasingly figured to be corrupt, embraced their social isolation as a constitutive characteristic of their intellectual makeup, and in so doing, turned away from the salons of Paris to what for centuries had represented the ultimate outsider space: the world of commercial publishing. His acute anxieties about control over his writing, and the tempestuousness of his relations with those that he then entrusted with the task of presenting his authorial self-presentation to a public, anticipate what in the modern era will come across as the typically temperamental behavior of an artist who engages the commercial sphere from a paradoxical, inherently unstable position: as an author whose claim to a transcendent autonomy from this sphere is at the same time, and inseparably, the anguished experience of his or her dependence on it.

Conclusion

THIS BOOK HAS ADVANCED two key arguments, contradictory at one level but in fact complementary. On one hand, it has reconsidered a traditional narrative emphasizing the development of the literary market as an alternative system representing a fundamental break with early modern intellectual culture. In this view, the market took shape fully exterior to the Old Regime literary field according to its own logic that, against the rigid, hierarchical nature of the established cultural sphere, valorized the freedom and individualism yet also the vulgarity of commercial exchange. I have argued, however, that the literary market did not emerge so autonomously, but took shape instead as part of a broader historical process by which the commercialization of intellectual activities—of writing, philosophy, letters, and "literature"—was charged with symbolic meaning. Indeed, as Marcel Hénaff has shown, this history easily reaches back into antiquity with the formulation of a new intellectual rhetoric that defined the philosopher and philosophical insight as "priceless [hors-de-prix]." Commercial exchange was precisely that which most undermined philosophical credibility; and correlatively, the authority to perceive and disseminate the truth was then tied more than anything to imperviousness before "pecuniary temptation."[1]

The "modern" writers of the market would, of course, turn to this ancient discourse in articulating their own legitimacy as selfless, dedicated servants to truth and to the greater good. The rhetorical move was, however, sharply inflected by the more specific resonance that "literary commerce" had acquired in the early modern period; I have highlighted the early part of the seventeenth century as an exemplary moment, though undoubtedly the roots of the trend stretch back into the Renaissance and earlier. In the overall movement, evolving patterns of elite socialization—the rise of what Norbert Elias called court culture, or in a wider perspective, the development of a culture of *mondanité* centered not only at the court but also in the households of an intellectualized, progressive elite—came to define and impose new standards against which intellectual activities might, as reflections of and contributions to the preeminence of this polished elite, be valorized, and in turn recognized as the basis of a social identity of those who undertook them as *hommes* or *femmes de lettres*. To the extent that the excellence of the emerging social, cultural, and intellectual configuration was measured by its superiority over what preceded – namely, the more physical, less "literate" court culture of the Renaissance – these writers and their activities were consecrated as "modern." In the "prevailing climate of honnêteté" that ensued and set the tone for the last two centuries of the Old Regime, literary venality figured not a generic negativity, but a far more specific lack of credibility associated with one's exclusion from this "civilizing process." "Commerce" marked a failure—whether willful or involuntary—to adapt to the behavioral and linguistic norms that upheld the new elite's cult of refined manners and harmonious, polished interaction. In such a framework, the writer's interest in the sale of his or her works spoke to isolation and marginality; it evoked an inability to be integrated into the community, and to this degree, it was inseparable from a series of disqualifying ethical attributes, all of which highlighted the writer's lack of sociability: awkwardness, inelegance, rudeness, and above all extravagant self-centeredness, arrogance, and driving ambition. These qualities stood out as potential tendencies in anyone who would take the step of converting writings into printed books. "Commerce" articulated them in such a way that the individual who engaged in the acts of writing and publication might, in the gesture of "rejecting" all things commercial in the name of aristocratic leisure, conviviality, or *honnête* self-effacement, then be able to inoculate him- or herself from the moral suspicion which authorial activities inevitably elicited. Anticommercial gestures were thus key signifiers of the writer's legitimacy, not simply as a polished individual adapted to the values of the court or *le monde*, but also *as* a writer whose presence in *le monde* was precisely based on that particular capacity to delight. It was, in this respect, the rejection of commerce and of authorship as a professional function that allowed "letters"—signifying writing as it was oriented toward the pleasures and entertainments of the intellectualized elite, and pointing ahead to what we will retrospectively define as "literature"—to become the basis of an acknowledged, valued social identity.

As an alternative to the traditional aristocratic field, the literary market did not emerge from outside, as a function of the objective expansion of commercial publishing in the period. Rather, it took shape, as an alternative, *within* elite culture, initially as a representation of what this culture, in its cohesion, had to exclude. If ultimately the market presented the mechanism for rejecting the aristocratic domestication of authorship in the Old Regime, it grew out of an intellectual vision that had been forged by early modern partisans of letters as a function of elite interaction and leisure, which later writers, fashioning themselves, in turn, as "modern," then inverted, revaluing as positive—outsiderhood and the refusal to pay court—what had originally been construed as decidedly negative. With its rootedness in an older rhetoric of literary selfhood, the development of the market can as such also be understood as a similarly rhetorical effect. It was, in other words, not the product of objective changes offering an outlet to the pent-up "natural" desires of intellectuals seeking freedom from the constraints of patronage. The market instead took form in the effort to impose on a public a new ideal of intellectual credibility, which reflected the ambiguous circumstances in which those writers who were committed to it found themselves, struggling in overlooked yet viable sectors of the literary field; neither basking in prestige nor wholly lacking in opportunities, they were inevitably discontent with their lot. Endeavoring to convert their relative marginality as the basis of a newly valorized notion of themselves—based on rather than despite a non-integration now reimagined as a powerful symbol of their dedicated, courageous refusal to alter their brutally truthful insights for the amusements of an over-indulged, corrupt aristocracy—these writers highlighted rather than hid their contacts with the commercial sphere, the meaning of which, as indicators of an individual's distance from the world of elites, was clearly understood and which, consequently, effectively conveyed their independence vis-à-vis this milieu.

At the same time, while expressive of its underappreciated rootedness in older notions, the rhetoricity of the market can also help us get at what is in fact distinctive about this commercialized model of the cultural field, and about the modernity with which it is so often associated. We must, though, understand "modernity" here not as an "objective" state but rather as a polemical claim that was increasingly central to the rising legitimacy of letters in the Old Regime, and more exactly, to the growing ability of letters to legitimize an esteemed social identity, that of *gens de lettres*. For as we saw in Chapter 1, the primacy of Alain Viala's "first literary field" lay largely in the ascendency of a new use of letters—one that transforms "traditional" intellectual activities into something increasingly identifiable to us as "literature"—that was tied to the efforts of individuals to incorporate themselves into a leisured elite, precisely on the basis of their capacity to please its members with their wit. As suggested by proliferating accounts of the "new Parnassus" in the seventeenth century, the aristocratic integration of writers unfolded entirely in the name of "modernity," conceived as a "purification" and refinement of authorial practices appreciable only through a stark break with the vulgarity and inelegance of earlier intellectual trends, most notably with the pedantry and the neo-Latin stylings of Renaissance humanism. Ironically, those figures who defined themselves so completely in their contributions to the cultures of court and salon nowadays tend to stand out as the prime representatives of that which modernity will negate. Vincent Voiture is mostly forgotten today for having dedicated himself to poetry that was wholly reducible to the dynamic of the leisured interaction of elites. Yet it was precisely on this basis, on his capacity to modulate his verse to the tastes of elite *divertissement*, that in the eyes of his contemporaries he remained in the vanguard of intellectual activity, representing a bracing departure from the past.

If the claim to modernity goes back to Voiture, the modernity of those who rejected the kind of authorial practice that he represented can, nonetheless, be distinguished from the earlier variants. In fact, we can through the comparison perhaps better understand the modernity of the market. For its specificity is then seen to lie not in a self-conscious break with what preceded, since this also characterized Voiture and his innovativeness, but in the complexity of the identity into which the break subsequently led the writer, defined by the radical nature of the disparity between the image that writers projected and the objective truth of their lives. The discrepancy functioned at a number of levels, reflecting, for one thing, the inconsistency inherent in the rhetorical claim to a sincere, "authentic" self premised on the freedom of a writer who no longer sought to entertain elite patrons, but instead spoke straight from the heart and voiced the truth without fear of offending. For another, it played out in the paradox of an image of authorial disinterest and transcendence that rested on endlessly evoking the writer's entanglement in the commercial sphere, even as an account of failure and exploitation. In either case, it is above all the sharp contradictoriness of these disparities that can be said to characterize the modernity of the market-based writer, and which offers, I would suggest, the essential contrast with the seventeenth-century modernity of a Voiture. Certainly, the writers of the first literary field also constructed themselves in and through the differences between an idealized self-presentation and the reality of their lives as writers. Georges de Scudéry was not the retired military commander that his prefaces and privileges declared him to be. It might be argued, moreover, that such discrepancies were equally constitutive of their modernity, given that the first literary field was characterized by the social mobility that it opened up to individuals who, with recourse to their intellectual skills, endeavored to reinvent themselves as something that they originally were not—a part of the social elite.

But the noncorrespondence of real and ideal in such cases was a function of hyperbole and sublimation more than of direct opposition. Invariably writers overplayed their cards; such a tendency was a defining trait of the intellectual, not an aberration of the latter's nature. As the basis of an identity recognized and valorized in society, authorship was always an exercise in transforming oneself into something that, in an initial state, the individual who "published" writing, meant in a broad sense, was not, whether a refined high-society *mondain*, a *philosophe* with the political clout to advise a monarch in the name of the public, or a moral leader articulating a vision of universal justice and truth. There was no "traditional" mechanism for validating such claims; no preestablished social status, nor any recognizable political or religious affiliation such as a position in the Parlement or Church. The authority rested exclusively on the writer's ability to articulate persuasively a self-image built on personal qualities—wit or charm; a dedication to the truth; courage; selflessness—that would resonate with a public ready, willing, and with the capacity to acknowledge the image as "true", and consequently validate the intellectual credibility to which it lay claim. Thus a writer became something more meaningful: an *homme* or *femme de lettres*; a *philosophe*; or in the latest "modern" permutation, an author or an intellectual. As the figuration of a "liberated" writer, the latter is in this respect the result of a new consensus about what constitutes intellectual legitimacy and authority, more than of an actual liberation of the writer.

The key, moreover, was the effort. Authorship was not a one-time transformation but a continual effort to affirm, enhance, maintain, and control the idealized self-presentation. The self-image postulated could be of varying degrees of extravagance, and the endeavor met with varying degrees of success or failure. In fact, the writer's trajectory through the cultural and social field was, at a basic level, inevitably going to be a mixture of both, and the precise balance of the two would clearly have serious implications for the writer's present and future reputation. The discrepancy between reality and ideal, though, became more extreme in the framework of the literary market, and rested more consistently on jarring contradictions rather on than shades of exaggeration. The writer's rhetoric sought to finesse a reality that was at bottom basically opposed to it, a reality that included not just the motivated presence of the writer in the book trade, but also the very need to resort to rhetoric in order to project the writer's legitimacy as a disinterested, sincere figure. The specific modernity of the "modern author"—meaning that particular representation of the intellectual whose history the histories of literary property, "droit d'auteur," and the market seek to tell—lies in the fact that the writer formulates his claim to authority—and foremost in the work that needs to be done in further accounting for this development is understanding how the market transformed authorship into such a masculinized identity, whereas the Old Regime world of letters had not been so exclusive—out of this tension, of which he is both the effect and the cause.

The paradox of "professionalism" follows from this fact, for the autonomous writer as a "modern" identity, no longer defined by integration into the world of aristocratic leisure but by an exceptional contribution, through tireless labors and selfless dedication, to the general good, always resided in the failure to be able actually to contribute in this way, a failure measured by the compensation to which the writer was clearly entitled but which a ruthless, cutthroat system would not pay. As the arena for such failure and for all the struggles, abuse, disappointments, and mistreatment that would highlight it, the literary market clearly stands in the sharpest of contrasts with the "market" theorized as an economic concept, which emphasizes the harmonization of diverse interests and their tendency to gravitate toward an equilibrium state that maximizes overall benefit. No such harmony could ever characterize the literary market as a model of the cultural field because its essence consists in its power to affirm and project as remarkably hostile the relationship of aspiring writers to an "objective" world in which, chances are, they are engaged in a more mundane struggle for visibility and recognition.

Notes

Introduction

1. The other writers comprising the famous *cinq auteurs* were François Boisrobert, Jean Rotrou, Claude de l'Estoile, and Guillaume Colletet.
2. Paul Pellisson-Fontanier and Pierre-Joseph Thoulier d'Olivet, *Histoire de l'Académie française*, 2 vols. (Paris: Coignard, 1743), 1:107. Pellisson's section was first published by Augustin Courbé in 1653 as *Relation contenant l'histoire de l'Académie françoise*. The abbé d'Olivet updated the history in the eighteenth century. Unless otherwise indicated, all the translations throughout this book are mine.
3. Pellisson-Fontanier and d'Olivet, *Histoire de l'Académie française*, 1: 107–8, emphasis in the original. The play opens with the Monologue, which describes in idyllic, gallant language a walk through the palace and its gardens: "It is of the greatest of Kings the superb home, / And the true paradise of the delicacies of love." The Carré d'eau refers to a basin of water in the gardens. The lines are in fact part of Colletet's description of the aviary. I have included the preceding sentence, which grammatically completes the verses cited by Pellisson.
4. Victor Hugo, *Oeuvres complètes: édition chronologique*, ed. Jean Massin, 18 vols. (Paris: Club du Livre, 1967–71), 3: 1248. The "Fragment d'histoire" appeared in the June 1829 edition of the *Revue de Paris* and was included in the 1834 collection *Littérature et philosophie mêlées*. Patrice Broussel and Madeleine Dubois cite the letter to Véron in their volume in the 1950s series in literary sociology, "De quoi vivait. . . ." See Broussel and Dubois, *De quoi vivait Victor Hugo* (Paris: Deux-Rives, 1952), 69.
5. Interestingly enough, since 1 pistole equaled 100 francs in the early seventeen century, the sums in the two stories are identical.
6. See Stephen Greenblatt, *Renaissance Self-Fashioning: From More to Shakespeare* (Chicago: University of Chicago Press, 1980) and Erving Goffman, *The Presentation of Self in Everyday Life* (New York: Anchor, 1959).
7. Denis Diderot, *Oeuvres complètes*, ed. J. Assézat and Maurice Tourneux, 20 vols. (Paris: Garnier, 1875–77), 18: 18. We shall see, of course, that authors were in fact deeply involved in the commercialization of their writings from these first years. What is transformed is the relationship between this involvement and their sense of themselves as intellectuals or authors, and thus the degree to which this involvement was incorporated into their self-images.
8. Pierre Bourdieu, *Outline of a Theory of Practice*, trans. Richard Nice (Cambridge: Cambridge University Press, 1977), 170.
9. There are others, of course. But these two are of specific relevance to this project. Bourdieu's concept of the *champ* has been enormously influential and, as such, the object of much commentary, refinement, and critique. It is thus hard

enough to summarize his articulation of the concept, as applied to literary, intellectual, or artistic activities, which evolved over thirty years, let alone to account for the many interpretations of other scholars. Some key texts for Bourdieu are "Flaubert's Point of View," trans. Priscilla Parkhurst Ferguson, *Critical Inquiry* 14, 3 (Spring 1988): 539–62; "Le champ littéraire," *Actes de la recherche en sciences sociales* 89 (September 1991): 3–46; *Les règles de l'art: genèse et structure du champ littéraire* (Paris: Seuil, 1992); and *The Field of Cultural Production: Essays on Art and Literature*, ed. Randal Johnson (New York: Columbia University Press, 1993). See William Paulson, "The Market of Printed Goods: On Bourdieu's Rules," *Modern Language Quarterly* 58, 4 (December 1997): 399–415; Priscilla Parkhurst Ferguson, "A Cultural Field in the Making: Gastronomy in 19th-Century France," *American Journal of Sociology* 104, 3 (November 1998): 597–641; and Gisèle Sapiro, "The Literary Field Between the State and the Market," *Poetics* 31 (2003): 441–64, for just a few discussions or refigurings of Bourdieu's concept of the field.

10. Bourdieu, *Les règles de l'art*, 76–77.

11. Bourdieu, *Les règles de l'art*, 154.

12. Bourdieu, "The Production of Belief: Contribution to an Economy of Symbolic Goods," in *The Field of Cultural Production*, 74–111.

13. Stephen Greenblatt, *Shakespearian Negotiations: The Circulation of Social Energy in Renaissance England* (Berkeley: University of California Press, 1988), 7.

14. For this reason, the term will, at key moments, appear in quotes to remind us that its meaning is in play; alternatively, I will often use the more general "intellectual" to allow for the fact that, whatever "literary value" meant in the Old Regime, it accounted for a much broader and more diverse range of writing practices, texts, and effects than it would in a later time. The rise of the market is, of course, concomitant with the narrowing of the definition of literature.

15. A classic formulation of the author-centered approach to the cultural sphere as a whole is the notion that great writers "form" their publics while mediocre writers cater to a desire already present. Paul Valéry, for instance, distinguished works "that are as if created by the public" from those that "tended to create their public." See Valéry, *Oeuvres*, 2 vols. (Paris: Gallimard, 1957), 1:1442. Cited in Bernard Lahire, *La condition littéraire: la double vie des écrivains* (Paris: La Découverte, 2006), 57.

16. For a variety of innovative approaches to the problem of publication in the Old Regime, many of which this book will build upon, see the essays gathered in the collection edited by Alain Viala and Christian Jouhaud, *De la publication: entre Renaissance et Lumières* (Paris: Fayard, 2002).

17. Lahire, *La condition littéraire*, 39.

18. The term *libraire* technically refers to a bookseller, but the individual identified as such played a much broader role in the world of letters of the Old Regime than today. In addition to selling books from a bookshop, the *libraire* also negotiated with authors and dealt directly with printers (*imprimeurs*). In other words, he played a role closer to today's publisher. The word "éditeur" would be used now, but did not exist until the nineteenth century. I will use the word *libraire* throughout the book in its early modern sense.

19. Alain Viala, *La naissance de l'écrivain: sociologie de la littérature à l'âge classique* (Paris: Minuit, 1985).

20. See Viala, "Institution littéraire, champ littéraire et périodisation: l'institution du siècle," *Littératures classiques* 34 (Autumn 1998): 119–29.

*Part I Introduction. The Story of a Transition:
When and How Did Writers Become "Modern"?*

1. See, e.g., Robert Darnton, *The Literary Underground of the Old Regime* (Cambridge, Mass.: Harvard University Press, 1982), 19–20. Emphasizing the overcrowding of the intellectual sphere in the second half of the eighteenth century, Darnton notes that "the marketplace could not support many more writers than in the days when Prévost and Le Sage proved that it was possible—barely possible—to live from the pen instead of pensions," and Hayden Mason, *French Writers and Their Society: 1715–1800* (London: Macmillan, 1982), 48: "At a time when, in the 1720s, Pope was growing rich by his pen, writers like Le Sage and Prévost were barely making ends meet, despite the great amount of hack-work which they undertook."
2. Wallace Kirsop, "Les mécanismes éditoriaux," in *Histoire de l'édition française*, ed. Roger Chartier and Henri-Jean Martin, 4 vols. (Paris: Fayard, 1990), 2:23.
3. See John Lough, *Writer and Public in France from the Middles Ages to the Present Day* (Oxford: Clarendon, 1978), 207–8.
4. John Lough, *An Introduction to Eighteenth-Century France* (London: Longmans, 1960), 231.
5. Henri-Jean Martin, "Auteurs et libraries," introduction to part 3 of *Histoire de l'édition française*, 2:495.
6. Jules Bertaut, *La vie littéraire en France au XVIIIe siècle* (Paris: Tallandier, 1954), 350.
7. Rémy Saisselin, *The Literary Enterprise in Eighteenth-Century France* (Detroit: Wayne State University Press, 1979), 150; Éric Walter, "Les auteurs et le champ littéraire," in *Histoire de l'édition française*, 2:516–17. See also Jacques Proust's studies of Diderot's interventions into the literary property debates of the 1760s: "Pour servir à une édition critique de *La lettre sur le commerce de la librairie*," *Diderot Studies* 3 (1961): 321–46; and the introduction to Proust's edition of Diderot's *Lettre sur le commerce*, retitled *Sur la liberté de la presse*, in volume 7 of Diderot's *Oeuvres choisies* (Paris: Éditions Socials, 1964), 7–37.
8. Georges d'Avenel, *Les revenus d'un intellectuel de 1200–1913: les riches depuis sept cent ans* (Paris: Flammarion, 1922), 303–6; and Raymond Birn, "Rousseau et ses éditeurs," *Revue d'histoire moderne et contemporaine* 40 (1993): 122–24.
9. Robert Escarpit, *La sociologie de la littérature* (Paris: Presses Universitaires de France, 1973), 54.
10. Michèle Vessillier-Ressi, *Le métier d'auteur: comment vivent-ils?* (Paris: Bordas, 1982), 180. Bernard Lahire's study of the literary condition similarly takes as its starting point the "double life of writers," which is the notion that writers are structurally forced to work on two planes simultaneously: a literary plane and another that sees to their economic survival. "If there nonetheless exists anything like a poetic condition, and more broadly a *literary condition*, it lies notably in this

division of the self—of one's time and one's social investments, both literary and extraliterary—which characterizes the social life of a great majority of authors, as we can define it." See *La condition littéraire: la double vie des écrivains* (Paris: Découverte, 2006), 19.

11. Sociologists of literature distinguish between "internal financing" (*financement interne*) and "external financing" (*financement externe*), with the former conveying the idea of a "direct" payment for intellectual labor concretized as a work, and enjoying a privileged relationship to the modern concept of authorial autonomy. See Escarpit, *La sociologie de la littérature*, 47.

12. Lahire notes that the Flaubertian model of the writer-*rentier*, who is able to absorb himself completely in his work, is "the exception which proves the rule of accumulated activities." See *La condition littéraire*, 46.

13. Bourdieu's concept of "the heteronomous principle" opposes the artistic autonomy of "l'art pour l'art," representing "non-artistic" pressures, judgments, and constraints such as those that the political, economic, and social worlds impose. See "The Field of Cultural Production, or: The Economic World Reversed," in *The Field of Cultural Production: Essays on Art and Literature*, ed. Randal Johnson (New York: Columbia University Press, 1993), 38.

14. Vessillier-Ressi, *Le métier d'auteur*, 179.

15. See Geraldine Sheridan, *Nicolas Lenglet Dufresnoy and the Literary Underworld of the Ancien Régime*, Studies on Voltaire and the Eighteenth Century 262 (Oxford: Voltaire Foundation, 1989); C. E. J. Caldicott, *La carrière de Molière entre protecteurs et éditeurs* (Amsterdam: Rodolpi, 1998); Alain Viala, "Corneille et les institutions littéraires de son temps," in *Pierre Corneille: actes du colloque tenu à Rouen (2–6 oct. 1984)*, ed. Alain Niderst (Paris: Presses Universitaires de France, 1985) and *La naissance de l'écrivain: sociologie de la littérature à l'âge classique (*Paris: Minuit, 1985); and Cynthia Brown, *Poets, Patrons, and Printers: Crisis of Authority in Late Medieval France* (Ithaca, N.Y.: Cornell University Press, 1995). Caldicott's and Viala's studies will be discussed at greater length in the following chapter.

16. See Brown, *Poets, Patrons, and Printers* for a potent investigation into how invested in commercialization and textual ownership writers were from the first arrival of the press in France around the turn of the sixteenth century.

17. I will add here that beginning in Chapter 2 and continuing into Part II, I will tend more often to use the masculine pronoun when referring abstractly to the writer, especially when working off the eighteenth-century texts. This reflects one highly significant effect of the development that I am tracing, which is that the literary market evolves as a space that is rhetorically more amenable to male authorship than female, even if, as Carla Hesse has shown, the modern market also nurtured an expansion in the numbers of women who wrote and published (as in those of men). The rhetorical difficulty arises in part due to the mediated access that women had to the mechanisms through which the writer engaged the market, such as literary property rights or payments from publishers. Françoise de Graffigny and Isabelle de Charrière often dispatched male intermediaries to present their demands into the book trade, which, while allowing them to pursue their authorial activities, impeded their abilities to incorporate these commercial contacts into their self-presentations, and thus to lay as direct a claim to the new identities

opened up by the market. There is, of course, a great deal of research to consult on the gender dynamics of the Old Regime intellectual fields, and in particular, on the growing alienation of women in those fields between the seventeenth century and the Revolutionary period. The following is only a partial list: Joan DeJean, *Tender Geographies: Women and the Origins of the Novel in France* (New York: Columbia University Press, 1984); Faith Beasley, *Mastering Memory, Salons, History, and the Creation of 17th-Century France* (Aldershot: Ashgate, 2006); Joan Landes, *Women and the Public Sphere in the Era of the French Revolution* (Ithaca, N.Y.: Cornell University Press, 1988); Dena Goodman, *The Republic of Letters: A Cultural History of the French Enlightenment* (Ithaca, N.Y.: Cornell University Press, 1994); Elizabeth Goldsmith and Dena Goodman, eds., *Going Public: Women and Publishing in Early Modern France* (Ithaca, N.Y.: Cornell University Press, 1995); and Carla Hesse, *The Other Enlightenment: How French Women Became Modern* (Princeton, N.J.: Princeton University Press, 2001).

Chapter 1. Literary Commerce in the Age of Honnête *Publication*

1. Henri-Jean Martin, *Livre, pouvoirs et société à Paris au XVIIe siècle*, 1969, 2 vols. (Geneva: Droz, 1999), 1:424–29. This short section addresses the condition of the author in the first part of the seventeenth century. Martin returns to the question of authors later in the book when focusing on 1665–1702. Though he indicates in the later section that there has been some modification with respect to the earlier period, the underlying premise continues to be that "overall, . . . little change with respect to the beginning of the century" (2:919).

2. Other investigations giving considerable space to a recitation of amounts paid as central to a narrative about the evolution of the literary sphere include John Lough, *An Introduction to Eighteenth-Century France* (London: Longmans, 1960), chap. 6, 231–76, and *Writer and Public* in *France from the Middle Ages to the Present Day* (Oxford: Clarendon, 1978), 43–45, 85–96, 207–15; Alain Viala, *La naissance de l'écrivain: sociologie de la littérature à l'âge classique* (Paris: Minuit, 1985), chap. 3; and Jules Bertaut, *La vie littéraire en France au XVIIIe siècle* (Paris: Tallandier, 1954), chap. 13. In a less systematic way, such numbers have also played prominent roles in studies of individual writers. See, for instance, Raymond Birn, "Rousseau et ses éditeurs," *Revue d'histoire moderne et contemporaine* 40 (1993): 120–21.

3. Martin, *Livre, pouvoirs et société*, 1:426–29.

4. Martin cites a 1685 *Mémoire* written by the Parisian *libraires* explaining why their books are more expensive than those of the Lyon printers: "In the past, authors gave booksellers money to contribute to the printing costs. . . . Today, it is the opposite," *Livre, pouvoirs et société*, 2:915. In his introduction to part three of the *Histoire de l'édition française*, Martin reaffirms the idea: "In the old situation, often the author received no remuneration at all for his manuscript and was even sometimes forced to pay for the printing expenses" (495). See Roger Chartier, *L'ordre de livres: lecteurs, auteurs, bibliothèques en Europe entre XVIe et XVIIIe siècles* (Aix-en-Provence: Alinea, 1992), 55–57, and Maurice Pellisson, *Les hommes de lettres au XVIIIe siècle* (1903; Geneva: Slatkine, 1970), 76–93. M. Nicolet notes that, even into the sev-

enteenth century, writers seeking to publish their texts often had to subsidize the substantial cost of having the four or more copies made of the manuscript that was to be used in the printing shop. See "La condition de l'homme de lettres au XVIIe siècle à travers l'oeuvre de deux contemporains: Ch. Sorel et A. Furetière," *Revue d'histoire littéraire de la France* 63, 3 (July–September 1963): 381.

5. See, for instance, Georges D'Avenel's survey of the income of intellectuals from 1200 to the modern period, in which he converts all prices to 1913 francs. A preliminary note on prices conveys just how complicated and strained the conversion process is: the original prices have first been changed into "intrinsic francs of 4.5 grams of silver (at 222fr. 22c. per kilo, following the legal equivalency between gold and silver of fifteen and a half), and these *intrinsic francs* were converted, according to their buying power at various dates compared with their buying power in 1913, into 1913 francs." *Les revenus d'un intellectuel de 1200 à 1913: Les riches depuis sept cents ans* (Paris: Flammarion, 1922), "Note sur les prix." Jacques Douvez proposes a more direct ratio for understanding eighteenth-century values based on a perhaps oversimplified premise that one early eighteenth-century franc was worth three 1913 francs, while a late century franc was worth only two; see *De quoi vivait Voltaire* (Paris: Deux Rives, 1949), 9. David Pottinger's discussion of attempts at establishing price equivalencies in Appendix A of *The French Book Trade in the Ancien Régime* (Cambridge, Mass.: Harvard University Press, 1958) casts a strong doubt on their accuracy and informativeness, though he does go on to propose his own unlikely conversion system based on comparing the annual incomes of university professors.

6. Viala, *Naissance de l'écrivain*, 113.

7. Bertaut, *La vie littéraire en France*, 350. Martin writes, "Most authors of the time, if they do get into the habit of requesting payment from their bookseller, cannot get what they need to subsist decently," "Auteurs et libraires," 1:429.

8. Lough, *Writer and Public in France*, 209.

9. See Foucault, "What Is an Author," *Language, Counter-Memory, Practice: Selected Essays and Interviews*, ed. Donald Bouchard (Ithaca, N.Y.: Cornell University Press, 1977), 115.

10. Birn, "Rousseau et ses éditeurs," 122, 124.

11. Carla Hesse, "Enlightenment Epistemology and the Laws of Authorship in Revolutionary France, 1777–1793," *Representations* 30 (Spring 1990), 112.

12. Bernard Edelman, *Le Sacre de l'auteur* (Paris: Seuil, 2004), 129. Edelman's title obviously evokes Paul Bénichou's classic study, *Le Sacre de l'écrivain, 1750–1830: essai sur l'avènement d'un pourvoir spirituel laïque dans la France moderne* (Paris: Corti, 1973).

13. Marc Fumaroli, *Héros et orateurs: rhétorique et dramatique cornéliennes* (Geneva: Droz, 1990), 32–33.

14. Claire Carlin, *Pierre Corneille Revisited* (New York: Twayne, 1998), 4. See also D'Avenel, *Les revenus d'un intellectuel*, 294–97.

15. Alain Viala, "Corneille et les institutions littéraires de son temps," in *Pierre Corneille: actes du colloque tenu à Rouen (2–6 octobre 1984)*, ed. Alain Niderst (Paris: Presses Universitaires de France, 1985), 198.

16. Viala, *Naissance de l'écrivain*, 98.

17. Viala, *Naissance de l'écrivain*, 99. The law of 1791 recognized the exclusive

property rights of dramatic authors until five years after their deaths. That of 1793 extended the protection to all authors, and lengthened the right to a period of ten years after the death of the author. For more on Revolutionary legislation, see Carla Hesse, *Publishing and Cultural Politics in Revolutionary Paris: 1789–1810* (Berkeley: University of California Press, 1991). For an updated and nuanced account of Beaumarchais' historical connection to intellectual property debates and the role played in them by the Société des auteurs dramatiques—the subject of much historiographical mythologizing—see Gregory Brown, *Literary Sociability and Literary Property in France, 1775–1793: Beaumarchais, the Société des auteurs dramatiques and the Comédie française* (Aldershot: Ashgate, 2006).

18. Viala, *Naissance de l'écrivain*, 99.

19. "Different action, but of the same order," writes Viala: in 1653, Quinault became the first playwright to be paid a percentage and not a one-time payment. Racine, in 1665, allowed the theater troupe of the Hôtel de Bourgogne to put on his tragedy *Alexandre* only eight days after Molière's rival troupe had premiered it, "thus breaking with the tradition of the theatre's initial exclusive rights," *Naissance de l'écrivain*, 99.

20. Viala, *Naissance de l'écrivain*, 100–103. Pierre Ronsard and René Descartes, the latter among the last to benefit, were famous recipients of a *privilège général*. Henri Falk made the practice of *privilège* renewal, beginning in the seventeenth century, central to his historical analysis of the evolution of literary property rights in the Old Regime. See Henri Falk, *Les privilèges de librairie sous l'ancien régime: étude historique du conflit des droits sur l'oeuvre littéraire* (Paris: Rousseau, 1906), 87.

21. Viala, *Naissance de l'écrivain*, 103.

22. Nicolas Boileau-Despréaux, "L'art poétique," in *Oeuvres complètes*, ed. Antoine Adam and Françoise Escal (Paris: Gallimard, 1966), 183.

23. Viala, *Naissance de l'écrivain*, 106. Like Viala, Edelman interprets Boileau's rhetoric as prescriptive, that is, as an effort to mitigate and "correct" what is the presumably mounting desire of writers to earn a living as professionals. See *Le Sacre de l'auteur*, 118–19.

24. Viala, *Naissance de l'écrivain*, 104.

25. Jacques Boncompain provocatively titled his study of late eighteenth-century literary debates on literary property (instigated by Beaumarchais), *La révolution des auteurs: naissance de la propriété intellectuelle (1773–1815)* (Paris: Fayard, 2002).

26. Jean de Préchac, *La Noble vénitienne, ou la Bassette, histoire galante* (Paris: Barbin, 1679), 189. Cited by Delphine Denis in *Le Parnasse galant: institution d'une catégorie littéraire* (Paris: Champion, 2001), 140. A card game, bassette proved addictive to gambling courtiers, and Louis XIV banned it in 1679.

27. C. E. J. Caldicott, *La carrière de Molière entre protecteurs et éditeurs* (Amsterdam: Rodolpi, 1998), 121.

28. Caldicott, *La carrière de Molière*, 138. In a conventional style, the prefaces that Molière wrote for the publication of his plays generally downplayed the printing of the work. *Précieuses ridicules* was the first play he had printed; in the preface, he underscores his reluctance by pointing out that he was offering the text against his will, only because an unauthorized copy had been put into circulation. He emphasizes that the real quality of the play consists in its performance: "But since a

large part of the grace that has been found [in *Précieuses*] depends on the action and the tone of voice, it was important to me that it wasn't robbed of these qualities; and I found that the success of the performance was good enough to stop there. I had resolved not to bring the play to light except by candlelight," in Molière, *Oeuvres completes*, 3 vols. (Paris: Gallimard, 1971), 1:262.

29. Caldicott, *La carrière de Molière*, 9, 138, 153. Joan DeJean formulates a similar argument in favor of considering Molière as "a modern author," emphasizing the playwright's entrepreneurial involvement in the marketing of his literary works. She complicates Caldicott's analysis, though, in two key ways: first, by incorporating the importance of the state censorship mechanism, which, she contends, increasingly determined the types of *privilèges* issued in 1640–60; second, by connecting Molière's publishing activities with his celebrity, seen as inseparable from his personal relationship with the king and his successes at the court beginning in 1662. The stark opposition between court and market is thus not operable; on the contrary, Molière's rise as a modern author rests on his status as playwright of the court. See Joan DeJean, *The Reinvention of Obscenity: Sex, Lies, and Tabloids in Early Modern France* (Chicago: University of Chicago Press, 2002), chap. 3, "Two-Letter Words: Molière's *L'École des femmes* and Obscenity Made Modern," 84–121.

30. The "Projet de lettres patentes" is included in Marty-Laveaux's nineteenth-century edition of the *Oeuvres de Corneille*, 12 vols. (Paris: Hachette, 1862), 1:lxxiv–lxxv. I should add that there was nothing unusual in the fact that the request was not articulated in Corneille's own voice, nor written by him. As Elizabeth Armstrong points out, petitions for *privilèges* were usually written by lawyers not the petitioner, to whom they generally referred in the third person. See Armstrong, *Before Copyright: The French Book Privilege System 1498–1526* (Cambridge: Cambridge University Press, 1990), 63. I mention it here only because the fact, while normal, still emphasizes how difficult it is in this period to determine the motives of writers who intervene into the publishing operation.

31. Carlin, *Pierre Corneille Revisited*, 4.

32. Alan Howe, "Corneille et ses premiers comédiens," *Revue d'histoire littéraire de la France* 106, 3 (July–September 2006): 529.

33. The first edition of *Cinna* was published by Toussaint Quinet; that of *Polyeucte* by Sommaville and Courbé.

34. This is S. Wilma Deierkauf-Holsboer's general interpretation of the *lettres patentes* project in her history of the Marais theater. She reads Corneille's request in light of the animosity that had existed between the playwright and Bellerose, the leader of the Hôtel de Bourgogne troupe. Deierkauf-Holsboer does acknowledge the financial stakes for Corneille, who, like all playwrights at the time, did not share in the profits theater companies made from reprisals of his plays, though she does not really make this about "literary property" in any philosophical sense. Moreover, her account of why the request was turned down accentuates court and theater politics, with the *conseillers du roi* concerned to protect the official troupe and to uphold conventional practices rather than to deny Corneille's "property rights." See S. Wilma Deierkauf-Holsboer, *Le théâtre du Marais*, 2 vols. (Paris: Nizet, 1954), 1:87–90.

35. Gédéon Tallement des Réaux, *Historiettes*, ed. Antoine Adam, 2 vols. (Paris: Gallimard, 1960–61), 2:908.

36. See fragment 56 of the chapter "Des jugements" in *Les caractères ou les moeurs de ce siècle*. Jean de La Bruyère, *Oeuvres complètes*, ed. Julien Benda (Paris: Gallimard, 1951), 361.

37. In his collected works published in 1634, several years before the *Querelle*, Antoine Gaillard writes: "Corneille is excellent, but he sells his works." *Oeuvres* (Paris: J. Dugast, 1634), 1:33. The line is cited in Georges Mongrédien, *Recueil de textes et des documents du XVIIe siècle relatifs à Corneille* (Paris: CNRS, 1972), 54.

38. See Edelman, *Le Sacre de l'auteur*, 131.

39. François-Hédelin, abbé d'Aubignac, *Troisième dissertation concernant le poème dramatique en forme de remarques: sur la tragédie de M. Corneille intitulée Oedipe, envoyée à Madame la Duchesse de R**, 1663, in *Dissertations contre Corneille*, ed. Nicholas Hammond and Michael Hawcroft (Exeter: University of Exeter Press, 1995), 87.

40. "Excuse à Ariste," in *Oeuvres complètes de Corneille*, ed. Georges Couton, 3 vols. (Paris: Gallimard, 1980–86), 1:780. The "Excuse à Ariste" was probably published in February 1637, and possibly circulated earlier. In the poem, Corneille politely refuses to write verse for a song, as "Ariste," whose identity has remained uncertain, had requested.

41. Jean Mairet, "L'autheur du vray Cid espagnol à son traducteur François, sur une Lettre en vers." The poem, along with all the other polemical documents that make up the *Querelle du Cid*, is included in Armand Gasté's invaluable collection, *La Querelle du Cid: pièces et pamphlets publiés d'après les originaux*, 1898 (Geneva: Slatkine, 1970). The "autheur du vray Cid espagnol" (*La Querelle du Cid*, 67–68) is a reference to Guillén de Castro, whose 1599 *Mocedades del Cid* was the most recent and undoubtedly significant literary model for Corneille; in fact, accusations that the latter plagiarized ("translated") Guillén de Castro's work were repeatedly leveled in the Querelle's polemic.

42. Gasté, *La Querelle du Cid*, 9.

43. Hélène Marlin, *Public et littérature en France au XVIIe siècle* (Paris: Belles Lettres, 1994), 156.

44. Georges de Scudéry, "Observations sur le Cid," in Gasté, *La Querelle du Cid*, 72. The publication date of the "Observations" has remained uncertain; Antoine Adam suggests somewhere around the beginning of April 1637. See Corneille, *Oeuvres complètes*, 1:1522. Scudéry's long critique elevated the dispute, transforming it into something that the newly formed Académie française was called in to adjudicate. Their judgment, penned, of course, by Jean Chapelain with the probable involvement of Richelieu, was published in late November 1637 as the "Sentiments de l'Académie françoise sur la Tragic-comédie du Cid," and is generally considered to have put an end to the affair, though it should be noted that a number of pamphlets continued to be printed afterward.

45. Scudéry, "Observations," 71, 73.

46. Scudéry, "Observations," 95–96.

47. Scudéry, "Observations," 72.

48. Jean Mairet, "Epistre familiere du sieur Mairet au sieur Corneille, sur la Tragi-Comédie du Cid," in Gasté, *La Querelle du Cid*, 289.

49. "L'accomodement du Cid et de son Censeur," in Gasté, *La Querelle du Cid*, 197. Corneille's second mistake was to have responded to Scudéry's *Observations* in a pamphlet that was not only printed, but that also named his antagonist in the title: "Lettre apologétique du sieur Corneille, contenant sa responce aux Observations faites par le Sieur Scuderi sur le Cid." Scudéry, for his part, had maintained what he deemed to be a very respectful anonymity in his initial critique. This dramatically raised the stakes of the dispute, according to the anti-Corneille camp, transforming it into a public *querelle*. And indeed, it is precisely on this basis, as the identifiable victim of a public attack, that Scudéry asks the Académie française to adjudicate. See his "Lettre à l'illustre Académie," in Gasté, *La Querelle du Cid*, 214–17.

50. Paul Scarron [?], "Apologie pour Monsieur Mairet contre les calomnies de sieur Corneille de Roüen," in Gasté, *La Querelle du Cid*, 342.

51. "La victoire du sieur Corneille, Scudéry et Claveret, avec une remonstrance par laquelle on les prie aimablement de n'exposer ainsi leur renommée à la risée publique," in Gasté, *La Querelle du Cid*, 199. As suggested by the title, this pamphlet is neutral in the debate, and satirizes both sides. On March 24, 1637, the Cour des aides of Normandy registered letters of nobility accorded to Corneille's father, Pierre Corneille, in recognition of service in "the office of master of Waters and Forests, in the viscounty of Rouen, during more than twenty years." The playwriting son is not specifically named; but included as "children and posterity," he is ennobled by the letters, which authorize him to assume the low-ranking title of *écuyer* and "enjoy and benefit from all the honors, privileges, and exemptions, rights, prerogatives, and preeminence" of that rank. Awarded in the months following Corneille's success with the *Le Cid*, it is difficult not to see a connection, though none is explicitly made. In fact, it is likely that the ennoblement was a result of his recent fame. See André Le Gall, *Pierre Corneille en son temps et en son oeuvre: Enquête sur un poète de théâtre au XVIIe siècle* (Paris: Flammarion, 1997), 126–27. Le Gall cites the letters.

52. Mairet, "Epistre familiere du sieur Mairet au sieur Corneille, sur la Tragi-Comédie du Cid," in Gasté, *La Querelle du Cid*, 289. Mairet attacks Corneille's "indiscretion in delivering it so quickly to his bookseller after his best friends had brought to his knowledge its defects."

53. Mairet, "Epistre familière," 289–90. Corneille's lack of generosity toward the acting troupe, who are viewed as the real architects of the playwright's success, is a motif that recurs in the anti-Corneille polemic. See, e.g., the "Apologie pour Monsieur Mairet," 342. Convention dictated that a playwright would wait an appropriate amount of time before contracting with a *libraire* to print his play. Indeed, Howe points out that Corneille had up to then studiously observed the norm, waiting a year before printing *Clitandre*, three years in the case of *Mélite*, and about two for *La Veuve*. By contrast, only a few weeks had passed since the first performance of *Le Cid* and the issuing of the *privilège* to Courbé for its publication on January 21, 1637. The play appeared in print by late March. See "Corneille et ses premiers comédiens," 529, and Alain Riffaud, "L'impression du Cid (1637–1648)," *Revue d'histoire littéraire de la France* 106, 3 (July–September 2006): 543–70.

54. Jean Claveret, "Lettre du sieur Claveret au sieur Corneille, soy disant autheur du Cid" in Gasté, *La Querelle du Cid*, 187.

55. Claveret, "Lettre du sieur Claveret au sieur Corneille," 191.

56. In the next chapter, we will address Claude-Adrien Helvétius's admiring comment in *De l'Esprit* that Corneille refused to be concerned about "the small details which make for the daily interaction of *gens du monde*," in order to focus on "reflections that, pertaining to man in general, belong to and please humanity." Helvétius, *De l'Esprit*, 1758 (Paris: Fayard, 1988), 109. John Iverson explores the Enlightenment reception of Corneille as a *grand homme*—"le Grand Corneille"—at the centenary of his death in 1784. See "L'apothéose du grand Corneille et le centenaire de 1784," *XVIIe Siècle* 225, 56 (2004): 559–66.

57. Corneille readily recognized in himself his lack of natural courtliness. In the *avertissement* to the 1644 edition of his *Oeuvres*, he writes, "God made me a bad courtier." See *Oeuvres complètes*, 2:187.

58. Corneille, "Excuse à Ariste," 1:780.

59. See Fumaroli's notion of "l'héroïsme littéraire," in *Héros et orateurs*, 28.

60. Claire Carlin depicts the project as the expression of Corneille's "lawyer's approach to the business of the theatre." See *Pierre Corneille Revisited*, 4.

61. See note 30 above, and Deierkauf-Holsboer, *Le théâtre du Marais*, 1:87–90.

62. D'Avenel, for one, conflates the two in *Les revenus d'un intellectuel*, 295, referring to the *lettres patentes* as a *privilège*. Gregory Brown underscores the importance of differentiating between the two forms; see *A Field of Honor: Writers, Court Culture, and Public Theater in French Literary Life from Racine to the Revolution* (New York, Columbia University Press, 2002), chap. 1, note 15, www.gutenberg-e.org. For an account of the legal mechanism of the *privilège en librairie*, see Armstrong's *Before Copyright*, which explores its first uses and early evolution; as well as Madeleine Dock, *Étude sur le droit d'auteur* (Paris: Librairie générale de droit et de jurisprudence, 1963) and Cynthia Brown, *Poets, Patrons, and Printers: Crisis of Authority in Late Medieval France* (Ithaca, N.Y.: Cornell University Press, 1995). Most discussions of the *privilège* do focus on its complex role in the history of literary property; see, for instance, Falk, *Les privilèges de librairie sous l'ancien régime*; and Pottinger, who describes the *privilège* system in a chapter entitled, "Protection of Literary Property," in *The French Book Trade*, 210–40. An alternative, and complementary, approach to the "property rights" analysis is to consider the *privilège* as a part of the efforts of the centralizing state to control and censor print. See Henri-Jean Martin's discussion of *privilèges* in *Livres, pouvoirs et société*, 1:440–71: "It must be noted at the outset that the system of *privilèges* assures the Royal State at least a theoretical means of control over everything that it published," 440.

63. Carlin, *Pierre Corneille Revisited*, 4.

64. See Nicolas Schapira, *Un professionnel des lettres au XVIIe siècle, Valentin Conrart: une histoire sociale* (Seyssel: Champ Vallon, 2003), chap. 2, "Quand le privilège de librairie publie l'auteur," 98–151. Conrart was a central figure in the administration of the mid-seventeenth-century book trade, among other things composing many of the *privilèges* that were issued. A shorter version of the chapter is included in *De la publication: entre Renaissance et Lumières*, ed. Christian Jouhaud and Alain Viala (Paris: Fayard, 2002), 121–37.

65. Schapira, *Un professionnel des lettres*, 124–25. Schapira notes that the prac-

tice of authors requesting *privilèges* was initially common in the sixteenth century, then disappeared, only to reemerge in the seventeenth. Armstrong's account of the evolution of the book *privilège* also shows that writers played an important role in its early development in Germany, Italy, and by the first decades of the sixteenth century, in France. Defying the concept of a "prehistory," authors were among the first to request such protections from various central authorities in the beginnings of the print era. See *Before Copyright*, 4, 21.

66. Armstrong also suggests that this legitimizing function of the *privilège* was not unknown in the early years of the book trade. See *Before Copyright*, 4.

67. Adrien Baillet, *La vie de Monsieur Des-Cartes*, 2 vols. (Paris: chez Daniel Horthemels, 1691), 1:275.

68. Cited in Schapira, *Un professionnel des lettres*, 122–24.

69. François Charpentier, *Carpentariana, ou Recueil des pensées historiques, critique, morale, et de bons mots*, 1724 (Amsterdam: n.p., 1741), 109–10. Tallement also ridicules Scudéry for obtaining *privilèges* that highlighted his military career and relations with elites: "he sent the *privilège* to d'Alaric back to Conrart, and told him that this wasn't the type of *privilège* he normally wrote for his friends. It therefore had to be amplified, to praise Scudéry as a great warrior and to praise as well the Queen of Sweden [to whom the work was dedicated]." In fact, Scudéry was granted just such a *privilège* for the 1653 in-quarto edition of the epic poem. See *Historiettes*, 2:689 and note 7. It should be noted that in the last two cases the reference to this use of the *privilège* is satirical, suggesting limits to its effectiveness, or perhaps the dangers that print always presented. Like print publication generally, the *privilège* could just as easily project the writer's vanity, foregrounding less his or her *honnêteté* as the efforts undertaken in order to establish this credibility.

70. George Hoffmann develops a highly illuminating account of the *privilège* and its connection to a very different cultural history than that of the "birth of the writer" in *Montaigne's Career* (Oxford: Clarendon, 1998). He examines its role in Montaigne's publication activities, and, correlatively, the importance of these acitivites for his identity as a noble magistrate.

71. The *Dictionnaire de l'Académie française*, 2 vols. (Paris: Coignard, 1694) in its entry "Société," defines it first as "Interaction [frequentation], commerce that men naturally like to have with each other," and third as "A group of people who ordinarily get together for enjoyable gatherings [pour des parties de plaisir]." The examples given underscore, I would say, the implicit focus on exclusive rather than inclusive groupings: "Agreeable society. He is a man of good company [de bonne compagnie], he must be admitted into our society. He is annoying, he must be banished from our society."

72. Charles Sorel, *La Bibliothèque Françoise*, 2nd ed. "reveuê et augmentée" (Paris: Compagnie de Libraires, 1667), 8.

73. Charles Sorel, "Le Nouveau Parnasse, ou les muses galantes," in *Oeuvres diverses ou discours meslez* (Paris: Compagnie des Libraires, 1663), 26. Sorel's text is one of several from the middle of the century that allegorize this transformation of intellectual practices as a battle pitting writers identified with antiquity and humanist erudition against an up-and-coming group, whose dominance over the first is rooted in their identification with the court, both through their actual

connections and through their immersion in its ethos. The most famous example would be Antoine Furetière's *Nouvelle allégorique ou Histoire des derniers troubles arrivés au royaume d'éloquence,* 1658, ed. Eva van Ginneken (Geneva: Droz, 1967); see also Gabriel Guéret, *Le Parnasse réformé* (1671; Geneva: Slatkine Reprints, 1968).

74. Denis, *Le Parnasse galant,* 47, 167.

75. See Domna Stanton, *The Aristocrat as Art: A Study of the Honnête Homme and Dandy in Seventeenth- and Nineteenth-Century French Literature* (New York: Columbia University Press, 1980).

76. Schapira, *Un professionnel des lettres,* 236.

77. See, for instance, Paul Pellisson-Fontanier's 1653 *Relation contenant l'histoire de l'Académie française,* continued and republished by Pierre-Joseph Thoulier d'Olivet in the eighteenth century as *Histoire de l'Académie française,* 2 vols. (Paris: Coignard, 1743).

78. See Pierre Bourdieu, "The Production of Belief: Contribution to an Economy of Symbolic Goods," in *The Field of Cultural Production: Essays on Art and Literature,* ed. Randal Johnson (New York: Columbia University Press, 1993), 74–111.

79. Jonathan Dewald, *Aristocratic Experience and the Origins of Modern Culture in France, 1570–1715* (Berkeley: University of California Press, 1993), chap. 6, "The Meanings of Writing."

80. Tallement des Réaux, *Historiettes,* 1:442–43.

81. Sorel, *La Bibliothèque Françoise,* 8. Sorel opens his survey of useful books with those that explore "la pureté de la langue françoise." Most prominent among these is, of course, Claude Vaugelas's *Remarques sur la langue françoise utile à ceux qui veulent bien parler et bien escrire* (Paris: Augustin Courbé, 1647), which both marked the shift in elite practices and was one of its most potent driving forces, offering an influential guide to "le bon usage" for those participating in *le monde.*

82. Nicolas Faret, *L'honneste homme ou l'art de plaire à la cour* (1630; Paris: Presses Universitaires de France, 1925), 30.

83. Faret, *L'honneste homme,* 31.

84. Jean-Baptiste Poquelin Molière, *Le Misanthrope* (i,2), in *Oeuvres complètes,* ed. Maurice Rat, 2 vols. (Paris: Gallimard, 1959), 2:54; Molière, *The Misanthrope,* trans. Richard Wilbur (New York: Harcourt, Brace, 1955), 27

85. Molière, *Le Misanthrope* (iv, 1), 2:85–86; Molière, *The Misanthrope,* 93.

86. Molière, *Le Misanthrope* (iv, 1), 2:86; Molière, *The Misanthrope,* 93.

87. Molière, *The Misanthrope,* 93, "Mais pour louer ses vers, je suis son serviteur."

88. Molière, *Le Misanthrope* (i, 2), 2:53; Molière, *The Misanthrope,* 23.

89. Molière, *Le Misanthrope* (i, 2), 2:55; my translation.

90. We might think of "Author" here as defined by Antoine Furetière: "it is said of those who have brought to light [mis en lumière] a book. Nowadays, it is said only of those who have had one printed." *Dictionnaire universel: contenant généralement tous les mots françois, tant vieux que modernes, et les termes de toutes les sciences et des arts* (La Haye: Arnout et Reinier Leers, 1690). Marc Fumaroli writes of this and other definitions, "The word *Author . . . ,* which is associated with the vainglory of the sophist, is frankly charged with disdain." See *L'âge de l'éloquence:*

rhétorique et 'res literaria' de la Renaissance au seuil de l'époque classique (Paris: Albin Michel, 1994), 25.

91. Boileau-Despréaux, *Oeuvres complètes*, 161.

92. François le Métel de Boisrobert, *Les epistres en vers et autres oeuvres poétiques* (Paris: Courbé, 1659), "Advis."

93. Gaultier de Coste, Seigneur de La Calprenède, *La mort de Mithridate* (Paris: Sommaville, 1637), "Au lecteur."

94. *Oeuvres de Voiture: lettres et poésies*, 1650, ed. M. A. Ubicini, 2 vols. (Geneva: Slatkine, 1967), 1:12.

95. See Roger Chartier, "Loisir et sociabilité: lire à haute voix dans l'Europe moderne," in *Littératures classiques* 12 (1990): 127–47.

96. In the preface to his *Remarques*, Vaugelas writes, "language [la parole] which is pronounced is first in order and dignity, because that which is written is but its image." It was then, of course, assumed that good writing was simply the reflection of good speech, as Du Plaisir affirmed "one cannot help but write better where one speaks better." See *Sentiments sur les lettres et sur l'histoire avec des scrupules sur le style*, 1683, ed. Philippe Hourcade (Geneva: Droz, 1975), 19. Marc Fumaroli, in *La diplomatie de l'esprit: de Montaigne à La Fontaine* (Paris: Hermann, 1994), 290, describes writing and the book as playing "the modest role of a pedagogical and mnemonic support" to the social practice of conversation. Myriam Maître discusses the complexity of the relationship between writing and speech in the context of "salon" culture in *Les Précieuses: naissance des femmes de lettres en France au XVIIe siècle* (Paris: Champion, 1999), 462–63, where she argues that far from "reflecting" the oral practices of the salon, writing actually invented the models of orality. As such, "conversation" evolved more as a written genre than an actual social practice. See also Dewald, *Aristocratic Experience*, 182, 202. Dewald views the problem of the "broad public" more literally. The danger is for him one of turning away from the elite public toward another, less refined audience, before which the aristocratic writer is in some sense sullied. I would argue, though, that the danger is not one of shifting between two distinct publics, but of altering the type of relationship that the writer maintained—by means of the ways he or she addressed it—with a fixed and inevitably small readership.

97. La Bruyère, *Oeuvres complètes*, 65.

98. Boisrobert, *Epistres en vers*, "Advis."

99. Tallement des Réaux, *Historiettes*, 1:415.

100. Viala, *Naissance de l'écrivain*, part I, "Le premier champ littéraire." Viala discusses the evolution of "belles-lettres" as the key term used to describe what in many instances we would refer to today as "literature" in his 1982 doctoral thesis, "La naissance des institutions de la vie littéraire (1643–1665): essai de sociopoétique" (Ph.D. diss., University de Lille-III, 1982), 93–94. He underscores a shift in the term's meaning in the mid-seventeenth century reflecting the rise of a modern idea of literature: "The semantic passage of *belles-lettres* from the sense of 'sciences' (for Furetière and thus for the traditionalists) to that of 'productions having at least in part an aesthetic character,' would seem to correspond to a new esteem accorded to literary activity." The aesthetic is an anachronistic category, much like "literature" itself. However, both Viala and Denis have used it in illuminating ways to reference

a new appreciation of writing rooted in a sense of "pleasure" and in a context of leisure and pastime. On the seventeenth-century meanings of "literature" and "lettres," see also Fumaroli's introduction in *L'âge de l'éloquence*, 24–25, and Philippe Caron's extended etymological study, *Des "belles lettres" à la "littérature": une archéologie des signes du savoir profane en langue française (1680–1760)* (Paris: Société pour l'information grammaticale, 1992).

101. Viala writes: "One of the signs of this institutionalization is the place given to literature in education." *Naissance des institutions littéraires*, 33.

102. Viala, *Naissance des institutions littéraires*, 34.

103. Christian Jouhaud, *Les pouvoirs de la littérature: histoire d'un paradoxe* (Paris: Gallimard, 2000), 10.

104. D'Aubignac, *Dissertations contre Corneille*, 73.

105. *Oeuvres de Voiture*, 1:13. Cited in Alain Génetiot, *Poétique du loisir mondain: de Voiture à La Fontaine* (Paris: Champion, 1997), 167.

106. Martin Warnke develops the parallel concept of "court freedom" in his analysis of Old Regime artists, who, integrated into the court under the tutelage of noble patrons, are then delivered from the rules and conventions imposed on them by the guild system. Warnke, *The Court Artist: On the Ancestry of the Modern Artist*, 1985, trans. David McLintock (Cambridge: Cambridge University Press, 1993), xiv, 34, 65. Peter Shoemaker's recent study *Powerful Connections: The Poetics of Patronage in the Age of Louis XIII* (Newark: University of Delaware Press, 2007) offers an extended and illuminating analysis of the ambiguous nature of patronage in seventeenth-century France. While patronage presented obvious constraints that intellectuals had to work around, at the same time, it was also clearly the only framework in which something like "intellectual freedom" could be thought and experienced in the period. See also Dustin Griffin, *Literary Patronage in England 1650–1800* (Cambridge: Cambridge University Press, 1996), who takes a similar approach to the phenomenon in England in showing patronage to be much more than an antiquated and purely negative imposition on the freedom and progress of writers.

107. See Génetiot, *Poétique du loisir mondain*.

108. Timothy Reiss, *The Meaning of Literature* (Ithaca, N.Y.: Cornell University Press, 1992), chap. 3, "The Invention of Literature," 70–96. Reiss situates the invention in this period, identifying it with the cultural political projects of Richelieu. Georges Molinié writes, of the inscription of salon-based "verbal virtuosity" in books, that it "turns discourse into literature [littérarise le discours]." Molinié, "Style et littérarité," *Littératures classiques* 28 (1996): 70.

109. *Oeuvres de Voiture*, 1:6.

110. "Lettre du Monsieur de Scudéry, à Messieurs de l'Académie françoise, Sur le jugement qu'ils ont fait du Cid, et de ses Observations," in Gasté, *La Querelle du Cid*, 465. The letter was published shortly after the publication of the Académie's *Sentiments* in November 1637, along with the two letters of a brief epistolary exchange on *Le Cid* between Guez de Balzac and Scudéry.

111. Georges de Scudéry, *Ligdamon et Lidias ou La Ressemblance. Tragi-Comédie* (Paris: Targa, 1631), "A qui lit."

112. Georges de Scudéry, *Ligdamon et Lidias*, "A qui lit."

113. See Charpentier, *Carpentariana*, 109–10. Tallement also mercilessly at-

tacked Scudéry for his pretentious claims to elite stature, particularly as these were advanced in printed editions of his plays. He notes, for instance, the edition from 1635 of *Le Trompeur puny*, which Scudéry arranged to include an engraved portrait of himself with a buffalo, "and around him these words: And poet and warrior / He will be crowned with laurel [Il aura du laurier]." See *Historiettes*, 2:684–85.

114. Claveret, "Lettre du sieur Claveret au sieur Corneille," 188. Scudéry was the author of the "Observations sur le Cid," and hence the Observateur.

115. Mairet, "Epistre familiere," 299.

116. Marc Antoine Gérard, sieur de Saint-Amant, *Les Oeuvres du sieur de Saint-Amant* (Paris: Estienne, 1629), "Avertissement au lecteur."

117. The point is to distinguish between the "salon" as a historiographical concept referring to specific imbrications of social and intellectual practices beginning in the mid-seventeenth century and the "salon" as it refers more concretely to an actual gathering of elite individuals in an aristocratic household. The conflation of the two has been a commonplace in much historical writing on the period, which often rigidly identifies the socialization of writing with the appearance of the elegant get-togethers that were only later called "salons." The conflation comes out of the seventeenth century itself in texts such as Tallement's account of the Marquise de Rambouillet's *chambre bleue*, which closely links the development of a new kind of interaction—refined, witty, with a central role afforded to belles-lettres—to the architectural creation of a space in an aristocratic household in which such elegant interactivity might take place. See *Historiettes*, 1:442–54. However, recent work by Antoine Lilti, among others, has argued for a more careful differentiation between the two meanings of "salon." In its latter sense, referring to a regular social gathering, the "salon" was greatly mythologized by nineteenth-century literary historians such as the Goncourt brothers and artists such as Gabriel Lemonnier, whose famous 1812 painting of the salon of Mme Geoffrin envisions a gathering that never took place. It is in its reference to the development of what Lilti calls *la sociabilité mondaine*, that is, the reorientation of intellectual practices toward the pleasures of an elite group, that the "salon" was, by contrast, a crucial part of the history of literary practices in the Classical era. See Lilti, *Le monde des salons: sociabilité et mondanité à Paris au XVIII siècle* (Paris: Fayard, 2005).

118. Scudéry, *Ligdamon et Lidias*, "A qui lit."

119. Claveret, "Lettre du sieur Claveret à Monsieur de Corneille," 310–11.

120. Mairet, "Epistre familiere," 291.

121. Scudéry, "Observations," 72.

122. Claveret, "Lettre du sieur Claveret au sieur Corneille," 189.

123. Vaugelas's concept of "le bon usage" of the French language is the most important articulation of this process: "It is the way that the most sensible part [la plus saine partie] of the Court speaks, in conformity with the way that the most sensible authors of the time write," in *Remarques sur la langue françoise*, "préface."

124. D'Aubignac, *Dissertations contre Corneille*, 79, 86.

125. Claveret, "Lettre du sieur Claveret au sieur Corneille," 191; Claveret, "Lettre à Monsieur de Corneille," 307.

126. See Viala, *Naissance de l'écrivain*, 106.

127. Tallement, *Historiettes*, 1:573–76. Tallement begins: "M. Chapelain is one

of the biggest self-promoters [caballeurs] in the kingdom; he is always paying court to a dozen people." See also Tallement's *historiette* on Boisrobert, which similarly punctuates an account of the poet as an arrogant author with a description of his profiteering: "He managed to cajole a female publisher [une librairesse] to pay him 100 livres for four Spanish novellas that he translated into bad French," 1:415.

Chapter 2. The Paradoxes of Enlightenment Publishing

1. Nicole Masson, "La condition de l'auteur en France au XVIIIe siècle: le cas de Voltaire," in *Le livre et l'historien: études offertes en l'honneur du Prof. Henri-Jean Martin*, ed. Frédéric Barbier et al. (Geneva: Droz, 1997), 554.

2. Robert Darnton, *The Literary Underground of the Old Regime* (Cambridge, Mass.: Harvard University Press, 1982), 20.

3. Masson, "La condition de l'auteur en France," 554.

4. Jules Bertaut, *Le vie littéraire en France au XVIIIe siècle* (Paris: Tallandier, 1954), 354.

5. Bertaut, *La vie littéraire*, 354.

6. Noting the lack of much solid, insightful material relating to intellectual property rights and freedom of the press in the *Encyclopédie*, Michel Gaulin similarly writes that these ideas "only developed slowly and it seems that the encyclopedists perhaps did not have all the elements which would have allowed them to adopt firmer attitudes on these topics. As we have already hinted, it would instead be the role of the nineteenth century to define and affirm these attitudes." The assumption is that the *philosophes* would have probed these ideas in much greater depth if they had been able to. See *Le concept d'homme de lettres en France à l'époque de l'Encyclopédie* (New York: Garland, 1991), 116–17.

7. Jacques Douvez, *De quoi vivait Voltaire* (Paris: Deux Rives, 1949), 114.

8. "Opinion de Linguet touchant l'arrêt sur les privilèges," in *La propriété littéraire au XVIIIe siècle: recueil de pièces et de documents publié par le comité de l'association pour la défense de la propriété littéraire et artistique*, ed. Edouard Laboulaye and Georges Guiffrey (Paris: Hachette, 1859), 232.

10. Éric Walter, for instance, also tempers the standard view of the *philosophes* as the initiators of new intellectual practices, pointing out that they were "believers in a traditional model." See Walter, "Les auteurs et le champ littéraire," in *Histoire de l'édition française*, vol. 2, ed. Roger Chartier and Henri-Jean Martin (Paris: Fayard, 1990), 511.

11. Maurice Pellisson, *Les hommes de lettres au XVIIIe siècle* (1911; Geneva: Slatkine, 1970), 1.

12. Masson, "La condition de l'auteur en France," 552.

13. Darnton, *The Literary Underground*, 3, 7.

14. Christian Jouhaud and Alain Viala, eds., *De la publication: entre Renaissance et lumières* (Paris: Fayard, 2002), 5–21.

15. David Smith's *Helvétius: A Study in Persecution* (Oxford: Clarendon, 1965) presents a detailed source for the Affaire de l'Esprit. Smith sketches an earlier account in "The Publication of Helvétius's *De l'Esprit* (1758–9)," *French Studies* 18

(1964): 332–43. Other pertinent studies include Albert Keim, *Helvétius, sa vie et son oeuvre, d'après ses ouvrages, des écrits divers et des documents inédits* (Paris: Alcan, 1907); Didier Ozanam, "La disgrâce d'un premier commis: Tercier et l'affaire de l'*Esprit* (1758–1759)," *Bibliothèque de l'Ecole des Chartes* 113 (1955): 140–70; E. R. Anderson, "Apropos of the *affaire de l'*Esprit," *Trivium* 1 (1966): 5–23; and Raymond Birn, *La censure royale des livres dans la France des lumières* (Paris: Odile Jacob, 2007), 80–94.

16. See Salley's letter to Malesherbes of July 6, 1758, in which he goes on to ask Malesherbes not to let anyone know that he was the source of the information regarding Helvétius's work. *Correspondance générale d'Helvétius*, ed. Alan Dainard, Jean Orsoni, David Smith, and Peter Allan, 5 vols. (Toronto: University of Toronto Press, 1981–2004), letter 287, 2:48.

17. Smith includes the suppressions in "The Publication of Helvétius's *De l'Esprit*," note 10. The identity of this second censor has always remained something of a mystery. Smith surmises that it was Père Plesse, a Jesuit priest and friend of the author, who would continue to play a prominent role in the *affaire*, mediating between the *philosophe* and his enemies. See Smith, *Helvétius*, 25. Raymond Birn proposes Jean-Jacques Barthélemy, who was a protégé of the duc de Choiseul and a guard in the Cabinet du roi. See Birn, *La Censure royale des livres*, 84.

18. See Jean-Baptiste-Antoine Suard, *Mélanges de littérature*, 5 vols. (Paris: Dentu, 1806), 1:30.

19. Ozanam, "La disgrâce d'un premier commis," 154. Like his request for a second round of censorship, this move was no doubt more about protecting Helvétius than anything else.

20. Helvétius's father had been the queen's physician; his mother remained in her entourage after her husband's death.

21. In the first retraction, Helvétius defends his intentions more than he repents for the positions that he staked out. As a result, the Jesuits called for a new retraction that would be "more precise, more detailed and above all humiliating." Cited in Smith, *Helvétius*, 33. These two retractions would be published in editions of about 300 copies each. Referring to the second one, Malesherbes wrote to Cardinal Nicolas-Charles de Saulx-Tavanes on September 6: "I am counting on this retraction being on sale the day after tomorrow at all bookshops," *Correspondance générale*, letter 339, 2:111.

22. Théophile-Imarigeon Duvernet, *La vie de Voltaire* (Geneva, 1786), 189–90.

23. J.-P. Belin recounts how the Parlement's response to *De l'Esprit* culminated in a burning of "philosophical books" in February 1759. Helvétius's treatise was joined in the conflagration by an eclectic mix of writings including Diderot's *Pensées philosophiques*, Voltaire's "Poème sur la loi naturelle," and the early volumes of the *Encyclopédie*. See Belin, *Le mouvement philosophique de 1748 à 1789: étude sur la diffusion des idées des philosophes à Paris d'après les documents concernant l'histoire de la librairie* (1913; New York: Burt Franklin, 1962), 119–20, 125.

24. This historiographical tradition is exemplified by Joseph Delort's 1829 study, *Histoire de la détention des philosophes et des gens de lettres à la Bastille et à Vincennes, précédée de celle de Foucquet, de Pellisson et de Lauzun, avec tous les documents authentiques et inédits* (1829; Geneva: Slatkine, 1967).

25. Belin, *Le mouvement philosophique*, 119.

26. See his letters to the abbé Henri-Philippe de Chauvelin of September 3, 1758; and to Malesherbes of September 6. Around September 24, he writes to Voltaire: "I do not know if I am safe or if I will be obligated to leave France." Around October 15, he writes again to Voltaire, "everyone persecutes me. . . . I know that they are plotting new horrors against me. They can do what they like; I will flee [je prendray mon party] when it is time." *Correspondance générale*, letters 335, 341, 346, 353; 2:106–7, 113–14, 119–21, 130–31.

27. Ann Goldgar, "The Absolutism of Taste: Journalists as Censors in 18th-Century Paris," in *Censorship and the Control of Print in England and France 1660–1910*, ed. Robin Myers and Michael Harris (Winchester: St. Paul's Bibliographies, 1992), 87–110. Goldgar illustrates the topos by citing the opening lines from Albert Bachman's 1934 *Censorship in France from 1715 to 1759: Voltaire's Opposition* (New York: Columbia University Press): "The history of censorship in the first half of the eighteenth century is really an episode of the struggle between the monarchical and religious conservatism, on the one hand, and the progressive *philosophical spirit*, on the other," 88.

28. Goldgar, "The Absolutism of Taste," 97. Véronique Sarrazin, in "Du bon usage de la Censure au XVIIIe siècle," *Lettre Clandestine* 5 (1996): 161–91, similarly emphasizes the imbrications of the worlds of censors and writers in the eighteenth century: "the censor is himself . . . a 'republican of letters.' Those that he reviews would know him, at least by his works. Moreover, as an author, he is himself subjected to censorship. Of the author whose manuscript he is given to assess, he might be a colleague in an academy, or he might share with him the same publisher. Thus not only might the censor and the censored know each other, but there even might be a certain familiarity in their relation," 165. This familiarity, according to Sarrazin, opens up possibilities for negotiation between writer and censor, which will, of course, be one decisive aspect of the Helvétius *affaire*. See also Birn's series of lectures to the Collège de France, *La Censure royale des livres en France*, which presents precisely as its central thesis the philosophical transformation of the state apparatus and its promotion of Enlightenment.

29. Roger Chartier, *Forms and Meanings: Texts, Performances, and Audiences: From Codex to Computer* (Philadelphia: University of Pennsylvania Press, 1995), 33–34. See also Edward Andrew, *Patrons of Enlightenment* (Toronto: University of Toronto Press, 2006) for a thorough analysis of the ambiguities of patronage in the eighteenth century.

30. Jacques Proust, *Diderot et l'Encyclopédie* (1962; Paris: Albin Michel, 1995), 47–50; Arthur Wilson, *Diderot* (Oxford: Oxford University Press, 1972), 73–82; and G. L. van Roosbroeck, "Who Originated the Plan of the *Encyclopédie*," *Modern Philology* 27 (1929–30): 382–84, who suggests that another publisher might have come up with the idea: J. Néaulme. Diderot and d'Alembert signed a contract to become editors of the *Encyclopédie* on October 16, 1747, though both had been involved, according to the publishers' account books, since early 1746. The question of who then decided to expand the project beyond the scope of a translation of an existing work is unresolved, with there being clearly some historiographical interest in seeing Diderot in this role. The evidence, however, is not conclusive. In any case, a second *privilège*, apparently reflecting the new expanded project, was granted in

April 1748, though the texts of the two documents are almost identical. See Wilson, *Diderot*, 81; and Proust, *Diderot et l'Encyclopédie*, 49.

31. Charles Collé, *Journal et mémoires sur les hommes de lettres, les ouvrages dramatiques, et les événements les plus mémorables du règne de Louis XV (1748–1772)*, ed. Honoré Bonhomie, 3 vols. (Geneva: Slatkine, 1967), 2:151–52.

32. Letter of August 6, 1758. *Correspondance générale d'Helvétius*, letter 300, 2:64–66.

33. See Birn, *Le Censure royale des livres*, 76–80.

34. Letter of August 7, 1758. *Correspondance générale d'Helvétius*, letter 304, 2:70.

35. Friedrich Melchoir, baron von Grimm, et al., *Correspondance littéraire, philosophique et critique par Grimm, Diderot, Raynal, Meister, etc.*, ed. Maurice Tourneux, 16 vols. (Paris: Garnier, 1877–82), 4:80, entry for February 15, 1759. Though the narrative highlighting the Helvétius affair as yet another instance in the official crackdown on the Enlightenment movement prevails, the view of the affair as somehow standing out does endure today, of course, in the idea that it represented a kind of tipping point. As E.R. Anderson puts it, "The ultimate effect of the publication of *De l'Esprit* inside France [. . .] was, then, to halt the *Encyclopédie* in mid career." See "Apropos of the *affaire de l'*Esprit," 20.

36. *Correspondance générale d'Helvétius*, letter 284, 2:43.

37. Ozanam advanced this interpretation in his 1955 article exploring the unfortunate fate of the censor, "La disgrâce d'un premier commis," which focused on two key documents: a draft letter that the censor had prepared to submit to the king, justifying his innocence; and the account of Pierre Michel Hennin, who was a colleague of the censor's in the Ministry of Foreign Affairs, and claims to have been "chez lui" when the censor began reading Helvétius's manuscript. Both David Smith, in *Helvétius*, and E. R. Anderson, in "Apropos of the *affaire de l'*Esprit," subsequently develop the approach.

38. Ozanam, "La disgrâce d'un premier commis," 146.

39. Ozanam, "La disgrâce d'un premier commis," 147–49; Smith, *Helvétius*, 20–22; Anderson, "Apropos of the *Affaire de l'*Esprit," 11–16.

40. Smith, *Helvétius*, 18; Anderson, "Apropos of the *Affaire de l'*Esprit," 16. Anderson writes, "the idea of publishing in France originated with Le Roy and Helvétius merely allowed himself to be persuaded. . . . Thus all that Helvétius can be reproached with is his weakness in acquiescing to Le Roy's plan and to his tricking of Tercier, at most his consenting to being an accessory to persuading Tercier to accept the task of censor."

41. Sarrazin, "Du bon usage de la censure," 164–67.

42. Letter of August 7, 1758. *Correspondance générale d'Helvétius*, letter 302, 2:67.

43. Ozanam, "La disgrâce d'un premier commis," 147. Hennin relates, in fact, that he himself tried to dissuade Tercier from taking on the censoring job; "I begged him not to do it, and to leave Helvétius the trouble of finding a censor. I even told him that the best course of action would be to pass on it because I was convinced by everything I knew about the author that the work was not of a type to survive an

examination." Hennin's "Relation de l'affaire de *l'Esprit*" is included as Appendix 15 of the *Correspondance générale d'Helvétius*, 2:423–29. Cited in Ozanam, 145–46.

44. Letter of August 11, 1758. *Correspondance générale d'Helvétius*, letter 312, 2:81.

45. Collé, *Journal et mémoire*, 2:151–52.

46. Hennin, "Relation," in Helvétius, *Correspondance générale de Helvetius*, 2:423; Collé, *Journal et mémoires*, 2:152.

47. Birn writes that Helvétius "allowed himself to be convinced [se laissa convaincre] by a long-time friend." See *De la censure royale*, 81.

48. Voltaire spent two years in England from 1726 to 1728 following his famous run-in with the chevalier de Rohan. He was also forced to stay away from Paris in 1734 when a French-language edition of the *Lettres philosophiques* was published in Rouen (the first edition appeared in English). Diderot spent the fall of 1749 in the prison of Vincennes after the publication of his *Lettre sur les aveugles*. I have discussed the brief suppression in 1752 of the *Encyclopédie* in the wake of the abbé de Prades's Sorbonne thesis above.

49. See Smith, *Helvétius*, 18; Keim writes, "It is certain that this highly honorific position enhanced the credibility and the relations of the *fermier-général*. Helvétius had thus the right to sidle through Versailles at his pleasure [de glisser à son aise], in red heels on the brilliant parquet of the Oeil de Boeuf [a reception room in the palace]." He also points to the fact that since he had not attacked anyone in his work, he would have felt safe from any possible reprisals. *Helvétius*, 179, 322.

50. Suard, *Mélanges de littérature*, 1:30.

51. Jean François de La Harpe, *Réfutation du livre de l'esprit, prononcée au Lycée républicain dans les séances des 26 et 29 mars et des 3 et 5 avril* (Paris: Mignaret, 1797), 6.

52. "car il n'y auroit pas moien de faire imprimer autre chose que la croix de par dieu." The "croix de par dieu" refers to a manual for teaching children the alphabet. By extension, it also comes to mean "the basics." Letter of July 2 or 3, 1758. *Correspondance générale d'Helvétius*, letter 283, 2:42.

53. Henri Falk develops this argument in *Les privilèges de librairie sous l'ancien régime: étude historique du conflit des droits sur l'oeuvre littéraire* (Paris: Rousseau, 1906). We explore the publishers' arguments in favor of literary property rights in much more detail in Chapter 4.

54. Roger Chartier, *L'ordre des livres: lecteurs, auteurs, bibliothèques en Europe entre le XIVe et XVIIIe siècles* (Aix-en-Provence: Alinea, 1992), 42; Carla Hesse, "Enlightenment Epistemology and the Laws of Authorship in Revolutionary France, 1777–1793," *Representations* 30 (Spring 1990): 112; and Raymond Birn, "The Profits of Ideas: *privilèges en librairie* in Eighteenth-Century France," *Eighteenth-Century Studies* 4, 2 (Winter 1970–71): 142.

55. The six *arrêts* decreed by the *Conseil du roi* on August 30, 1777, are included in Laboulaye and Guiffrey, eds., *La propriété littéraire au XVIIIe siècle*, 127–50.

56. *Encyclopédie ou Dictionnaire raisonné des sciences, des arts et des métiers, par une Société de Gens de lettres*, ed. Denis Diderot and Jean le Rond d'Alembert, 17 vols. (Paris: Le Breton, 1751–72), 7:599.

57. *Encyclopédie*, 12:510. This entry was adapted from a 1743 text by the grammarian César-Chesneau Dumarsais.

58. The *sociability* of the philosophe has commanded considerable attention in recent years. Scholars have explored the theme in a fruitful challenge to a tradition that has overly intellectualized these figures and their movement. A focus on the social practices of the *philosophes*—rather than exclusively on their ideas—presents a means for revalorizing underappreciated aspects of their history, which were critical to the development of the Enlightenment in France, the most important being the context of the "salon," frequented by almost every recognized *philosophe* that one could name, and the role of the women who created and presided over these spaces. See Dena Goodman, *The Republic of Letters: A Cultural History of the French Enlightenment* (Ithaca, N.Y.: Cornell University Press, 1994); Daniel Gordon, *Citizens Without Sovereignty: Equality and Sociability in French Thought 1670–1789* (Princeton, N.J.: Princeton University Press, 1994); Antoine Lilti, "Vertus de la conversation: l'abbé Morellet et la sociabilité mondaine," *Littératures classiques* 37 (1999): 213–28; *Le monde des salons: sociabilité et mondanité à Paris au XVIIIe siècle* (Paris: Fayard, 2005); and, Elena Russo, *Styles of Enlightenment: Taste, Politics, and Authorship in Eighteenth-Century France* (Baltimore: Johns Hopkins University Press, 2007).

59. Charles Pinot Duclos, *Considérations sur les moeurs de ce siècle*, 1751, ed. F. C. Green (Cambridge: Cambridge University Press, 1946), 135–36.

60. Jean le Rond d'Alembert, "Essai sur la société des gens de lettres et des Grands, sur la réputation, sur les mécènes, et sur les récompenses littéraires," in *Oeuvres complètes de d'Alembert*, 4 vols. (Geneva: Slatkine, 1967), 4:335–73. D'Alembert's text initially appeared in his *Mélanges de littérature, d'histoire et de philosophie*, the first edition of which was published in Paris in 1753, with no *privilège* and Berlin indicated as the place of publication.

61. D'Alembert, "Essai sur les gens de lettres," 4:339–40.

62. John Pappas, "D'Alembert et la nouvelle aristocratie," *Dix-huitième siècle* 15 (1983): 336–37.

63. Darnton, *The Literary Underground*, 13. Darnton will of course quickly tack back to a discussion of d'Alembert's embrace of the Old Regime social order, as we shall see.

64. Jürgen Habermas, *The Structural Transformation of the Public Sphere: An Inquiry into a Category of Bourgeois Society*, 1962, trans. Thomas Burger and Frederick Lawrence (Cambridge, Mass.: MIT Press, 1995), 31.

65. Dinah Ribard, "D'Alembert et la 'société des gens de lettres': utilité et autonomie des lettres dans la polémique entre Rousseau et d'Alembert," *Littératures classiques* 37 (Fall 1999): 238–39.

66. D'Alembert, "Essai sur les gens de lettres," 4:336.

67. "[T]his suppleness [souplesse] is one of the overriding principles of our art," Nicolas Faret, *L'Honneste homme ou l'art de plaire à la cour*, 1630 (Paris: Presses Universitaires de France, 1925), 70.

68. In the preface to his *Caractères*, La Bruyère wrote: "We should neither speak nor write but to instruct; yet, if we happen to please, we should not be sorry for it, since by such means we render those instructive truths more palatable and ac-

ceptable." Jean de La Bruyère, *Characters*, trans. Henri Van Laun (New York: Howard Fertig, 1992), ii.

69. D'Alembert, "Essai sur les gens de lettres," 4:345.

70. Helvétius, *De L'Esprit* (1758; Paris: Fayard, 1988), 113–14, 96.

71. D'Alembert, "Essai sur les gens de lettres," 4:359.

72. D'Alembert, "Essai sur les gens de lettres," 4:359.

73. Helvétius, *De l'Esprit*, 109.

74. D'Alembert, "Portrait de l'auteur, fait par lui-même, et adressé, en 1760, à Madame ***," *Oeuvres complètes*, 1:9–10.

75. Helvétius refers at one point to a "man [who] offers himself to the public, either in a work or in an important post [grande place]," *De l'Esprit*, 95. The "place" would surely refer to something specifically non-leisured, such as an academic, ministerial, or ambassadorial position. See also D'Alembert, "Essai sur les gens de lettres," 4:345.

76. D'Alembert, "Essai sur les gens de lettres," 4:346–47. Daniel Gordon argues that the eighteenth-century notion of the "public" as an institution of reasoned judgment, to be differentiated from "le peuple" as the irrational masses, grew out of the experience of *le monde*. Those who have the most consistent recourse to the term "were authors or public officials who spent a great deal of their lives in the salon and *Académie française*," such as Duclos, Suard, and Morellet. See "'Public Opinion' and the Civilizing Process in France: The Example of Morellet," *Eighteenth-Century Studies* 22, 3 (Spring 1989): 307–9. Much recent literature on the rise of the "public" in Old Regime France begins with the literary discussions that preoccupied the world of social elites, from the *Querelle du Cid* through the *Querelle des Anciens et des modernes* and into the Enlightenment, and demonstrates a fairly direct correlation between *le monde* and the public for literary and philosophical works, in contrast, of course, with the opposition emphasized by d'Alembert and Helvétius. See Hélène Merlin, *Public et littérature en France au XVIIe siècle* (Paris: Belles lettres, 1994); and Joan DeJean, *Ancients Against Moderns: Culture Wars and the Making of a Fin de Siècle* (Chicago: University of Chicago Press, 1997).

77. D'Alembert, "Essai sur les gens de lettres," 4:340–41, 360, 358–59.

78. D'Alembert, "Essai sur les gens de lettres," 4:344, 346.

79. Helvétius, *De l'Esprit*, 91–92.

80. Helvétius, *De l'Esprit*, 109.

81. D'Alembert, "Essai sur les gens de lettres," 4:346.

82. Referring to "men curious to learn of the science of morality [la morale]," Helvétius writes: "It is only with the help of history and on the wings of meditation that they will be able, according to the uneven strength of their intellect, to elevate themselves to varying heights, where one will see cities and another the whole universe. It is only by contemplating the world from that point of view, by rising to such heights, that it [the world] will be reduced before a philosopher to a small space, and that it takes, in his eyes, the form of a tiny hamlet inhabited by different families called Chinese, English, French, Italian, indeed all those names that we give to different nations. It is from there that, considering the spectacle of manners, laws, customs, religions and diverse passions, a man, who has become as immune to the praise as to the satire of nations, can break with all the ties of prejudice, examine

with a calm eye the contradictoriness of men's opinions, [. . . and] contemplate with pleasure the vast extent of human folly." See *De l'Esprit*, 110–11.

83. D'Alembert, "Portrait de l'auteur," in *Oeuvres complètes*, 1:11. The Marquise du Deffand in her portrait of d'Alembert also reports the use of this phrase in reference to the *philosophe*. The portrait is included in a "Galerie des portraits intimes" that is appendixed to the recently published *Lettres de Madame du Deffand, 1742–1780* (Paris: Mercure de France, 2002), 928–30.

84. Lilti, "Vertus de la conversation," 215.

85. Daniel Gordon's and Dena Goodman's arguments about the importance of sociability for the *philosophes* would, of course, fall into the same category. They rethink the cultural history of the Enlightenment, not by rethinking the figure of the "philosophe," but by exploring the transformation of elite social practices, as they were oriented away from leisure toward "serious" discussion; indeed, the adjective "serious" is used extensively by Goodman in her attempts to define the kind of "working space" that the salon provided for writers in the eighteenth century as an "institution of Enlightenment," in contrast to that of the seventeenth, which operated as "a leisure institution of the nobility," *The Republic of Letters*, 53. In this respect, d'Alembert and the hostility toward aristocracy that he represents, precisely the image that Gordon and Goodman rightly seek to nuance, is nonetheless compatible with the "philosophe mondain." In both cases, the *philosophe*'s autonomy, defined in terms of a repudiation of traditional aristocratic social practices, remains unquestioned.

86. Habermas, *The Structural Transformation of the Public Sphere*, 33.

87. Against a tradition highlighting the "salon" as an egalitarian milieu in which social differences were, temporarily, forgotten, Lilti argues that *mondanité* was a fundamentally hierarchical cultural framework, in which the "freedom" accorded to writers to address their elite hosts and fellow guests as equals was possible only to the degree that everybody implicitly recognized and accepted the obvious distinctions in stature separating the commoner writers from the aristocrats enjoying their productions. See Lilti, *Le monde des salons*, 155–59.

88. La Harpe, *Réfutation du livre de l'esprit*, 5. Keim writes, "Helvétius appears to us first of all as a *mondain*. His high position, his fortune, his name open up all doors to him." See his "portrait" in *Helvétius*, 21–33, quote 23.

89. Madame du Deffand, "Portrait de d'Alembert," in *Lettres*, 928–30.

90. Letter of November 1, 1760, in Deffand, *Lettres*, 90.

91. Ronald Grimsley, *Jean d'Alembert (1717–1783)* (Oxford: Clarendon, 1963), 8–9.

92. *Mémoires de Marmontel*, ed. Maurice Tourneau, 2 vols. (Paris: Librairie des Bibliophiles, 1891), 2:88.

93. Habermas, *The Structural Transformation of the Public Sphere*, 33.

94. La Harpe, *Réfutation du livre de l'esprit*, 3–4.

95. In her study of the enduring aesthetic and ethical influence of *mondanité* in the eighteenth century, Elena Russo characterizes the fraught position assumed by the *philosophes*, who in the name of neoclassical ideals decried the frivolous, ludic, and ironic tendencies of salon culture, yet invariably incorporated these same qualities into their own productions and activities. Diderot, for instance, in his article

on *Génie* for the *Encyclopédie*, emphasizes seriousness and systematic thought, and "deprived [genius] of its intuitive, impetuous side." But Russo notes the irony that, in downplaying "simultaneity, digression, and multiplicity," he discounted "the very qualities that characterize Diderot's own approach to science and culture." See *Styles of Enlightenment*, 153.

96. Darnton, *The Literary Underground*, 13.

97. Collé, *Journal et mémoires*, 2:151.

98. La Harpe, *Réfutation du livre de l'Esprit*, 5.

99. Henri-Jean Martin and Antoine Lilti evoke the elite readers of the *philosophes*—"l'aristocratie des lumières"—who sought ambivalently to protect and enhance their prestige through the cultivation of an intellectual culture in which their status was systematically attacked. See Martin, *Histoire et pouvoirs de l'écrit* (Paris: Albin Michel, 1996), 355, and Lilti, *Le monde des salons*, 79.

100. D'Alembert, "Essai sur les gens de lettres," 4:371–72. Helvétius will also emphasize exceptions as a way to ensure that his elite readers remain engaged, even as his project takes shape around a repudiation of *mondaine* culture and noble crudeness: "it behooves me to point out that I do not mean here, by *gens du monde*, all people of the Court: the Turennes, the Richelieus, the Luxembourgs, the La Rochefoucaults, the Retzes and several other men of their caliber prove that frivolity is not the inevitable prerogative [l'apanage nécessaire] of elevated rank; and that by *hommes du monde*, one should solely understand those who only live in its whirlwind." *De l'Esprit*, 98–99.

101. D'Alembert, *Mélanges de littérature, d'histoire et de philosophie. Nouvelle édition, revue, corrigée et augmentée très-considérablement par l'auteur*, 5 vols. (Amsterdam: Zacharie Chatelain, 1759), 1:ii–iii.

102. D'Alembert, "Essai sur les gens de lettres," 4:355.

103. Lilti, *Le monde des salons*, 104. See also Andrew's unmasking of Gibbon's self-mythologization as an independent author: "I cannot boast of the friendship and favour of princes." In reality, Gibbon's success rested on a series of patronage appointments, including a position in the Board of Trade obtained for him from George III by Lord North. See *Patronage of Enlightenment*, 81.

104. "Mémoire de d'Alembert par lui-même," in *Oeuvres complètes*, 1:4.

105. Deffand, "Portrait de d'Alembert," 929.

106. D'Alembert, "Essai sur les gens de lettres," 4:339.

107. See the entry for d'Alembert in Jean de Viguerie's *Histoire et dictionnaire du temps des lumières* (Paris: Laffont, 1995), 700–702. "A solitary man, he is, however, not isolated.... He is not *mondain*, but he has friends and he is loyal to them," 701.

108. Letter to Nicolas Claude Thieriot, October 18, 1758 (D7912), in Voltaire, *The Complete Works*, ed. Theodore Besterman et al., 135 vols. (Geneva: Voltaire Foundation, 1968–), 103:219–20.

109. See the passage from Grimm cited above: "Philosophy will long suffer the effects of the almost universal uproar that this author has unleashed with his work. And for having too freely written a book of bad and false morality, M. Helvétius will have to reproach himself for all the difficulties that those sublime and lofty geniuses who still remain will have to face," *Correspondance littéraire*, 4:80, entry for February 15, 1759.

110. Collé, *Journal et mémoires*, 2:153.
111. La Harpe, *Réfutation du livre de l'esprit*, 5.
112. Ribard, "D'Alembert et la 'Société des gens de lettres,'" 229.
113. Deffand, letter to d'Alembert, March 22, 1753; in Deffand, *Lettres*, 51.
114. D'Alembert, "Essai sur les gens de lettres," 341.
115. Deffand, letter to d'Alembert, March 22, 1753; in *Lettres*, 51.
116. D'Alembert, *Mélanges de littérature, d'histoire et de philosophie*, 1:ii.
117. Frederick II, *Oeuvres*, 31 vols. (Berlin: Imprimerie Royale, 1846–57), 24:370. The letter to d'Alembert is dated Potsdam, July 2, 1754. Cited in Grimsley, *Jean d'Alembert*, 158.
118. Frederick II, *Oeuvres*, 24:370. Andrew writes, "The ideal of independent thought was fabricated in conditions of royal and aristocratic patronage. Indeed, important patrons, such as Lord Brute, instructed reliable clients to write with greater appearance of independence." He further notes the "satisfaction" that the protector enjoys for being in a position to exercise such magnanimous self-restraint. See *Patrons of Enlightenment*, 27, 51.
119. See, of course, Natalie Zemon Davis, "Beyond the Market: Books as Gifts in Sixteenth-Century France," *Transactions of the Royal Historical Society* 5, 33 (1983): 69–88.
120. *Mémoires secrets pour server à l'histoire de la République des lettres en France*, 36 vols. (London: John Adamsohn, 1777–1789), 3:125.
121. Letter to Étienne Noël Damilaville, January 27, 1764 (D11664); in Voltaire, *The Complete Works*, 111:190–91.
122. Letter to Elie Bertrand, March 30, 1759 (D8226); in Voltaire, *Complete Works* 104: 85–86.
123. Jouhaud and Viala, *De la publication*, 5.
124. François-Hédelin, abbé d'Aubignac, *Troisième dissertation concernant le poème dramatique* in *Dissertations contre Corneille*, ed. Nicholas Hammond and Michael Hawcroft (Exeter: University of Exeter Press, 1995), 74.

Part II Introduction. Reconsidering the Alternative

1. David Pottinger, *The French Book Trade in the Ancien Régime 1500–1791* (Cambridge, Mass.: Harvard University Press, 1958), 82. We might recall here Robert Darnton's characterization of the eighteenth-century book trade as illustrative of "the phase of economic history known as booty capitalism." See Darnton, *The Business of Enlightenment: A Publishing History of the Encyclopédie 1775–1800* (Cambridge, Mass.: Harvard University Press, 1979), 4.

2. Robert Darnton's portrait of Jean Ranson, the La Rochelle merchant and obsessive reader of Rousseau, illustrates the nonelite reader to whom the "market" catered. See "Readers Respond to Rousseau: The Fabrication of Romantic Sensitivity," in Darnton, *The Great Cat Massacre and Other Episodes in French Cultural History* (New York: Vintage, 1985), 215–56.

3. Daniel Roche, *Les républicains des lettres: gens de culture et Lumières au XVIIIe siècle* (Paris: Fayard, 1988), 255, and Henri-Jean Martin's short text, "Auteurs

et libraires," in *Histoire de l'édition française*, ed. Roger Chartier and Henri-Jean Martin, 4 vols. (Paris: Fayard, 1990), 2:496.

4. Alain Viala, *La naissance de l'écrivain: sociologie de la littérature à l'âge classique* (Paris: Minuit, 1985), 104–6.

5. Despite moments when he does conflate this more general sense of the term with the specifically antinoble one, particularly in his discussions of literary property, the former is Viala's basic understanding of "autonomy" in *Naissance de l'écrivain* when he refers to the "autonomization of the first literary field," a process that has nothing to do with a break with elites, but with the elevation of the "literary" or the "intellectual" as the basis of a plausible, recognizable, and ultimately valorized social identity. See my discussion of Viala's use of the concept in Chapter 1.

6. As we have seen, in the opening pages of *Les pouvoirs de la littérature: histoire d'un paradoxe* (Paris: Gallimard, 2000), 10, Christian Jouhaud poses the question that his study endeavors to answer: "Everything takes off from an observation that seemed paradoxical to me, and to which everything can be reduced: in the seventeenth century, *hommes de lettres* and their activities benefited from a new-found recognition and a growing autonomy, in which we can discern the contours of an emerging social status—the birth of the writer—and yet, their dependence on political authorities, and especially State authorities, seems never to have been so constraining. How can a process of autonomization proceed by such reinforced dependence?"

Chapter 3. "Living by the Pen": Mythologies of Modern Authorial Autonomy

1. See John Lough, *An Introduction to Eighteenth-Century France* (London: Longmans, 1960), 231, and Jules Bertaut, *La vie littéraire en France au XVIIIe siècle* (Paris: Tallandier, 1954), 350–51.

2. See Darrin McMahon, *Enemies of the Enlightenment: The French Counter-Enlightenment and the Making of Modernity* (Oxford: Oxford University Press, 2001).

3. See "Les *Oui*" and "Les *Quand*," François Marie Arouet de Voltaire, *Oeuvres complètes*, ed. Louis Moland, 52 vols. (Paris: Garnier, 1877–85), 10:563–64 and 24:112. The first poem was part of a series of six poems gathered under the title "L'assemblée des monosyllables," and published by Gabriel Cramer in 1760 in a *Recueil des Facéties parisiennes, pour les six premiers mois de l'an 1760*. This collection offered the polemical writings of mostly Voltaire, but also others, against their critics. The six poems, following a similar structure with the repetition at the beginning of a line of a short word such as "Qui," "Pour," or "Que," excoriated Le Franc de Pompignan as a provincial pedant. These poems were preceded by a prose piece from April 1760 called "les Quand, notes utiles sur un discours prononcé devant l'Académie française, le 10 mars, 1760": "*When* one is admitted into a respectable assembly," observes Voltaire, "one should, in one's harangue, hide behind a veil of modesty one's insolent arrogance, which is the common trait of hotheads and mediocre talents," Voltaire, *Oeuvres complètes*, ed. Moland, 24:111. On Le Franc de Pompignan, see Theodore

Braun, *Un ennemi de Voltaire: Le Franc de Pompignan, sa vie, ses oeuvres, ses rapports avec Voltaire* (Paris: Minard, 1972).

4. Charles Palissot de Montenoy, *Les philosophes* (Paris: Duchesne, 1760).

5. André, l'abbé Morellet, *Préface de la Comédie des Philosophes* (Paris: chez l'auteur, 1760), 6, 7. Italics in the original. This pamphlet would earn Morellet two months in the Bastille for its satirical portrayal of the princesse de Robecq, who was a patron of Palissot.

6. Morellet, *Préface de la Comédie des Philosophes*, 16–18.

7. Morellet, *Préface de la Comédie des Philosophes*, 15.

8. Abraham Chaumeix was the author of a two-volume *Préjugés légitimes contre l'Encyclopédie* published in 1758; Guillaume-François Berthier was the editor from 1745 to 1762 of the Jesuit journal *Mémoires de Trévoux*, which was a vehicle for anti-Encyclopedia attacks; and Élie-Catherine Fréron, about whom more will be said below, started his journal *l'Année littéraire*, another anti-philosophical organ, in London in 1754, and would direct it until his death in 1776.

9. The Fréron character was named Wasp in the first theatrical version of the play.

10. Voltaire, *Le café ou l'Ecossaise*, I, i, in *The Complete Works*, ed. Theodore Besterman et al. (Geneva: Voltaire Foundation, 1968–), 50:363.

11. "Le Pauvre diable, ouvrage en vers aisés, de feu M. Vadé, mis en lumière par Catherine Vadé, sa cousine," in Voltaire, *Oeuvres complètes*, ed. Moland, 10:97–113. Voltaire made pseudonymous use on several occasions of the name Vadé, which he apparently borrowed from an author named Jean-Joseph Vadé, who had died in 1757. In 1764 he published a collection of stories with Gabriel Cramer under the authorship of Guillaume Vadé, preceded like the "Pauvre diable" by a preface by his cousin Catherine. Catherine "dedicated" the "Pauvre diable" to Abraham Chaumeix, one of the poem's principal targets, calling him "one of the most absurd scribblers [barbouilleurs de papier] who has ever tried to reason." See *Oeuvres*, ed. Moland, 10:97.

12. Robert Darnton in particular adopts the term in characterizing more broadly not *anti-philosophes* but those writers "who were overcrowding the bottom ranks in the republic of letters, much to the consternation of those on the top," though there was, clearly, significant overlapping of the two groups. See "The Life of a 'Poor Devil' in the Republic of Letters," in *Essays on the Age of Enlightenment in Honor of Ira O. Wade*, ed. Jean Macary (Geneva: Droz, 1977), 39–92, which focuses on the obscure figure of the abbé Le Senne, who is a "perfect representative of the 'poor devils.'"

13. Denis Diderot, *Rameau's Nephew and Other Works*, trans. Jacques Barzun and Ralph Bowen (Indianapolis, Ind.: Library of Liberal Arts, 1964), 47. "Tous les poètes qui tombent [. . .], tous les musiciens décriés, tous les auteurs qu'on ne lit point, toutes les actrices sifflées, tous les acteurs hués," Diderot, *Oeuvres*, ed. André Billy (Paris: Gallimard, 1951), 435.

14. Diderot is represented by the character of Dortidus, a leading figure in a group of what are repeatedly described as "charlatans" and "imposters." Palissot, *Les philosophes*, I, 1; II, 4. Rousseau is portrayed in Crispin, who famously enters the stage in scene 9 of act V on all fours: "As for Philosophy, a taste to which all cedes /

Has made me choose the condition of a quadruped [Pour la Philosophie un gout à qui tout cède / M'a fait choisir exprès l'état de quadrupède]."

15. Michèle Duchet and Michel Delaunay discuss the chronology of Diderot's composition of the text in *Entretiens sur "Le Neveu de Rameau"* (Paris: Nizet, 1967), "Cinquième Entretien," 137–72.

16. We can in this respect recall Arthur Wilson's memorable subtitle: "The Appeal to Posterity" to Part II of his biography; see *Diderot* (1957), 2 vols. (Oxford: Oxford University Press, 1972). The *Neveu* was not published until 1805, when it appeared in a German translation by Goethe, who, for his part, had received the manuscript from Friedrich Schiller. Schiller's attention was drawn to the text by a Russian acquaintance, who found the manuscript among the writings of Diderot that had been sent to Saint Petersburg at his death, as per the agreement with Catherine II by which she had "bought" his library. Famously, there are no references to the work in Diderot's correspondence, nor in any contemporaneous account, which is generally taken to mean that Diderot had not allowed the dialogue, which he appears to have initially put to paper in 1761 or 1762, to circulate: "Indeed, it is evident that he wrote it for his own satisfaction and for posterity," writes Otis Fellows in *Diderot* (Boston: Twayne, 1989), 82. Diderot did regularly return to the manuscript, however, revising it as late as 1775. See Wilson, *Diderot*, 417, and Herbert Dieckmann, *Inventaire du fonds Vandeul, et inédits de Diderot* (Geneva: Droz, 1951), 72. Marian Hobson's forthcoming edition of *Le Neveu Rameau* (Paris: Gallimard, 2009) will shed further light on this obscure publication history.

17. Diderot, *Rameau's Nephew*, 9; "Son premier soin, le matin, quand il est levé, est de savoir où il dînera; après dîner, il pense où il soupera," Diderot, *Oeuvres*, 396.

18. Diderot, *Rameau's Nephew*, 78, 82; "il vaudrait mieux se renfermer dans son grenier, boire de l'eau, manger du pain sec, et se chercher soi-même," "il n'est pas du bon ordre de n'avoir pas toujours de quoi manger," Diderot, *Oeuvres*, 466, 469–70.

19. Jean le Rond d'Alembert, "Essai sur la société des gens de lettres et des Grands, sur la réputation, sur les mécènes, et sur les récompenses littéraires," in *Oeuvres complètes de d'Alembert*, 4 vols. (Geneva: Slatkine, 1967), 4:368.

20. Voltaire, *Oeuvres complètes*, ed. Moland, 10:113.

21. Diderot, *Rameau's Nephew*, 11; "ce que vous, moi, et tous les autres font, du bien, du mal et rien. Et puis j'ai eu faim, et j'ai mangé," Diderot, *Oeuvres*, 398.

22. Diderot, *Rameau's Nephew*, 83; "Ma foi, ce que vous appelez la pantomime des gueux, est le grand branle de la terre," Diderot, *Oeuvres*, 471.

23. Diderot, *Rameau's Nephew*, 84; "un être dispensé de la pantomime," Diderot, *Oeuvres*, 471.

24. Diderot, *Rameau's Nephew*, 9; Diderot, *Oeuvres*, 396.

25. Voltaire, *Complete Works*, ed. Besterman, 50:500.

26. Voltaire, *Complete Works*, ed. Besterman, 50:500–501.

27. In his biography of Fréron, François Cornou cites the original contract with Duchesne from 1750, which required the polemicist to cede his rights "permanently, such that under no pretext, whether a change of title, a tacit permission, or more generally, any kind of privilege, can he opt out of the present agreement." A

second contract from 1752 offered better terms, but all in all, for Cornou, Fréron's breach was justified by the exploitative practices of the publisher. *Élie Fréron: trente années de luttes contre Voltaire et les philosophes au XVIIIe siècle* (Paris: Champion, 1922), 107–8. See also Jean Balcou's note 26 in Voltaire, *Complete Works*, ed. Besterman, 50:502, which puts Voltaire's account of Fréron's scheming in perspective.

28. Roche's discussion of "Les modèles économiques du mécénat" is in chapter 10 of *Les républicains des lettres: gens de culture et Lumières au XVIIIe siècle* (Paris: Fayard, 1988), 254–62, quote 254.

29. Palissot, *Les Philosophes* (II, 4), 54.

30. Simon-Henri-Nicolas Linguet, *Le fanatisme des philosophes* (London, 1764), 8, 12.

31. Diderot, *Rameau's Nephew*, 73; "De l'or, de l'or. L'or est tout, et le reste, sans or, n'est rien," Diderot, *Oeuvres*, 461.

32. Diderot, *Rameau's Nephew*, 75; "Ah! si j'avais vos talents," "Je parle mal. Je ne sais que dire la vérité, et cela ne prend pas toujours, comme vous savez," Diderot, *Oeuvres*, 463.

33. Voltaire, *Oeuvres complètes*, ed. Moland, 10:103

34. Voltaire, *Oeuvres complètes*, ed. Moland, 18:141.

35. See *The Great Cat Massacre and Other Episodes in French Cultural History* (New York: Vintage, 1985), chap. 4, "A Police Inspector Sorts His Files: The Anatomy of the Republic of Letters," 145–89. D'Hémery's files are gathered in three registers entitled "Historique des auteurs" in the Nouvelles acquisitions françaises collection of the Bibliothèque nationale, 10781–3.

36. Joseph d'Hémery, "Historique des auteurs," BNF, nouv. acq. fr. 10782.

37. D'Hémery, "Historique des auteurs," BNF, nouv. acq. fr. 10781. It is difficult to ascertain the identity of the *libraire* referenced in this entry, which in the handwritten dossier appears as something closer to "La Foliot" than "La Billiot." Darnton rendered the name as La Foliot in citing this passage in *The Great Cat Massacre*. However, no bookseller by that name is listed in Augustin-Martin Lottin's *Catalogue chronologique des libraires et des imprimeurs-libraires de Paris, depuis l'an 1470, époque de l'établissement de l'Imprimerie dans cette Capitale, jusqu'à présent*, 2 vols. (Paris: chez Jean-Roch Lottin de St. Germain, 1789). La Foliot could, of course, be a provincial *libraire*, and thus not included in Lottin's catalogue. This might seem unlikely, though, given her relatively prominent role in d'Hémery's files, most notably as an important source of information on many of the writers haunting the Parisian literary scene. On the other hand, the *Catalogue* does include a La Billiot, who was the daughter of Esprit Billiot, a *libraire* from the first half of the eighteenth century, and the widow of the bookseller Jean-Barthélemi Alix, whose business she took over when he died in 1740. In 1789, she is listed by Lottin as the "doyenne des veuves."

38. D'Hémery, "Historique des auteurs," BNF, nouv. acq. fr. 10783. Though they were themselves unsuccessful as playwrights, François and Claude Parfaict did, of course, produce a number of works on the theater that remain of great interest today to historians, including an *Histoire générale du théâtre Français depuis son origine jusqu'à présent*, published between 1734 and 1749. Their 7–volume *Dictionnaire des théâtres de Paris* (1767) has been made available online at the *Calendrier*

électronique des spectacles sous l'Ancien Régime (CESAR) electronic database at www.cesar.org.uk.

39. D'Hémery, "Historique des auteurs," nouv.acq.fr. 10781.

40. Daniel Roche, *Les républicains des lettres*, 254–55. Éric Walter, "Les Auteurs et le champ littéraire," in *Histoire de l'édition française*, ed. Henri-Jean Martin and Roger Chartier, 4 vols. (Paris: Fayard, 1990), 2:509. Charles Duclos defines as *considération* the kind of recognition that intellectuals have acquired and to which they increasingly aspire through their contacts with *le monde*. See *Considérations sur les moeurs de ce siècle* (1750), ed. F. C. Green (Cambridge: Cambridge University Press, 1946), 135–46.

41. Darnton's most famous exposition of this thesis is in *The Literary Underground of the Old Regime* (Cambridge, Mass.: Harvard University Press, 1982); see also "The High Enlightenment and the Low-Life of Literature in Pre-Revolutionary France," *Past and Present* 51 (May 1971): 81–115. Darnton highlights key revolutionaries such as Jean-Paul Marat, Jean-Louis Carra, and his most famous example, Jacques-Pierre Brissot. It should be noted, as we have seen, that the acute sense of a divide characterizes both camps: the insiders as well as the outsiders. Chartier refers to a "reciprocal hostility," in *Les origines culturelles de la Révolution française* (Paris: Seuil, 1990), 231.

42. Chartier, *Les origins culturelles*, 231.

43. Darnton, *The Literary Underground*, 16.

44. Roche, *Les républicains des lettres*, 254. Henri-Jean Martin writes in a similar vein of the development of a "proletariat of intellectuals frustrated in their hopes, deprived of positions or pensions, exploited or ignored by the publishing business [le capitalisme éditorial]." See *Histoire de l'édition française*, 2:497.

45. Both texts quoted in this paragraph are from D'Hémery, "Historique des auteurs," BNF, nouv. acq. fr. 10783.

46. Friedrich Melchoir, baron von Grimm et al., *Correspondance littéraire, philosophique et critique par Grimm, Diderot, Raynal, Meister, etc*, ed. Maurice Tourneux, 16 vols. (Paris: Garnier, 1877–82), 8:274.

47. Mathieu François Pidansat de Mairobert, *L'espion anglois, ou correspondance secrète entre milord All'Eye et milord All'Ear*, 10 vols. (London: John Adamson, 1779–84), 3:44. The figure is cited by Rémy Saisselin in *The Literary Enterprise in Eighteenth-Century France* (Detroit: Wayne State University Press, 1977), 78.

48. See Darnton's discussion in *The Literary Underground*, 3–10, of the earnings of established *gens de lettres*, typified by the career of Jean-Baptiste Suard. Darnton estimates that Suard enjoyed an income of somewhere over 10,000 livres, consisting exclusively of pensions and other "traditional" forms of revenue, such as income from his membership in the Académie française. John Lough offers a similar appraisal of the varieties and amounts of revenues that writers received through state and aristocratic patronage, including pensions, one-off gifts and sinecurial positions. Most of these brought sums to the writer in the range of 1,000 to 3,000 livres, with successful writers able to accumulate income from diverse sources. See *Writer and Public in France from the Middle Ages to the Present Day* (Oxford: Clarendon Press, 1978), 227–34.

49. Pidansat de Mairobert, *L'espion anglois*, 3:43.

50. The entry on the abbé de la Porte in Hoefer's nineteenth-century *Nouvelle biographie générale* describes the *Voyage au séjour des ombres* as having "some success." The partial bibliography makes reference to the re-edition of 1751. A 1753 edition

can be found in the collections of the Bibliothèque nationale de France. See "de la Porte" in Jean C. E. Hoefer, *Nouvelle biographie générale depuis les temps les plus reculés jusqu'a nos jours, avec les renseignements bibliographiques et l'indication des sources à consulter*, 46 vols. (Paris: Firmin Didot, 1852–66), 29:558–59. Although d'Hémery's dossier on de la Porte is dated January 1, 1748, the reference to the *Voyage* indicates that, as with many of the files, much of the information was added later.

51. Jean-François de la Harpe, *Correspondance littéraire, addressée à son altesse impériale, Mgr le grand-duc, aujourd'hui, empereur de la Russie, et à m. le comte André Schowalow, chambellan de l'impératrice Catherine II, depuis 1774 jusqu'à 1789*, 5 vols. (Paris: Migueret, 1801–7), 3:44.

52. In order, the citations are from a pamphlet entitled *Mémoire sur Fréron*, from the *Anecdotes sur Fréron*, and from *Le café ou l'Ecossaise* (I,i), all included in *Complete Works*, ed. Besterman, 50:500, 520, and 363.

53. Charles Nisard, *Les ennemis de Voltaire* (Paris: Amyot, 1853), 204–6.

54. For instance, Chartier's discussion of the hardening divide between insiders and outsiders, in its emphasis not only on divergent economic results but also on the separation of writers into opposed camps of the "well-off [nantis]" and those "without quality [sans qualité]," at some level, appears to echo the *philosophes*' own efforts to justify their status as the guests of aristocrats based on their talents rather than social skills, connections, and wealth. In line with Voltaire's views, Chartier implies, even if this is not his intention, that those who remained on the outside as "poor devils" did so at some level because they were not good enough. See *Les origines culturelles*, 231.

55. Louis-Gabriel Michaud, ed., *Nouvelle biographie universelle ancienne et moderne: histoire par ordre alphabétique de la vie publique et privée de tous les hommes*, 2nd ed., 45 vols. (Paris: Vivès, 1880), 35:143–44.

56. Michaud, *Biographie universelle*, 24:566–68. Darline Gay Levy offers an even more comprehensive list in her biography of Linguet, which includes his journalism as well as legal writings. In all, Linguet's corpus is comprised of 127 published texts. Levy, *The Ideas and Careers of Simon-Nicolas-Henri Linguet: A Study in Eighteenth-Century French Politics* (Urbana: University of Illinois Press, 1980), 345–52. Darnton calls Linguet "the most influential outsider in pre-Revolutionary France." See *The Literary Underground*, 24.

57. Jean-Claude Bonnet provides a complete bibliography in *Louis-Sébastien Mercier (1740–1814): un hérétique en littérature* (Paris: Mercure de France, 1995), 471–83.

58. Saisselin, *The Literary Enterprise*, 88: "Between the low life of Grub Street and the exalted and rarefied air at the summit of Mount Parnassus, there were thus a great many intermediate levels on which the writer might find a modest place."

59. Elizabeth Eisenstein, *Grub Street Abroad: Aspects of the French Cosmopolitan Press from the Age of Louis XIV to the French Revolution* (Oxford: Clarendon, 1992), 135–38. John Lough's analysis of midlevel activities also underscores their viability rather than the suffering of their practitioners. Discussing the "contemporary demand for works of popularization, for dictionaries, encyclopaedias, works of references, and the like," he concludes that "The compilations of such works could help struggling authors pay their rent and even provide them with a comfortable

income." *An Introduction to Eighteenth-Century France* (London: Longmans, 1960), 248. In tone, this seems a far cry from the "dirty work" highlighted by the *philosophes* and Darnton, even though the specific tasks are, in many instances, identical.

60. See the introduction to Part I; Michèle Vessillier-Ressi, *Le métier d'auteur: comment vivent-ils?* (Paris: Bordas, 1982), 179–80; and Bernard Lahire, *La condition littéraire: la double vie des écrivains* (Paris: La Découverte, 2006), 19. "La préhistoire du droit d'auteur" is the subtitle given to a section on the place of the writer in the early seventeenth-century book trade in Henri-Jean Martin, *Livre, pouvoirs et société à Paris au XVIIe siècle*, 1969, 2 vols. (Geneva: Droz, 1999), 1:424–29.

61. Alexis Piron's 5-act comedy, *La Métromanie ou le poète* was a tremendous success when it was first performed by the Comédie française on July 7, 1738.

62. Simon-Henri-Nicolas Linguet, *L'aveu sincère ou lettre à une mère sur les dangers que court la jeunesse en se livrant à un goût trop vif pour la sincère littérature* (London: Cellot, 1768), 24.

63. Linguet, *L'aveu sincère*, xv; and Louis-Sébastien Mercier, *Tableau de Paris*, 1781–88, ed. Jean-Claude Bonnet, 2 vols. (Paris: Mercure de France, 1994), 2:1260.

64. Mercier, *Tableau de Paris*, 2:1260.

65. Mercier, *Tableau de Paris*, 2:1261.

66. Mercier, *Tableau de Paris*, 2:1261.

67. Mercier, *Tableau de Paris*, 2:1260.

68. Mercier, *Tableau de Paris*, 1:332.

69. Mercier, *Tableau de Paris*, 2:1260.

70. Brissot, *Mémoires (1754–1793)*, ed. Claude Perroud, 2 vols. (Paris: Picard, 1911), 1:2.

71. Mercier, *Tableau de Paris*, 1:332.

72. Charles-Joseph Fenouillot de Falbaire de Quingey *Avis aux gens de lettres* (Liège, 1770), 37–38.

73. For more on Linguet's career change, see Levy, *The Ideas and Careers of Simon-Nicolas-Henri Linguet*, 29–31; Daniel Baruch, *Linguet, ou l'irrécupérable* (Paris: François Bourin, 1991), 84; Jean Cruppi, *Un avocat journaliste au XVIIIe siècle: Linguet* (Paris: Hachette, 1896), 43; and Charles Monselet, *Les oubliés et les dédaignés; figures de la fin du 18ème siècle* (Paris: Charpentier, 1876), 7–8.

74. The case of de la Barre counts among Voltaire's famous campaigns against judicial intolerance, following in 1765 on the affairs of Calas and Sirven in the early 1760s. Linguet spent time in Abbéville in 1763–64, where he taught mathematics to military officers and was supported by a local notable and counselor, Jean-Nicolas Douville. Douville summoned Linguet when the former's own son was implicated in the events leading to the trial and execution of de la Barre. See Levy, *The Ideas and Careers of Simon-Nicolas-Henri Linguet*, 23–37, and Cruppi, *Un avocat journaliste*, 69–154.

75. Cited without reference in Monselet, *Les oubliés et les dédaignés*, 9–10, and Cruppi, *Un Avocat journaliste*, 46. Levy cites Cruppi's reference, *The Ideas and Careers of Simon-Nicolas-Henri Linguet*, 30. Whether he actually wrote these words or not, the sentiment is certainly consistent with other writings from the period highlighting his abandonment of letters. In a letter from September 1764 to Charles Duclos, with whom he had been in contact in the hopes of promoting his works and advancing his career, Linguet, while not mentioning his switch to law, writes of

being resolved to "live in total obscurity, and to depend for my living [de devoir ma vie], if necessary, on manual labor [au travail de mes mains]." Further on, he speaks of a manuscript on *Les révolutions de l'Empire Romain*, which he hopes to publish with Duclos's support, as "the last that will I write [le dernier qui m'échappera]." Jacques Brengues published these letters to Duclos in his article, "Duclos dupé par Linguet ou quatre lettres inédites de Simon-Nicolas-Henri Linguet à Charles Duclos," *Revue des sciences humaines* 137 (1970), 71. In addition, the dedication to Douville from Linguet's *Fanatisme des philosophes* also conveys a sentiment of writing his last work; see as well *L'Aveu sincère* from four years later.

76. Levy, *The Ideas and Careers of Simon-Nicolas-Henri Linguet*, 30.

77. Diderot, *Oeuvres*, 404.

78. Mercier, *Tableau de Paris*, 1:332.

79. Furetière's definition of "Auteur" states, "it is said of those who have brought to light [mis en lumière] a book. Nowadays, it is said only of those who have had one printed." *Dictionnaire universel: contenant généralement tous les mots français, tant vieux qui modernes, et les termes de toutes les sciences et des arts* (La Haye: Arnout et Reinier Leers, 1690).

80. Paul Bénichou, *Le sacre de l'écrivain: essai sur l'avènement d'un pouvoir spirituel laïque dans la France moderne* (Paris: J. Corti, 1973).

81. Mercier, *Tableau de Paris*, 1:961. See also Mercier's, *De la littérature et des littérateurs*, 1778 (Geneva: Slatkine, 1970).

82. Brissot, *Mémoires*, 1:2.

83. Brissot, *Mémoires*, 1:2.

84. Brissot, *Mémoires*, 1:103.

85. Brissot, *Mémoires*, 1:227.

86. Among his supporters at various stages in his career were Edme Mentelle, historiographer for the comte d'Artois, the Genevan financier Etienne Clavière, and the duc d'Orléans, in whose Chancellery he was employed in 1786 as the secretary to the marquis Du Crest, brother of Madame Genlis. In addition, his mobilization against slavery in the 1780s enlisted the support of the Marquis de Lafayette. In 1788, Brissot travelled to the United States where a letter of introduction from Lafayette procured a meeting with George Washington at Mount Vernon ("To stroll along the banks of the Potomac is surely far from being trapped in the gutters of Paris," writes Eisenstein). Brissot also won two prizes from the Châlons Academy in the early 1780s, with the second one leading to his membership into the Academy. See Frederick de Luna, "The Dean Street Style of Revolution: J-P Brissot, *Jeune Philosophe*," *French Historical Studies* 17:1 (Spring 1991): 159–90; and Eisenstein, *Grub Street Abroad*, 145–52 (quote 148).

87. Robert Darnton, "J.-P. Brissot and the Société Typographique de Neuchâtel (1779–1787)," in *SVEC* 2001:10: 7–47. Brissot exchanged 167 letters with the STN publishers, and particularly with Frédéric Samuel Ostervald. See also Eisenstein, *Grub Street Abroad*, 150.

88. De Luna, "The Dean Street Style of Revolution," 169. Brissot was bailed out by his mother-in-law and Etienne Clavière.

89. Jean-Jacques Rousseau, *Discourse on the Sciences and Arts* in *Collected Writings of Rousseau*, ed. Roger Masters and Christopher Kelly, trans. Judith Bush, Roger

Masters, and Christopher Kelly, 12 vols. (Hanover, N.H.: University Press of New England for Dartmouth College, 1990–), 2:21; "Tel qui sera toute sa vie un mauvais versificateur, un géomètre subalterne, serait peut-être devenu un grand fabricateur d'étoffes," Rousseau, *Discours sur les sciences et les arts*, in *Oeuvres complètes*, ed. Bernard Gagnebin and Marcel Raymond, 5 vols. (Paris: Gallimard, 1959–), 3:29.

90. Brissot, *Mémoires*, 1:2.

91. Alexis Piron, *La métromanie ou le poëte: comédie en vers et en cinq actes* (La Haye: Antoine van Dole, 1738), III, 7. In line with the Classical frame of reference, Damis's uncle is paraphrasing lines from Boileau's Satire IX: "Et ne sçavez-vous pas, que sur ce mont sacré [Mount Parnassus], / Qui ne vôle au sommet tombe au plus bas degré." See Boileau, *Oeuvres complètes*, ed. Antoine Adam and Françoise Escal (Paris: Gallimard, 1966), 49.

92. Saisselin, *The Literary Enterprise*, 88.

93. Daniel Roche, *Les républicains des lettres*, 255, and Henri-Jean Martin, "Auteurs et libraires," in *Histoire de l'édition française*, ed. Henri-Jean Martin and Roger Chartier, 4 vols. (Paris: Fayard, 1990), 2:496.

Chapter 4. Economic Claims and Legal Battles: Writers Turn to the Market

1. Roger Chartier, *Les origines culturelles de la Révolution française* (Paris: Seuil, 1990), 77.

2. Pierre Bourdieu, *Les règles de l'art: génèse et structure du champ littéraire* (Paris: Seuil, 1992), 86.

3. Robert Darnton, *The Literary Underground of the Old Regime* (Cambridge, Mass.: Harvard University Press, 1982), 27.

4. Darnton, *The Literary Underground*, 19–21.

5. See Daniel Roche, *Les républicains des lettres: gens de culture et Lumières au XVIIIe siècle* (Paris: Fayard, 1988), 255; and Henri-Jean Martin's short text, "Auteurs et libraires," in *Histoire de l'édition française*, ed. Henri-Jean Martin and Roger Chartier, 4 vols. (Paris: Fayard, 1990), 2:496.

6. Roger Chartier, *L'ordre des livres: lecteurs, auteurs, bibliothèques en Europe entre XIVe et XVIIIe siècles* (Aix-en-Provence: Alinea, 1992), 56.

7. A good portion of this correspondence—about 350 letters to Gabriel Cramer, the Genevan *libraire* who published Voltaire's most memorable writings, including *Candide*, *Essai sur les moeurs*, the *Dictionnaire philosophique*, and several editions of Voltaire's collected works—was published in a separate 1952 edition by Bernard Gagnebin: *Lettres inédites à son imprimeur Gabriel Cramer* (Geneva: Droz, 1952).

8. Voltaire's most pressing strategy was to ensure that the guise of anonymity be maintained for which he would send Cramer letters asking who had authored the works being imputed to him, such as *Candide* (see the letters to Cramer dated early March and March 1759, in *Lettres inédites*, 29–30). The letters provided Cramer with deniability in the case of police searches. Carefully crafted to protect the publisher as well—he would, for instance, disingenuously ask whether Cramer had received his copies of *Candide* from Paris or Lyon, and would recommend that the publisher

not print the work himself—the letters were thus also the effects of Voltaire's own pseudo-aristocratic generous concern for the *libraire*'s well-being, a recurring motif both in Voltaire's reflections on his activities, and in the larger repertoire of *honnête* publication. Voltaire's strategies, including his anxieties about delays and mistakes, are explored in Chapter 5.

9. David Pottinger, among others, surveys the growing prices that were paid to authors for their manuscripts beginning in the seventeenth century, noting the 600 livres paid to d'Aubignac for the *Pratique du théâtre* and to La Fontaine in 1669 for his *Psyché*, the 2,000 livres paid to Molière for *Tartuffe*, and the 3,000 to Chapelain for *La Pucelle*. Though the focus of Pottinger is on the fact of the sums themselves, what is notable is the eclectic nature of the situations and transactions evoked, including 1,000 livres paid not to Honoré d'Urfé but to his *valet* for the third part of *L'Astrée*. In other words, what is striking is that, for the frequency of payments to writers from publishers, there seems to be no discernable *system* in operation. See Pottinger, *The French Book Trade in the Ancien Régime 1500–1791* (Cambridge, Mass.: Harvard University Press, 1958), 95–96.

10. In a "Liste de quelques Gens de Lettres François vivans en 1662," drawn up at the request of Colbert to identify writers as deserving of state pensions, Jean Chapelain includes a recommendation for César D'Estrées, bishop of Laon and since 1658 a member of the Académie française: "he has not had anything printed of which we are aware; but we have seen several very beautiful French and Latin letters"; and for a Montmor: "We have not seen anything by him in print, though we have heard that he has many works in progress [il a force choses commencées]." Chapelain's list is included in A. H. de Salengre, *Continuation des mémoires de littérature et d'histoire*, vol. 2 (Paris: chez Simart, 1726), 21–56. In his dossier *Historique des auteurs*, compiled in the years around 1750, Joseph d'Hémery identifies the abbé Ninon: "He is the canon of Reims and is good friends with the abbé de Batteux and the abbé de Latteignant. He is a tenth-grade teacher [professor de seconde] at the Collège de Navarre. He has written a lot of French verse [il a fait beaucoup de vers François] but he has never published anything in print." Nouv. acq. fr. 10783.

11. Of course, Mercier represents a shift toward a new book-centered paradigm of literary identity that we studied in Chapter 3—the intellectual as a hardworking, productive Author who distills his privileged insight into a published work—a fact that is obviously reflected in the irony of his attitude toward the older model. It is true, however, that a commercially published book was not necessary for admission into the Académie, many of the seats of which were traditionally reserved for aristocratic members who did not "seriously" write at all. By extension, such publication was not considered to be essential for acquiring an authoritative status in the cultural sphere as "lettered." Roche notes that the category of "homme de lettres" designated in the Old Regime cultural field a "comportment, a style or way of life" rather than any creative or self-expressive practices. See *Les républicains des lettres*, 219. Gregory Brown similarly observes: "Those seeking acceptance as men of letters had to demonstrate personal worthiness . . . , not through published words showing creative talent, but instead through direct interaction with those of higher social status. *A Field of Honor: Writers, Court Culture, and Public Theater in French Literary Life from Racine to the Revolution* (New York: Columbia University Press, 2002). See

also James Swenson, *On Jean-Jacques Rousseau, Considered as One of the First Authors of the Revolution* (Stanford, Calif.: Stanford University Press, 2000), 12, who writes that "homme de lettres," as the "key term of social consecration in the Enlightenment," was "primarily a social category."

12. For instance, the *philosophes*, for all their intellectual feistiness, "did not show the same combativeness when it came to [. . . their] literary interests," to recall the words of Jules Bertaut, *La vie littéraire en France au XVIIIe siècle* (Paris: Tallandier, 1954), 354. As we saw in Chapter 2, Bertaut is referring to Voltaire. Nicole Masson offers a similar assessment in "La condition de l'auteur en France au XVIIIe siècle: le cas de Voltaire," also cited in Chapter 2, in *Le livre et l'historien: études offertes en l'honneur du Prof. Henri-Jean Martin*, ed. Frédéric Barbier et al. (Geneva: Droz, 1997), 554.

13. What J. P. Belin tellingly describes as Diderot's faithfulness to his Parisian *libraires* has been a flashpoint for this type of historiographical discomfort, leading to the characteristic account of Diderot who works "despite" his mistreatment by his publishers: "Despite the endless difficulties that he had to overcome," writes Belin; see *Le commerce des livres prohibés à Paris de 1750 à 1789* (New York: Burt Franklin, 1967), 73. Jacques Proust's studies of Diderot's relations with his publishers are rife with similarly awkward formulae, seemingly destined to highlight the *philosophe*'s resistance to his *libraires* in the absence of much explicit evidence of any sustained resistance (with the famous 1764 letter to Le Breton, angrily denouncing the latter's modifications of *Encyclopédie* entries, ultimately notable as an outlier). See above all *Diderot et l'Encyclopédie* (Paris: Albin Michel, 1962, 1995), chap. 3, "L'*Encyclopédie* et la fortune de Diderot," 81–116. The discomfort plays out in appraisals of what is perhaps Diderot's best-known expression of this faithfulness, the *Lettre sur le commerce de la librairie*, which he wrote in 1763 at the behest of the Parisian publishers' guild and its syndic, Le Breton (who was also the principal publisher of the *Encyclopédie*), to make their case for permanent rather than temporary *privilèges* to the works that they bought from writers. Much more will be said about this document and its context, as well as about Diderot's relations with his publishers in this chapter.

14. Examples of the Diderot/Rousseau opposition used to describe modernization alternatives include Rémy Saisselin, *The Literary Enterprise in Eighteenth-Century France* (Detroit: Wayne State University Press, 1979), 150; and Éric Walter, "Les auteurs et le champ littéraire," in *L'histoire de l'édition française*, ed. Henri-Jean Martin and Roger Chartier, 4 vols. (Paris: Fayard, 1990), 2:515–17.

15. Many examples could be cited here. Two early discussions of eighteenth-century writers and the book trade in terms of individual entrepreneurialism can be found in Georges d'Avenel, "Les riches depuis sept cents ans: VIII honoraires des Gens de lettres," *Revue des deux mondes* 48 (Nov. 15, 1908): 335–67; and Maurice Pellisson, *Les hommes de lettres au XVIIIe siècle* (1911; Geneva: Slatkine 1970), 64–75.

16. Denis Diderot, "Salon de 1763" in *Oeuvres complètes*, ed. Herbert Dieckmann, Jacques Proust, and Jean Varloot, 25 vols. (Paris: Hermann, 1975–), 13:390.

17. In this respect, the French situation might seem to stand in sharp contrast with an earlier state of affairs in England, which has inspired much scholarship on the rise of the "proprietary author." See, for instance, Mark Rose, *Authors and Owners: The Invention of Copyright* (Cambridge, Mass.: Harvard University Press, 1993) and Joseph Loewenstein, *The Author's Due: Printing and the Prehistory of Copyright*

(Chicago: University of Chicago Press, 2002). In *The Trouble with Ownership: Literary Property and Authorial Liability in England: 1660–1730* (Philadelphia: University of Pennsylvania Press, 2005), Jody Greene emphasizes the costs of "ownership," which were increased regulation and accountability.

18. Carla Hesse writes, "the argument that ideas were the property of the individual author was first advanced in defense of the monopoly of the Parisian Publisher's Guild." Hesse, "Enlightenment Epistemology and the Laws of Authorship in Revolutionary France, 1777–1793," *Representations* 30 (Spring 1990): 112. Roger Chartier notes: "The first important revision: far from developing from a particular application of the individual right to property, the affirmation of literary property derives directly from a defense of the *privilège*." See Chartier, *L'ordre des livres: lecteurs, auteurs, bibliothèques en Europe entre XIVe et XVIIIe siècles*, 42. It would be interesting to consider parallels with the English debates about copyright, as they took shape before and after the passage of the Statute of Anne in 1709–10. Unlike the Parisian publishers, the members of the Stationers Company had already enjoyed de facto permanent rights to their purchased manuscripts up until the lapse of the previous Licensing Act in the 1690s. The mobilization for "property rights," which would similarly highlight the figure of the "possessive author" as the source of that property, would have the effect, indeed by connecting that right to Authorship and to the life of the writer, of temporally limiting it. See Loewenstein, *The Author's Due*, chap. 2, 27–51.

19. We have, of course, already discussed the *privilège* in Chapters 1 and 2. According to Elizabeth Armstrong, the first *privilège* for the printing of a particular book was granted in 1479 by the bishop of Würzburg to a group of printers for the exclusive rights to a breviary. The first to be found in France dates from 1498. See Armstrong, *Before Copyright: The French Book Privilege System 1498–1526*, Cambridge Studies in Publishing & Printing History (Cambridge: Cambridge University Press, 1990), 2–3, 7. Clearly, such "firsts" are always hard to pin down. Madeleine Dock identifies "the first authentic *privilège*" as that accorded by the Venice College to Jean de Spire in 1469. See Dock, *Étude sur le droit d'auteur* (Paris: Librairie générale de droit et de jurisprudence, 1963), 63. For a rich and detailed analysis of the legal framework of the early years of printing in France, with emphasis on how writers around the turn of the sixteenth century engaged the system, see Cynthia Brown, *Poets, Patrons, and Printers: Crisis of Authority in Late Medieval France* (Ithaca, N.Y.: Cornell University Press, 1995).

20. Claude-Marin Saugrain's *Code de la librairie et imprimerie de Paris* (Paris: Communauté des libraires et des imprimeurs, 1744) synthesizes the accumulation of ordinances dating from 1332 that provided the legal framework for the *privilège* system. Among these is a 1645 *déclaration* requiring the full text or an excerpt of the *privilège* itself to be printed into each copy of the book, 89–90. The *Code* was established in 1723 for Paris, then was extended in 1744 to the nation as a whole. See Henri Falk, *Les privilèges de librairie sous l'ancien régime: étude historique du conflit des droits sur l'oeuvre littéraire* (Paris: Rousseau, 1906). Séguier's definition of the *privilège* is cited by Falk, 66, who further characterizes the device as "a simple measure for the protection of an industry, called for by royal solicitude."

21. D'Héricourt, "Mémoire à M. le Garde des Sceaux," in Edouard Laboulaye and Georges Guiffrey, *La propriété littéraire au XVIIIe siècle: recueil de pièces et de documents publié par le comité de l'association pour la défense de la propriété littéraire et*

artistique (Paris: Hachette, 1859), 24. This relatively new pro-property rhetoric from the *libraires* in the 1720s comes in the context of the 1723 synthesis of the *Code de la librairie*. See Falk, *Les privilèges en librairie*, 90; and Raymond Birn, "The Profits of Ideas: *Privilèges en librairie* in Eighteenth-Century France," *Eighteenth-Century Studies* 4, 2 (Winter 1970–71): 143–44.

22. D'Héricourt, "Mémoire," 26–27.

23. D'Héricourt, "Mémoire," 27.

24. D'Héricourt, "Mémoire," 24.

25. The "Requête au roi pour la librairie et l'imprimerie de Paris au sujet des deux arrêts du 30 août 1777" was signed by "l'avocat Cochut," and presented to the administration by the syndic of the guild and his adjuncts in 1778. The text is in Laboulaye and Guiffrey, *La Propriété littéraire au XVIIIe siècle*, 160–90. In August 1777, the Conseil du Roi promulgated six *arrêts* that aimed to limit in some measure the dominance of the Parisian booksellers' guild over the French book trade and aid the increasingly impoverished provincial *libraires*. The two *arrêts* mentioned in the title are the fifth and the sixth. The fifth was the most significant, and set out broadly to reform the *privilège* system as a whole, shortening the duration of the *privilège* to ten years for publishers (while notably lengthening it for authors). It also made the renewal process more rigorous by requiring "an expansion of the book by at least a quarter." Above all, perhaps, this *arrêt* reaffirmed the traditional view of the *privilège* as "a grace founded in justice." The sixth *arrêt* offered amnesty to publishers for past counterfeiting, with the proviso that now, with the chokehold of the Parisians on the market broken, there would be no need to resort to piracy. All six articles of the reforms are included in Laboulaye and Guiffrey, *La propriété littéraire au XVIIIe siècle*, 127–50. See also Birn, "The Profits of Ideas," 131–68.

26. D'Héricourt, "Mémoire," 24.

27. Chartier, *L'ordre des livres*, 55. Chartier references thirty contracts between authors and Parisian publishers from 1535 to 1560, which were discovered by Annie Parent-Charron, and discussed in her *Les métiers du livre à Paris au XVIe siècle: 1535–1560* (Geneva: Droz, 1974).

28. For Henri Falk, the historic shift by which *libraires* increasingly published the works of living authors with whom they had to negotiate directly was decisive for the emergence of the new conceptualization of the *privilège* as a permanent property right. See *Les privilèges de librairie*, 92. Diderot had in fact anticipated this argument in his *Lettre sur le commerce de la librairie* (1763), in *Oeuvres complètes*, ed. Jules Assézat and Maurice Tourneux, 20 vols. (Paris: Garnier, 1875–77), 18:18–19.

29. André Chevillier, *L'origine de l'imprimerie de Paris, dissertation historique et critique* (Paris: J. de Laulne, 1694), 380. Cited in Dock, *Étude sur le droit d'auteur*, 81.

30. D'Héricourt, "Mémoire," 28–29.

31. D'Héricourt, "Mémoire," 28.

32. As we saw in Chapter 3, the abbé de la Porte published and sold enormous quantities of works, in the process earning impressive profits; yet he never acquired much respectability: "he does not raise his expectations so high," wrote Pidansat de Mairobert, "his goal is more concrete, to amass money." See *L'espion anglois, ou correspondance secrète entre milord All'Eye et milord All'Ear*, 10 vols. (London: John Adamson, 1779–84), 3:43–44.

33. "Publishing," of course, did have the broader signification in the early modern period of "making public," and was less closely tied to the specific variant of "print publication" than it is in our day. It would therefore not be strange in Old Regime France to use the word in order to refer to the reading of a poem in a salon. The question is further complicated by the continuing importance of manuscript circulation, especially in the exclusive social networks of *le monde*. See Christian Jouhaud and Alain Viala's introduction to *De la publication: entre Renaissance et Lumières*, ed. Jouhaud and Viala (Paris: Fayard, 2002), 5–21. Harold Love offers a counterpoint to the monopoly that print has held on the attention of scholars. He examines the importance of "scribal publication" in seventeenth-century England, highlighting among other aspects of the phenomenon the "societal functions" of the manuscript, which bonded "groups of like-minded individuals into a community, sect or political faction, with the exchange of texts in manuscript serving to nourish a shared set of values and to enrich personal allegiances." Love, *The Culture and Commerce of Texts: Scribal Publication in Seventeenth-Century England* (Amherst: University of Massachusetts Press, 1998), 177. See also Margaret Ezell's study *Social Authorship and the Advent of Print* (Baltimore: Johns Hopkins University Press, 1999), which similarly reconsiders the role of print publication in Restoration England against a broader intellectual context in which the manuscript remained a medium of choice.

34. "Opinion de Linguet touchant l'arrêt sur les privilèges," 1778, in *La propriété littéraire au XVIIIe siècle*, ed. Laboulaye and Guiffrey, 232.

35. Roche, *Les républicains des lettres*, 260.

36. D'Héricourt, "Mémoire," 24.

37. In his *Lettre sur le commerce de la librairie*, which, as we will see, was directly influenced by d'Héricourt's tract, Diderot famously evaluates his lifetime earnings from publishing at 40,000 écus. It must be recalled, of course, that this sum was mostly compensation for editorial rather than authorial activities. See Diderot, *Oeuvres complètes*, 18:47. Bernardin de Saint-Pierre's account of his conversations with Rousseau addresses the question of the latter's earnings and whether they were sufficient to support him. Having noticed various individuals stopping by Rousseau's house to drop off or pick up scores of music, and seeing the financial transactions that each visit entailed, Bernardin wonders why Rousseau does not cash in on his talents. "Your works must have brought you basic comforts; they enriched so many publishers!" Bernardin states. Rousseau then reveals exactly how much he had made (barely 20,000 livres), explaining that this sum was spread over many years and was spent as it came in. In additon, "a Dutch publisher, out of gratitude, set up a 600 livres pension for me, of which 300 are transferable to my wife after my death. This is my entire fortune. It costs me 100 louis [the louis was worth 24 livres] to maintain my household; I have to earn more." See *La vie et les ouvrages de Jean-Jacques Rousseau*, ed. Maurice Sourian (Paris: Hachette, 1907), 60–64.

38. See Chapter 1.

39. Alain Viala, *Naissance de l'écrivain* (Paris: Minuit, 1985), 113. See, again, Chapter 1.

40. Hesse, "Enlightenment Epistemology," 113. On "modern authorship" in Germany, oriented by Romantic claims to originality and singularity, see Martha Woodmansee, *The Author, Art and the Market: Rereading the History of Aesthetics*

(New York: Columbia University Press, 1994), particularly chap. 2, "Genius and the Copyright," 35–55. On England, where the debates played out earlier and were shaped by more strictly "professional" concerns, see Rose, *Authors and Owners*; Lowenstein, *The Author's Due*; and Greene, *The Trouble with Ownership*.

41. Far from it, in fact. Louis d'Héricourt's mémoire was received with great hostility by the Garde des Sceaux, Joseph Jean Baptiste Fleuriau d'Armenonville in 1726. The syndic of the Parisian guild and his adjunct were forced to resign; the latter, a printer named Vincent who had published the mémoire, had to flee Paris. See Lucien Brunel, "Observations critiques et littéraires sur un opuscule de Diderot," *Revue d'histoire littéraire de la France* 10 (1903): 7. Even with more "liberal" magistrates running the book trade by the mid-eighteenth century, the Old Regime administration would never recognize permanent *privilèges*, with the 1777 reforms reaffirming the status of the *privilège* as a temporary "grace." Of course, literary property will never exist as a legally permanent possession, though the clear long-run trend has been for the term of the copyright protection to be steadily lengthened.

42. D'Héricourt, "Mémoire," 23.

43. Birn, "The Profits of Ideas," 145. We will explore in more detail the case of Luneau de Boisjermain, who was sued in 1769 by the Parisian Guild for illegally selling books, sparking polemics in the press about the relationship between authors and publishers.

44. John Lough, *An Introduction to Eighteenth-Century France* (London: Longmans, 1960), 231–32; Martha Woodmansee, "The Genius and the Copyright: Economic and Legal Conditions of the Emergence of the 'Author,'" *Eighteenth-Century Studies* 17, 4 (Summer 1984): 425–48.

45. Walter, "Les auteurs et le champ littéraire," in *Histoire de l'édition française*, 2:515–17; and Lough, *Writer and Public in France from the Middle Ages to the Present Day* (Oxford: Clarendon, 1978), 212.

46. Darnton, *The Literary Underground*, 189. See my article "Conceptualising the Literary Market: Diderot and the *Lettre sur le commerce de la librairie*," *SVEC* 2003:01 (January 2003): 137–70, for a discussion of the negative and positive reactions to the text. Both deal with the central problem of disassociating Diderot's voice from that of the guild. Those who believe that they can do it consider the *Lettre* to be an important item in the *philosophe*'s corpus—Jacques Proust being a leading advocate of this view, argues that the *Lettre* is "of capital importance"—those who do not, deem it to be weak and forgettable. Either way, the problem of Diderot's complicity with the guild is a central one. See Jacques Proust, "Pour servir à une édition critique de la *Lettre sur le commerce de la librairie*," *Diderot Studies* 3 (1961): 337.

47. For a detailed account of the affair, see John Lough, "Luneau de Boisjermain v. the Publishers of the *Encyclopédie*," *Studies on Voltaire and the Eighteenth Century* 23 (1963): 115–77.

48. *Mémoires secrets pour servir à l'histoire de la République des Lettres en France depuis MDCCLXII jusqu'à nos jours*, 36 vols. (London: John Adamsohn, 1777–1789), 4:360.

49. Charles-Josheph Fenouillot de Falbaire de Quingey, *Avis aux gens de lettres* (Liège: n.p., 1770), 37–38.

50. Fenouillot de Falbaire, *Avis aux gens de lettres*, 38.

51. Fenouillot de Falbaire, *Avis aux gens de lettres*, 1, 12.

52. Nicolas-Simon-Henri Linguet, *Mémoire signifié pour le sieur Luneau de Boisjermain, Défendeur: Contre les Syndic & Adjoints des Libraires & Imprimeurs de Paris, Demandeurs* (Paris: Imprimerie de Grangé, [1769]), 5. The *mémoire judiciaire* was a lawyer's brief. Though originally handwritten and destined only for circulation among those concerned with a particular case, it was increasingly printed beginning in the seventeenth century, and thanks to a loophole in print trade regulations, which continued to consider the *mémoire judiciaire* as a specialized document meant only to be read in the framework of a specific trial, the only requirement for printing and circulating it was that the lawyer's and printer's names appear. No prepublication approval was needed, which, as Sarah Maza points out, meant that not only could certain issues be engaged in a *mémoire judiciaire* that would have been more difficult to address in a conventional pamphlet, but the time to publication was also considerably shorter. The *mémoire judiciaire* thus played a central role in a range of public debates from the late eighteenth century. See Maza, *Private Lives and Public Affairs: The Causes Célèbres of Prerevolutionary France* (Berkeley: University of California Press, 1993), 33–38. David Bell explores the intellectual culture of barristers and the culture's connection with the Enlightenment, emphasizing in particular the role played by lawyers in a critical engagement with absolutism in the name of public opinion and the Nation. See *Lawyers and Citizens: The Making of a Political Elite in Old Regime France* (Oxford: Oxford University Press, 1994).

53. Linguet, *Memoire signifié*, 2, and *Dernière réponse signifiée et consultation pour le sieur de Luneau de Boisjermain contre les Syndic et Adjoints des Libraires de Paris* (Paris: Imprimerie de Gueffier, 1769), 12.

54. *Mémoires secrets*, entry for February 14, 1770, 5:79. See Birn, "Privilèges en librairie," 156–57. Birn emphasizes the administration's interest in the case as a way of opposing the Parisian guild's efforts to solidify their control over the French book trade. The final judgment was in this view a kind of "technicality." The director of the book trade, Gabriel de Sartine, did not believe that he was authorized to allow a writer with a *privilège* to self-publish.

55. Fenouillot de Falbaire, *Avis aux gens de lettres*, 1.

56. *Mémoires secrets*, entry for December 27, 1769, 5:40.

57. Fenouillot de Falbaire, *Avis aux gens de lettres*, 12, 33–34.

58. Fenouillot de Falbaire, *Avis aux gens de lettres*, 12.

59. Fenouillot de Falbaire, *Avis aux gens de lettres*, 12.

60. See Fabre d'Eglantine, *Les gens de lettres; ou le Provincial à Paris*, which had a run of exactly one night on September 21, 1787, and was only later published in an 1827 *Mélanges littéraires* (Paris: n.p., 1827), 9–117. Clar is a very serious, scrupulous, and impoverished provincial poet who is harassed by his imperious publisher Musophage. Darnton discusses this play in "The Facts of Literary Life in Eighteenth-Century France," in *The Political Culture of the Old Regime*, vol. 1 of *The French Revolution and the Creation of Modern Political Culture*, ed. Keith Michael Baker, 4 vols. (Oxford: Pergamon, 1987), 261–91.

61. Louis-Sébastien Mercier, *Tableau de Paris*, 1781–88, ed. Jean-Claude Bonnet (Paris: Mercure de France, 1994), 2:1260.

62. Louis-Sébastien Mercier, *De la littérature et des littérateurs* (1778; Geneva: Slatkine, 1970), 59.

63. Linguet, *Dernière réponse signifiée*, 31. In a different framework after the reforms of 1777, which had rejected the pro-property argument, Linguet presents in an article appearing in the *Annales politiques, civiles et littéraires* the same arguments for understanding the *privilège* as a guarantee of property rights. He returns, however, to a more conciliatory tone toward the Parisian publishers, whose abusiveness is rooted not in their avaricious character but in a badly devised system. If publishers act like "vampires," writes Linguet, "it is not by the nature of things; it is only due to the abuses generated by bad legislation. Neither the publisher, nor publishers in general, deserve this slur." See "Opinion de Linguet touchant l'arrêt sur le privilèges," in Laboulaye and Guiffrey, *La propriété littéraire au XVIIIe siècle*, 247–48.

64. Fenouillot de Falbaire, *Avis aux gens de lettres*, 45.

65. Darnton, *The Literary Underground*, 189 and note 38.

66. Falk, *Les privilèges en librairie*, 96.

67. Falk, *Les privilèges en librairie*, 96. The *notice préliminaire* to the *Lettres* in the Assézat/Tourneux edition contends that the text holds a "premier rank" in the list of works "which Diderot took on in order to provide for his minor expenses." See Diderot, *Oeuvres complètes*, 18:5. We might recall, as part of Diderot's complicated legacy, that during the Luneau trial, he intervened on the side of the *Encyclopédie* publishers, who had asked him to support their cause. He did so, moreover, in his guise as an editor rather than as an author, defending his decisions to expand the work from the original proposal: "I wanted my edition to be as it pleased me [être à ma fantaisie]." The "Lettre de Monsieur Diderot à Messieurs Briasson et Le Breton, Libraires associés à l'Encyclopédie" was appended to one of the publishers' mémoires against Luneau: *Mémoire pour les Libraires associés à l'Encyclopédie contre le sieur Luneau de Boisjermain* (Paris: Imprimerie de Le Breton, 1771), 68–74, quote 68. Diderot had a famous falling out with Le Breton, recorded in a letter to the publisher from November 12, 1764 (Diderot, *Correspondance*, ed. Georges Roth, 16 vols. [Paris: Minuit, 1955–], 4:300–306), which the *philosophe* penned after discovering that Le Breton had been editing the articles as a cautionary measure in the wake of the debacle of 1759, when the *Encyclopédie* publishers lost their *privilège*. Diderot angrily denounces "an atrocity of which there is no example since the origins of printing." The letter has attracted much attention; the arc of Diderot's career suggests, however, a more ambivalent view of his *libraires* and of the commerce of letters.

68. Diderot refers specifically to the *Mémoire* by "one of our most celebrated jurists," going on to add, "I had the satisfaction of discovering that I adhered to the same principles as he did, and that we both drew from them the same consequences," *Lettre sur le commerce de la librairie*, 31.

69. Letter to Nicolas-René Berryer, lieutenant-general of the police, August 10, 1749, in Diderot, *Correspondance*, 1:83.

70. Diderot, *Lettre sur le commerce de la librairie*, 18:47.

71. Darnton, *The Literary Underground*, 189, note 38.

72. Diderot, *Lettre sur le commerce de la librairie*, 18:7.

73. Diderot, *Lettre sur le commerce de la librairie*, 18:29.

74. Diderot, *Lettre sur le commerce de la librairie*, 18:54.

75. See, e.g., Lucien Brunel's painstaking comparison of Diderot's *Lettre sur le commerce de la librairie* and the *Représentations des libraires de Paris sur l'état de la*

librairie, which was the version of Diderot's text that the guild ultimately delivered to Sartine. The latter document included many stylistic and substantive changes, including the elimination of all the negative images of the *libraires*. See Brunel, "Observations critiques et littéraires sur un opuscule de Diderot," 17. Brunel's approach can be contrasted with, for instance, Jacques Proust's less compelling attempt to differentiate Diderot's *Lettre* from the guild's discourse by pointing to its ideological focus on "freedom of the press," based on Diderot's own reference to his text in a letter to Mme de Meaux as a "a short piece on freedom of the press." See Proust, "Pour servir à une édition critique de la *Lettre sur le commerce de la librairie*," 335. Proust published an edition of Diderot's *Lettre* under the title "Sur la liberté de la presse," which he considers to be its "definitive title." Laurent Versini's introduction to the *Lettre* included in his edition of Diderot's *Oeuvres*, vol. 3, "Politique" (Paris: Robert Laffont, 1995) similarly deems Diderot's text to be "one of the most important of the eighteenth century concerning the freedom to think, write and publish," 55.

76. Diderot, *Lettre sur le commerce de la librairie*, 18:51–52.

77. D'Héricourt, "Mémoire au Garde des Sceaux," 21.

78. Lucien Febvre and Henri-Jean Martin describe the rise of pro-Catholic printing monopolies in Paris during the Religious Wars, nurtured by Charles IX and Henri III, who granted a core group of publishers lucrative *privilèges* for the works of the Church Fathers and other *livres de piétés*. See Febvre and Martin, *The Coming of the Book: The Impact of Printing 1450–1800*, ed. Geoffrey Nowell-Smith and David Wotton, trans. David Gérard, (London: Verso, 1986), 241.

79. D'Héricourt, "Mémoire au Garde des Sceaux," 22.

80. Diderot, *Lettre sur le commerce de la librairie*, 18:11–12.

81. Diderot, *Lettre sur le commerce de la librairie*, 18:13.

82. Diderot, *Lettre sur le commerce de la librairie*, 18:13.

83. Diderot, *Lettre sur le commerce de la librairie*, 18:34.

84. Diderot, *Lettre sur le commerce de la librairie*, 18:58–59.

85. See Wallace Kirsop, "Les mécanismes éditoriaux," in *L'histoire de l'édition française*, ed. Chartier and Martin, 2:26–29. About one-third to one-half of production costs went toward the paper.

86. Diderot, *Lettre sur le commerce de la librairie*, 18:38–39. It goes without saying that these press runs were small by modern-day standards, usually in the range of 500–1,000 copies, and rarely exceeding 3,000. See Kirsop, "Les mécanismes éditoriaux," 28.

87. Kirsop, "Les mécanismes éditoriaux," 17. Kirsop remarks that "even the treatises of natural history that begin to flourish in this period of discovery and scientific research present themselves ostensibly as precious objects created for an elite clientele." For a breakdown of the reading public in eighteenth-century France, see Roger Chartier and Daniel Roche, "Les pratiques urbaines de l'imprimé," in *L'histoire de l'édition française*, ed. Chartier and Martin, 2:521–28. Darnton reminds us that books on the whole were beyond the means of the relatively well-paid artisans who made them. A print-shop worker earned somewhere in the neighborhood of forty sous per day, according to Darnton, which was about twice what artisans in other trades might make. The price of a book, of course, varied greatly with its quality. For instance, Rey's original 1761 edition of Rousseau's "best-selling" *Nouvelle Héloïse*, 3 vols. in 12, went for around 15–16 livres, just over a week's pay for a print laborer. More luxurious books

were farther out of reach; the cost of the first edition of the *Encyclopédie* finally came to 980 livres for seventeen volumes. However, much cheaper books could be found. Printed plays were more affordable. Duchesne appended to his 1760 edition of Palissot's *Les Philosophes* a catalogue of dramatic works available in his store, most of which cost under five francs. The cheapest were collections of songs and vaudevilles bearing a 1 franc 40 sols price tag. It should be stressed, though, that this still represented about a day's work for an average urban tradesman. See Darnton, *The Business of Enlightenment: A Publishing History of the Encyclopédie, 1775–1800* (Cambridge, Mass.: Harvard University Press, 1979), 11, and chap. 5, "Bookmaking"; and Rousseau, *Correspondance complète*, ed. R. A. Leigh, 52 vols. (Geneva: Institut et musée Voltaire, 1965–), 7:264.

88. Diderot, *Lettre sur le commerce de la librairie*, 18:10.

89. Darnton, *The Literary Underground*, 189.

90. This conflation was much larger than Diderot and reflected what Darnton famously called the "typographical consciousness" of the Old Regime; that is, its fetishization of the material text in an age when these were made by hand and acquired at great expense. The cult of the format is a good illustration, according to which a book's quality and size (folio, quarto, octavo, etc.) were assumed to reflect each other. Indeed, throughout his *Lettre*, Diderot interchangeably characterizes the type of "grande entreprise" that publishers are increasingly reluctant to undertake as "folios" or as "livres savants." See Darnton, *The Business of Enlightenment*, 180, 236.

91. Diderot, *Lettre sur le commerce de la librairie*, 18:38.

92. Fenouillot de Falbaire, *Avis aux gens de lettres*, 33.

93. Diderot, *Lettre sur le commerce de la librairie*, 18:30. Linguet makes a similar case in his *Dernière réponse signifiée*, 12–13.

94. Mercier, *De la littérature et des littérateurs*, 59.

95. Mercier, *Tableau de Paris*, 1:363–64.

96. Diderot, *Lettre sur le commerce de la librairie*, 18:16.

97. Diderot, *Lettre sur le commerce de la librairie*, 18:16, and Fabre d'Eglantine, *Les Gens de lettres* in *Mélanges littéraires*, 97–100.

98. Voltaire, "Lettre à un premier commis," in *Politique de Voltaire*, ed. René Pomeau (Paris: Armand Colin, 1994), 226. The letter is dated June 20, 1733. Guillaume-Chrétien de Lamoignon de Malesherbes' *Mémoires sur la librairie* were written at the request of his father, the Chancellor Lamoignon in 1759 following the controversies surrounding *De l'Esprit* and the revocation of the *privilège* for the *Encyclopédie*. Malesherbes' reflections are driven by a sense of the futility of censorship, which does not stop illegal publication but forces it abroad: "In this way, we would lose an important branch of commerce, or rather we would give away an active commerce to foreigners, which would be disadvantageous for France." See *Mémoires sur la librairie*, ed. Roger Chartier (Paris: Imprimerie nationale, 1994), 86.

99. Voltaire's epistle was the only other text mentioned by Versini in the introduction to Diderot's *Lettre* naming the latter, as we saw above, "one of the most important of the eighteenth-century concerning the freedom to think, write and publish." See Diderot, *Oeuvres*, 3:55.

100. Voltaire, "Lettre à un premier commis," 226. Voltaire echoes Mandeville, who exercised a considerable influence on his thinking at this time. Georges May has famously analyzed what would soon become a very repressive atmosphere for novel

publication, which culminates in the late 1730s with the decision of the Chancellor, Henri-François d'Aguesseau, who at the time was directly in charge of the book trade, to refuse all *privilèges* for a genre that was both popular and considered to be morally corrupting. See May, *Le dilemme du roman au XVIIIe siècle: étude sur les rapports du roman et de la critique, 1715–1761* (New Haven, Conn.: Yale University Press, 1963).

101. Voltaire, "Letter à un premier commis," 226. Martha Woodmansee points to a similar representation of authorship as nothing more than a node in a broad production process in a German commercial dictionary from 1735, in which the book was defined as the output of a plurality of artisans, whose contributions were invoked according to no obvious hierarchy other than the sequence of production itself: "Many people work on the ware before it is completed and becomes an actual book. . . . The scholar and the writer, the papermaker, the type founder, the typesetter and the printer, the proofreader, the publisher, the book binder, sometimes even the gilder and the brass worker, etc. Thus many mouths are fed by this branch of commerce." See Woodmansee, "The Genius and the Copyright," 425. The dictionary to which she is referring is Georg Heinrich Zinck's *Allgemeines Oeconomisches Lexicon* published in Leipzig in 1735.

102. Even, as we saw in Chapter 2, if this philosphical *honnêteté* mediated an image of the opposite: the writer's autonomy from elite society.

103. Bourdieu, *Les règles de l'art*, 76–77.

104. Bourdieu, *Les règles de l'art*, 121–23.

105. Molière, *Precious Provincials*, scene 9, in *Don Juan and Other Plays*, trans. George Graveley and Ian Maclean (Oxford: Oxford University Press, 1998), 16; "Cela est au dessous de ma condition; mais je le fais seulement pour donner à gagner aux libraires," *Les précieuses ridicules*, scene 9, *Oeuvres complètes*, ed. Maurice Rat, 2 vols. (Paris: Gallimard, 1959), 1:232. Needless to say, the following clause "who plague me [qui me persécutent]" should not be understood as an indication of mistreatment but as a self-congratulatory reference to the demand for his poems.

106. No doubt there are exceptions to this observation. But overall in the seventeenth century, even the most satirically "commercial" depictions of transactions between writers and publishers—those for instance offered by Furetière in the *Roman bourgeois* or by Charles Sorel in the *Histoire comique de Francion*—tend to point more to the crude economic nature of the writer than the *librairie*, who remains a peripheral untargeted character. In his *Entretiens sur les contes de fées* from 1699, Pierre de Villiers lambastes the commercial degradation of letters but his attack is directed pointedly at writers not *libraires*, who are only doing what they would be expected to do. "They have no other motive in printing books than to sell them," he writes, excusing them; "I only have a grief against Authors who, with their terrible Works, give them the opportunity to use this expertise." See *Entretiens sur les contes de fées, et sur quelques autres ouvrages du temps, pour servir de préservatif contre le mauvais goût* (Paris: Jacques Collombat, 1699), 214, 221.

107. Malesherbes, *Mémoires sur la liberté de la presse*, 153–54.

108. Pierre-Jacques Blondel, *Mémoire sur les véxations qu'exercent les libraires & imprimeurs de Paris*, 1725, ed. Lucien Faucou (Paris: Moniteur du Bibliophile, 1879), 18. Like d'Héricourt's *Mémoire*, Blondel's text comes out of the polemics surrounding the synthesis of the *Code de la librairie* in 1723.

109. Fenouillot de Falbaire, *Avis aux gens de lettres*, 39.

110. Blondel, *Mémoires sur les véxations qu'exercent les libraires et imprimeurs de Paris*, 18.

111. Darnton notes, for instance, that the Protestant publishers were interested in printing a breviary for the Cistercians, as proposed by the abbé Le Senne. See Darnton, "The Life of a 'Poor Devil' in the Republic of Letters," in *Essays on the Age of Enlightenment in Honor of Ira O. Wade*, ed. Jean Macary (Geneva: Droz, 1977), 66.

112. Elisabeth Eisenstein, *Grub Street Abroad: Aspects of the French Cosmopolitan Press from the Age of Louis XIV to the French Revolution* (Oxford: Clarendon, 1992), 28.

113. Fenouillot de Falbaire, *Avis aux gens de lettres*, 12.

114. Fenouillot de Falbaire, *Avis aux gens de lettres*, 43–44. Linguet had gone over the numbers in detail in his *Dernière réponse signifiée*, accusing the *Encyclopédie* editors in another mémoire of "excessive and illegitimate profit." See *Mémoire et Consultation pour M. de Luneau de Boisjermain, Souscripteur de l'Encyclopédie. Contre le sieur Briasson, Libraire, Syndic des Librairies & Imprimeurs, ancien Adjoint de sa Communauté, et le sieur de Le Breton, Libraire, ancien Syndic et Adjoint de la même Communauté, associé avec le sieur Briasson pour l'impression de l'Encyclopédie* (Paris: Imprimerie de Louis Cellot, 1770), 4. The figures were duly recorded in the *Mémoires secrets*, entries for December 27 and 29, 1769, 5:39–40, 43. "Where is the fortune of the authors of the *Encyclopédie*?" Mercier asks in *De la littérature et des littérateurs*, 60. Diderot, by contrast, consistently defended his publishers against such accusations; he closes his letter in support of Le Breton and Briasson against Luneau de Boisjermain, addressing them directly: "I admit that it is sad, after twenty years of persecutions which I shared with you, that you are now troubled in your enjoyment of a fortune that you have certainly merited by your work." See his "Lettre de Monsieur Diderot à Messieurs Briasson et Le Breton," 74.

115. Blondel, *Mémoire sur les véxations*, 48; and Linguet, *Mémoire signifié pour le sieur Luneau de Boisjermain*, 4.

116. For a detailed examination of Rousseau's conceptualization of his own literary career as a prolonged effort of "consecrating [his] life to the truth"—adapting Juvenal's phrase as his motto in the *Lettres à d'Alembert*—an effort conceived in terms of struggle, authorial responsibility, and the assumption of personal risk and deprivation, see Christopher Kelly, *Rousseau as Author: Consecrating One's Life to the Truth* (Chicago: University of Chicago Press, 2003).

Chapter 5. The Reality of a New Cultural Field: The Case of Rousseau

1. André, l'abbé Morellet, *Préface de la Comédie des philosophes* (Paris: chez l'auteur, 1760), 16–17.

2. Robert Darnton, "The Life of a 'Poor Devil' in the Republic of Letters," in *Essays on the Age of Enlightenment in Honor of Ira O. Wade*, ed. Jean Macary (Geneva: Droz, 1977), 78–79.

3. See Pierre Bourdieu, *In Other Words: Essays Towards a Reflexive Sociology*, trans. Matthew Adamson (Stanford, Calif.: Stanford University Press, 1990), chap. 3, "From Rules to Strategies," 59–75.

4. Diderot, *Lettre sur le commerce de la librairie*, in *Oeuvres complètes*, ed. Jules Assézat and Maurice Tourneux, 20 vols. (Paris: Garnier, 1875–77), 18:47.

5. The theater presents a significant exception to this identification of print with a universal public, although as Gregory Brown argues, the "theater" increasingly meant print for self-fashioned outsiders in the eighteenth century. See Gregory Brown, *A Field of Honor: Writers, Court Culture, and Public Theater in French Literary Life from Racine to the Revolution* (New York: Columbia University Press, 2002), chap. 3, "'Politesse perdue': The Patriot Playwright Between Court and Public." Brown explores the growing recourse to print among playwrights whose access to the Comédie française had been impeded, despite the fact that printing an unperformed play represented a contravention of established norms: it undermined the profitability of the play for the troupe. Brown highlights "an alternative identity" elaborated by dramatic writers who emphasized "not face-to-face encounters with urban elites or the court but the medium of print: prefaces to plays, treatises, *mémoires judiciaires*, and journalistic criticism. In claiming to speak through print to and for a much broader audience, these writings thereby presented an alternative conception of their role as playwrights—and, by extension, men of letters—as 'patriots.'" On the importance of the theater as an institution in which battles over the new identity of the intellectual played out, see also Jeffrey Ravel, *The Contested Parterre: Public Theater and French Political Culture, 1680–1791* (Ithaca, N.Y.: Cornell University Press, 1999); Paul Friedland, *Political Actors: Representative Bodies and Theatricality in the Age of the French Revolution* (Ithaca, N.Y.: Cornell University Press, 2002); Susan Maslan, *Revolutionary Acts: Theater, Democracy and the French Revolution* (Baltimore: Johns Hopkins University Press, 2005); and Elena Russo, *Styles of Enlightenment: Taste, Politics, and Authorship in Eighteenth-Century France* (Baltimore: Johns Hopkins University Press, 2007), chaps. 7 and 8.

6. *Mémoires de Marmontel*, ed. Maurice Tourneau, 2 vols. (Paris: Librairie des Bibliophiles, 1891), 2:88.

7. Letter to Rey of August 10, 1758, in Rousseau, *Correspondance complète*, ed. R. A. Leigh, 52 vols. (Geneva: Institut et musée Voltaire, 1965–), 5:126.

8. Jean-Jacques Rousseau, *Oeuvres complètes*, ed. Bernard Gagnebin and Marcel Raymond, 5 vols. (Paris: Gallimard, 1959–), 1:380, 513. Editorial positions at official journals such as the *Journal des Sçavants* or the *Mercure de France* were positions of considerable prestige.

9. Rousseau, *Oeuvres complètes*, 1:843. In fact, Rousseau never had to rely on copying music to make a living. This was an instance of self-mythologization connected with his efforts to disassociate himself from the world of Parisian cultural and intellectual elites, beginning in the early 1750s. In the *Confessions*, Rousseau points to this period, after the success of his first discourse, as one during which the tension between himself and others was first manifested. The latter, he contends, were jealous, not of his celebrity but of his personal reform, a key part of which was his repudiation of social ambition: "I forever renounced any project of fortune and advancement," he wrote, and in this context, as central to this rejection—and its image—he formulated a plan to earn his keep: "I imagined a very simple way to do it: this was to copy music for so much per page." From this point, Rousseau became an avowed enemy of the *philosophes* and an outsider, all the while continuing to live off the hospitality of notables such as the duc and duchesse de Luxembourg. The idea of copying music played

up his social independence as a simple laborer. Significantly, it was also around this time that Rousseau began to receive higher compensation from his literary endeavors, in part as a result of the duchesse de Luxembourg's lobbying on his behalf. Thus he was paid 6,000 livres by the *libraire* Duchesne in 1761 for *Emile*, which was an enormous sum at the time. The 2,000 livres that he had received three years earlier for *La Nouvelle Héloïse* was already an impressive amount. Benoît Mély rightly concludes, "the real relation between literary activity and remunerative work at this time differs significantly from that which the *Confessions* . . . ideally describes." Mély, *Jean-Jacques Rousseau: un intellectuel en rupture* (Paris: Minerve, 1985), 114. See also Roland Mortier's appraisal of Rousseau's willful lack of lucidity regarding the role of music copying in his economic life: "Paresse et travail dans l'introspection de Rousseau," in *Rousseau and the Eighteenth Century: Essays in Memory of R. A. Leigh*, ed. Marian Hobson, J. T. A. Leigh, and Robert Wokler (Oxford: Voltaire Foundation, 1992), 132.

10. Rousseau, *Letter to Beaumont*, in *Collected Writings*, ed. Roger Masters and Christopher Kelly, trans. Judith Bush, Christopher Kelly, and Roger Masters, 12 vols. (Hanover, N.H.: University Press of New England for Dartmouth College, 1990–), 9:81; "je n'aspirai jamais à ce titre, auquel je reconnais n'avoir aucun droit; et je n'y renonce assurément pas par modestie," *Oeuvres complètes*, 4:1004. My thanks to Ourida Mostefai for calling my attention to this passage, which she discusses in her ongoing investigation into Rousseau, censorship and celebrity. See also Christopher Kelly, *Rousseau as Author: Consecrating One's Life to the Truth* (Chicago: University of Chicago Press, 2003), 172–73, who cites these lines.

11. Blondel, *Mémoire sur les véxations qu'exercent les libraires et imprimeurs de Paris*, 1725, ed. Lucien Faucou (Paris: Le Moniteur du Bibliophile, 1879), 48.

12. *Mémoires secrets pour servir à l'histoire de la République des Lettres en France depuis MDCCLXII jusqu'à nos jours*, 36 vols. (London: John Adamsohn, 1777–1789), entry for October 20, 1769, 4:362. "Colporteurs" is a derisive term in this context, since it would normally refer to ambulant peddlers, rather than established shopkeepers or businesspeople.

13. A satirical representation of how inevitably bad suggestions from publishers were assumed to be can be found in Fabre d'Eglantine's play *Les gens de lettres*, in which the publisher Musophage insists that Clar change the title of his book to *Je veux vendre*. See *Les gens de lettres; ou le provincial à Paris* in *Mélanges littéraires*, vol. 1 (Paris: Musophage, 1827), 99.

14. Letter to Gabriel and Philibert Cramer of (probably) February 1762 (D10331). Voltaire, *The Complete Works*, ed. Theodore Besterman et al., 135 vols. (Geneva: Voltaire Foundation, 1968–), 108:288–89.

15. Letter to Gabriel Cramer of (probably) December 1763 (D11564). Voltaire, *Complete Works*, ed. Besterman, 111:107–8. I explore a number of the issues and texts that follow, with a somewhat different emphasis, in "The Enlightenment Literary Market: Rousseau, Authorship, and the Book Trade," *Eighteenth-Century Studies* 36, 3 (Spring 2003): 387–410.

16. Letter to Rey of June 28, 1758, in Rousseau, *Correspondance complète*, 5:102.

17. Letter to Gabriel Cramer of around December 15, 1761 (D10213), Voltaire, *Complete Works*, ed. Besterman, 108:173–74. On the notion of "typographi-

cal consciousness," see Darnton, *The Business of Enlightenment: A Publishing History of the Encyclopédie, 1775–1800* (Cambridge, Mass.: Harvard University Press, 1979), 236.

18. Letter to Gabriel Cramer of around February 10, 1773 (D18196), Voltaire, *Complete Works*, ed. Besterman, 123:295. The work in question was the *Lois de Minos*.

19. Letter to Gabriel Cramer of November 20, 1772 (D18032), Voltaire, *Complete Works*, ed. Besterman, 123–63. Voltaire adds: "As for Louis XV, I don't think he would enjoy reading these scribblings [ces rogatons]."

20. In a letter to Gabriel Cramer of about March 25, 1773, Voltaire writes, in regard to a short text on the court battle of the nobleman Morangiès that was to be appended to Cramer's 1773 edition of the *Lois de Minos*: "A strange mistake has slipped into the declaration on the trial of Mr de Morangiès. It reads *Réponse d'un avocat* instead of *Réponse à l'écrit d'un avocat*. I don't know how else to correct this other than by hand in the copies that you will be sending me." Voltaire, *Complete Works*, ed. Besterman, 123:351 (D18271). The implication is that a given edition would entail two sub-editions: one circulated through the bookstores, including the mistakes and possibly an errata sheet, and another distributed by Voltaire himself with handwritten corrections. In fact, every edition of a Voltaire work followed this pattern in that, while he asked for no monetary compensation from his *libraires*, he always demanded a large number of copies—as many as 75 or 100—which he would send to his network of elite readers. These personal copies would, of course, be printed using higher-quality materials: "I am counting on you to send on Friday . . . two copies, covered in crimson satin, to Mr le duc de Choiseul, and two to Mr le duc de Praslin; and a dozen bound copies to me," letter of December 31, 1766 (D13782), Voltaire, *Complete Works*, ed. Besterman, 115:186. For more regarding the Morangiès affair, see John Renwich, *Voltaire et Morangiès 1772–1773: où les lumières l'ont échappé belle*, Studies on Voltaire and the Eighteenth Century 202 (Oxford: Voltaire Foundation, 1982) and Sarah Maza, *Private Lives and Public Affairs: The Causes Célèbres of Prerevolutionary France* (Berkeley: University of California Press, 1993), chap. 1, 19–67.

21. Letter to Rey of June 9, 1764, in *Correspondance complète*, 20: 169. In this letter, Rousseau is proposing to Rey his *Lettres écrites de la Montagne*, which he warns "will be difficult to print correctly due to the many notes, citations, numbers, and quotation marks that it includes, and which require the greatest care from the printer [du Prote], pressman or corrector."

22. In his classic study, Jean Starobinski underscores the writer's defensiveness: "From now on, Rousseau's gestures are less initiatives than counterattacks [ripostes]." See *L'oeil vivant* (Paris: Gallimard, 1961), 95–96.

23. Voltaire reprimands Cramer for delays in sending a copy of his 1764 edition of Corneille's complete works to the Académie française: "I beseech you . . . not to make me fall out with thirty-nine colleagues." Letter to Gabriel Cramer of around January 20, 1765 (D12336), Voltaire, *Complete Works*, ed. Besterman, 112:339. On Voltaire's involvement of the Académie, long-time critics of the seventeenth-century playwright (from the days of the *Sentiments* in 1637) but now called upon to sponsor the new edition, see David Williams, "Voltaire and

the Patronage of Corneille," *Eighteenth-Century Studies* 6, 2 (Winter 1972–73): 221–37.

24. Letter to Rey of May 29, 1755, in *Correspondance complète*, 3: 129–30. There is a veiled threat here; namely, Rousseau might himself take his manuscript to a London publisher.

25. Letter to Rey of March 14, 1759, in *Correspondance complète*, 6: 44. Part of the issue relates to Rousseau's desire to have the provincial characters of *La Nouvelle Héloïse* communicate using a "natural" language, in contrast with the affected, polished language of sophisticated urban elites, to whom, indeed, the former would always seem "incorrect." "The style will offend *gens de goût*," writes Rousseau in the first preface. "Whoever decides to read these letters will have to be patient with regards to the language-related mistakes [fautes de langue], to the emphatic and unexciting style, to the banal thoughts rendered in grandiose terms." See Rousseau, *Oeuvres complètes*, 3: 5–6.

26. Letter to Rey of May 25, 1760, in *Correspondance complète*, 7:107.

27. The *Dialogues* is Rousseau's least accessible text, with rambling excursions into paranoia. Despite or perhaps because of this fact, as Christopher Kelly and Roger Masters indicate, it is also the work "in which Rousseau undertakes his most comprehensive reflection on the relations between himself as an author, his books, and his audience." See Kelly and Masters, "Rousseau on Reading 'Jean-Jacques': The *Dialogues*," *Interpretation: A Journal of Political Philosophy* 17 (Winter 1989–90): 239–53.

28. Rousseau, *Rousseau Judge of Jean-Jacques: Dialogues*, in *Collected Writings*, 1:23, 27. "le plus crapuleux, le plus vile débauché qui puisse exister," Rousseau, *Oeuvres complètes*, 1:688, 694.

29. Rousseau, *Collected Writings*, 1:30; "lisez vous-mêmes les livres dont il s'agit et sur les dispositions où vous laissera leur lecture jugez de celle où étoit l'Auteur en les écrivant," *Oeuvres complètes*, 1:697. On the extremely rich topic of reader responses to Rousseau, see James Swenson, *On Jean-Jacques Rousseau, Considered as One of the First Authors of the Revolution* (Stanford, Calif.: Stanford University Press, 2000), 116–35; Robert Ellrich, *Rousseau and His Reader: The Rhetorical Situation of the Major Works*, Studies in the Romance Languages and Literatures 83 (Chapel Hill: University of North Carolina Press, 1969); Robert Darnton, "Readers Respond to Rousseau: The Fabrication of Romantic Sensitivity," in *The Great Cat Massacre* (New York: Vintage, 1985), 215–56; and Nicholas Paige, "Rousseau's Readers Revisited: The Aesthetics of *La Nouvelle Héloïse*," *Eighteenth-Century Studies* 42, 1 (Fall 2008): 131–54.

30. Rousseau, *Collected Writings*, 1:212; "j'y ai trouvé des maniéres de sentir et de voir qui le distinguent aisement de tous les écrivains de son tems et de la plus part de ceux qui l'ont précédé," *Oeuvres complètes*, 1:933–34.

31. "No, Sir, I don't even need to see J.J. to know what I think about him." Rousseau, *Collected Works*, 1:218 and *Oeuvres complètes*, 1:942.

32. Rousseau, *Collected Writings*, 1:24; "le langage intrepide et fier d'un écrivain qui, consacrant sa plume à la vérité, ne quête point les suffrages du public et que le témoignage de son coeur met au dessus des jugements des hommes," *Oeuvres complètes*, 1: 689.

33. Rousseau, *Collected Writings*, 1:212; "un habitant d'une autre sphère où rien ne ressemble à celle-ci," *Oeuvres complètes*, 1:934.

34. Albert Schinz, "Jean-Jacques Rousseau et le librairie-imprimeur Marc-Michel Rey," *Annales de la Société Jean-Jacques Rousseau* 10 (1914–15): 11.

35. Only with eighteenth-century writers are the letters exchanged between an author and a publisher deemed to be an autonomous correspondence, worthy in and of itself of an edition. Johannes Bosscha did for Rousseau in 1858 what would have been inconceivable for a seventeenth-century writer and published his letters with Rey as a separate, stand-alone volume: *Lettres inédites de Jean-Jacques Rousseau à Marc-Michel Rey*, ed. J. Bosscha (Amsterdam: Frédéric Muller, 1858). In 1952, Bernard Gagnebin did the same for Voltaire and Gabriel Cramer with the *Lettres inédites à son imprimeur*, ed. Bernard Gagnebin (Geneva: Droz, 1952).

36. As we saw in Chapter 1, Conrart was a *secrétaire du roi* responsible between the 1630s and 1650s for issuing *privilèges en librairie*. In this capacity, he played a broker role between writers and printers. Nicolas Schapira has explored Conrart's importance in *Un professionnel des lettres au XVIIe siècle, Valentin Conrart: Une Histoire sociale* (Seyssel: Champ Vallon, 2003).

37. Letter of January 20, 1652, in Jean-Louis Guez de Balzac, *Lettres du feu M. de Balzac à M. Conrart* (Paris: Courbé, 1659), 149. *Aristippe ou de la cour* was finally published in 1658, four years after Balzac's death.

38. Molière, *Precious Provincials*, scene 9, in *Don Juan and Other Plays*, trans. George Graveley and Ian Maclean (Oxford: Oxford University Press, 1998), 16; "Cela est au dessous de ma condition; mais je le fais seulement pour donner à gagner aux libraires," *Les Précieuses ridicules*, scene 9, *Oeuvres complètes*, ed. Maurice Rat, 2 vols. (Paris: Gallimard, 1959), 1:232.

39. The article, "Von der Unrechtmäßigkeit des Büchernachdrucks," appeared in May 1785 in the *Berlinische Monatsschrift*. It was recently included in a small collection of Kant's and Fichte's writings on literary property translated into French by Jocelyn Benoist, entitled *Qu'est-ce qu'un livre* (Paris: Quadrige PUF, 1995). Martha Woodmansee draws on these and other writings from late eighteenth-century German debates in "The Genius and the Copyright: Economic and Legal Conditions of the Emergence of the 'Author,'" *Eighteenth-Century Studies* 17, 4 (Summer 1984): 425–48, and in *The Author, Art and the Market: Rereading the History of Aesthetics* (New York: Columbia University Press, 1994).

40. Rousseau, *Oeuvres complètes*, 1:561. Rey set up the small pension for Thérèse in the early part of 1762, which, as we have seen, was a time of increasing paranoia for Rousseau. Initially, Rey's offer was a pension that would start to pay off at the author's death. But the writer asked instead for a smaller pension beginning January 1, 1763. Rey agreed to this and set up a 150 livres/year pension. Rousseau's anxieties were, of course, vindicated by events a few months later when both *Emile* and *Le contrat social* were condemned by the Paris Parlement, forcing Rousseau into exile.

41. Rousseau, *Oeuvres complètes*, 1:561.

42. Letter to Rey of June 9, 1964, in *Correspondance complète*, 20:169.

43. The daughter was born on May 3, 1762.

44. Bosscha, *Lettres inédites de Jean-Jacques Rousseau à Marc-Michel Rey*, v–vi. See also Schinz, "Jean-Jacques Rousseau et le librairie-imprimeur Marc-Michel Rey,"

and Elisabeth Eisenstein, "The Libraire-Philosophe: Four Sketches of a Group Portrait," in *Le livre et l'historien: études offertes en l'honneur du Prof. Henri-Jean Martin*, ed. Frédéric Barbier et al., Histoire et civilisation du livre 6, 24 (Geneva: Droz, 1997), 539–50. Bernard Lahire surveys contemporary writers who express similar ideas, suggesting that this intensely personalized commercial relationship is an enduring model: "Ultimately, they often have personal and almost intimate relations with their publishers, more than rational, professional relations." One of his interviewees reports: "The work of the writer is more affective than that of an electrician. An author cannot, at least at the beginning, have strictly professional relations [with others] because he is not convinced of the value of his work. If I am a mason and I build a wall, I don't need anyone to tell me that the wall is straight; I see it; I have an implicit recognition of this. But simply writing 300 pages doesn't make someone a writer. . . . The publisher is the first reader, he who thinks that these 300 pages merit the attention of the public." *La condition littéraire: la double vie des écrivains* (Paris: Éditions de la découverte, 2006), 44.

45. Cassirer, *The Question of Jean-Jacques Rousseau*, ed. and trans. Peter Gay (New Haven, Conn.: Yale University Press, 1989), 43–44.

46. Rousseau recounts the whole affair in a long letter to Paul-Claude Moltou of December 12, 1761, in *Correspondance complète*, 9:312–14.

47. Letter to Moltou of December 12, 1761, in *Correspondance complète*, 9:313.

48. Letter to Rousseau of December 7, 1761, in *Correspondance complète*, 9:297. The duchesse de Luxembourg would also report finding nothing suspicious, and conveyed Duchesne's explanation for the irregularities: "If you haven't gotten proofs as often as you should, it's because you make a lot of corrections and add a lot of notes, which he [Duchesne] showed me in your handwriting, such that the sheets have to be reprinted and sent back to you a second time when you've made changes." Letter to Rousseau of December 15, 1761, in *Correspondance complète*, 9:321.

49. Letter to Malesherbes of December 23, 1761, in *Correspondance complète*, 9:347. Rousseau's subsequent efforts to explain his state of mind to Malesherbes, who had opined that Rousseau's "somber melancholy" was the result of his solitude, constitute the famous four letters to Malesherbes of January 4, 12, 26, and 28, 1762. In their autobiographical, self-justificatory, and thematic focus, these letters anticipate the *Confessions* and the *Rêveries*.

50. Ralph Leigh points out that the episode marked one of the earliest instances of Rousseau thinking in terms of a plot (*complot*) against him. See his introduction to volume 9 of *Correspondance complète*, xxiii–xxv. Ellrich, too, points out that this affair was Rousseau's "first paranoid crisis." Ellrich, *Rousseau and His Reader*, 56.

51. Rousseau, *Oeuvres complètes*, 1:561.

52. See Rousseau's letter to Rey of December 6, 1773, in *Correspondance complète*, 39:212. Rousseau tried to print a "Déclaration relative à différentes réimpressions de ses ouvrages" in various newspapers. However, none would publish the short text. He then took matters into his own hands and distributed copies himself in the Tuileries and on the boulevards. According to Johannes Bosscha, it was finally published in the *Gazette de littérature, des sciences et des arts* on February 19, 1774. See *Oeuvres complètes*, 1:1186–87, note 3. In spite of this, the exemplary reader of Rous-

seau highlighted by Darnton, the La Rochelle merchant Jean Ranson, knew about Rousseau's disavowal of all subsequent editions. Ranson in fact presents an interesting counterpoint, offering a glimpse into the complex dynamic on the other side, since his relationship with Rousseau was also mediated through his interactions with the publishers of the Société Typographique de Neuchâtel, and especially with one of its founders, Frédéric-Samuel Ostervald, with whom Ranson had gone to *collège* as a youth. Of course, they began as friends; still, it is striking to see how the *libraire* assumed a similarly equivocal role, being called upon, inasmuch as he was a bookseller, to play much more than a commercial function. Ranson would, for instance, chide Ostervald for refusing to share news of any meeting he might have had with the author: "What! You have seen l'*Ami* Jean-Jacques and you do not tell me about it!" In this way, the reader's transcendent experience also hinged on his or her belief in the transparency of the publication process. See Darnton, "Readers Respond to Rousseau," 235.

53. In the 1774 *Déclaration*, Rousseau, writing in the third person, disavowed all but the first editions of his works as forgeries: "Thus since his writings, as he wrote and published them, exist only in the first edition of each work that he made, and which have long ago disappeared from the eyes of the world, he declares that all old and recent books which are and will be printed in his name, wherever it might be, are incorrect, altered, mutilated or falsified with the cruelest spite, and he disavows them, some for no longer being his work and others for being falsely attributed to him." See *Oeuvres complètes*, 1:1187.

54. See Schinz, "Jean-Jacques Rousseau et le libraire-imprimeur Rey," 115–30.

55. Rousseau, *Oeuvres complètes*, 1:1186; see Gagnebin's note 3.

56. Rousseau, *Oeuvres complètes*, 1:1186, note 3. Karel Rudolf Gallas points out that Rey refused to publish a new edition of Palissot's *Les philosophes* in 1760 so as not to hurt Rousseau. See "Autour de Marc-Michel Rey et de Rousseau," *Annales de la Société Jean-Jacques Rousseau* 17 (1926): 73–90.

Conclusion

1. Marcel Hénaff, *Le prix de la vérité: le don, l'argent, la philosophie* (Paris: Seuil, 2002), 38.

Bibliography

"L'accomodement du Cid et de son Censeur." In Gasté, 197.
Aldridge, A. Owen. *Voltaire and the Century of Light*. Princeton, N.J.: Princeton University Press, 1975.
Alembert, Jean le Rond d'. *Mélanges de littérature, d'histoire et de philosophie. Nouvelle édition, revue, corrigée et augmentée très-considérablement par l'auteur*. 5 vols. Amsterdam: Zacharie Chatelain, 1759.
_____. *Oeuvres complètes*. 4 vols. Geneva: Slatkine, 1967.
Anderson, E. R. "Apropos of the *affaire de l'Esprit*." *Trivium* 1 (1966): 5–23.
Andrew, Edward. *Patrons of Enlightenment*. Toronto: University of Toronto Press, 2006.
Armstrong, Elizabeth. *Before Copyright: The French Book Privilege System, 1498–1526*. Cambridge: Cambridge University Press, 1990.
Aubignac, François-Hédelin, abbé d'. *Dissertations contre Corneille*. Ed. Nicholas Hammond and Michael Hawcroft. Exeter: University of Exeter Press, 1995.
Avenel, Georges d'. *Les revenus d'un intellectuel de 1200–1913: les riches depuis sept cent ans*. Paris: Flammarion, 1922.
_____. "Les riches depuis sept cents ans: VIII honoraires des Gens de lettres." *Revue des Deux Mondes* 48 (November 15, 1908): 335–67.
Baillet, Adrien. *La vie de Monsieur Des-Cartes*. 2 vols. Paris: chez Daniel Horthemels, 1691.
Balzac, Jean-Louis Guez de. *Lettres du feu M. de Balzac à M. Conrart*. Paris: Courbé, 1659.
Barbier, Fréderic, Annie Parent-Charon, François Dupuigrenet Desroussilles, Claude Jolly, Dominique Varry, and Robert Dawson, eds. *Le livre et l'historien: études offertes en l'honneur du Prof. Henri-Jean Martin*. Geneva: Droz, 1997.
Baruch, Daniel. *Linguet, ou l'irrécupérable*. Paris: François Bourin, 1991.
Beasley, Faith. *Salons, History, and the Creation of 17th-Century France: Mastering Memory*. Aldershot: Ashgate, 2006.
Belin, J. P. *Le commerce des livres prohibés à Paris de 1750 à 1789*. New York: Burt Franklin, 1967.
_____. *Le mouvement philosophique de 1748 à 1789: étude sur la diffusion des idées des philosophes à Paris d'après les documents concernant l'histoire de la librairie*. 1913. New York: Burt Franklin, 1962.
Bell, David. *Lawyers and Citizens: The Making of a Political Elite in Old Regime France*. Oxford: Oxford University Press, 1994.
Bénichou, Paul. *Le sacre de l'écrivain: essai sur l'avènement d'un pouvoir spirituel laïque dans la France moderne*. Paris: J. Corti, 1973.
Benoist, Jocelyn. *Qu'est-ce qu'un livre*. Paris: Quadrige PUF, 1995.

Bernardin de Saint-Pierre, Jacques-Henri. *La vie et les ouvrages de Jean-Jacques Rousseau*. Ed. Maurice Sourian. Paris: Hachette, 1907.

Bertaut, Jules. *La vie littéraire en France au XVIIIe siècle*. Paris: Jules Tallandier, 1954.

Birn, Raymond. *La censure royale des livres dans la France des lumières*. Paris: Odile Jacob, 2007.

——. *Forging Rousseau: Print, Commerce and Cultural Transformation in the Late Enlightenment*. SVEC 2001:08. Oxford: Voltaire Foundation, 2001.

——. "The Profits of Ideas: *Privilèges en librairie* in Eighteenth-Century France." *Eighteenth-Century Studies* 4, 2 (Winter 1970–71): 131–68.

——. "Rousseau et ses éditeurs." *Revue d'histoire moderne et contemporaine* 40 (1993): 120–36.

Blondel, Pierre-Jacques. *Mémoire sur les véxations qu'exercent les libraires & imprimeurs de Paris*. 1725. Ed. Lucien Faucou. Paris: Moniteur du Bibliophile, 1879.

Boileau-Despréaux, Nicolas. *Oeuvres complètes*. Ed. Antoine Adam and Françoise Escal. Paris: Gallimard, 1966.

Boisrobert, François le Métel de. *Les épistres en vers et autres oeuvres poétiques*. Paris: Courbé, 1659.

Bonnet, Jean-Claude. *Louis-Sébastien Mercier (1740–1814): un hérétique en littérature*. Paris: Mercure de France, 1995.

Bourdieu, Pierre. "Le champ littéraire." *Actes de la recherche en sciences sociales* 89 (September 1991): 3–46.

——. *The Field of Cultural Production: Essays on Art and Literature*. Ed. Randal Johnson. New York: Columbia University Press, 1993.

——. "Flaubert's Point of View." Trans. Priscilla Parkhurst Ferguson. *Critical Inquiry* 14, 3 (Spring 1988): 539–62.

——. *In Other Words: Essays Towards a Reflexive Sociology*. Trans. Matthew Adamson. Stanford, Calif.: Stanford University Press, 1990.

——. *Outline of a Theory of Practice*. Trans. Richard Nice. Cambridge: Cambridge University Press, 1977.

——. *Les règles de l'art: genèse et structure du champ littéraire*. Paris: Seuil, 1992.

Braun, Theodore. *Un ennemi de Voltaire: Le Franc de Pompignan, sa vie, ses oeuvres, ses rapports avec Voltaire*. Paris: Minard, 1972.

Brengues, Jacques. "Duclos dupé par Linguet ou quatre lettres inédites de Simon-Nicolas-Henri Linguet à Charles Duclos." *Revue des sciences humaines* 137 (1970): 61–74.

Brissot de Warville, Jacques-Pierre. *Mémoires (1754–1793)*. Ed. Claude Perroud. 2 vols. Paris: Picard, 1911.

Broussel, Patrice and Madeleine Dubois. *De quoi vivait Victor Hugo*. Paris: Deux-Rives, 1952.

Brown, Cynthia. *Poets, Patrons, and Printers: Crisis of Authority in Late Medieval France*. Ithaca, N.Y.: Cornell University Press, 1995.

Brown, Gregory. *A Field of Honor: Writers, Court Culture, and Public Theater in French Literary Life from Racine to the Revolution*. New York: Columbia University Press, 2002. Electronic file available at www.gutenberg-e.org.

——. *Literary Sociability and Literary Property in France, 1775–1793: Beaumarchais,*

the Société des auteurs dramatiques, and the Comédie française. Aldershot: Ashgate, 2006.
Brunel, Lucien. "Observations critiques et littéraires sur un opuscule de Diderot." *Revue d'histoire littéraire de la France* 10 (1903): 1–24.
Caldicott, C. E. J. *La carrière de Molière entre protecteurs et éditeurs*. Amsterdam: Rodolpi, 1998.
Carlin, Claire. *Pierre Corneille Revisited*. New York: Twayne, 1998.
Caron, Philippe. *Des "belles lettres" à la "littérature": une archéologie des signes du savoir profane en langue française (1680–1760)*. Paris: Société pour l'information grammaticale, 1992.
Cassirer, Ernst. *The Question of Jean-Jacques Rousseau*. Ed. and trans. Peter Gay. New Haven, Conn.: Yale University Press, 1989.
Charpentier, François. *Carpentariana, ou Recueil des pensées historiques, critique, morale, et de bons mots. 1724*. Amsterdam: n.p., 1741.
Chartier, Roger. "Espaces sociales et imaginaire sociale: les intellectuels frustrés au XVIIe siècle." *Annales ESC* 37, 2 (March–April 1982): 389–400.
_____. *Forms and Meanings: Texts, Performances, and Audiences from Codex to Computer*. Philadelphia: University of Pennsylvania Press, 1995.
_____. "Loisir et sociabilité: lire à haute voix dans l'Europe moderne." *Littératures classiques* 12 (1990): 127–47.
_____. *L'ordre de livres: lecteurs, auteurs, bibliothèques en Europe entre XVIe et XVIIIe siècles*. Aix-en-Provence: Alinea, 1992.
_____. *Les origines culturelles de la Révolution française*. Paris: Seuil, 1990.
Chartier, Roger and Henri-Jean Martin, eds. *Histoire de l'édition française*. 4 vols. Paris: Fayard, 1990.
Chevillier, André. *L'origine de l'imprimerie de Paris, dissertation historique et critique*. Paris: J. de Laulne, 1694.
Clark, Priscilla Parkhurst, *Literary France: The Making of a Culture*. Berkeley: University of California Press, 1987.
Claveret, Jean. "Lettre à Monsieur de Corneille." In Gasté, 307–12.
_____. "Lettre du sieur Claveret au sieur Corneille, soy disant autheur du Cid." In Gasté, 187–92.
Cochut. "Requête au roi pour la librairie et l'imprimerie de Paris au sujet des deux arrêts du 30 août 1777." In Laboulaye and Guiffrey, 154–90.
Collé, Charles. *Journal et mémoires sur les hommes de lettres, les ouvrages dramatiques, et les événements les plus mémorables du règne de Louis XV (1748–1772)*. Ed. Honoré Bonhomie. 3 vols. Geneva: Slatkine, 1967.
Corneille, Pierre. *Oeuvres*. Ed. Charles-Joseph Marty-Laveaux. 12 vols. Paris: Hachette, 1862.
_____. *Oeuvres complètes*. Ed. Georges Couton. 3 vols. Paris: Gallimard, 1980–86.
Cornou, François. *Elie Fréron: trente années de luttes contre Voltaire et les philosophes au XVIIIe siècle*. Paris: Champion, 1922.
Cruppi, Jean. *Un avocat journaliste au XVIIIe siècle: Linguet*. Paris: Hachette, 1896.
Darnton, Robert. *The Business of Enlightenment: A Publishing History of the Encyclopédie 1775–1800*. Cambridge, Mass.: Harvard University Press, 1979.
_____. "The Facts of Literary Life in Eighteenth-Century France." In *The Political*

Culture of the Old Regime. Vol. 1 of *The French Revolution and the Creation of Modern Political Culture*. Ed. Keith Michael Baker. 4 vols. Oxford: Pergamon Press, 1987. 261–91.

———. *The Great Cat Massacre and Other Episodes in French Cultural History*. New York: Vintage, 1985.

———. "The High Enlightenment and the Low-Life of Literature in Pre-Revolutionary France." *Past and Present* 51 (May 1971): 81–115.

———. "J.-P. Brissot and the Société Typographique de Neuchâtel (1779–1787)." SVEC 2001:10. Oxford: Voltaire Foundation, 2001. 7–47.

———. "The Life of a 'Poor Devil' in the Republic of Letters." In *Essays on the Age of Enlightenment in Honor of Ira O. Wade*, ed. Jean Macary. Geneva: Droz, 1977. 39–62.

———. *The Literary Underground of the Old Regime*. Cambridge, Mass.: Harvard University Press, 1982.

Davis, Natalie Zemon. "Beyond the Market: Books as Gifts in Sixteenth-Century France." *Transactions of the Royal Historical Society* 5, 33 (1983): 69–88.

Deffand, Marie Anne de Vichy-Chamrond, marquise du. *Lettres 1742–1780*. Paris: Mercure de France, 2002.

Deierkauf-Holsboer, S. Wilma. *Le théâtre du Marais*. 2 vols. Paris: Nizet, 1954.

DeJean, Joan. *Ancients Against Moderns: Culture Wars and the Making of a Fin de Siècle*. Chicago: University of Chicago Press, 1997.

———. *The Reinvention of Obscenity: Sex, Lies, and Tabloids in Early Modern France*. Chicago: University of Chicago Press, 2002.

———. *Tender Geographies: Women and the Origins of the Novel in France*. New York: Columbia University Press, 1984.

Delort, Joseph. *Histoire de la détention des philosophes et des gens de lettres à la Bastille et à Vincennes, précédée de celle de Foucquet, de Pellisson et de Lauzun, avec tous les documents authentiques et inédits*. 1829. Geneva: Slatkine, 1967.

de Luna, Frederick. "The Dean Street Style of Revolution: J-P Brissot, *Jeune Philosophe*." *French Historical Studies* 17, 1 (Spring 1991): 159–90.

Denis, Delphine. *Le Parnasse galant: institution d'une catégorie littéraire*. Paris: Champion, 2001.

Dewald, Jonathan. *Aristocratic Experience and the Origins of Modern Culture in France, 1570–1715*. Berkeley: University of California Press, 1993.

D'Hémery, Joseph. "Historique des auteurs." Bibliothèque nationale de France. Nouvelles acquisitions françaises 10781–3.

D'Héricourt, Louis. "Mémoire à M. le Garde des Sceaux." In Laboulaye and Guiffrey, 21–39.

Dictionnaire de l'Académie française. 2 vols. Paris: Coignard, 1694.

Diderot, Denis. *Correspondance*. Ed. Georges Roth. 16 vols. Paris: Minuit, 1955–.

———. "Lettre de Monsieur Diderot à Messieurs Briasson et Le Breton, Libraires associés à l'Encyclopédie." In *Mémoire pour les Libraires associés à l'Encyclopédie contre le sieur Luneau de Boisjermain*. Paris: Imprimerie de Le Breton, 1771. 68–74.

———. *Oeuvres*. Ed. André Billy. Paris: Gallimard, 1951.

———. *Oeuvres*. Ed. Laurent Versini. Vol. 3, *Politique*. Paris: Robert Laffont, 1995.

———. *Oeuvres complètes*. Ed. Jules Assézat and Maurice Tourneux. 20 vols. Paris: Garnier, 1875–77.
———. *Oeuvres complètes*. Ed. Herbert Dieckmann, Jacques Proust, and Jean Varloot. 25 vols. Paris: Hermann, 1975–.
———. *Rameau's Nephew and Other Works*. Trans. Jacques Barzun and Ralph Bowen. Indianapolis: Library of Liberal Arts, 1964.
———. *Sur la liberté de la presse*. Ed. Jacques Proust. Vol. 7 of *Oeuvres choisies*. Paris: Éditions Socials, 1964.
Diderot, Denis and Jean le Rond d'Alembert, eds. *Encyclopédie ou Dictionnaire raisonné des sciences, des arts et des métiers, par une Société de Gens de lettres*. 17 vols. Paris: Le Breton et al., 1751–72.
Dieckmann, Herbert. *Inventaire du fonds Vandeul, et inédits de Diderot*. Geneva: Droz, 1951.
Dock, Madeleine. *Étude sur le droit d'auteur*. Paris: Librairie générale de droit et de jurisprudence, 1963.
Douvez, Jacques. *De quoi vivait Voltaire*. Paris: Deux Rives, 1949.
Duchet, Michèle, and Michel Delaunay. *Entretiens sur "Le Neveu de Rameau"*. Paris: Nizet, 1967.
Duclos, Charles Pinot. *Considérations sur les moeurs de ce siècle*. 1751. Ed. F. C. Green. Cambridge: Cambridge University Press, 1946.
Du Plaisir, *Sentiments sur les lettres et sur l'histoire avec des scrupules sur le style*. 1683. Ed. Philippe Hourcade. Geneva: Droz, 1975.
Duvernet, Théophile-Imarigeon. *La vie de Voltaire*. Geneva: 1786.
Edelman, Bernard. *Le sacre de l'auteur*. Paris: Seuil, 2004.
Eisenstein, Elizabeth. *Grub Street Abroad: Aspects of the French Cosmopolitan Press from the Age of Louis XIV to the French Revolution*. Oxford: Clarendon, 1992.
———. "The Libraire-Philosophe: Four Sketches of a Group Portrait." In Barbier et al., 539–50.
Elias, Norbert. *The Court Society*. Trans. Edmund Jephcott. New York: Pantheon, 1983.
———. *Mozart: Portrait of a Genius*. Ed. Michael Schröter, trans. Edmund Jephcott. Berkeley: University of California Press, 1993.
Ellrich, Robert. *Rousseau and His Reader: The Rhetorical Situation of the Major Works*, Studies in the Romance Languages and Literatures 83. Chapel Hill: University of North Carolina Press, 1969.
Escarpit, Robert. *La sociologie de la littérature*. Paris: Presses Universitaires de France, 1973.
Ezell, Margaret. *Social Authorship and the Advent of Print*. Baltimore: Johns Hopkins University Press, 1999.
Fabre d'Eglantine, Philippe-François-Nazaire. *Les gens de lettres; ou le provincial à Paris*. Vol. 1 of *Mélanges littéraires*. 2 vols. Paris: n.p., 1827.
Falk, Henri. *Les privilèges de librairie sous l'ancien régime: étude historique du conflit des droits sur l'oeuvre littéraire*. Paris: Rousseau, 1906.
Faret, Nicolas. *L'honneste homme ou l'art de plaire à la cour*. 1630. Paris: Presses Universitaires de France, 1925.

Febvre, Lucien, and Henri-Jean Martin. *The Coming of the Book: The Impact of Printing 1450–1800*. Ed. Geoffrey Nowell-Smith and David Wotton, trans. David Gérard. London: Verso, 1986.
Fellows, Otis. *Diderot*. Boston: Twayne, 1989.
Fenouillot de Falbaire de Quingey, Charles-Joseph. *Avis aux gens de lettres*. Liège: n.p., 1770.
Ferguson, Priscilla Parkhurst. "A Cultural Field in the Making: Gastronomy in 19th-Century France." *American Journal of Sociology* 104, 3 (November 1998): 597–641.
Foucault, Michel. "What Is an Author?" In Foucault, *Language, Counter-Memory, Practice: Selected Essays and Interviews*, ed. Donald Bouchard. Ithaca, N.Y.: Cornell University Press, 1977.
France, Peter. "The Commerce of the Self." *Comparative Criticism* 12 (1990): 39–56.
Frederick II. *Oeuvres*. 31 vols. Berlin: Imprimerie Royale, 1846–57.
Friedland, Paul. *Political Actors: Representative Bodies and Theatricality in the Age of the French Revolution*. Ithaca, N.Y.: Cornell University Press, 2002.
Fumaroli, Marc. *L'âge de l'éloquence: rhétorique et 'res literaria' de la Renaissance au seuil de l'époque classique*. Paris: Albin Michel, 1994.
———. *La diplomatie de l'esprit: de Montaigne à La Fontaine*. Paris: Hermann, 1994.
———. *Héros et orateurs: rhétorique et dramatique cornéliennes*. Geneva: Droz, 1990.
Furetière, Antoine. *Dictionnaire universel: contenant généralement tous les mots français, tant vieux qui modernes, et les termes de toutes les sciences et des arts*. La Haye: Arnout and Reinier Leers, 1690.
———. *Nouvelle allégorique ou Histoire des derniers troubles arrivés au royaume d'éloquence*. 1658. Ed. Eva van Ginneken. Geneva: Droz, 1967.
Gaillard, Antoine. *Oeuvres*. Paris: J. Dugast, 1634.
Gallas, Karel Rudolf. "Autour de Marc-Michel Rey et de Rousseau." *Annales de la Société Jean-Jacques Rousseau* 17 (1926): 73–90.
Gaulin, Michel. *Le concept d'homme de lettres en France à l'époque de l'Encyclopédie*. New York: Garland, 1991.
Gasté, Armand, ed. *La Querelle du Cid: pièces et pamphlets publiés d'après les originaux*. 1898. Geneva: Slatkine, 1970.
Génetiot, Alain. *Poétique du loisir mondain: de Voiture à La Fontaine*. Paris: Champion, 1997.
Goffman, Erving. *The Presentation of Self in Everyday Life*. New York: Anchor, 1959.
Goldgar, Ann. "The Absolutism of Taste: Journalists as Censors in 18th-Century Paris." In *Censorship and the Control of Print in England and France 1660–1910*, ed. Robin Myers and Michael Harris. Winchester: St. Paul's Bibliographies, 1992. 87–110.
Goldsmith, Elizabeth, and Dena Goodman, eds. *Going Public: Women and Publishing in Early Modern France*. Ithaca, N.Y.: Cornell University Press, 1995.
Goodman, Dena. "Enlightenment Salons: The Convergence of Female and Philosophic Ambitions." *Eighteenth-Century Studies* 22, 3 (Spring 1989): 329–50.

---. *The Republic of Letters: A Cultural History of the French Enlightenment.* Ithaca, N.Y.: Cornell University Press, 1994.
Gordon, Daniel. *Citizens Without Sovereignty: Equality and Sociability in French Thought 1670–1789.* Princeton, N.J.: Princeton University Press, 1994.
---. "'Public Opinion' and the Civilizing Process in France: The Example of Morellet." *Eighteenth-Century Studies* 22, 3 (Spring 1989): 302–28.
Greenblatt, Stephen. *Renaissance Self-Fashioning: From More to Shakespeare.* Chicago: University of Chicago Press, 1980.
---. *Shakespearian Negotiations: The Circulation of Social Energy in Renaissance England.* Berkeley: University of California Press, 1988.
Greene, Jody. *The Trouble with Ownership: Literary Property and Authorial Liability in England: 1660–1730.* Philadelphia: University of Pennsylvania Press, 2005.
Griffin, Dustin. *Literary Patronage in England 1650–1800.* Cambridge: Cambridge University Press, 1996.
Grimm, Friedrich Melchoir, Baron von, et al. *Correspondance littéraire, philosophique et critique par Grimm, Diderot, Raynal, Mesiter, etc.* Ed. Maurice Tourneux. 16 vols. Paris: Garnier, 1877–82.
Grimsley, Ronald. *Jean d'Alembert (1717–1783).* Oxford: Clarendon, 1963.
Guéret, Gabriel. *Le Parnasse réformé.* 1671. Geneva: Slatkine, 1968.
Habermas, Jürgen. *The Structural Transformation of the Public Sphere: An Inquiry into a Category of Bourgeois Society.* 1962. Trans. Thomas Burger and Frederick Lawrence. Cambridge, Mass.: MIT Press, 1995.
Helvétius, Claude-Adrien. *Correspondance générale.* Ed. Alan Dainard, Jean Orsoni, David Smith, and Peter Allan. 5 vols. Toronto: University of Toronto Press, 1981–2004.
---. *De l'esprit.* 1758. Paris: Fayard, 1988.
Hénaff, Marcel. *Le prix de la vérité: le don, l'argent, la philosophie.* Paris: Seuil, 2002.
Hesse, Carla. "Enlightenment Epistemology and the Laws of Authorship in Revolutionary France, 1777–1793." *Representations* 30 (Spring 1990): 109–37.
---. *The Other Enlightenment: How French Women Became Modern.* Princeton, N.J.: Princeton University Press, 2001.
---. *Publishing and Cultural Politics in Revolutionary Paris: 1789–1810.* Berkeley: University of California Press, 1991.
---. "Reading Signatures: Female Authorship and Revolutionary Law in France, 1750–1850." *Eighteenth-Century Studies* 22, 3 (Spring 1989): 469–87.
Hoefer, Jean C. E., ed. *Nouvelle biographie générale depuis les temps les plus reculés jusqu'a nos jours, avec les renseignements bibliographiques et l'indication des sources à consulter.* 46 vols. Paris: Firmin Didot, 1852–66.
Hoffmann, George. *Montaigne's Career.* Oxford: Clarendon, 1998.
Howe, Alan. "Corneille et ses premiers comédiens." *Revue d'histoire littérature de la France* 106, 3 (July–September 2006): 519–42.
Hugo, Victor. *Oeuvres complètes: édition chronologique.* Ed. Jean Massin. 18 vols. Paris: Club du livre, 1967–71.
Iverson, John. "L'apothéose du grand Corneille et le centenaire de 1784." *XVIIe siècle* 225, 56 (2004): 559–66.

Jouhaud, Christian. *Les pouvoirs de la littérature: histoire d'un paradoxe*. Paris: Gallimard, 2000.

Jouhaud, Christian, and Alain Viala, eds. *De la publication: entre Renaissance et lumières*. Paris: Fayard, 2002.

Kamuf, Peggy. *Signature Pieces: On the Institution of Authorship*. Ithaca, N.Y.: Cornell University Press, 1988.

Keim, Albert. *Helvétius, sa vie et son oeuvre, d'après ses ouvrages, des écrits divers et des documents inédits*. Paris: Alcan, 1907.

Kelly, Christopher. *Rousseau as Author: Consecrating One's Life to the Truth*. Chicago: University of Chicago Press, 2003.

Kelly, Christopher, and Roger Masters. "Rousseau on Reading 'Jean-Jacques': The *Dialogues*." *Interpretation: A Journal of Political Philosophy* 17 (Winter 1989–90): 239–53.

Kirsop, Wallace. "Les mécanismes éditoriaux." In Chartier and Martin, 2:15–34.

Laboulaye, Edouard and Georges Guiffrey, eds. *La propriété littéraire au XVIIIe siècle: recueil de pieces et de documents publié par le comité de l'association pour la défense de la propriété littéraire et artistique*. Paris: Hachette, 1859.

La Bruyère, Jean de. *Oeuvres complètes*. Ed. Julien Benda. Paris: Gallimard, 1951.

———. *Characters*. Trans. Henri Van Laun. New York: Howard Fertig, 1992.

La Calprenède, Gaultier de Coste, seigneur de. *La mort de Mithridate*. Paris: Sommaville, 1637.

La Harpe, Jean François de. *Correspondance littéraire, addressée à son altesse impériale, Mgr le grand-duc, aujourd'hui, empereur de la Russie, et à m. le comte André Schowalow, chambellan de l'impératrice Catherine II, depuis 1774 jusqu'à 1789*. 5 vols. Paris: Migueret, 1801–1807.

———. *Réfutation du livre De l'esprit, prononcée au Lycée républicain dans les séances des 26 et 29 mars et des 3 et 5 avril*. Paris: Mignaret, 1797.

Lahire, Bernard. *La condition littéraire: la double vie des écrivains*. Paris: La Découverte, 2006.

Landes, Joan. *Women and the Public Sphere in the Era of the French Revolution*. Ithaca, N.Y.: Cornell University Press, 1988.

Le Gall, André. *Pierre Corneille en son temps et en son oeuvre: enquête sur un poète de théâtre au XVIIe siècle*. Paris: Flammarion, 1997.

Levy, Darline Gay. *The Ideas and Careers of Simon-Nicolas-Henri Linguet: A Study in Eighteenth-Century French Politics*. Urbana: University of Illinois Press, 1980.

Lilti, Antoine. *Le monde des salons: sociabilité et mondanité à Paris au XVIIIe siècle*. Paris: Fayard, 2005.

———. "Vertus de la conversation: l'abbé Morellet et la sociabilité mondaine." *Littératures classiques* 37 (1999): 213–28.

Linguet, Simon-Nicolas-Henri. *L'aveu sincère ou lettre à une mère sur les dangers que court la jeunesse en se livrant à un goût trop vif pour la littérature*. London: chez Cellot, 1768.

———. *Dernière réponse signifiée et consultation pour le sieur de Luneau de Boisjermain contre les Syndic et Adjoints des Libraires de Paris*. Paris: Imprimerie de Gueffier, 1769.

———. *Le fanatisme des philosophes*. London: 1764.

_____. *Mémoire et Consultation pour M. de Luneau de Boisjermain, Souscripteur de l'Encyclopédie. Contre le sieur Briasson, Libraire, Syndic des Libraires & Imprimeurs, ancien Adjoint de sa Communauté, et le sieur de Le Breton, Libraire, ancien Syndic et Adjoint de la même Communauté, associé avec le sieur Briasson pour l'impression de l'Encyclopédie*. Paris: Imprimerie de Louis Cellot, 1770.

_____. *Mémoire signifié pour le sieur Luneau de Boisjermain, Défendeur. Contre les Syndic & Adjoints des Libraires & Imprimeurs de Paris, Demandeurs*. Paris: Imprimerie de Grangé, [1769].

_____. "Opinion de Linguet touchant l'arrêt sur les privilèges." In Laboulaye and Guiffrey, 224–59.

Loewenstein, Joseph. *The Author's Due: Printing and the Prehistory of Copyright*. Chicago: University of Chicago Press, 2002.

Lottin, Augustin-Martin. *Catalogue chronologique des libraires et des imprimeurs-libraires de Paris, depuis l'an 1470, époque de l'établissement de l'Imprimerie dans cette Capitale, jusqu'à present*. 2 vols. Paris: chez Jean-Roch Lottin de St. Germain, 1789.

Lough, John. *An Introduction to Eighteenth-Century France*. London: Longmans, 1960.

_____. "Luneau de Boisjermain v. the Publishers of the *Encyclopédie*." *Studies on Voltaire and the Eighteenth Century* 23 (1963): 115–77.

_____. *Writer and Public in France from the Middles Ages to the Present Day*. Oxford: Clarendon, 1978.

Love, Harold. *The Culture and Commerce of Texts: Scribal Publication in Seventeenth-Century England*. Amherst: University of Massachusetts Press, 1998.

Mairet, Jean. "L'autheur du vray Cid espagnol à son traducteur François, sur une lettre en vers." In Gasté, 67–68.

_____. "Epistre familière du sieur Mairet au sieur Corneille, sur la Tragi-Comédie du Cid." In Gasté, 283–305.

Maître, Myriam. *Les précieuses: naissance des femmes de lettres en France au XVIIe siècle*. Paris: Champion, 1999.

Malesherbes, Chrétien-Guillaume de Lamoignon de. *Mémoires sur la librairie*. Ed. Roger Chartier. Paris: Imprimerie nationale, 1994.

Marais, Mathieu. *Journal et mémoires sur la régence et le règne de Louis XV*. Ed. M. De Lescure. 4 vols. Paris: Didot, 1863–68.

Marmontel, Jean-François. *Mémoires*. Ed. Maurice Tourneau. 2 vols. Paris: Librairie des Bibliophiles, 1891.

Martin, Henri-Jean. "Auteurs et libraires." In Chartier and Martin, 2:495–97.

_____. *Histoire et pouvoirs de l'écrit*. Paris: Albin Michel, 1996.

_____. *Livre, pouvoirs et société à Paris au XVIIe siècle*. 2 vols. 1969. Geneva: Droz, 1999.

Maslan, Susan. *Revolutionary Acts: Theater, Democracy, and the French Revolution*. Baltimore: Johns Hopkins University Press, 2005.

Mason, Hayden. *French Writers and Their Society: 1715–1800*. London: Macmillan, 1982.

Masson, Nicole. "La condition de l'auteur en France au XVIIIe siècle: le cas de Voltaire." In Barbier et al., 551–55.

May, Georges. *Le dilemme du roman au XVIIIe siècle: étude sur les rapports du roman et de la critique, 1715–1761*. New Haven, Conn.: Yale University Press, 1963.
Maza, Sarah. *Private Lives and Public Affairs: The Causes Célèbres of Prerevolutionary France*. Berkeley: University of California Press, 1993.
McMahon, Darrin. *Enemies of the Enlightenment: The French Counter-Enlightenment and the Making of Modernity*. Oxford: Oxford University Press, 2001.
Mellot, Jean-Dominique. "Entre 'librairie française' et marché du livre au XVIIIe siècle: repères pour un paysage éditorial." In Barbier et al., 493–517.
Mély, Benoît. *Jean-Jacques Rousseau: un intellectuel en rupture*. Paris: Minerve, 1985.
Mémoires secrets pour servir à l'histoire de la République des lettres en France depuis MDCCLXII jusqu'à nos jours. 36 vols. London: John Adamson, 1777.
Menger, Pierre-Michel. *Portrait de l'artiste en travailleur: métamorphoses du capitalisme*. Paris: Seuil, 2002.
Mercier, Louis-Sébastien. *De la littérature et des littérateurs*. 1778. Geneva: Slatkine, 1970.
———. *Tableau de Paris*. 1781–1788. Ed. Jean-Claude Bonnet. 2 vols. Paris: Mercure de France, 1994.
Merlin, Hélène. *Public et littérature en France au XVIIe siècle*. Paris: Belles lettres, 1994.
Michaud, Louis-Gabriel, ed. *Nouvelle biographie universelle ancienne et moderne: histoire par ordre alphabétique de la vie publique et privée de tous les hommes*. 2nd. ed. 45 vols. Paris: Vivès, 1880.
Molière, Jean-Baptiste Poquelin. *Don Juan and Other Plays*. Trans. George Graveley and Ian Maclean. Oxford: Oxford University Press, 1998.
———. *The Misanthrope*. Trans. Richard Wilbur. New York: Harcourt, Brace, 1955.
———. *Oeuvres complètes*. Ed. Maurice Rat. 2 vols. Paris: Gallimard, 1959.
Molinié, Georges. "Style et littérarité." *Littératures classiques* 28 (1996): 69–74.
Mongrédien, Georges. *Recueil de textes et des documents du XVIIe siècle relatifs à Corneille*. Paris: CNRS, 1972.
Monselet, Charles. *Les oubliés et les dédaignés; figures de la fin du 18ème siècle*. Paris: Charpentier, 1876.
Morellet, André, l'abbé. *Préface de la Comédie des philosophes*. Paris: chez l'auteur, 1760.
Mortier, Roland. "Paresse et travail dans l'introspection de Rousseau." In *Rousseau and the Eighteenth Century: Essays in Memory of R. A. Leigh*, ed. Marian Hobson, J. T. A. Leigh, and Robert Wokler. Oxford: Voltaire Foundation, 1992. 125–34.
Mostefai, Ourida. "The Author as Celebrity and Outcast: Authorship and Autobiography in Rousseau." In *Approaches to Teaching Rousseau's* Confessions *and* Reveries of the Solitary Walker, ed. John O'Neal and Ourida Mostefai. New York: Modern Language Association, 2003. 68–72.
Nicolet, M. "La condition de l'homme de lettres au XVIIe siècle à travers l'oeuvre de deux contemporains: Ch. Sorel et A. Furetière." *Revue d'histoire littéraire de la France* 63, 3 (July–September 1963): 369–93.
Nisard, Charles. *Les ennemis de Voltaire*. Paris: Amyot, 1853.
Ozanam, Didier. "La disgrâce d'un premier commis: Tercier et l'affaire de l'*Esprit* (1758–1759)." *Bibliothèque de l'École des Chartes* 113 (1955): 140–70.

Paige, Nicholas. "Rousseau's Readers Revisited: The Aesthetics of *La Nouvelle Héloïse*." *Eighteenth-Century Studies* 42, 1 (Fall 2008): 131–54.
Palissot de Montenoy, Charles. *Les philosophes*. Paris: Duchesne, 1760.
Pappas, John. "D'Alembert et la nouvelle aristocratie." *Dix-huitième siècle* 15 (1983): 335–43.
Parent-Charron, Annie. *Les métiers du livre à Paris au XVIe siècle: 1535–1560*. Geneva: Droz, 1974.
Paulson, William. "The Market of Printed Goods: On Bourdieu's Rules." *Modern Language Quarterly* 58, 4 (December 1997): 399–415.
Pellisson, Maurice. *Les hommes de lettres au XVIIIe siècle*. 1911. Geneva: Slatkine, 1970.
Pellisson-Fontanier, Paul and Pierre-Joseph Thoulier d'Olivet. *Histoire de l'Académie française*. 2 vols. Paris: Coignard, 1743.
Pidansat de Mairobert, Mathieu François. *L'espion anglois, ou correspondance secrète entre milord All'Eye et milord All'Ear*. 10 vols. London: John Adamson, 1779–84.
Piron, Alexis. *La métromanie ou le poëte: comédie en vers et en cinq actes*. La Haye: Antoine van Dole, 1738.
Pottinger, David. *The French Book Trade in the Ancien Régime*. Cambridge, Mass.: Harvard University Press, 1958.
Préchac, Jean de. *La Noble Vénitienne, ou la Bassette, histoire galante*. Paris: Barbin, 1679.
Proust, Jacques. *Diderot et l'Encyclopédie*. 1962. Paris: Albin Michel, 1995.
_____. "Pour servir à une édition critique de *La lettre sur le commerce de la librairie*." *Diderot Studies* 3 (1961): 321–46.
Ravel, Jeffrey. *The Contested Parterre: Public Theater and French Political Culture, 1680–1791*. Ithaca, N.Y.: Cornell University Press, 1999.
Reiss, Timothy. *The Meaning of Literature*. Ithaca, N.Y.: Cornell University Press, 1992.
Renwich, John. *Voltaire et Morangiès 1772–1773: où les lumières l'ont échappé belle*. Studies on Voltaire and the Eighteenth Century 202. Oxford: Voltaire Foundation, 1982.
Ribard, Dinah. "D'Alembert et la 'société des gens de lettres': utilité et autonomie des lettres dans la polémique entre Rousseau et d'Alembert," *Littératures classiques* 37 (Fall 1999): 229–45.
Riffaud, Alain. "L'impression du Cid (1637–1648)." *Revue d'histoire littéraire de la France* 106, 3 (July-September 2006): 543–70.
Roche, Daniel. *Les républicains des lettres: gens de culture et Lumières au XVIIIe siècle*. Paris: Fayard, 1988.
Rose, Mark. *Authors and Owners: The Invention of Copyright*. Cambridge, Mass.: Harvard University Press, 1993.
Rousseau, Jean-Jacques. *Collected Writings of Rousseau*. Ed. Roger Masters and Christopher Kelly, trans. Judith Bush, Roger Masters, and Christopher Kelly. 12 vols. Hanover, N.H.: University Press of New England for Dartmouth College, 1990–.
_____. *Correspondance complète*. Ed. R. A. Leigh. 52 vols. Geneva: Institut et musée Voltaire, 1965–.

_____. *Lettres inédites de Jean-Jacques Rousseau à Marc-Michel Rey*. Ed. J. Bosscha. Amsterdam: Frédéric Muller, 1858.
_____. *Oeuvres complètes*. Ed. Bernard Gagnebin and Marcel Raymond. 5 vols. Paris: Gallimard, 1959–.
Russo, Elena. *Styles of Enlightenment: Taste, Politics, and Authorship in Eighteenth-Century France*. Baltimore: Johns Hopkins University Press, 2007.
Saint-Amant, Marc-Antoine-Gérard, sieur de. *Les oeuvres du sieur de Saint-Amant*. Paris: Estienne, 1629.
Saisselin, Rémy. *The Literary Enterprise in Eighteenth-Century France*. Detroit: Wayne State University Press, 1979.
Salengre, A. H. de. *Continuation des mémoires de littérature et d'histoire*. vol. 2. Paris: chez Simart, 1726.
Sapiro, Gisèle. "The Literary Field Between the State and the Market." *Poetics* 31 (2003): 441–64.
Sarrazin, Véronique. "Du bon usage de la Censure au XVIIIe siècle." *Lettre clandestine* 5 (1996): 161–91.
Saugrain, Claude-Marin. *Code le la librairie et imprimerie de Paris*. Paris: Communauté des libraires et des imprimeurs, 1744.
Scarron, Paul [?]. "Apologie pour Monsieur Mairet contre les calomnies de sieur Corneille de Rouen." In Gasté, 328–32.
Schapira, Nicolas. *Un professionnel des lettres au XVIIe siècle, Valentin Conrart: une histoire sociale*. Seyssel: Champ Vallon, 2003.
_____. "Quand le privilège de librairie publie l'auteur." In Jouhaud and Viala, 121–37.
Schinz, Albert. "Jean-Jacques Rousseau et le libraire-imprimeur Marc-Michel Rey." *Annales de la société Jean-Jacques Rousseau* 10 (1914–15): 1–133.
Scudéry, Georges de. "Lettre de Monsieur de Scudéry à l'illustre Académie." In Gasté, 214–17.
_____. "Lettre de M. de Scudéry à Messieurs de l'Académie française, sur le jugement qu'ils ont fait du 'Cid,' et de ses 'Observations.'" In Gasté, 464–65.
_____. *Ligdamon et Lidias ou La Ressemblance. Tragi-Comédie*. Paris: Targa, 1631.
_____. "Observations sur le *Cid*." In Gasté, 71–111.
Sheridan, Geraldine. *Nicolas Lenglet Dufresnoy and the Literary Underworld of the Ancien Régime*. Studies on Voltaire and the Eighteenth Century 262. Oxford: Voltaire Foundation, 1989.
Shoemaker, Peter. *Powerful Connections: The Poetics of Patronage in the Age of Louis XIII*. Newark: University of Delaware Press, 2007.
Simon, Julia. *Mass Enlightenment: Critical Studies in Rousseau and Diderot*. Albany, N.Y.: SUNY Press, 1995.
Smith, David. *Helvétius: A Study in Persecution*. Oxford: Clarendon, 1965.
_____. "The Publication of Helvétius's *De l'Esprit* (1758–9)." *French Studies* 18 (1964): 332–43.
Sorel, Charles. *La Bibliothèque Françoise* [1664]. 2nd ed. "reveuê et augmentée." Paris: Compagnie de Libraires, 1667.
_____. *Oeuvres diverses ou discours meslez*. Paris: Compagnie des Libraires, 1663.
Stanton, Domna. *The Aristocrat as Art: A Study of the Honnête Homme and Dandy in*

Seventeenth- and Nineteenth-Century French Literature. New York: Columbia University Press, 1980.
Starobinski, Jean. *L'oeil vivant.* Paris: Gallimard, 1961.
Suard, Jean-Baptiste-Antoine. *Mélanges de littérature.* 5 vols. Paris: Dentu, 1806.
Swenson, James. *On Jean-Jacques Rousseau, Considered as One of the First Authors of the Revolution.* Stanford, Calif.: Stanford University Press, 2000.
Tallement des Réaux, Gédéon. *Historiettes.* Ed. Antoine Adam. 2 vols. Paris: Gallimard, 1960–61.
Trousson, Raymond. *Rousseau et sa fortune littéraire.* Paris: Nizet, 1977.
Turnovsky, Geoffrey. "Conceptualising the Literary Market: Diderot and the *Lettre sur le commerce de la librairie*. SVEC 2003:01. Oxford: Voltaire Foundation, 2003. 135–70.
_____. "The Enlightenment Literary Market: Rousseau, Authorship, and the Book Trade." *Eighteenth-Century Studies* 36, 3 (Spring 2003): 387–410.
_____. "Identité littéraire et librairie au XVIIe siècle: le cas Pierre Corneille." *SVEC* 2004:10. Oxford: Voltaire Foundation, 2004. 35–45.
_____. "Marginal Writers and the 'Literary Market': Defining a New Field of Authorship in Eighteenth-Century France." *Studies in Eighteenth-Century Culture* 33 (2004): 101–23.
_____. "'Vivre de sa plume': Réflexions sur un topos de l'auctorialité moderne." *Revue de synthèse* 128, 1–2 (2007): 51–70.
Valéry, Paul. *Oeuvres.* 2 vols. Paris: Gallimard, 1957.
van Roosbroeck, G. L. "Who Originated the Plan of the *Encyclopédie*." *Modern Philology* 27 (1929–30): 382–84.
Vaugelas, Claude. *Remarques sur la langue françoise.* Paris: Augustin Courbé, 1647.
Verèb, Pascal. *Alexis Piron, poète (1689–1773), ou la difficile condition d'auteur sous Louis XV.* Studies on Voltaire and the Eighteenth Century 359. Oxford: Voltaire Foundation, 1997.
Vessillier-Ressi, Michèle. *Le métier d'auteur: comment vivent-ils?* Paris: Bordas, 1982.
Viala, Alain. "Corneille et les institutions littéraires de son temps." In *Pierre Corneille: Actes du colloque tenu à Rouen (2–6 oct. 1984),* ed. Alain Niderst. Paris: Presses Universitaires de France, 1985. 197–204.
_____. "Institution littéraire, champ littéraire et périodisation: l'institution du siècle." *Littératures classiques* 34 (Autumn 1998): 119–29.
_____. *La naissance de l'écrivain: sociologie de la littérature à l'âge classique.* Paris: Minuit, 1985.
_____. "La naissance des institutions de la vie littéraire (1643–1665): essai de sociopoétique." Ph.D. dissertation, Université de Lille-III, 1982.
Viala, Alain and Christian Jouhaud. *De la publication: entre Renaissance et Lumières.* Paris: Fayard, 2002.
"La victoire du sieur Corneille, Scudéry et Claveret, avec une remonstrance par laquelle on les prie aimablement de n'exposer ainsi leur renommée à la risée publique." In Gasté, 198–201.
Viguerie, Jean de. *Histoire et dictionnaire du temps des lumières.* Paris: Laffont, 1995.
Villiers, Pierre de. *Entretiens sur les contes de fées, et sur quelques autres ouvrages du*

temps, pour servir de préservatif contre le mauvais goût. Paris: Jacques Collombat, 1699.

Voiture, Vincent. *Oeuvres: lettres et poésies.* 1650. Ed. M. A. Ubicini. 2 vols. Geneva: Slatkine, 1967.

Voltaire, François-Marie Arouet. *Lettres inédites à son imprimeur Gabriel Cramer.* Ed. Bernard Gagnebin. Geneva: Droz, 1952.

_____. *The Complete Works.* Ed. Theodore Besterman et al. 135 vols. Geneva, Banbury, Oxford: Voltaire Foundation, 1968–.

_____. *Oeuvres complètes.* Ed. Louis Moland. 52 vols. Paris: Garnier Frères, 1877–85.

_____. *Politique de Voltaire.* Ed. René Pomeau. Paris: Armand Colin, 1994.

Walter, Éric. "Les auteurs et le champ littéraire." In Chartier and Martin, 2:499–518.

Warnke, Martin. *The Court Artist: On the Ancestry of the Modern Artist.* 1985. Trans. David McLintock. Cambridge: Cambridge University Press, 1993.

Weil, Françoise. "Les libraires parisiens propriétaires d'éditions sans véritable privilège: l'exemple de Voltaire." *Studies in Voltaire and the Eighteenth Century* 249 (1987): 227–39.

Williams, David. "Voltaire and the Patronage of Corneille." *Eighteenth-Century Studies* 6, 2 (Winter 1972–73): 221–37.

Wilson, Arthur. *Diderot.* 2 vols. Oxford: Oxford University Press, 1972.

Woodmansee, Martha. *The Author, Art, and the Market: Rereading the History of Aesthetics.* New York: Columbia University Press, 1994.

_____. "The Genius and the Copyright: Economic and Legal Conditions of the Emergence of the 'Author.'" *Eighteenth-Century Studies* 17, 4 (Summer 1984): 425–48.

Woodmansee, Martha and Peter Jaszi, eds. *The Construction of Authorship: Textual Appropriation in Law and Literature.* Durham, N.C.: Duke University Press, 1994.

Index

Académie française, 1, 39, 45–46, 55, 66, 91, 115, 124, 149, 156, 219n44, 220n49, 241n48, 246nn10–11, 260–61n23

Alembert, Jean le Rond, d': on authorial poverty, 119–20, 126, 137, 167, 187; as editor of *Encyclopédie*, 74, 229n30; relations with patrons and social elites, 82–101, 187, 195, 234nn83, 85, as target of anti-philosophical attacks, 64, 66, 68, 101, 114. *See also* "Essai sur les gens de lettres et les grands"

Andrew, Edward, 229n29, 235n103, 236n118

"Anti-philosophe," 114–17, 121, 184, 238n12

Aubignac, François-Hédelin, abbé d', 37–38, 54, 60, 101, 246n9

Baillet, Adrien, 44
Balzac, Honoré de, 148
Balzac, Jean-Louis Guez de, 198, 225n110
Beaumarchais, Pierre-Augustin Caron de, 29, 31, 217nn 17, 25
Belin, J. P., 72, 228n23, 247n13
Bell, David, 252n52
Belles-lettres, 20, 47, 53–54, 70, 108, 224n100, 226n117
Bénichou, Paul, 141, 216n12
Bernis, François Joachim de Pierres, comte de, 76
Bertaut, Jules, 16, 65
Birn, Raymond, 29, 158, 228n17, 229n28, 231n47, 252n54
Blondel, Pierre-Jacques, 181, 189, 256n108
Boileau-Despréaux, Nicolas, 31–33, 36, 50, 108, 245n91
Boisrobert, François le Métel de, 50, 52, 227n127
Bosscha, Johannes, 200, 262n35, 263n52
Bourdieu, Pierre: on concept of "literary" or "cultural" field, 7–11, 22, 180, 211–12n9; and "heteronomous principle," 17, 214n13; on "literary underground," 147; on strategy, 184. *See also* Cultural/intellectual/literary field

Brissot de Warville, Jacques-Pierre: "living by the pen" and independence, 127, 142–45, 244n86; on wealth of *philosophes*, 138; as representative of "literary underground," 241n41

Brown, Cynthia, 214n16, 248n19
Brown, Gregory, 217n17, 221n62, 246–47n11, 258n5

Caldicott, C. E. J., 34
Carlin, Claire, 30, 221n60
Catherine II, czarina of Russia, 92, 94, 191
Cassirer, Ernst, 200
Champion, Antoinette, 170
Chapelain, Jean, 61, 219n44, 226–27n127, 246nn9, 10
Charpentier, François, 44–45
Charrière, Isabelle de, 214nn17
Chevillier, André, 155
Choiseul, Étienne-François, duc de, 71, 97, 228n17, 260n20
Christine of Sweden, 198
cinq auteurs, 1, 211n1
Claveret, Jean, 41–43, 55, 58–59
Collé, Charles, 74, 76, 91, 95–96
Conrart, Valentin, 198, 221n64, 222n 69, 262n36
Corneille, Pierre, 1, 30, 38, 88, 219nn40–41, 220nn49, 51, 221nn56–57, 260–61n23; attacked as bad example, 54–56, 58–60, 101, 121, 124; and Hôtel de Bourgogne troupe, 35, 218n34; and *Lettres patentes*, 31, 34–35, 43, 113, 218n30; as commercially oriented writer, 21, 37–43, 45, 60, 219n37, 220n53. *See also* *Querelle du Cid*

Cornou, François, 122, 239–40n27
Cramer, Gabriel, 190, 237n3, 238n11, 245n7, 245–46n8, 260nn20, 23, 262n35
Cramer, Philibert, 190
Cultural/intellectual/literary field, 19, 26, 69, 99, 106–7, 110, 118, 121, 125, 128–30, 141, 144, 153, 156–57, 161, 163, 165–66, 191, 203–5, 208, 215n17, 246n11; concept, 7–10, 180, 212n9; "first literary field," 11–12, 21, 46, 51, 53–54, 56, 61, 63, 106, 108, 206–7, 237n5; literary market as, 6—7, 11, 62–63, 102, 112–13, 129, 146–47, 150, 179, 182–83, 185–88, 195–97, 199, 206, 209; place of book trade in, 20, 36–37, 64–65, 130–32, 149, 178–79, 182–84, 188, 196, 199

Darnton, Robert, 64, 128, 130, 133, 143, 145, 148, 152, 181, 184, 190, 213n1, 236nn1–2, 238n12, 240n37, 241nn40, 48, 242n56, 242–43n59, 254n86, 257n110, 264n52; on Diderot's *Lettre sur le commerce de la librairie*, 169, 174; on *philosophes*, 66–68, 83, 91. See also Literary underground
Deierkauf-Holsboer, S. Wilma, 218n34
DeJean, Joan, 218n29, 233n76
de la Barre, Jean-François, chevalier, 139, 243n74
de la Porte, Joseph, abbé, 122, 131–33, 175, 241–42n50, 249n32
De l'Esprit (Helvétius), 70–78, 84, 91, 95–97, 100, 221n56, 228nn17, 23, 230n35, 255n98
de Luna, Frederick, 143
Denis, Delphine, 46, 217n, 224–25n100
Descartes, René, 44, 85, 217n20
Dévots, mobilization against Helvétius, 71–72, 100
D'Hémery, Joseph, 128–32, 143, 240nn35, 37, 241–42n50, 246n10
D'Héricourt, Louis, 153–55, 157–58, 163, 170–71, 173, 250n51
Diderot, Denis, 6, 77, 115, 118–20, 140, 197, 231n48, 234–35n14, 239n15, 16, 255n90; ambivalent relations with publishers, 247n13, 251n46, 253n67, 253–54n75, 257n114; as early professional author, 16, 18, 64, 152; earnings from literary activities, 157, 170, 177, 183, 185; as editor of *Encyclopédie*, 64, 74, 118, 229n30; and literary property debates, 29, 111, 160–62, 169–76, 197. See also *Lettre sur le commerce de la librairie*; *Neveu de Rameau*
Douvez, Jacques, 65, 216n5
Duclos, Charles Pinot, 66, 82–83, 89, 95, 126, 130, 233n76, 241n40, 243–44n75
Du Deffand, Marie-Anne de Vichy Chamrond, marquise, 90, 95, 97–98, 234n83
Duchesne, Nicolas Benaventure, 122, 200–201, 239n27, 254–55n87, 259n9, 263n48
Durand, Laurent, 70–71

Edelman, Bernard, 30, 216n12, 217n23
Eisenstein, Elizabeth, 133–34, 143, 182, 200, 244n86
Elias, Norbert, 204
Encyclopédie, 64, 70–71, 74, 77, 81, 97, 100, 114, 116, 118, 162, 169, 227n6, 229n30, 230n35, 235n95, 247n13, 253n67, 255n98, 257n114. See also Diderot
Escarpit, Robert, 17, 214n11
Ezell, Margaret, 250n33

Fabre d'Eglantine, Philippe-François-Nazaire, 166, 252n60, 259n13
Falk, Henri, 169–70, 217n20, 221n62, 231n53, 248–49n20, 249n28
Faret, Nicolas, 47, 83
Febvre, Lucien, 254n78
Fenouillot de Falbaire de Quingey, Charles-Joseph, 139, 162–70, 175–16, 181–83
Foucault, Michel, 29
Frederick II, king of Prussia, 92, 98–99, 191
Fréron, Élie-Catherine, 72, 133, 138, 238nn8–9, 239–40n27; as object of Voltairean satire, 116–17, 121–22, 127, 132
Fumaroli, Marc, 30, 221n59, 223n90, 224n96, 225n100
Furetière, Antoine, 223nn75, 90, 224n100, 244n79, 256n106

Gagnebin, Bernard, 202, 245n7, 262n35
Gibbon, Edward, 94, 235nn103

Goldgar, Ann, 73, 229n27
Goodman, Dena, 89, 232n58, 234n85
Gordon, Daniel, 89, 232n58, 233n76, 234n85
Graffigny, Françoise Paule d'Issembourg de, 214n17
Grimm, Friedrich Melchoir, baron von, 75, 131
Grimsley, Ronald, 90

Habermas, Jürgen, 89
Helvétius, Claude-Adrien; attacked by outsiders, 101, 115, 138; and *De l'Esprit* controversy, 70–78, 95–97, 228nn16–17, 19–21, 23, 230nn35, 37, 231n47; and ideal of public, 84–86, 89, 233n82; as *mondain*, 89–92, 235n100. See also *De l'Esprit*
Hénaff, Marcel, 204
Hennin, Pierre-Michel, 76, 230n37, 230–31n43
Hesse, Carla, 29, 80, 158, 214–15n17, 217n17, 248n18
Honnête, honnêteté, 193; commerce signifying lack of, 60; culture of, 20, 22, 47–48, 51, 63, 80, 83, 205; and writers, publication, and literary culture, 10–12, 23, 45, 49, 56–59, 63, 65, 79–81, 99–100, 148, 150, 157, 161, 168, 179, 185, 187, 198, 246n8, 256n102
Hôtel de Rambouillet, 46–47, 85, 195, 226n. See also Rambouillet
Hugo, Victor, 2–3, 211n4

Iverson, John, 221n56

Joly de Fleury, Jean-Omer, 71, 74, 76, 97
Jouhaud, Christian, 53–54, 69, 100, 237n6

Kant, Immanuel, 199

La Bruyère, Jean de, 37, 52, 84, 182, 232n68
La Calprenède, Gaultier de Coste, seigneur de, 25, 50
Lafayette, Gilbert du Motier, marquis de, 244n86
Lafayette, Marie-Madeleine Pioche de la Vergne, comtesse de, 46

La Harpe, Jean-François de, 77, 90–92, 96, 131, 133
Lahire, Bernard, 10, 213n10, 214n11, 263n44
La Mettrie, Julien Offray de, 91
La Rochefoucauld, François IV, duc de, 84
Le Breton, André-François, 74, 162, 169–70, 182, 247n13, 253n67, 257n114
Le Franc de Pompignan, Jean-Jacques, 115, 117, 237–38n3
Le Roy, Charles, 75–77
Le Sage, Alain-René, 15–16, 213n1
Lettre sur le commerce de la librairie (Diderot), 160–61, 169–77, 185, 247n13, 249n28, 251n46, 253n67, 253–54n75
Levasseur, Thérèse, 199, 262n40
Lilti, Antoine, 89, 94, 226n117, 232n58, 234n87, 235n99
Linguet, Simon-Henri-Nicolas, 131; as "anti-philosophe," 66, 125; literary career, 133, 242n56, 243n74, 243–44n75; and literary property debates, 111, 156, 162–65, 167–70, 175, 189, 197, 253n63, 257n114; as outsider, 136–40
Literary/intellectual property, 4, 209, 214n17, 216–17n17, 217nn20, 25, 251n41; authors and neglect of, 6, 22, 29, 61–62, 65–66, 68, 93, 97, 101–2, 227n6; eighteenth-century debates, 79, 111, 147–83; France compared with England, 248n18; marginal writers and, 162–64, 166–68, 253n63; as rhetorical device, 111, 159, 164, 168; role of publishers in debates, 29, 152–59, 249nn21, 28; seventeenth-century claims, 30–32, 34, 43–44, 56, 218n. See also Diderot; Luneau de Boisjermain affair; *Privilège*
"Literary Underground," 130, 133, 148, 152
Lough, John, 15–16, 215n2, 241n48, 242–43n59
Love, Harold, 250n33
Luneau de Boisgermain affair, 162–66, 189, 253n67, 257n114
Luxembourg, Madeleine-Angélique de Neufville-Villeroy, duchesse de, 201, 259n9, 263n48

Mairet, Jean, 38–41, 43, 55–56, 60
Maître, Myriam, 224n96
Malesherbes, Chrétien-Guillaume de Lamoignon de, 91, 118; on economic benefits of freedom of press, 178, 181, 255n98; relation with Rousseau, 188, 201, 263n49; role in Helvétius affair, 70–71, 74–76, 78, 97, 228nn16, 21
Marmontel, Jean-François, 66, 90, 95
Martin, Jenri-Jean, 16, 25–26, 32, 146, 215nn1, 4, 216n7, 221n62, 235n99, 241n44, 254n78
Masson, Nicole, 64–65, 67, 247n12
Maupertuis, Pierre-Louis Moreau de, 77
Maza, Sarah, 252n12
Mémoire judiciaire, 164, 252n52, 258n5
Mémoires secrets, 99, 163, 165, 189, 257n114
Mercier, Louis-Sébastien, 133; on Académie française, 149; on author as moral leader, 141; on literary outsiders and poverty, 136–40, 156, 177
Merlin, Hélène, 39, 233n76
Le misanthrope (Molière), 47–50
Molière, Jean-Baptiste Poquelin, 47–50, 180, 198; and commercial publishing, 34–35, 217n19, 217–18n28, 218n29, 246n9
Moltou, Paul-Claude, 201
Le monde, mondain, mondanité: as configuration of elite culture, 47, 52, 60–62, 85, 91, 95, 97, 101, 204, 223n81, 234n87; foreignness and resistance of writers to, 37, 41–42, 68, 82, 84–88, 95, 99, 101, 114, 124–26, 146, 151, 167, 186, 196, 221n56, 235n100; Helvétius as *homme du monde*, 77–78, 80, 96, 100; integration of writers into, 36, 47, 50, 52, 56, 59, 79–82, 84, 89–90, 91, 93–100, 114, 121, 124–25, 136, 179, 187, 205, 234n85, 241n40, 250n33; philosophical apology of, 89; as public, 84, 90, 92–95, 98, 195, 233n76. See also *Philosophes*; Sociability; *Sociabilité mondaine*
Morellet, André, abbé de, 89, 95, 115–16, 118, 120, 184, 233n76, 238n5

Neveu de Rameau (Diderot), 118–21, 126, 132, 140, 184, 239n16
Nicolet, M., 215–16n4

Palissot de Montenoy, Charles, 72; and *philosophes*, 115, 118, 125, 238–39n14, 264n56; mocked by Morellet, 115–16, 120, 184, 238n5
Pappas, John, 83
Parlement, role in Helvétius affair, 71–72, 74, 228n23
"Le pauvre diable" (Voltaire), 114, 117–21, 127, 132, 136, 140, 238n11
Pellisson, Maurice, 67
Pellisson-Fontanier, Paul, 1–2, 211n2
Philosophes: autonomy, 22–23, 67–69, 88, 90–94, 97–100, 124–25, 187, 196, 234n85; censorship and relation to political authorities, 71–75, 78–79, 83; as hypocrites, 91–92, 96, 101–2, 124–27, 167; integration into elite society, 68–69, 79, 81–82, 84–100, 124–26, 187, 195–96, 227n10, 232n58, 234n85, 234–35n95; as negative models of literary identity, 114, 125, 135–38, 167–68, 188; polemics against critics, 114–23, 127, 132, 184; publishing practices and neglect of literary property, 22, 64–69 85–87, 94, 96–102, 160, 187, 227n6, 247n12
Pidansat de Mairobert, Mathieu Franfçois, 131, 249n32
Pinchesne, Martin, 44–45, 51, 54
Piron, Alexis, 136, 145, 243n61, 245n91
Pompadour, Jeanne-Antoinette Le Normant d'Étioles, marquise de, 71, 92, 97
Pottinger, David, 105, 216n5, 221n62, 246n9
Prades, Jean-Martin, abbé de, 72
Les précieuses ridicules (Molière), 180, 198, 217–18n28
Préchac, Jean de, 33
Prévost, Antoine-François, abbé de, 15–16, 213n1
Privilège (en librairie), 35, 218n, 221n64, 248n20, 254n78, 256n100; and literary property, 29, 43–44, 79–80, 153–55, 158–60, 168–69, 171–73, 217n20, 221n62, 247n13, 248n18, 249nn25, 28, 251n41, 252n54; as medium of *honnête* self-presentation, 44–45, 56, 59, 80–81, 220n53, 222nn69–70; and Molière, 34–35; origins, 248n; renewal of, 31, 217; revocation of for *Encyclopédie*, 74, 118, 229–30n30, 253n67,

255n97, role in Helvétius affair, 70–79, 96–98

Querelle du Cid, 5, 21–22, 30, 38–43, 55–56, 58–61, 63–64, 88, 219nn41, 44, 220n49, 233n76
Quinault, Philippe, 31, 217n19

Racine, Jean, 31, 162, 217n19
Rambouillet, Catherine de Vivonne, marquise de, 46–47, 226n. *See also* Hôtel de Rambouillet; Salon
Ranson, Jean, 236n2, 264n52
Reforms of 1777, 66, 80, 154, 249n25, 253n63
Reiss, Timothy, 54, 225n108
Rey, Marc-Michel, 112, 188, 190, 192, 197, 199–202, 254–55n87, 260n21, 262nn35, 40, 264n56
Ribard, Dinah, 83, 97
Richelieu, Armand-Jean du Plessis, duc de, 1–3, 219n44, 225n108
Roche, Daniel, 106–7, 123, 126, 130, 146, 246n11
Rousseau, Jean-Jacques, 91, 115, 144, 238n14, 254–55n87, 257n116, 263nn49–50; against writing as *métier*, 152, 258–59n9; earnings of, 157, 177, 183, 258–59n9; as intellectual outsider, 64, 68, 127, 185–86; as precursor, 16, 18, 29, 247n14; publishing strategies compared to Voltaire, 11, 189–92, 260n21; and readers, 192–94, 236n2, 261nn27, 29, 264n52; relation with publisher, 188, 197–203, 262nn35, 40
Rulhière, Claude-Carloman de, 67–68
Russo, Elena, 234–35n95

Saint-Amant, Marc-Antoine-Gérard, sieur de, 57
Saisselin, Rémy, 145, 241n47, 247n14
Salley, Charles-Alexandre, 70, 228n16
Salon, 50–51, 106, 108, 194, 203; as historiographical concept, 226n; importance in seventeenth-century intellectual culture, 46–47, 68–70, 207, 224n96; as institution of literary field, 45–46, 53, 56, 58, 232n58; and intellectual outsiders, 138, 186, 203; and *philosophes*, 66, 81, 83, 85–86, 89–91, 95, 124, 130, 179, 187,

195, 232n58, 233n76; as publication venue, 156, 250n33
Sarrazin, Véronique, 76, 229n
Sartine, Antoine-Raymond-Jean-Gualbert Gabriel de, 169, 172, 252n54, 253–54n75
Schapira, Nicolas, 44, 46, 80, 221–22n65
Schinz, Albert, 197, 200, 202
Scudéry, Georges de, 39–40, 45, 55–56, 58–59, 207, 219n44, 220n49, 222n69, 225n110, 226n113
Scudéry, Madeleine de, 46
Smith, David, 72, 228n17
Sociability, *sociabilité* (*mondaine*): and autonomy of *philosophes*, 85, 87, 91, 94, 98–101, 232n58, 234n85; and cultural or intellectual legitimacy of writers, 20–21, 52, 56, 58, 68–69, 81, 84, 121, 226n17; writers and resistance or lack of, 41, 64, 105, 114, 205
Société typographique de Neufchâtel (STN), 143, 181, 244n87, 264n52
Sorel, Charles, 45, 47, 223n81
Statute of Anne, 248n18
Suard, Jean-Baptiste-Antoine, 71, 77, 233n76, 241n48

Tallement des Réaux, Gédéon, 37, 47, 52, 61, 222n69, 225–26n113, 226n117, 226–27n127
Tercier, Jean-Paul, 75–76, 230nn40, 43

Valéry, Paul, 212n15
Vaugelas, Claude Favre de, 223n81, 224n96, 226n123
Vessillier-Ressi, Michèle, 17
Viala, Alain: on cost of upholding image as writer, 27, 157; and "first literary field," 11, 21–22, 45, 53, 206, 237n5; importance of literary commerce and property in seventeenth century, 30–33, 36, 43, 61, 108; on publication, 69, 100, 250n33. *See also* Belles-lettres
Vigny, Alfred de, 166
Villiers, Pierre de, 256n106
Voiture, Vincent, 51, 54, 207
Voltaire, François-Marie Arouet, 68, 70, 72, 77–78, 81, 83, 91, 95, 129, 138, 167, 228n23, 231n48, 243n75; as exemplary literary figure, 22, 64, 67, 145, 175; and

Voltaire, François-Marie Arouet *(cont.)*
"Lettre à un premier commis," 178–79, 255nn99–100; and literary property, 65–66, 161; as polemicist, 114–20, 122, 127, 132, 136–37, 139–49, 237n3, 238n11; and publishing strategies, 99–100, 126, 148, 189–92, 245n8, 260n20

Walter, Éric, 160, 227n10
Warnke, Martin, 225n106
Woodmansee, Martha, 250n40, 256n101, 262n39

Acknowledgments

THIS PROJECT HAS BEEN a long time in the making, and would not have been possible without the generous intellectual and financial support of many individuals and institutions. It is with pleasure that I acknowledge them. Priscilla Parkhurst Ferguson has from the earliest stages offered her encouragement, interest, and exacting reading. My deepest thanks to her, as well as to Pierre Force and Andreas Huyssen. Many people have, over the years, read or heard portions of the manuscript and offered vital advice. In 2002–2003, participants in the seminar on "The Book," organized by Peter Stallybrass at the Penn Humanities Forum of the University of Pennsylvania, read an early version of Chapter 1. In 2007–2008, colleagues in the Society of Fellows seminar at the University of Washington Simpson Center for the Humanities gave me feedback on Chapter 4. I am grateful to Christian Jouhaud for providing me with a forum in his seminar in the spring of 2005, and to Alain Viala, Dinah Ribard, Mathilde Bombart, and Nicholas Schapira for their ideas. My thanks also to many others who have taken the time and effort to read or hear parts of the text and who have shared with me their thoughts on how to make it better: Daniel Brewer, Gregory Brown, Lance Donaldson-Evans, George Hoffmann, Antoine Lilti, Jennifer Milligan, Karlis Racevskis, Robert Romanchuk, Maurice Samuels, Heather Webb, and the late Charles Williams; my colleagues at the UW including Marshall Brown and members from our early modern reading group, Kevin Donnelly, Susan Gaylard, Donald Gilbert-Santamaria, and Louisa Mackenzie. Nicholas Paige offered extensive input on Chapter 1. And I am grateful as well to the two anonymous readers from the Press for their extremely thoughtful and constructive recommendations.

I am lucky to have been affiliated with a series of institutions that have provided me with tremendously supportive environments in which to make progress on this book. My warmest thanks to former and current colleagues and students at Colgate University, Ohio State University, and now at the University of Washington, including Diane Birckbichler, Douglas Collins, Katherine Deimling, Denyse Delcourt, Frederick Luciani, Paul Reitter, Albert Sbraggia, and many others. All of these institutions have, in addition, been generous in their financial support of my work. Grants from the OSU College of Humanities allowed me to spend parts of the summer of 2004 and the spring of 2005 in Paris. The Simpson Center for the Humanities at the UW provided me with teaching leave in 2007–2008, giving me time to complete the manuscript, and a Summer Stipend in 2008 to fund a trip to Paris. My thanks to Kathy Woodward and the Simpson Center staff for all their help; and to the Graduate School of the UW and the College of the Arts and Sciences for support preparing the manuscript. I am also particularly grateful to the Penn Humanities Forum and the Mellon Foundation for a postdoctoral fellowship in 2002-2003, which came at a critical juncture as the project was getting underway.

Portions of this book have drawn on previous published articles. Parts of Chapter 1 were initially developed in "Identité littéraire et librairie au XVIIe siècle: le cas Pierre Corneille," which appeared in *SVEC* 2004:10 (October 2004): 35–45. Chapter 3 extends an argument that I first sketched out in "Marginal Writers and the 'Literary Market': Defining a New Field of Authorship in Eighteenth-Century France," in *Studies in Eighteenth-Century Culture* 33 (2004): 101–23. Chapter 4 draws on "Conceptualising the Literary Market: Diderot and the *Lettre sur le commerce de la librairie*," in *SVEC* 2003:01 (January 2003): 135–70. And Chapter 5 builds from an analysis that I first presented in "The Enlightenment Literary Market: Rousseau, Authorship, and the Book Trade," *Eighteenth-Century Studies* 36, 3 (Spring 2003): 387–410. I am grateful to these journals (and their readers) for offering me a forum in which to present my research, and now for allowing me to draw on these articles in this book.

Finally, none of this would have been possible without the support of my family. My thanks and love to my sister Jacqueline and her new family; to my parents, Stephen and Michelle; and to my wife, Carolyn.